Monitoring Sweatshops

*Workers, Consumers, and the
Global Apparel Industry*

Monitoring Sweatshops

Workers, Consumers, and the Global Apparel Industry

JILL ESBENSHADE

TEMPLE UNIVERSITY PRESS
Philadelphia

9-14-2004
WW
$22.95

JILL ESBENSHADE is an assistant professor of sociology at San Diego State University.

Temple University Press
1601 North Broad Street
Philadelphia PA 19122
www.temple.edu/tempress

Copyright © 2004 by Temple University
All rights reserved
Published 2004
Printed in the United States of America

⊛ The paper used in this publication meets the requirements of the American National Standard for Information Sciences—Permanence of Paper for Printed Library Materials, ANSI Z39.48-1992

Library of Congress Cataloging-in-Publication Data

Esbenshade, Jill Louise.
    Monitoring sweatshops : workers, consumers, and the global apparel industry / Jill Esbenshade.
       p.   cm.
    Includes bibliographical references and index.
    ISBN 1-59213-255-3 (cloth : alk. paper) — ISBN 1-59213-256-1 (pbk. : alk. paper)
    1. Sweatshops.   2. Clothing trade.   3. Clothing workers.   4. Wages—Clothing workers.   5. Globalization.   6. Consumers—Attitudes.   I. Title.
    HD2337.E83 2004
    331.25–dc22   2003067209

2   4   6   8   9   7   5   3   1

For my mother and father
and the family they have nurtured

And in memory of
Patricia Sanabria-Candido (1979–2003)
Quien en vida tuvo al cielo por sombrero

Contents

Preface

HOW DID I come to study monitoring in the apparel industry? As the great-granddaughter, granddaughter, and niece of Jewish garment retailers, one could say that I was born to the subject. As the sister-in-law of two Salvadoran garment workers, one could say that I married into it. As a former staff member at the International Ladies' Garment Workers' Union (ILGWU), I seemed to come to it through my own professional and political development. And as someone who has been schooled in ethnic studies and focused her graduate career on the plight of immigrants, especially in regard to labor, I was educated into it. But perhaps, as they say, all roads lead to Rome.

In any case, I came upon the subject of monitoring in the garment industry in 1996, as the Gap campaign took off and the press began to link maquilas in El Salvador to garment makers in the United States. I was searching for a dissertation topic at the time. As I embarked on my research, I discovered that there was a ripe case study much closer to home. In my native Los Angeles, garment manufacturers were engaging in a new and innovative experiment of monitoring contractors, and it appeared to be having some positive effects. The monitoring program was winning awards, receiving praise, and apparently making a difference. Yet it had detractors. My imagination was captured. Were these improvements real? And most interesting for me, how did workers themselves feel about this apparent solution?

I was intrigued by the problem and, to boot, it appeared that there was a ready-made collection of data waiting to be explored. The ILGWU (now part of a merged union, UNITE) and numerous workers had filed lawsuits against jeans-maker GUESS?, Inc., and obtained boxes of documentation on the company's monitoring practices, including workers' testimony, monitoring reports, and depositions of company officials and monitors. What graduate student could walk away from an interesting question accompanied by thousands of pages of primary data? Unfortunately, a judge's confidentiality order indefinitely delayed my access to the legal files. But by the time I discovered this, I was already hooked.

So I turned to the live sources themselves rather than their paper counterparts, which turned out to be a wholly positive turn of events. Nothing could have substituted for actually observing during monitoring visits. The people I talked with were more forthcoming than I had imagined, thanks in no little measure to my sympathetic female ear, I am sure. Moreover, walking into a hot, dim tenth-floor factory in a downtown Los Angeles tenement and then drinking cold soda on a plush leather couch in a manufacturer's air-conditioned lobby was a contrast that only the lived experience could really capture.

During my fieldwork in Los Angeles, monitoring was for the most part still an intellectual curiosity for me. It was a concrete phenomenon that existed in the real world of workers, *and* I felt that it had some potentially important theoretical implications. On returning to Berkeley and becoming active in the student movement and with a group of anti-sweatshop activists in the San Francisco Bay area, it became a passion.

However, I would contend that my analysis led me to my passion, not vice versa. I became involved with the student movement and with constructing an alternative to private monitoring after conducting fieldwork in Los Angeles. It was my research, not my a priori political sense, that led me to a thorough understanding of the flaws in the current system. I wanted to use the information I gathered, and my analysis of it, to change that system. This, of course, is not novel. There is a strong tradition of applied research in many fields, including sociology and ethnic studies.

From my research I wrote a policy paper that was distributed widely in the anti-sweatshop movement and probably influenced the debate. I also testified before a California State Senate committee on new garment legislation, which was passed and is discussed in this book. In addition, I participated, as I said, in the student movement in the University of California system to force the administrators to adopt a strong code of conduct and to convince them to join the Worker Rights Consortium (WRC), an alternative monitoring organization. I was the graduate-student representative on the system-wide advisory committee on these issues. I believe that my in-depth knowledge of the subject significantly contributed to the committee's work. I also helped coordinate a local group of anti-sweatshop activists, lawyers, and students to develop a model monitoring plan (known as the UCAS, or University Coalition Against Sweatshops, proposal). I then represented UCAS in discussions of our proposal with activists and unionists in New York. From these meetings we developed a working group. After making drastic revisions, we submitted the plan to the United Students Against Sweatshops (USAS), and I continued to participate in the development of what is now the WRC, serving on its advisory council and then the governing board.

Did I influence the developments that are described in this book? I believe I did. Is that bad? I would argue that it is not. I am committed to good scholarship; I am also committed to social justice. I hope that the former can contribute to the latter. I believe it can. But it cannot in a time lapse, and it cannot by dividing our world into "academic interests" and "political interests." My greatest contribution to the movement for social justice may be the information and analysis that I, as an academic, can provide. To withhold such contributions would, for me, be ethically inappropriate; to delay such contributions would cripple them. I am proud that at the very least I contributed to improvements within the area I was studying. These improvements have helped some workers achieve concrete changes in their workplaces and their lives. I hope workers will continue to be able to capitalize on alternative forms of monitoring. I also hope that my scholarship can inform the academic community and move forward theoretical debates. In that hope, I offer this book.

Acknowledgments

MANY, MANY PEOPLE and institutions have helped make this book possible. I cannot begin to name or thank them all, but I will recognize those who have been most involved in the process, although I am, of course, solely responsible for the findings and conclusions of this book.

I will begin my acknowledgments by recognizing the person without whom I could not have made it through the dissertation, or graduate school, for that matter. Edna Bonacich has been a committed mentor, discussing ideas, reading drafts and revisions, faithfully responding to my tidal wave of e-mails, and showing unbounded enthusiasm for the project. More important, perhaps, she has been an inspiring role model. I am always amazed by her unflagging energy and diligence. And I am constantly impressed by her ability to balance and maintain her strong commitment to politics, scholarship, students, and family. She showed me that it could be done—that a woman could raise a family, get a Ph.D., be an activist, and maintain her integrity as a teacher and scholar. On top of it all, she has been a dear and caring friend.

Several other professors and fellow graduate students helped me immeasurably along the way with guidance, chapter critiques, and emotional support. I particularly thank Nerissa Balce-Cortez, Michael Burawoy, Julie Guthman, Beatriz Manz, Jean Molesky, Evelyn Nakano-Glenn, Liz Ogelsby, and Caroline Streeter.

In regard to surviving as a student-parent, no one deserves more thanks than the wonderful and dedicated teachers at UC Child Care, especially Mary Hartman-Clark and Cynthia Steele, without whom many academic careers would have met untimely ends.

My extended family in El Salvador made conducting fieldwork possible by providing shelter, food, and babysitting assistance. Don Pablo, Liseth, Carlos, Sonia, and Pablo Delgado were especially generous. Jeff Steeno spent an entire summer with us in El Salvador helping to keep my children entertained and my spirits up.

My family has been extremely supportive. As a fellow graduate student, my brother Rick (to whom I owe my political conscience) offered solidarity, as always. His wife, Zsuzsa, patiently answered my unending questions about the dissertation and the sociological profession, providing invaluable advice. Lee answered my editorial, as well as my metaphysical, questions. Anne and Mike sent pick-me-ups by phone and mail to brighten my days. And as a co-Berkeleyite, Andy was a companion and favorite uncle to my children. My parents helped in innumerable ways, from housing and homemade meals during fieldwork in Los Angeles to meticulous editing on the final manuscript. Mostly they provided reassurance, as they always have. Becky Rosenfeld, my ever true best friend, provided a rock to cling to (be it on the other side of the country) when all else seemed to falter.

On a final personal note, I thank Julio, Timoteo, and Noemi Delgado. Julio survived eight years of Bay area rain, conference trips, and dissertation- and then book-writing tension. I thank him for always insisting that I keep my academic career in perspective, for bringing spontaneity into my life, and for loving me enough to persevere far from the home he loves. Timoteo and Noemi are my miracle and my angels.

The book would never have seen light outside the University of Michigan dissertation archives if it had not been for the unflagging support and encouragement of my editor Peter Wissoker at Temple University Press. His calm advice always brought me back to what needed to be done and how to get there. And he found diligent and astute reviewers. Rich Appelbaum and Robin Broad gave comments that helped fill out and strengthen the manuscript. Lance Compa was incomparable in both detailed and big-picture feedback. I cannot thank him enough for his truly focused attention to this project. His two reviews made the manuscript a much better piece of writing, with a clearer and more nuanced argument.

I could not conclude without thanking the many anti-sweatshop activists with whom I have worked for offering me inspiration and assuring me that my research was indeed useful. I cannot name all those whose support and inspiration was much appreciated, but I will mention a few. Jeremy Blasi and the other United Students Against Sweatshop activists, Katie Quan, Nikki Bas, Maria Roeper, and my colleagues in the Worker Rights Consortium gave me sustenance over the long haul.

On a practical note, I thank various entities that provided grants to make this research possible. The Inter-American Foundation supplied the original fellowship for fieldwork in El Salvador. The University of California provided fellowships through the President's Dissertation Fellowship and the Institute for Labor and Employment. At Berkeley, the Center for Latin American Studies, the Human Rights Center, the Vice-Chancellor's Office for Research, the Chicano/Latino Policy Project, and the Institute for Industrial Relations all provided research grants. Thanks to Michael Reich and the generous and supportive staff, the Institute for Industrial Relations also provided an office and a community of labor scholars that I was very sad to leave.

My new home, San Diego State University, has also provided invaluable support in revising, updating, and overhauling the dissertation into a book. My colleagues in the sociology department have been warm and supportive. Kristen Hill-Maher gave me insightful critiques on my drafts, as well as the confidence to send them off. Mary Sanwald provided essential logistical support to the entire bureaucratic process. The university supported me with two research grants.

And finally, I thank all those whom I interviewed for so generously sharing their perspectives, knowledge, and experiences of such a controversial topic. I particularly thank all the garment workers in Los Angeles and El Salvador, as well as around the world, for clothing me and my family and offering inspiration in their struggle for justice. I hope that one day they will be allowed to represent themselves, work in decent conditions, and receive a dignified wage for the essential labor they perform day in and day out.

Introduction
Monitoring, Sweatshops, and Labor Relations

Monitoring is the anti-sweatshop movement's great hope.
—*New York Times*, April 24, 2001

IN A FACTORY in downtown Los Angeles, 130 Latino immigrants toil away producing garments for Los Angeles's largest apparel company, GUESS?, Inc. The Korean-owned factory is one of many sewing shops in Los Angeles that contract to make the stylish jeans, chic tops, and other fashion-forward items GUESS? is known for. Less well known are the backward labor conditions under which these high-priced items are made. Five of the 130 workers are children younger than sixteen. One child, a thirteen-year-old, has been working forty hours a week for more than a year. A U.S. Department of Labor investigation finds that only seventy workers are listed on the payroll and that although workers begin arriving at seven o'clock in the morning and stay as late as six at night, the payroll reflects only eight hours of work. Many workers are paid as little as $3 per hour. The DOL concludes that 127 workers are owed overtime pay, and 118 are owed for violations of the minimum wage. They assess the owner of Jay's Fashions more than $750,000 in back wages. The owner closes down and files for bankruptcy.

This is the fifth GUESS? contractor to be found in violation of labor law between 1991 and 1992. However, GUESS? does not technically employ these workers—even though the company unilaterally sets the contract price and thereby the conditions in the contract shop; its quality-control staff spend from one to three hours per day in the shop overseeing the work; and it reaps the profit from the sweat of these workers.

Because of the flagrancy and repeated nature of the violations found in GUESS?'s shops, the DOL threatens to take the company to court. In lieu of court proceedings, GUESS? agrees to pay the DOL more than $500,000 in back wages and pledges scholarships to the five children. Most notably, GUESS? agrees to monitor its own contractors, becoming the first company to do so. On August 5, 1992, the solicitor-general of the DOL, Marshall Berger, describes the monitoring agreement as follows: "The Guess–DOL agreement is truly historic. . . . Guess stands as a bellwether in the fight to eliminate widespread wage and hour violations among apparel industry sewing and assembly contractors."[1] What had seemed a defeat quickly becomes a public-relations victory. GUESS? boasts about its pioneering role in monitoring and claims that its program is a model for the industry. In December 1995, as part of its anti-sweatshop campaign, the DOL begins a Trendsetters List and includes GUESS? among this well-publicized group of manufacturers that are touted as the "Good Guys of Fashion."

Less than a year later, in July 1996, the California Division of Labor Standards Enforcement raids fifteen apartments in Los Angeles for illegal homework violations and finds GUESS? clothing in most of them. The division also finds in-shop violations at four GUESS? contractors, including nonpayment of the minimum wage, nonpayment of overtime, falsification of time cards, and cash payments. One of the workers, Enriqueta Soto, later described the situation to a Congressional committee as follows:

> I have worked in the garment industry for seventeen years. And I worked in about seven different shops. My experience in this industry has been a very difficult one. In most of the shops minimum wage is not guaranteed. Overtime is not paid. Holidays are not paid. There is no paid vacations. We have no medical insurance. . . . My experience at Jeans Plus [a GUESS? contractor], where they had a monitoring system, the conditions there were the same. We couldn't complain to the people who were doing the monitoring. . . . Because those people who were monitoring only spoke to those employees who were selected by the contractor. When one of my co-workers decided to speak to the manufacturer, when she decided to speak up, they simply decided to punish us and they removed the work. So 400 of us lost our jobs. They shut down the plant. . . .
>
> How can we feel secure . . . if the consequences of [reporting violations] mean losing our employment? We have no assurances, either from the monitoring system or from the Department of Labor.[2]

In August 1996, a group of workers files a class-action lawsuit for minimum-wage and hour violations at sixteen GUESS? contracting shops. Part of the workers' argument is that workers should be considered third-party beneficiaries of the monitoring agreement and thus should be able to sue for breach of contract. Ironically, as part of its defense strategy, GUESS? sends the head of its monitoring program into shops—where she is supposed to be protecting workers' rights—to urge workers to waive their right to participate in the lawsuit. In spite of the monitoring agreement and the court action, violations continue. Between January 1996 and January 1997, state and federal investigators assess nearly $250,000 in back pay owed to workers at some twenty GUESS? contractors. Cal-Safety Compliance Corporation, a monitoring company that GUESS? has hired and whose reports became court documents, finds many more violations.

Meanwhile, the garment workers' union, UNITE, is organizing workers in various contracting shops, as well as at GUESS?'s own "inside" shop. According to a finding of the National Labor Relations Board, GUESS? harasses, intimidates, fires, and lays off workers in response to the unionization drive. GUESS? also forms anti-union worker committees and threatens workers that it will move production abroad if the workers unionize. In January 1997, GUESS? agrees to reinstate workers and pay $80,000 in back wages. The next day, the company announces that it will move more than half of its Los Angeles production to Mexico and elsewhere in Latin America over the coming year. Until this point, GUESS? has produced more than 75 percent of its apparel in Los Angeles, making its contractors the largest group of garment employers in the region.

Despite all the findings of violations and its decision to send production offshore rather than allow workers in Los Angeles to unionize, GUESS? continues to advertise itself as a company with progressive labor practices. In the summer of 1997, state inspectors find illegal homework being done for GUESS? contractors. Although none of the garments are actually GUESS? products, GUESS? is supposedly monitoring the shops for such behavior. GUESS?'s lawyer Daniel Petrocelli boasts to the *New York Times*, "This voluntary policing mechanism that GUESS? pioneered has become a model for the country."[3] In the fall of 1997, in response to a consumer-boycott campaign, GUESS? hands out leaflets at its stores saying that it is on the Trendsetters List and that the union's allegations are untrue. In fact, in November 1996 GUESS? had been put on probationary status on the Trendsetters List, and in January 1997 that status had been extended indefinitely.

In December 1997, GUESS? runs full-page ads in the *Los Angeles Times,* *La Opinion* (the major Spanish newspaper), and elsewhere guaranteeing that its products are "Sweat-Free" and declaring, "Voluntary Monitoring Works." GUESS? also refers to the DOL's "No Sweat" campaign in its ads, implying government endorsement. When the DOL publicly reproaches the company, GUESS? drops the reference to the government-sponsored program but continues to advertise as 100 percent sweat-free and to publicly proclaim that it is a leader in monitoring, with the strongest program in the country. In addition, GUESS? hangs tags on its clothing advertising the products as "Sweat-Free."

Meanwhile, the press, policymakers, and academics all praise the DOL's "No Sweat" program. In 1996, the DOL wins the Kennedy School of Government's prestigious Innovations in American Government award for its monitoring program. The program is touted as a huge success, significantly raising levels of compliance in the United States. In the same year, the president calls together companies, unions, and human-rights organizations to begin a worldwide voluntary monitoring program. By 2000, however, DOL data show that the effects of the program are limited. Disappointment over the results, combined with a change from the Clinton to the Bush administration, leads the agency to pull back from aggressively pursuing the program. The central DOL office drops the "No

Sweat" program from its website, including numerous screens devoted to monitoring. It also halts systematized public reporting of violators, one of the major sticks of the program. Meanwhile, the Los Angeles office switches to pursing informal rather than legally binding agreements. Despite the weakening of the program, it is still the centerpiece of any focused effort on the garment industry that remains. Moreover, on the international level, monitoring continues to proliferate unabated.

The GUESS? case highlights many important questions about monitoring. How does the process actually function and why? What are the costs and benefits to workers? Why is the practice proliferating internationally, despite obvious weaknesses? How have the government and others envisioned the participation of companies, workers, and consumers in monitoring—and more broadly, in addressing the sweatshop crisis?

MONITORING SWEATSHOPS

The current exploitation of production workers in the garment industry is widely acknowledged (Bonacich and Appelbaum 2000; Bonacich et al. 1994; Leibhold and Rubenstein 1999; Ross 1997, 2002; Rothstein 1989; Sajhau 1997; U.S. DOL 1996, 1997; U.S. GAO 1988; Varley 1998). In the United States, these workers are largely immigrants from Latin America and Asia.[4] In Los Angeles, the largest production site in the country, 94 percent of the workers are immigrants.[5] Most are women, and a high proportion are undocumented. This highly vulnerable workforce is subject to a degree of exploitation that for decades had been marginal in the garment industry in the United States. Abroad, women who are often very young, with little education and few alternatives, have become the mainstays of new export industries, which provide needed dollars to their indebted governments. With a surge in the internationalization of production, the decline in unionization, deregulation, and a renewed reliance on vulnerable labor, sweatshops have reemerged and proliferated. Domestically, violations of wage and hour laws are rampant, and violations of health and safety laws are almost universal. Internationally, the use of child labor and verbal and physical abuse often accompany low wages and long hours.

The focus of the U.S. government's policy initiatives to address the "sweatshop crisis" has been privatized monitoring. Beginning with the GUESS? case in 1992, the DOL instituted a program in Los Angeles and elsewhere to force manufacturers to monitor their contractors for labor-law compliance. In 1996, President Bill Clinton formed a task force to replicate monitoring on an international scale, and in 2001 he presented the task force's newly formed monitoring organization, the Fair Labor Association, with $750,000 in start-up funding. Although federal support for monitoring has waned under President George W. Bush, the

FLA continues to grow, and the Los Angeles DOL continues to promote domestic monitoring.

Monitoring has been implemented as a means of addressing the contracting system, which allows manufacturers to avoid responsibility and sweatshops to flourish. Under this system, retailers (e.g., Macy's, Bloomingdale's),[6] who sell the clothes, generally order from manufacturers or jobbers (e.g., Liz Claiborne, Polo Ralph Lauren),[7] who design and market the clothes and use numerous contractors to produce the garments. Although a manufacturer may have "inside shops" that it owns, most manufacturers now use inside shops in a very limited fashion: to produce samples, cut cloth, and warehouse garments. The companies rely on dozens to hundreds of contractors to actually produce their apparel. These contractors range in size from small entrepreneurs to large and occasionally powerful multinational corporations. However, within the United States contractors are generally small and mainly immigrant enterprises averaging thirty employees. Layers may be added when buying agents, traders, and other intermediaries are involved and when contractors farm work out to subcontractors or, in many countries, to women who sew in their homes. Thus, workers may be many steps removed from the manufacturers and retailers who most profit from their labor.

With the globalization of production, garment manufacturers are now insulated from workers not only by a lack of legal responsibility but also by distance and anonymity. Contracting has been expanded and complicated by economic globalization. Companies currently produce in dozens of countries at once using hundreds of contractors. Workers often do not know whom they are actually producing for, and in any case they have no access to the manufacturer to rectify any grievances. Manufacturers have the ability to rapidly move production from one plant or country to the next. Most contractors have no brand-name reputation to protect and few assets; they are also quite mobile. They can quickly rent another location, register under another name, or sometimes even move to another country.[8] Workers and government agencies have had a difficult, often impossible, time recouping back wages and demanding other redress from such ephemeral entities. The challenge for workers, government officials, and anti-sweatshop crusaders has been to hold the real profit makers (the manufacturers and retailers) accountable for the conditions under which their products are made. Limited national enforcement capacity and an absence of effective international regulatory regimes have created a regulatory vacuum.

Activists, unionists, and government labor officials have devised alternative forms of pressure to complement, bolster, or substitute for direct worker resistance and effective government enforcement. In the garment industry, the most notable examples have been public pressure campaigns involving consumers and investors and the related approach of non-state regulation in the form of monitoring. Monitoring mechanisms supposedly ensure that domestic labor laws are complied with—or, in the case of international production, that a company's own code of conduct is implemented.

Codes of conduct are lists of principles that manufacturers develop to guide the conditions of production in their contracting factories. The codes usually include such issues as numbers of required hours, minimum working age, minimum wages, and rights such as freedom of association. Codes always demand compliance with local laws (for example, legal working age in the country) or specify higher standards (for example, minimum of fifteen years old). Manufacturers provide each of their contractors with their code and usually request that the contractor sign an agreement to comply. Monitoring—visits to and investigations of factories—is an additional step that a subset of manufacturers has adopted to confirm whether contractors are actually complying.

While codes of conduct are written documents that can be easily examined and analyzed for weaknesses or unacceptable principles (for example, legal minimum wage versus living wage; sixty required hours of work per week versus forty), monitoring is a set of practices that remains largely hidden from scrutiny. The concept and structure of monitoring are now the subject of worldwide debate among nongovernmental organizations, unions, manufacturers, academics, and others.

It should be noted that domestic and international monitoring differ in significant ways. For instance, companies that monitor abroad do so for compliance with their codes of conduct; most companies who monitor domestically do so only to insure compliance with U.S. laws that govern wage and hour standards, child labor, and, to a lesser degree, health and safety regulations. Issues such as discrimination, freedom of association, and collective-bargaining rights are ignored in the domestic monitoring process.

This difference in monitoring is partly due to the fact that international and domestic monitoring arise from two different pressures on the manufacturer. Monitoring, both domestic and international, was originally forced on manufacturers. Domestically, companies are monitoring partly in fear of negative publicity if sweatshop conditions are uncovered with their labels present but more immediately in response to a concerted campaign by the federal government. In 1992, GUESS?, Inc., became the first manufacturer to agree to a self-monitoring program of its domestic production after the DOL confiscated products made in violation of labor codes. At that time, GUESS? had more than $700 million in sales and employed 3,000 production workers in Southern California through an estimated 100 contractors.

Domestically, the federal government's effort has been concentrated in Los Angeles. Recognizing that it was not making progress enforcing labor law at the contractor level, the Los Angeles branch of the DOL began to enforce the "hot goods" provisions of the 1938 Fair Labor Standards Act against garment manufacturers by not allowing products made in violation of federal law to cross state lines.[9] In this way, the DOL forced manufacturers to pay back wages and repeat violators to agree to monitor their contractors. The companies agreed to monitor and guarantee remediation of back wages; the DOL agreed not to object to the shipment of goods.

However, the DOL has promoted monitoring far beyond those who sign the agreement. The department launched an education and training program for manufacturers and contractors. It widely disseminated information on how to create a monitoring program, including through its website. It continues to promote the practice of voluntary, not compulsory, participation through its Manufacturer Compliance Assistance Program. Almost all large manufacturers and many smaller ones in Los Angeles have some type of monitoring program as a result of the DOL's outreach program and other, more coercive efforts to compel participation.

In the 1990s, the DOL used the threat of bad publicity to compel manufacturers to monitor. A central component of the monitoring program from 1995 through 2000 was the DOL's quarterly publication of the *Garment Enforcement Report*. The *GER,* which was posted on the Internet, listed all contractors found in violation and the manufacturers for which they were working. The idea was that retailers (and potentially consumers, as well) would check the list and not purchase from repeat violators. The list also noted whether a company had or was adopting a monitoring program, supposedly a mitigating factor in potential repercussions. However, the *GER* has not been updated since President George W. Bush took office, further weakening the continuing program.

The DOL has attempted to enlist retailers' participation by pressuring them to require monitoring programs of all manufacturers that wish to sell to them. Retailers are exempt from "hot goods" if they are bona fide purchasers who buy the assembled goods (and do not own the cloth during production). Retailers qualify for the "good faith" exemption of the FLSA if they receive written assurances that the goods were not made in violation of the act. Beyond the *GER,* the DOL established a Retailer Contact Program to inform retailers of violations linked to manufacturers who sell to them and to urge retailers to use their leverage to promote monitoring. The DOL even threatened retailers that, once informed of a pattern of violations, they might lose their "good faith" exemption if they did not require more than written assurances.[10]

The DOL has also tried to tap in to the potential leverage of factors and banks—those who lend money to the manufacturers. In 1998, the DOL met with some of these entities and explained that they should consider "hot goods" violations a "risk factor" in their loans and should urge monitoring on their borrowers as a form of "insurance."[11] In 2003, the Los Angeles DOL planned to renew the factor strategy, hoping again to reach more manufacturers through these lenders. Thus, while more than sixty companies signed formal agreements with the DOL to monitor, hundreds of others do so "voluntarily" because of pressure from the government, retailers, and lenders.

In contrast, companies that conduct international monitoring have done so primarily in response to the pressure of social movements and the negative publicity these movements have generated about sweatshops abroad. In 1995, the Gap became the first manufacturer to agree to "independent monitoring" of a foreign contractor by human- and labor-rights organizations. After a long-fought campaign by workers and human-rights activists in El Salvador and the United States, the Gap signed an agreement with the National Labor Committee that specifically concerned a factory in El Salvador where workers had been mistreated and hundreds had been fired for union activities.[12] Later, Kathie Lee Gifford, the TV personality who serves as the celebrity endorser for a line of clothing sold at Wal-Mart, burst into tears on national television over the NLC's discovery that children in Honduras were sewing clothes with her name on the label. Meanwhile, Disney was exposed for exploiting workers in Haiti, and Nike was criticized for paying poverty wages to Indonesian workers. These incidents, together with the revelation of the virtual slave labor of Thai immigrants in a factory in El Monte, California, led to the formation of President Clinton's Apparel Industry Partnership and a surge in international monitoring activity.

Monitoring is now being touted as an international solution to the well-publicized sweatshop crisis. The AIP, a coalition of manufacturers and NGOs, has begun to expand monitoring into an institutionalized regime of certification through its successor organization, the FLA. Several other monitoring-oversight organizations have been formed to promote and regulate international monitoring, as well. Meanwhile, extensive labor violations have been found in monitored factories in Los Angeles.

Monitoring in Los Angeles consists entirely of "private monitoring"— that is, manufacturers hire a commercial firm or use their own employees to monitor. Although the vast majority of international monitoring is also private, a growing number of local nonprofit organizations with expertise in human- and labor-rights advocacy have been formed to conduct third-party, or "independent," monitoring.[13] While this alternative has created enthusiasm within the anti-sweatshop activist community, the role of independent monitoring continues to be the center of much debate among students, unions, and NGOs. This book does not fully evaluate the effectiveness of independent monitoring; however, I will conclude with an argument about the potential of independent monitoring vis-à-vis private monitoring. New models of independent monitoring (still limited to relatively few work sites) stand in sharp contrast to the practices of the private monitoring that is currently being conducted in thousands of factories in Los Angeles and around the world.

PRIVATE MONITORING AND LABOR RELATIONS

This book considers the meaning of the burgeoning practice of monitoring, or "social accounting." What has private monitoring meant for labor relations in the global apparel industry in terms of affecting employment conditions and structuring relations between workers and employers?

The clothing industry has always played an important role in capitalist development and the configuration of relations between workers and employers. The first wave of industrialization in the United States was based on textile production, and it has been argued that garment assembly was the first production process to become truly globalized (Dicken 1992). Moreover, the "prototype of collective bargaining agreements" emerged in the garment industry (Ross 1997). In 1910, in the wake of the uprising of 20,000 shirtwaist makers in New York City, more than 40,000 cloak makers sustained a two-month strike that ended in a general agreement signed between union and manufacturer representatives. The Protocols of Peace mandated preferential hiring for union members, guaranteed workers' participation in overseeing factory conditions, and instituted a joint grievance procedure (Stein 1977). This pact began the movement toward America's social contract built on an industrial democracy that involved workers in the regulation of the industry (Brandeis 1977 [1915]; Howard 1997; Ross 1997). From the late 1930s on, unionization and government promulgation and enforcement of labor laws increasingly balanced power relations in the industry. However, in the 1980s, with the globalization of production and the undermining of both unionization and government regulation, sweatshops reemerged.

It is not surprising, then, that a new form of labor relations is now developing within the apparel industry in response to changing economic conditions. Whereas the social contract that prevailed in the post–World War II period brought workers, business, and the government into an alliance, the "social-accountability contract," as I will call it, is a pact strictly among employers, their contractors, and the government or, in the case of international monitoring, public-interest organizations rather than governments. Thus, the violent struggle of the early twentieth century and the mid-century consensus were being succeeded at century's end by a new paternalism in labor relations.

OVERVIEW

In this book, I begin with a review of the historical trajectory of the sweatshop and then delve into the current response. I document the practices of private monitoring, domestic and international, and analyze its ramifications and theoretical import. I conclude by exploring the potential significance of the alternative independent model. To conduct research on monitoring, I relied primarily on the qualitative methods of in-depth interview, observation (sometimes participatory), and document analysis. I also used quantitative analysis of DOL data and a brief survey to ground my research. Intensive fieldwork took place in Los Angeles and El Salvador, and additional interviews were conducted in Washington, D.C., New York City, and the San Francisco Bay area. In all, I conducted more than 135 in-depth interviews with monitors, workers, contractors, manufacturers, government officials, unionists, academics, and NGO staff. I have included a complete list of those interviews, as well as a detailed description of each aspect of the research methods used (see Appendixes 2 and 3).

In the first chapter, I provide a historical context for my argument, detailing the rise and fall of a social contract in U.S. labor relations, particularly within the garment industry. Here I follow three trends and their relationship to one another and to the emergence, marginalization, and reemergence of the sweatshop. My focus is on industry structure, unionization, and government enforcement of labor laws. A clear understanding of the rise and fall of the social contract leads the way to the subsequent discussion of my concept of a social-accountability contract.

In the second chapter, I ask why monitoring arose in the 1990s and what monitoring means for labor relations. I posit that the nature of the global economy—with its proliferation of subcontracting, buyer-driven chains of production, government deregulation, attacks on unionization, and use of vulnerable labor—has sustained the development of a new form of labor relations. I argue that private monitoring reflects this new economic system because as a process it addresses multilevel production chains, privileges consumer concerns, privatizes a government function, can undermine unionization, and treats workers as passive and in need of protection.

Private monitoring is adapted to the globalized production system, *but it does not challenge that system.* Private monitoring accepts as given the industry's production practices—such as mobility and hidden chains of production—and its multilayered structure, both of which foster sweatshops. Thus, although monitoring purports to, and may minimally, improve conditions for workers, it cannot systemically address the sweatshop problem. This hypothesis is sustained by evidence from Los Angeles that private monitoring does not effectively change working conditions because it neither alters the structural practices under which sweatshops flourish nor allows workers to address their own exploitation.

The second chapter also lays out a theoretical framework for understanding the phenomenon of monitoring. By viewing private monitoring through the lens of shifting power relations, one can grasp its broader import. I theorize that monitoring represents a new paradigm in which the social-contract triangle of government, business, and workers is replaced by a social-accountability contract that involves government, business, and its contractors (the factory owners) and excludes workers. This triangle of power can be seen to reside within a triangle of resistance composed of civil society, consumers/investors, and workers. In this way, we can imagine the three methods of addressing sweatshops as embedded within these relations of power and resistance. Civil society pressures government for stronger enforcement; workers organize to win concessions from factory owners; and consumers and investors mount campaigns against brand-name companies. Monitoring, which represents a privatization of enforcement and an avoidance of worker organizing, caters to the powerful players in each triangle—the consumers/investors and the brand-name manufacturers. These companies use monitoring primarily to avoid bad publicity and to address consumer concerns.

Chapters 3 and 4 address the empirical questions of how monitoring is practiced through a case study of private monitoring in Los Angeles. The DOL program began in that city in 1992, and it has the longest-standing and most developed system of monitoring. Chapter 3 lays out the mechanics of this system: who is monitoring; what the actual practices of monitoring are; and how effective monitoring is. Chapter 4 assesses why monitoring has not been more effective by analyzing the weaknesses, conflicts, and issues involved in the practice in Los Angeles. Two central questions in this discussion are: Who controls monitoring, and what is the role of workers in the process?

The detailed description and analysis of monitoring as practiced in Los Angeles lays the groundwork for an exploration of international monitoring, which has grown exponentially since 1998. Chapter 5 moves into the international arena, documenting the rise and effectiveness of monitoring on a global scale. That chapter provides historical background for codes of conduct, which make up the relevant standards at this level, as well as a description of the forms of implementation being used. It also provides a context for the global phenomenon by detailing the internationalization of the industry and the conditions faced by workers around the world.

Chapter 6 is devoted to reviewing the vast body of reports, studies, and articles evaluating the effectiveness of monitoring across the globe. In its totality, this body of research reflects many of the conclusions I have drawn from evidence in Los Angeles: that monitoring practices are erratic; that monitoring is only marginally effective; and that workers are usually unaware of the programs and are not real participants in them.

I argue in this book that through private monitoring workers are "protected" rather than empowered; consumers are placated; and transnational companies maintain their power and profits. Yet monitoring is also a site of contestation. A struggle is being waged among those who promote private commercial monitoring; those who support independent NGO monitoring; those who denounce monitoring altogether; and those who believe that these seemingly opposed efforts may indeed be complementary.

This struggle is covered in Chapter 7. There I explore the development and politics of independent monitoring. Chapter 7 details the history of the first NGO monitoring initiative, located in El Salvador, and the campaign that brought it about. Such alternative forms of monitoring are being proposed and practiced on a small scale throughout Central America. The formation of the FLA triggered a focused interest in international monitoring on the part of anti-sweatshop activists, some of whom took up the idea of independent monitoring. Students, unionists, and other academics began formulating a different vision of monitoring—one that challenged the premises of private monitoring and of the industrial system on which it is built. This process resulted in the Worker Rights Consortium. The chapter describes how the public space of the university became the battleground between supporters of the WRC and the FLA and how that struggle has been partially resolved.

The question remains as to whether a different system of monitoring could promote workers' organizing by opening spaces for workers and providing access for their allies in otherwise constrained circumstances. Recent organizing successes in factories monitored by the WRC suggest real potential in this direction. I argue that these victories are largely due to a different conceptualization of the role of workers and consumers. In the conclusion, this conceptualization will provide the basis for a discussion of potential synergy between protest at the point of consumption and protest at the point of production. A monitoring model that focuses on workers' rights to organize, rather than on conditions, may succeed in bringing workers back into the social contract.

1 The Rise and Fall of the Social Contract in the Apparel Industry

THE GARMENT INDUSTRY ended the twentieth century as it began, with the stain of sweatshops on its clothes. At midcentury, government regulation and unionization combined to marginalize sweatshops within the industry. After hard-fought struggles in the early 1900s, garment workers gained a high degree of unionization. Immigrant garment workers literally marched their way out of the sweatshop and joined many of their working-class brothers and sisters in forcing employers and the government into a tripartite agreement constituting America's social contract. This "National Bargain," as former Secretary of Labor Robert Reich refers to it, involved employers' commitment to share their rising profits; workers' commitment to contain their struggle within rigid guidelines (most significantly, not to strike at will); and the government's commitment to regulate and mediate the relationship and to provide a crucial safety net (Reich 1991).

Although this bargain never included all workers—particularly, it excluded many unskilled and semiskilled workers of color (Harrison and Bluestone 1988)—by midcentury it did apply to much of the garment industry. In 1954, garment workers in the women's sector earned 85 percent of the average manufacturing wage, as opposed to 59 percent today.[1] But workers' position was greatly undermined as imports took their toll. The need for competitive pricing and manufacturers' threats to move production abroad combined with deregulation and the lack of enforcement of labor laws. With the new terms of economic globalization, the balance of power shifted, and the social contract was broken. By the 1980s, sweatshops had reemerged.

This chapter provides a brief history of labor relations in the garment industry from the sweatshops of New York tenements at the turn of the twentieth century, through the period of increasing unionization and government regulation, to the decline of both and the reemergence of abusive conditions. The first section sets the groundwork by discussing what constitutes a sweatshop, historically and currently. The next two sections follow the rise and fall of the social contract in relationship to the garment industry. The focus is on tracing the developments in unionization and regulation and the changing structure of the industry as three key factors in the marginalization and reemergence of sweatshops.

WHAT IS A SWEATSHOP?

The term "sweatshop" conjures up the image of a small, hot, dimly lit room with women bent over machines surrounded by piles of fabric. The truth is that exploitative conditions can exist in the best-lit, most spacious facilities, such as the airplane-hangar-like factories of Central America's export-processing zones. In its report *Sweatshops in the U.S.*, the U.S. General Accounting Office (1988: 16) defined a sweatshop in legal terms as "a business that regularly violates BOTH safety or health AND wage or child labor laws." Pamela Varley, in *The Sweatshop Quandary* (1998: iv), chose to use the term in the very general sense of factories that pay low wages and are otherwise criticized for their conditions. Some use the term to refer not to specific conditions of work but, rather, to the powerlessness of the workers. In his introduction to *Out of the Sweatshop*, Leonard Stein (1977: xv) posited that "the sweatshop, whether in a modern factory building or a dark slum cellar, exists where the employer controls the working conditions and the worker cannot protest." It is common for authors to refer to both miserable conditions and the imbalance of power that drives workers to suffer sweatshop employment (Arnold and White 1961; Bonacich and Appelbaum 2000).

The original definition of "sweatshop" was directly tied not only to the abuse of the workers but also to the way in which the structure of the garment industry fostered such exploitation. In 1901, the historian John Commons noted that the "'sweating system' originally denoted a system of subcontract" (Commons 1977 [1901]: 44). Contracting out is a system of compounded competition. Competing manufacturers give work to the lowest bidding contractors, who make their profit from the margin between the contract price and the lowest possible labor costs. This margin is "sweated" out of workers who toil under the pressure of a piece-rate system of pay. In a piece-rate system, workers are paid for each piece (seam, pants leg, or shirt) rather than by the hour. As the fastest workers become more efficient at sewing the given style, the piece rate drops, and everyone must sew faster to maintain the same pay. This system thus forces workers into competition with one another. Moreover, as Commons pointed out, the subcontracting itself renders the workers more vulnerable: "In the factory system the workmen are congregated where they can be seen by the factory inspectors and where they can organize or develop a common understanding. In the sweating system they are isolated and unknown" (Commons 1977 [1901]: 45). The struggle of garment workers has thus always been structured by the subcontracting system and their ability to combat it.

The subcontracting system, in which workers are divided and always in competition and garment manufacturers remain at arms' length from them, has been a major obstacle to both unionization and government enforcement of regulation. The garment industry is especially prone to subcontracting because it is highly labor-intensive and marked by large fluctuations in production (in terms of seasons, demand, and fashion changes). Within the hierarchy of retailers, manufacturers, and sewing contractors, risk is easily shifted down to smaller, more mobile companies able to enter the business with only enough capital to rent space and purchase or lease a few sewing machines. These companies often have neither reputation nor assets to protect.

The subcontracting system creates a situation in which abuses abound but a chain of legal accountability is absent. Retailers and manufacturers have been insulated from legal liability for working conditions because workers do not have a direct relationship to these companies, although the companies clearly profit from their labor. Domestically, manufacturers, as well as retailers with private labels, have actually owned the material throughout the entire process of production. They do not buy garments; they lease labor.[2] Internationally, the situation can differ, with some contractors offering "full-package" services in which they procure the cloth and cut and assemble the articles.

The first subcontracting system preceded garment factories and involved the distribution of cloth throughout an area to women who sewed the goods in their homes. This system was referred to as "putting out." Women sewing ready-made goods rather than garments only for family use began in the early 1800s. According to the historians Ava Baron and Susan Klepp, several factors led to the growth of ready-made clothing and the proliferation of sewing factories: the "democratization" of clothing, the availability of inexpensive textiles, and the mass-production of sewing machines, which did not happen on any large scale until the 1870s (Baron and Klepp 1984). Even at the beginning of the factory system, combining an "inside" shop with contracting out of seasonal work allowed manufacturers to minimize the risk they faced from the uneven and unpredictable nature of the women's clothing industry.

The recorded history of the sweatshop extends back as far as the 1840s, according to the journalist and labor activist Alan Howard (1997). However, it was in the 1880s, when the mass-production of garments took off, that sweatshops proliferated. Mechanization and factory-based production led to an ever higher degree of division of labor and a severe deskilling of the craft that custom tailors and dressmakers had performed. No longer did a single skilled craftsperson produce an entire garment; rather, many workers repetitively stitched only their portion: seams, buttonholes, cuffs, or collars. The seamstress no longer controlled her pace of work and maintained relations with her customers. Instead, she sat among dozens or hundreds of others at lines of sewing machines working under the watchful eye of supervisors who demanded ever increasing speed. The large expansion of sewing factories was facilitated by the concomitant influx of poor immigrants from Eastern Europe and Italy who swelled the low-wage labor market. In *The Needle Trades*, the historian

Joel Seidman documents the horrific abuses of the 1880s and 1890s, when sweatshop conditions in the industry reached their abyss. In New York, where the overwhelming majority of production occurred, immigrant workers lived and worked in crowded, unsanitary tenements with no water or ventilation. Hours commonly stretched to fifteen a day, with only a few minutes to eat lunch. Wages were miserable, and child labor was widespread (Seidman 1942). As far back as 1892, Congress recommended a system of labeling sweatshop goods after investigating the horrors of the subcontracting system (Arnold and White 1961).

THE RISE OF THE SOCIAL CONTRACT AND THE MARGINALIZATION OF SWEATSHOPS

In the first decades of the 1900s, workers banded together to fight exploitative conditions. Collective action was made possible by structural shifts within the industry. Electrically powered machines and a more stable distribution system (owing to newly established department stores and mail-order catalogues) lent themselves to increased capital investment, larger factories, and a decline in small contracting shops. Workers gathered in large factories with more stable employment were easier to organize, and large employers who reaped less of their profit simply from sweating had an interest in standardizing production and somewhat less reason to fiercely resist unionization, although many of them still did (Waldinger 1985).

One hundred and fifty thousand workers participated in strikes in the decade between 1905 and 1915, the most famous action being the "Uprising of 20,000." In New York City, a strike of 20,000 Jewish and Italian female garment workers exploded in 1909. A walkout by women at the Triangle Shirtwaist Company had galvanized other workers who saw the protesting seamstresses beaten by police and company-hired ruffians. Thousands of workers met in response and declared a strike. Middle-class female reformers joined women workers on the picket lines in hopes of halting arrests and police brutality. Union negotiators and the newly formed manufacturers' association were at loggerheads over union recognition, although they reached agreements on wages, hours, and conditions. Accounts of the outcome of the strike range from victory to defeat (Dye 1980; Jensen and Davidson 1984; Schofield 1984; Stein 1977). Many dozens and perhaps hundreds of individual employers signed agreements over wages, conditions, union recognition, and a cessation of subcontracting—the workers' principal demands (Finn Scott 1977 [1910]; Jensen and Davidson 1984). However, a still weak union was unable to enforce individual agreements with dozens of small manufacturers, in part because the union's male leadership did not commit the resources to the women workers that it would soon offer the men (Dye 1980; Waldinger 1985).

This prolonged mass action had in any case heightened awareness of the conditions in the industry, raised public support, strengthened the union, and prepared the way for broader changes. In 1910, the men followed suit, with 60,000 cloak makers taking to the city's streets. This second general strike ushered in a new era, with the manufacturers' association agreeing to recognize the union, standardize piece rates, institute an industry-wide joint grievance procedure, and establish a Joint Board of Sanitary Control to monitor health conditions (Dye 1980; Stein 1977).

Many argue that this Protocol of Peace, as the agreement was called, influenced "the course of industrial relations" (Howard 1997: 155). While the agreement did not eradicate the sweatshop, it did firmly establish the concept of an "industrial democracy." As Judge Louis Brandeis, who brokered the agreement and later served on the U.S. Supreme Court, wrote: "It was the purpose of the Protocol to introduce into the relations of the employer and the employee a whole new element; that is, the element of industrial democracy; that there should be a beginning, at least, of a joint control, and with joint control a joint responsibility for the industry" (Brandeis 1977 [1915]: 122). A Board of Grievances and a Board of Arbitration were established as part of the protocol to determine the outcome of any complaint. The former was a joint system of employers and union representatives resolving complaints. The latter served as a neutral body that would decide unresolved grievances. Employers agreed to abide by the board's decisions, and the union agreed not to strike for anything beyond that which had been agreed to in the accord. John Dyche, a union leader who fully supported the protocol, said at the time, "The Board of Grievances replaces the strike" (Dyche 1977 [1914]).

Some labor researchers have argued that such a system of arbitration ultimately stifled the power of unions by constraining them to bureaucratic channels (Brody 1993; Fantasia 1988). This arrangement did give workers an institutionalized voice in their conditions for the first time. But the complaint system was soon clogged, and the workers' ability to withhold work, their only real power, was greatly restricted. A fierce debate ensued within the union over the benefits of the protocol. Ultimately, it was the employers who abandoned the protocol in 1916, locking out workers and provoking a strike. Nevertheless, as the cultural critic Andrew Ross notes, the protocol was at least a condemnation of the unbridled abuse of the workers and the beginning of a social contract: "Thus were sown the seeds of labor-capital's social contract, conceived of as the joint control of industrial democracy, governed by the modernist creed of production efficiency and committed to a more rational form of capitalism than that symbolized by the sweatshop" (Ross 1997: 30). Although a step toward union recognition had been taken, the abuse of garment workers was not eradicated by the protocol. Six months after it was signed, on March 11, 1911, a fire at the same Triangle Shirtwaist factory killed 146 workers who were locked inside, many of whom jumped to their deaths rather than burn. Manufacturers also increasingly closed their inside shops and contracted out work in the wake of these uprisings and the subsequent union contracts.[3] Between the mid-1910s and 1920s, the percentage of work in the men's suit and coat industry that was contracted out tripled, rising from 25 percent to 75 percent (Howard 1997). The 1920s also saw an increase of non-union and independent contracting shops in the women's apparel industry. The percentage of small shops (most likely to be contractors) rose dramatically after 1917, reaching almost 80 percent by 1922.

The sociologist Roger Waldinger argues that the increase in contracting was brought about by increased competition based on slower growth. By the 1920s, market expansion based on the substitution of mass-produced clothing for homemade had been exhausted. Moreover, a new fashion consciousness contributed to the instability of the industry, which returned to its pre-turn-of-the-century dependence on small-scale shops (Waldinger 1985). In an increasingly competitive and volatile market, manufacturers sought to lower labor costs and outsource risk.

The membership of the ILGWU reflects both the activism described and these structural changes. Two thousand workers formed the ILGWU in 1900 (Arnold and White 1961). Membership census data show a huge jump in 1909, continued steady growth until 1920, and then a decline. However, after a mass uprising, with hundreds of thousands of workers striking in 1933, membership in the ILGWU shot up from 40,422 a year earlier to more than 198,000. As shown in Figure 1, membership continued to rise for the next four decades.[4]

Legal reforms instituted during the New Deal supported growing unionization and provided a regulatory apparatus to enforce labor laws. Protective legislation that limited working hours for women had been passed in many states during the Progressive era, but debate raged as to whether such gender-specific laws helped protect women or hindered them by limiting their opportunities in some of the most exploitative industries (Kessler-Harris 1982). Clearly, limiting hours without mandating pay standards meant restricting income. Minimum-wage bills had been passed in the 1920s but were struck down.[5] It was not until the New Deal that comprehensive and lasting protections were enacted. In 1933, shortly after President Franklin D. Roosevelt came into office, the National Recovery Administration was established. Under the NRA, business and labor were to work together to set wage and hour standards. Workers' legal rights to join unions and bargain collectively were secured.

Although the NRA was declared unconstitutional in 1935, many of its principal components were embedded in successive legislation, and the concept of a new tripartite arrangement for regulating industry continued. The Wagner Act, or National Labor Relations Act of 1935, reestablished workers' legally protected rights to organize and bargain collectively. It also created a National Labor Relations Board with the power

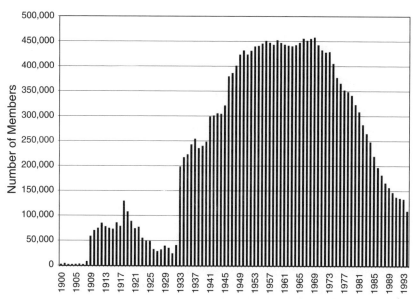

FIGURE 1. Membership in the International Ladies' Garment Workers' Union, 1900–94.
Source: Figures for 1902–91, from ILGWU research department; for 1900, from Arnold and White 1961; for 1993–94, from *Statistical Abstract of the United States,* comp. U.S. House of Representatives Committee on Education and the Workforce, Subcommittee on Oversight and Investigations, for hearing on August 6, 1998.

to enforce decisions on issues of employee elections, employers' obligation to bargain with majority-elected representatives, and a prohibition on coercing or restraining workers in regard to their union activities. The 1938 Fair Labor Standards Act (FLSA) set standards and established enforcement mechanisms in areas such as minimum wage, overtime pay, and child labor. To prevent widespread violations of wage and hour laws, the Department of Labor issued regulations in 1943, under the FLSA, outlawing homework in seven apparel-related industries, including women's garments.[6] In addition to new labor laws, the institutionalization of social-welfare policies in which the government took a measure of responsibility for the well-being of workers strengthened the workers' position vis-à-vis employers and consolidated the social contract.

With a profound increase in organizational strength and in legal standing, the unions were able to achieve a measure of joint liability, despite the lack of legislatively mandated accountability. "Joint liability" refers to the manufacturers' being mutually liable with the contractor for the wages and conditions in the contracting shops, despite the technicality that they are not the direct employers. As early as 1926, a New York State commission recommended that joint liability be established based on its findings that the manufacturers actually determined the conditions in those shops (Stein 1977). However, manufactures resisted, and such legislation was not passed.[7]

By the 1930s, though, the strengthened union was able to achieve a measure of accountability through its collective bargaining. Jobber (or manufacturer) contracts became standard in the industry and are an important practice that continues to this day (Howard 1997). Manufacturer-level contracts often include provisions that manufacturers pay the union health and pension benefits based on the number of workers in their contracting shops. Manufacturers also agree to use only union contractors and to pay the union "liquidated damages" based on the number of jobs lost if they do not.[8]

In 1959, manufacturer-level bargaining was codified in the Garment Industry Proviso amendment to the NLRA. This amendment states that garment manufacturers are *not* covered under the prohibition against secondary boycotts. The secondary-boycott provision was meant to protect neutral parties in a dispute from economic damage—for instance, cannery workers' asking shoppers to boycott a store selling the canned goods they produce may be considered a secondary boycott because the cannery owners, not the store, are the primary employers in the dispute. Apparel, however, is a highly integrated process in which manufacturers determine wages and conditions in contract shops by setting prices, shipment schedules, and amount of work ordered. The manufacturer also owns the cloth, and then the clothing, during the production process, although it does not own the shop in which it is being sewn. Garment manufacturers thus are not considered a neutral third party and are therefore subject to boycotts, contract bargaining, and other actions involved in unionization campaigns. The proviso helped clarify the standing of the joint liability provisions of contracts, which manufacturers had challenged in courts on numerous occasions.[9]

Throughout the post–World War II period, the union remained strong, and government enforcement of labor laws was comparatively effective. ILGWU membership reached 400,000 in 1948 and remained between 400,000 and 460,000 throughout the next two and a half decades. Social legislation was expanded during the War on Poverty years, and new labor legislation continued to be enacted. For example, the Occupational Safety and Health Administration was established in 1970. The country's economic boom and an expanding clothing market contributed greatly to improvements in factory conditions. Data on shop size reflect this growth and stability. Figure 2 shows that there was an increase in large shops, which continued through the late 1960s.

Garment workers benefited from the social-contract era, whose creed included companies' commitment to national economic well-being and government protection of vulnerable workers through social welfare and controls on the excesses of free-market capitalism. Scholars studying the garment industry agree that sweatshops became marginal in the middle

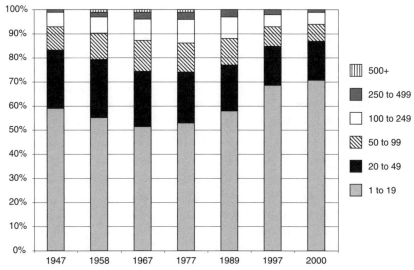

FIGURE 2. Establishment Size in the U.S. Garment Industry, 1947–2000.
Source: Census of Manufacturers for 1947, 1958, and 1967 (after 1982, the census does not report establishment size). County Business Patterns: 1977, 1989, 1997, and 2000. Bureau of the Census.

part of the century, emphasizing the role of union power, government enforcement, or both (Bonacich and Appelbaum 2000; Howard 1997; Jensen and Davidson 1984; Piore 1997; Ross 1997). There is also a clear consensus that the reemergence of sweatshops in the latter part of the century is directly attributable to changes wrought by the globalization of production (Bonacich and Appelbaum 2000; Bonacich et al. 1994; Howard 1997; Ross 1997; Ross 2002).

THE FALL OF THE SOCIAL CONTRACT AND THE REEMERGENCE OF SWEATSHOPS

The reemergence of sweatshops is a direct outgrowth of the increasing power of global capital in relation to the declining power of both workers and the state. Many multinational companies are valued at higher rates than the gross domestic products of most countries in the world. The average chief executive officer now earns more than sixty times the earnings of the president of the United States, as opposed to twice the president's earnings in 1960. In fact, according to *Business Week*'s 2001 annual report, CEOs at 365 of the largest publicly traded companies earned 531 times the earnings of the average worker in their companies (Gill 2001). The global apparel industry is no exception to this pattern. A 1999 comparison of the salaries of the CEOs of publicly traded companies in the apparel industry with the yearly gross earnings of a maquila worker in

Los Angeles and in Mexico is instructive: retail CEOs' earnings on average were 150 and 1,500 times as high as those of the workers in Los Angeles and Mexico, respectively, and manufacturing-company CEOs' salaries on average were 200 and 2,000 times as high (Dreier and Appelbaum 1999).

Economic power has also been translated into corporate rights through unprecedented global trade agreements. Under such agreements, corporations can weaken hard-won environmental and labor regulations by asserting their claims to free trade over restrictions imposed by local entities. As the political analyst John Cavanagh has stated: "If you combine the strong twenty-first century global rights for corporations with weak twentieth-century national rights for labor and the environment, the result is a return to something more like the brutal capitalism of the nineteenth century" (Cavanagh 1997: 49). The stark power imbalances between labor and capital, epitomized by the sweatshop, reemerged in the last quarter of the twentieth century in the United States with the decline of the welfare state, the government's increasingly pronounced preference for business rights over unions, and a rise in runaway shops.

Many social and economic policies of the social-contract era were abandoned in the 1980s. This included renouncing the redistributive mission of the federal government. During the middle part of the century, average family incomes rose steadily, even for the lowest-wage workers. But after the mid-1970s, inequality resurged. Not only did wages diverge greatly, but new tax policies reinforced the growing inequities. In 1960, the ratio of wages of a CEO of a large U.S. corporation and his factory workers averaged about 40 to 1. However, after taxes the difference dropped to 12 to 1. By the late 1980s, that executive earned 93 times the wage of the factory worker and 70 times as much after taxes (Reich 1991: 7). Not only were the taxes of wealthy Americans reduced during this period; the taxes of corporations were reduced, as well. Companies operating in the United States paid 39 percent of all federal income taxes in the 1950s, as opposed to 17 percent in the 1980s. Moreover, government policy favored businesses over jobs. Tax changes that allowed companies to deduct interest payments helped finance leveraged buyouts that resulted in job loss for tens of thousands (Barnet and Cavanagh 1994: 344). Government further weakened the position of workers as it yanked the safety net of social programs out from under them just as many workers lost their jobs. As political economists Bennett Harrison and Barry Bluestone have pointed out, this "Great U-Turn" in American social and economic policy had profound effects on the ability of labor to defend itself. Starting in 1978, and accelerating after Ronald Reagan's election as President, the balance of power between capital and labor shifted dramatically: "Washington began to adopt policies that effectively forced workers to accept wage concessions, discredited the trade-union movement and reduced the cost to business of complying with government regulation"

(Harrison and Bluestone 1988: 14). Under Reagan, there was a consistent and unceasing policy of deregulation that included cutting budgets of regulatory agencies, relaxing certain laws and regulations (for example, in some areas of industrial homework), and delegating more regulatory responsibility to state legislatures. There was also a near-freeze of the minimum wage and government promotion of the use of contingent labor. The government legalized its own hiring of temporary workers for up to four years, as well as its contracting out of many previously unionized jobs, such as janitorial, food-service, and data-processing services (Harrison and Bluestone 1998).

Unions were also directly attacked by the presidential administration for the first time since the New Deal. Reagan began by permanently replacing striking air-traffic controllers. His actions undermined labor's use of the strike and legitimated a fiercely anti-union stance of business on a broader scale. The openly hostile atmosphere fundamentally changed the nature of labor relations (Johnston 1994: 39). The worst blows were struck by the newly appointed National Labor Relations Board, which reversed existing board policy in many areas, including such crucial decisions as allowing companies to relocate if their workers organized (Harrison and Bluestone 1988).

Relocation was a major issue for the garment industry. As early as the 1930s, New York had begun to decline as the main production center because of the growing number of runaway shops seeking lower wages and non-unionized workers (Waldinger 1986). This flight was originally to other areas of the Northeast, then to the South, and finally to California. Beginning in the late 1950s, some U.S. production was moved to Asia. Meanwhile, the newly industrializing countries began to produce their own garments for export with aid from the United States, which sought to bolster capitalist development there (Ong et al. 1994). The low-cost imports from Asia increased competitive pressures in the industry.

By the late 1980s, there was an all-out race to secure the cheapest supplies of labor. As shown in Figure 3, foreign imports in apparel grew dramatically from just over $1 billion in 1970 to more than $60 billion in 2000, with rapid growth occurring in the 1980s and astronomical growth in the 1990s. By 1995, apparel imports accounted for more sales than domestically produced goods (Bonacich et al. 2000). This trend has only intensified in the past few years: by 2002, industry experts estimated, 70–80 percent of apparel sold in the United States was produced elsewhere.[10] Even Levi Strauss, which UNITE's president, Bruce Raynor, dubbed "the last of the big domestic producers," could not withstand the import competition. As opposed to every other major brand, Levi Strauss—which is a privately held company with a long-standing commitment to social issues—owned and operated dozens of plants in the United States until 1997. By 2002, the company had closed most of those plants and was contracting with 500 factories in 50 countries. In January

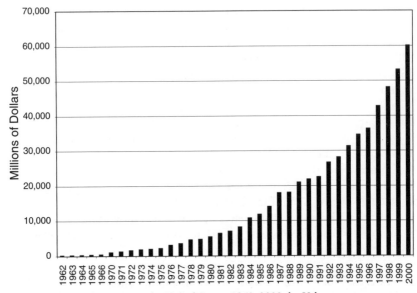

FIGURE 3. Apparel Imports to the United States, 1962–2000, by Value.
Source: Data for 1962–89 (1967–69 missing), from *Focus: An Economic Profile of the Apparel Industry,* American Apparel Manufacturers Association. Data for 1990–2000 provided by U.S. Department of Commerce, Office of Textiles and Apparel.

2004, Levi Strauss closed its last two domestic plants. After a century and a half as the classic symbol of American fashion, no Levi's jeans are now made in the United States.[11]

Logically, the growth of imports was inversely related to the number of production jobs in the U.S. apparel industry, which dramatically declined over the same period. After four decades of growth, the number of apparel jobs in the United States decreased by more than half between 1970 and 2000. The dramatic decline of the past quarter-century brought employment in the industry from a height of 1.2 million operatives to 517,000 in 2000, as shown in Figure 4.

Offshore production has been facilitated by technological advances in transportation and communication; encouragement by the U.S. government; and promotion by foreign governments. The technological revolution in transportation and communication that occurred from the 1960s on enabled garment firms to base their competitiveness on a new drive for ever cheaper labor rather than on developing a "high road" based on mechanization and value-added production. Satellites, fiber-optic cables, and faxes allowed for immediate communication with a worldwide network of producers. New information technology sped up communication and provided the organizational ability necessary to coordinate production efficiently on an international basis. As the sociologist Manuel Castells puts it, with information technology production could take place "on a planetary scale in real time" (Castells and Carnoy 1996). Computers and bar coding allowed for easy tracking of inventory and ordering from a complex network of suppliers. The spread of air travel from the 1960s on meant that executives could personally inspect factories and make deals, and that quality-control staff could visit factories regularly from headquarters. Also, advances in shipping, super-freighters, and containerization reduced the time and cost of transporting goods (Dicken 1992). Technology, however, was only one part of making offshore production feasible.

The U.S. government supported companies' movement abroad through a number of measures. It included assistance programs as well as tax relief, subsidized insurance, and incentives offered through the tariff code (Cavanagh 1997). The U.S. government also offered training programs, customer-matching services, and engineering and marketing assistance to companies that produced offshore rather than in the United States (Rothstein 1989). Moreover, as early as the 1960s, the tariff code was revamped to allow cheaper importation of assembled goods. Under Item 807 of the code, duties were required only on the value added abroad. Thus, a manufacturer would pay duty only on the ten cents it cost to pay a Mexican worker to sew the already cut shirt pieces together, not on the value of the shirt itself.

FIGURE 4. Production Employees in the U.S. Apparel Industry, 1900–2000.
Source: For 1900–60, from Historical Statistics of the United States, Colonial Times to 1970, U.S. Department of Commerce, Bureau of the Census, 1975; for 1970–2000, from Statistical Abstracts of the United States, U.S. Department of Commerce, Bureau of the Census.

In Latin America, this program was expanded with the Border Industrialization Program and the Caribbean Basin Initiative. The Border Industrialization Program, instituted in 1965, allowed the free importation of product parts to Mexico, where they were assembled and shipped practically duty-free back to the United States (Fernandez-Kelley 1983). This led to the growth of the maquiladora industry near the Mexico–U.S. border, an industry that has greatly expanded into other regions of the country since the 1994 implementation of the North American Free Trade Agreement (Fernandez-Kelley 1983; Sklair 1994). Mexican apparel and textile imports into the United States under Item 807 rose tenfold from 1987 to 1997 (U.S. ITC 1998). The Caribbean Basin Initiative, enacted in 1983, excluded garments, but a Special Access Program of the initiative established in 1986 gave guaranteed access to the U.S. market for goods assembled in specified Caribbean countries (Safa 1994; U.S. ITC 1998). Under Item 807, imports from Caribbean Basin Initiative countries rose more than 600 percent from 1987 to 1997 (U.S. ITC 1998). In the past five years, Caribbean Basin Initiative imports have risen at a much less dramatic pace and are far exceeded by Mexican imports, which have grown enormously with the full implementation of NAFTA (U.S. ITC 2002).

Mexico and the Dominican Republic are among the top exporters to the United States, but Asia plays an important role, as well. Under the Multi-Fiber Arrangement of the General Agreement on Tariffs and Trade, which was in effect from 1974 to 1994, imports from each country were limited to a certain quota. However, under the Uruguay Round Agreement on Textiles and Clothing, this quota system is being phased out. By 2005, trade policy, now administered by the World Trade Organization, will allow companies to seek the lowest-cost labor wherever they may find it, with no restrictions.[12] In 1997, China was already the largest exporter of textiles and apparel to the United States, at more than $6 billion worth of goods (U.S. ITC 1998). It is generally expected that the phaseout of the Multi-Fiber Arrangement will lead to a further shifting of production from the United States to developing countries, with China and its vast and controlled labor force gaining the largest share of production (Diao and Somwaru 2001; Hale 2000).

The U.S. government has been instrumental in facilitating the infrastructural conditions that developing countries need to attract multinational production. The U.S. Agency for International Development contributed extensively to the construction of many free-trade zones, as well as of the roads leading to and electrical facilities serving them (Kernaghan 1997). US-AID also financed local business groups that promoted investment from the United States. Such groups in El Salvador guaranteed businesses union-free factories and placed ads in U.S. trade magazines. US-AID encouraged U.S. companies to operate in specifically targeted countries by offering them financial and tax incentives (Varley 1998). In many cases, this was part of a Cold War policy to shore up capitalist development in conflictive regions (Ross 1997).

Also instrumental in shaping the policies of developing countries were global financial institutions that loaned money to those countries under the condition that they shift from import-substitution industrialization plans to export-oriented development—that is, shift from producing goods for local consumption to producing for export. The International Monetary Fund and World Bank pressured many countries to set up "free-trade" or "export-processing" zones to facilitate this process (Enloe 1993; Varley 1998). Export-led industrialization was supposed to garner hard currency, technological development, and skills and jobs for developing nations (Martens and Mitter 1994). Garment production was the first step on the road to development because it took little capital investment, technology, or highly trained skills. Electronics and durable goods were supposed to follow, according to this model. However, for many countries— particularly in Latin America, and now in Southeast Asia—there has been little transfer of skills and technology or diversification into more stable, higher-value goods (Fernandez-Kelly 1983).

Policies around export-oriented industrialization were part of the World Bank's and International Monetary Fund's imposition of larger structural-adjustment programs, which weakened the position of the labor movement and working people in general in those countries by cutting government services, freezing wages, and privatizing jobs and enterprises that had often been unionized. Moreover, low-wage countries competing for foreign investment, be it direct or through contracting work, gave infrastructural subsidies, tax breaks, exemption from customs duties, and often low-rent buildings or leased land. They also promised a docile work-force and ensured it with police protection and guarded plants (Enloe 1993; Fuentes and Ehrenreich 1983).

Third World countries continue to seek transnational investment because it furnishes a means to industrialization, dollars, and jobs. Moreover, women in these countries often find formal-sector employment and the independence it can offer appealing. Many of the women move to these jobs from declining rural areas or transfer from lower-paid sectors such as domestic employment (which often involves more exploitation and sometimes abuse) or street vending (which is often unstable). However, as explained, both the workers and the governments are acting within limited options structured in great part by the current neoliberal global financial system, which requires export-oriented development. This has often led to the devastation of locally based production and leaves little in the way of public support systems.

Sourcing apparel offshore has been part of a broader trend in the changing relationship between North and South from one of exploitation through the extraction of raw materials to the extraction of labor (Phizacklea 1983).[13] There has been a shift from bringing the materials to the

First World to taking the production to the Third World. An intermediary step—workers' moving to labor in the industrialized countries (extracting labor through migration)—is still used, to some extent, in combination with offshore production.[14]

Developing countries have provided workers for the U.S. apparel industry not only abroad but in the United States, as well. Changes in U.S. immigration law in 1965, the popularization of airline transportation, political turmoil, and economic shifts brought a new wave of immigration to the United States from Asia and Latin America (Reimers 1985). This was accompanied by a rise in undocumented immigration, which followed the 1964 ending of the *bracero* program, a guest worker agreement between the United States and Mexico that brought hundreds of thousands of Mexican workers per year, primarily to the agricultural fields of the United States. The numbers of undocumented people increased greatly in the 1980s, as did the number of countries from which they originated (Meier and Ribera 1993). Many of these immigrants came from garment-producing areas such as Mexico, the Caribbean, the Philippines, and China. Civil wars in the 1980s spurred new flows from Central America. The U.S. government is implicated in the initiation of many of these immigrant streams, from its colonial possession of the Philippines to its intervention in the civil wars of El Salvador, Guatemala, and Nicaragua. Moreover, many observers blame the United States' economic policies supporting globalization for the economic and social dislocation that has brought many immigrants, particularly from Mexico, to the United States and its garment factories. The maquilas themselves, which were supposed to offer jobs, disrupt lives by bringing workers to the border and to other industrialized areas. Once these workers have been uprooted and proletarianized, emigration seems a much more viable option (Sassen 1998).

The U.S. garment industry began to depend heavily on the growing number of undocumented immigrants when it shifted to Southern California. The Los Angeles region is the only region in which garment employment rose throughout most of the 1990s. This was due in part to the city's being both the entertainment center, where fashion is figuratively and literally "produced," and a global city with sufficient industrial, financial, and human resources, chiefly a large low-wage workforce (Appelbaum 1999). In addition, Los Angeles's apparel sector has grown because of the type of production that dominates in the city: women's fashion. In 1994, women's outerwear accounted for 65 percent of apparel production in Los Angeles, as opposed to only 25 percent in the rest of the country (Bonacich and Appelbaum 2000). Women's fashion is based on many short seasons and is highly dependent on changing trends. Therefore, batches are shorter and often smaller, and changeover is quicker. In this sector, offshore production is at somewhat of a disadvantage because of time constraints, difficulty of quality control with ever changing products, and the need to restock popular items quickly, although some companies overcome these obstacles with extremely well coordinated and efficient production systems.

There are clear indications that companies are increasingly able to surmount the logistical challenges of offshore production, even in the women's apparel sector. Given trade liberalization, the strength of the dollar against the peso, the move of the DOL toward stronger enforcement, the improved quality of Mexican producers, and ever increasing competition, many companies have done so (Gereffi et al. 2002). The number of garment workers in Los Angeles has declined significantly in the past five years. Beginning in 1998, the rise in garment employment in Los Angeles County—which had added nearly 20,000 jobs in the previous four years—began to turn around. In 1999, the industry suffered its worst decline, with a loss of 5,000 jobs. Although the number was large, Los Angeles actually fared better than the rest of the nation, which lost a total of 82,000 jobs over that period.[15] A further decline was documented in early 2002 and is predicted to continue. It should also be noted that some employment may have gone underground (numbers that are not considered in these figures), and other jobs may have moved to neighboring Orange County, where employment has been on the rise in recent years.[16] However, researchers attribute a large portion of this decline to the ramping up of NAFTA and to Mexico's increasing ability to provide full-package production. Surveys of Los Angeles-based apparel companies show that in 1992 only 25 percent were using offshore production, while in 2000, 75 percent were doing so (Kessler 2002).

The continuing movement of production offshore not only signifies multinational corporations' relentless pursuit of a more docile, cheaper workforce abroad. It also serves to discipline the remaining workforce in the United States (Bonacich et al. 1994). Offshoring strategies have reduced union membership not only by actually exporting unionized jobs, but also by creating the credible threat of moving, which has been used to squelch new unionization drives. The garment workers' union has been unable to successfully respond, given workers' lack of legal protections and leverage and the harassment they face when organizing, as described in the GUESS? case. Employers regularly lay off, fire, deny raises to, spy on, interrogate, and intimidate workers; they also threaten to or actually call in the Immigration and Naturalization Service and threaten to or actually move production to another shop or abroad. Internal conflicts within UNITE—between the two merging union leaderships, between the priorities of servicing old members and organizing new ones, and between the East Coast-centered white bureaucracy and the realities of immigrant organizing in Los Angeles—also hindered success.

The immigrant makeup of the Los Angeles workforce added to the difficulties of unionization there. Under the 1986 Immigration Reform and Control Act, employers could more easily fire workers involved in organizing, and judges could not order reinstatement—or now, back pay—

for fired workers if they were undocumented.[17] However, IRCA only aggravated an already dismal situation.

Union numbers dropped dramatically in two decades. By 1995, when the ILGWU merged with ACTWU to form UNITE, the ILGWU had only 109,000 members, the lowest number in more than sixty years (see Figure 1). In Los Angeles, union membership had also declined, even though production jobs had dramatically increased, as shown in Figure 5. By 1990, union density in Los Angeles, now the center of the U.S. garment industry, had dropped from an all-time high of nearly 60 percent to less than 3 percent, and union membership continued to decline in the 1990s.

Part of the decline in union membership throughout the country can be attributed to manufacturers' decreasing use of inside shops. From the 1970s on, many companies that had had their own facilities or relied on long-term union contractors, such as Liz Claiborne, Levi Strauss, and Koret of California, began to move their production abroad. Flexibility through outsourcing to small shops in the United States has been another strategy to increase competitiveness. According to the General Accounting Office's report on sweatshops, the number of establishments with 1–19 employees working in women's and misses' outerwear, the largest sector of the domestic garment industry, rose 51 percent between 1977 and 1982 (U.S. GAO 1988). My own analysis of the data shows that the number of small contractors in the United States increased starting in the 1970s but rose most dramatically from the late 1980s on. These changes parallel the rise in the 1970s and sharp increase in the 1980s of imports

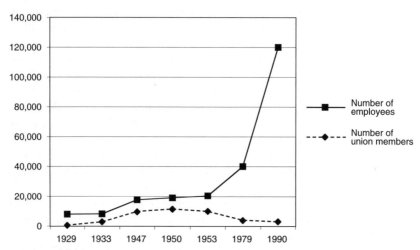

FIGURE 5. Number of Garment Workers and Union Members in Los Angeles, 1929–90. *Source:* Bonacich 1994; Laslett and Tyler 1989. Note that the data drawn from each year are from disparate sources.

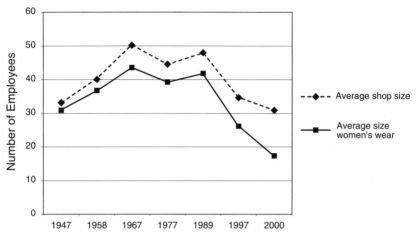

FIGURE 6. Average Shop Size in the U.S. Apparel Industry, 1947–2000.
Source: Census of manufacturers for 1947, 1958, and 1967 (after 1982, the census does not report establishment size). County Business Patterns: 1977, 1989, 1997, and 2000. Bureau of the Census.

with which these factories compete. The use of smaller shops further destabilized the jobs that remained in the United States. Small shops are more likely to have fluctuating production schedules and to run on small margins, leading to cycles of long hours and temporary layoffs; they are more likely to violate labor laws; and they are harder to organize.

As the percentage of workers employed in small shops grew, average shop size decreased. Shop size peaked in the late 1960s, at the same time as union membership, and then declined. Average shop size decreased even more dramatically in the women's outerwear sector, which dominates production in the Los Angeles area. Figure 6 demonstrates the dramatic decline.

Many small shops are obviously harder to regulate than a few large factories. The difficulties of enforcement have been greatly magnified by the lack of personnel in investigatory agencies. The ratio of workers to investigators rose 333 percent between 1957 and 1995. Whereas in 1957 there was one investigator for every 46,000 employees, by 1995 there were more than 150,000 workers and more than 8,500 workplaces for each investigator (Ross 2002). Although the numbers improved slightly in 1997, there were cuts again in 1999, and according to a DOL official in Los Angeles speaking in 2003, there has been a hiring freeze for the past two years.[18] The government's decreasing commitment to ensuring resources for enforcement began in the 1970s, coinciding with the proliferation of offshore production and contributing to the demise of the social contract.

CONCLUSION

The reliance on small contractors, declining power of workers, and decreasing government regulation served to create an atmosphere in which sweatshops once again flourished. By the 1980s, the government no longer attempted to balance power by redistributing wealth and supporting—at least, to some extent—workers' organizing. There was a change in the dominant view of unions. Strong unions were no longer seen as a means of providing a stable and reliable workforce and, ultimately, stable economic growth. Instead, they were represented as a barrier to competitiveness.

The internationalization of production had allowed for and driven the intensification of competition. Cutting costs was at a premium, and instability was part and parcel of the new economy, which revolved around flexible production systems. What was needed was a cheap labor force, not a stable one. Companies no longer benefited from unions, so the fragile partnership was broken. With the decline in tax revenues and the rise of a neoliberal philosophy of deregulation, the government no longer held up its end of the bargain by providing strong enforcement of laws or a safety net of social programs. The social contract had been shattered. Companies were searching the globe for cheap labor or trying to get U.S. labor to compete on the same terms. The 1990s ushered in the concept of monitoring to address the increasing problems that resulted from these shifts.

2   The Social-Accountability Contract

THE FALL of the social contract left a void in mechanisms to protect workers' rights. The resulting rise of the sweatshop caused waves of public consternation as the issue gained currency in the popular media. In response, the U.S. government devised the concept of monitoring to address the domestic problem and promoted codes of conduct for international production. A new model of labor relations was under construction.

What took shape in response to late-twentieth-century sweatshops is a new social contract—the "social-accountability contract"—in which employers make an agreement with the government, signed on to by the contractors, to protect the workers. Workers themselves are passive participants in the arrangement. A new triangle has thus emerged. This triangle of power, with employers, contractors, and the government forming its points, correlates to a triangle of resistance in which consumers and investors pressure manufacturers to change their practices, workers organize to force concessions from contractors, and civil society lobbies government to strengthen enforcement. With the weakening of unions and government enforcement, consumer and investor campaigns appear to be the dominant methods of addressing sweatshops. Monitoring, which companies use to advertise goodwill, to claim clean production, and to prevent exposés, is a means of simultaneously responding to and combating such campaigns.

Monitoring arises from an economic configuration in which consumers have increasing leverage and workers have decreasing power. Private monitoring is a means of removing workers, particularly female and ethnic-minority workers, from participation in the mechanism of rights enforcement. Private monitoring thereby reinforces rather than challenges workers' vulnerability.

This chapter begins with an explanation of how both the garment industry and monitoring are related to important facets of economic globalization, including horizontal webs of production, buyer-driven commodity chains, deregulation, the undermining of unions, and the use of vulnerable labor. Here I place the phenomenon of monitoring in the context of the literature on economic globalization and racialized and gendered labor. I then analyze the meaning and implications of the social-accountability contract that monitoring entails. By creating a theoretical framework, I place private monitoring in the broader context of power relations of the global economy and the shift away from the social contract.

Globalization, the Garment Industry, and the Rise of Private Monitoring

Mainstream economic, as well as Marxist, theory predicted that sweat-shops would disappear through progressive standardization and formal-ization of the economy (Edwards 1979; Varley 1998). This view under-lies the mainstream media's portrayal of sweatshops in the United States as remnants of a previous era. A corollary of this hypothesis is that the increase of sweatshops in the "industrialized world" is due to the influx of Third World immigrants, who import these practices or whose vul-nerability allows the practices to continue (Ross 2002; U.S. GAO 1998). However, there is much evidence that sweatshops are an integral part of the global economy, permitting companies to survive the intense compe-tition facilitated by modern technology (Bonacich and Appelbaum 2000; Bonacich et al. 1994; Piore 1997; Portes et al. 1989). Arrangements using ever more complex networks of contractors—where sweatshop condi-tions flourish—exemplify the international "webs of production" that form the structural basis of the global economy (Reich 1991).

Every period of capitalist development has its own particular form of labor relations (Gordon et al. 1982). The globalization of production emerged in part as an escape from traditional unionization strategies (Bonacich et al. 1994) and has proved successful in that respect (Chap-kis and Enloe 1993; Fuentes and Ehrenreich 1983; Martens and Mitter 1994; Ward 1990). With the period of globalization, the logic of the pre-vious labor-relations regime—collective bargaining between workers gath-ered in one factory and their employer—has broken down. The organi-zation of the global apparel industry is based on the fragmentation of the workplace and the workforce and a reliance on disenfranchised workers.

Emerging in the garment industry at the turn of the twenty-first cen-tury is a new social contract of sorts—what I call the social-accountabil-ity contract. This arrangement, solidified through the monitoring regime, shifts the position of workers to one outside the contract itself. Monitoring also allows profit makers to control labor relations in various sites at once while workers remain isolated from one another.

What about monitoring makes it suitable for the apparel industry of the global era? Table 1 connects aspects of globalization that scholars have identified as critical to the new economy, their role in the garment indus-try in particular, and their relationship to monitoring. I will discuss each of these areas in detail.

Webs of Production

Robert Reich, who oversaw the Department of Labor's monitoring pro-gram and initiated the Apparel Industry Partnership as secretary of labor under President Bill Clinton, well understood the nature of the global economy and laid forth its contours in his book *The Work of Nations*.

TABLE 1. Relationship of Global Economy to Garment Industry and Private Monitoring

Facet of global economy	Role in garment industry	Relationship to private monitoring
Horizontal webs of production	Industry structure based on complex subcontracting system in which manufacturers and retailers do not directly employ production workers; webs often international in scope	Attempts to create measure of joint liability between manufacturers and contractors for conditions of production; voluntary codes an international regulatory regime
Buyer-driven chains of production	Industry increasingly controlled by large retail chains that set prices; production consumption driven by market-specific demand and backward ordering	Caters to consumers by appearing to ensure "sweat-free" clothes; point-of-consumption response
Deregulation and privatization	Lack of effective government enforcement of labor laws	Emergence of private companies to enforce labor laws on a commercial basis
Undermining of union strength	Unionization levels extremely low because of internationalized labor-market competition and government's failure to protect workers' right to unionize	Undermines unionization by offering companies cover and mediating problems without worker organization
Use of vulnerable labor	Most workers are Third World women, many young and with little education; U.S. workers are also women, mainly immigrant and largely undocumented	Treats workers paternalistically; "protects" workers without involving them in the defense of their rights

Reich described the emergence of a new production system that involved horizontal production "webs" as opposed to the vertical enterprises that had grown up under Fordism. He detailed the shift from U.S. companies' owning their production chains, from design and marketing at the top to large production facilities at the bottom, to companies' operating through mind-boggling networks of smaller production units located across the globe (Reich 1991). Although Reich to some degree decries the demise of the social contract in this process, he assumes that it was an inevitable outcome of the optimal efficiency offered by new technology. This technology allowed for production to be relocated where the comparative advantage was greatest—labor-intensive work to low-wage countries and high-value-added work to countries with skilled and educated workforces. Although his theory cannot explain the reemergence of sweatshops in the industrialized world,[1] his account of globalization does describe the growing complexity of garment production in which companies such as Liz Claiborne and the Gap use an international network of buyers to arrange production with hundreds of sewing contractors in dozens of countries on several continents.

Although Reich gives an ultimately rosy picture of the prospects of globalization, other scholars analyze the deleterious effect that the reliance on far-flung networks of contractors has on labor. Manuel Castells notes that the key elements of the global economy—flexibility and networking—have led to a disaggregation of the labor process, a reversal of the socialization of production over the past fifty years, and a greater division in the workforce between "core" and "disposable" workers (Castells and Carnoy 1996). In the garment industry, this has meant the rise of small and offshore shops; a dispersion of production; and an organizational division between well-paid brand-name-employed designers, marketers, and managers and miserably paid, ever changing legions of sewing-machine operators. Saskia Sassen also points out that the rise of Reich's global managers and the exportation of steady-wage manufacturing jobs has led to a higher demand for labor-intensive products in industrialized countries. She argues that not everyone in Los Angeles and New York will benefit from globalization and that the resulting great disparities in wealth lead to sweatshops (for example) at both ends. The rich want handmade boutique items while the poor can afford only two-dollar T-shirts. The mass-produced-jeans-wearing middle class is disappearing (Sassen 1994).

An increased dependence on the subcontracting system allows core companies to respond to globalization by shifting risk through increased flexibility and lowered labor costs (Bonacich et al. 1994; Fernandez-Kelly and Garcia 1989; Ong et al. 1994). Contracting out work reduces the inputs related to labor not only by reducing overhead and paying less per hour or piece, but also because contractors often compete by avoiding such expenses as taxes, workers' compensation, insurance, registration fees, medical and other benefits, and expenditures associated with maintaining a safe and healthy work environment (Bonacich and Appelbaum 2000; Bonacich et al. 1994; Ong et al. 1994; Portes et al. 1989). Contracting out—particularly offshore—is also a means of avoiding unionization, as discussed earlier. In the garment industry, the increased use of subcontracting abroad and smaller units of production domestically are clearly related to the imperatives of competition created by globalization. Sweatshops by and large are not renegade garment producers selling out of alleys; they are part of much larger production chains tied to major manufacturers and retail stores (Bonacich and Appelbaum 2000).

The concept of monitoring is an acknowledgment of the relationship between sweatshops and large brand-name companies. Monitoring was meant to address the complications of a subcontracting system in which the legal link between garment manufacturers and production workers is tenuous, at best. Manufacturers were forced to take, and then accepted, the responsibility of supposedly keeping an eye on the conditions of work at the lowest level in their production chain, not just the quality of the garments those workers were producing. Moreover, voluntary codes of conduct are a type of pseudo-regulatory regime that reaches beyond a particular government's power to enforce its laws and thereby addresses the globalized nature of production chains.

Buyer-Driven Chains of Production

Scholars have addressed the issue of locating power and control in the global economy. Reich presents globalization as a diffusion of power through these webs of production. The concept of commodity chains also contradicts the notion that power is concentrated in a single site; rather, it is present at various nodes. However, the commodity-chain theory recognizes and analyzes the strong power differentials that exist within the production systems. Gary Gereffi distinguishes between producer-driven commodity chains and buyer-driven commodity chains operating in the global economy (Gereffi 1994). The first category consists of industries such as automobiles, computers, and aircraft, in which large integrated firms determine and carry out production in facilities they own as well as through networks of subsidiaries and component-supplying subcontractors. On the other side of the spectrum are buyer-driven commodity-chain industries, such as apparel, toys, and small electronics, in which the manufacturing process takes place entirely through contractors and it is the retailers, or "buyers," of the items that really determine production. The latter grouping, where the producer is subordinate, is made up of labor-intensive industries with low capitalization. Profit derives primarily not from production determinants such as labor process, scale, and technology, as in the first group, but from the selling-end factors of design, marketing, and consumer niches. Control is exercised at the point of consumption, not at the point of production (Gereffi 1994).

In the garment industry, the leverage exercised by retailers has grown substantially in recent decades. The consolidation of retailers in the 1970s and 1980s was accompanied by an enormous proliferation of sewing factories worldwide (Appelbaum et al. 1994). Six retail chains now sell more than half of all apparel bought in the United States (Mazur 1998). As a result, a few large retailers can almost unilaterally determine price, delivery time, and quality for manufacturers and ultimately for thousands of tiny competing factories. As one apparel executive stated, "You don't tell Wal-Mart your price. Wal-Mart tells you" (as quoted in Varley 1998: 95). Retailers are further reducing expenses and adding to cost pressures on producers by requiring them to pay for warehousing and delivery while the retailers maintain markups of 45–60 percent (Appelbaum et al. 1994; Gereffi 1994). Retailers are also using new computer technology to institute just-in-time provision of garments on their shelves for an increasing number of seasons. Retailers' traditional two seasons grew to Fall 1,

Fall 2, Holiday, Cruise, Spring, and Summer and now change even more often in stores such as the Gap, which presents a new line every month or two (Bonacich and Appelbaum 2000). While retailers cut their back inventory and provide consumers with an ever changing array of products, workers are under increasing time pressure. Unable to learn a style well before another is brought in, they cannot increase the number of pieces they sew in a day and, thus, their pay (Piore 1997). Retailers are further dominating the industry by eliminating the manufacturer, using their private labels or producing knock-offs of brand names (Appelbaum et al. 1994; Varley 1998).

It should be noted that retailers are even more protected than manufacturers from responsibility for sweatshop conditions. Even when retailers act like manufacturers, they are not covered by many of the laws passed in the social-contract era, such as the Garment Industry Proviso and the Fair Labor Standards Act prohibition of the shipment of "hot goods." Retailers are considered to be "bona fide" purchasers of goods rather than directly involved in their production.

Segmentation of the U.S. clothing market partially accounts for the rise of control at the point of consumption. Buyer-driven chains dominate the fashion, rather than mass-production, sectors of the industry (Gereffi 1994). Manufacturers no longer prosper by offering unending quantities of a limited variety of goods, such as Levi's 501 jeans. Instead, manufacturers must cater to a consuming public with myriad tastes, ages, and incomes. Department stores of the 1950s to 1970s assumed that a mother was buying for an entire middle-class suburban family. Now companies cater to all family members as they buy their own clothes. Moreover, the middle-class suburbanites represent a small portion of the consuming public (Gereffi 1994). A gap between rich and poor has also led to a diversification in demand, with large discounters (such as Wal-Mart and Kmart) and high-end specialty stores booming. Niche markets have proliferated with such brands as Quiksilver, which caters to surfers; FUBU (For Us By Us) for inner-city black youth; Abercrombie and Fitch for the gay community; and Gymboree, Baby Gap, and Gap Kids for yuppie offspring. Consumers play a greater role in an industry based on specialized products, ever changing fashion, and image, as shown by the enormous amounts of money apparel companies spend on advertising. Between 1993 and 1997, Nike quadrupled its yearly advertising budget to almost $1 billion (Shaw 1999).

The growth in branded products and the hype surrounding them is part of an increasing focus on the dynamics of consumption rather than production. The value of the logo now is often higher than the value of the product itself (Klein 1999). For example, the difference in the price of a Nike versus a no-name shoe is not the sum difference in the costs of the materials and labor; it is largely the added value of the swoosh symbol.

Because a brand's reputation is so central to profits, the consumers who are willing to pay for that brand, rather than the workers who produce the goods, have gained potential leverage with the companies.

Monitoring really caters to consumers' concerns. It is a point-of-consumption, not a point-of-production, response to sweatshops. The concept of monitoring rests on supposedly informing consumers about the conditions under which the products they buy are made. It does not empower the workers to put pressure on the companies; rather, it empowers the consumers to do so. From a Marxist perspective, monitoring can be seen as a move to demystify production, to de-fetishize the product. Monitoring potentially reveals to the consumer the actual labor involved in a worker's *making* an item, rather than the item's simply appearing in the store with its ostensible value represented by a price tag. Combined with worker organizing, this demystification could contribute to a powerful movement. However, as the apparel companies almost wholly control the process of private monitoring, it serves to remystify garment production by providing impossible and unsubstantiated assurances. A struggle over the public's awareness of production conditions has ensued, with companies claiming compliance and anti-sweatshop activists attempting to belie those claims through exposés.

Government Deregulation

The period of globalization has been accompanied by a dominant neoliberal economic philosophy that includes free trade, privatization, and deregulation as its principal tenets. Sassen argues that the deregulation of trade and financial flows was crucial to the development of the global economy (Sassen 1994). Within the United States, deregulation also played a principal role in the reemergence of sweatshops. Alejandro Portes, Manuel Castells, and Laura Benton argue that the informal economy, which includes sweatshops, has developed as a whole under government tolerance (Portes et al. 1989). The previous chapter detailed many of the trade initiatives, tax policies, and government loans that encouraged runaway shops and did nothing to protect workers in the countries to which garment production was transferred, resulting in low standards abroad and consequently lowered standards in the United States (Barnet and Cavanagh 1994; Rothstein 1989; Sklair 1994; Varley 1998). Also discussed were many changes in government policies in the late 1970s and through the 1980s that led to de-unionization and looser regulation of many domestic industries, including apparel (Bluestone and Harrison 1982; Carnoy et al. 1981).

While local directors of the U.S. Department of Labor in Los Angeles have certainly targeted the garment industry, they have tried to walk a very fine line, attempting to "clean up" the industry while not pushing manufacturers too far, lest they move production over the border. The

DOL's offices in Washington, D.C., took a more conservative stand in the establishment of the monitoring program than did local officials, clearly because they were more concerned about accusations of forcing jobs overseas, killing the industry, or slowing the economy.

The DOL has not been willing to consistently or effectively impose fines for violations, sue manufacturers for breaching monitoring agreements, or take other hard-line steps that might have a strong impact on the industry. Without fines, there is little incentive to comply with the law. If a contractor fails to pay the minimum wage or overtime and gets caught—a remote possibility, given the number of inspectors—he most likely will have to pay only what is already owed the worker. In other words, he loses nothing by cheating unless fined, and fines are so minimal that they have little effect. Although $3.5 million in back pay was collected for garment workers in 2000, less than $500,000 in fines were assessed nationwide.[2] In other words, on average, a contractor could pay a worker $3,500 when owed or take a very low risk of having to pay $4,000 later. Under the George W. Bush administration, the DOL has taken an even less confrontational tack. The word "sweatshop" has been removed from the DOL's vocabulary; legal monitoring agreements have been supplanted by voluntary commitments; and the department now focuses on "compliance assistance" and following up on workers' complaints rather than on proactive enforcement through random investigations and response to anonymous complaints.[3]

Enforcement, which has been significantly curtailed in Los Angeles since 2000, was already inadequate. In its report on sweatshops, the GAO (1988) notes that staffing levels of both federal and state investigators are too low, penalties are insufficient, and labor statutes are weak. In 1998, the DOL had 950 investigators for 6.5 million work sites (120 million workers). In Los Angeles, 42 inspectors cover 5,000 registered garment shops, probably another 2,000 underground shops, and all other industries, including restaurants, construction, retail, and filmmaking. Enforcement on the state level has also declined, with lower levels in 2000 than in 1990, 1980, and 1970 (Kessler 2002). While the number of employers in California doubled between 1982 and 2000, the enforcement staff of the state's DLSE decreased 6 percent. Even when workers file complaints, they may be fired for doing so; moreover, the cases languish for years, and even if they settle, the state is often unable to collect on judgments.[4]

The federal government cited its own limited capacity to enforce the law as the rationale behind the monitoring program. Given the ratio of investigators to shops, the DOL has called for the monitoring program as a partnership between manufacturers and the government. DOL staff have also publicly referred to monitors as an extended arm of the government. Once created, the capacity of the private sector far outstrips that of government. In 1998, the DOL and state investigators together conducted 1,000 garment investigations in the Los Angeles area while a few commercial firms conducted more than 10,000 compliance audits.

Because the monitors are either manufacturers' employees or employees of private commercial firms, monitoring can clearly be seen as a privatization of the enforcement of labor law. Private monitoring is a place where deregulation and privatization are fused, in that the deregulation drive includes a shift toward more privatized regulation. Environmental regulation has seen the same shift toward the private sector to a great extent. It has been argued that trends toward the privatization of regulation are happening in other arenas of workplace law enforcement, as well. For instance, Laura Edelman and colleagues have documented the trend toward courts' deferring to companies' internal grievance procedures in their decisions about the enforcement of sexual harassment and discrimination statutes (Edelman et al. 1999). The government's ceding the protection of workers' rights even partially to the private sector—and more egregiously, to the same private actors who benefit from the exploitation of those workers—is perhaps the most alarming facet of privatization.

Undermining Union Strength

The attack on unions has taken place not only directly through the changes in governmental policies discussed in the previous section, but also through a reorganization of work in the globalized era. In their book on the informal economy, Portes, Castells, and Benton argue that there is a systematic connection between the informal and the formal economy and that globalization has resulted in enormous growth of the former. They cite the effort to undermine unions as one cause of this growth. The power of organized labor is undermined by arranging production in small units, through homework, and by creating divisions among workers of different nations, races, and genders. The results are dramatic. As Castells and Portes put it, the new arrangements "deprive workers of even the meaning of a proletarian work relationship" (Castells and Portes 1989: 13). The growth in the heterogeneity of work sites and the number of intermediaries makes it harder for workers to form a class consciousness and subverts the logic of class struggle (Portes 1989). Workers are not brought together in ever larger work sites where their common experience unites them. Instead, they are separated into thousands of small shops isolated from one another by distance and anonymity, as well as by borders and language. They also have no clear adversary—each small grouping has its own relatively powerless boss. Intermediaries obfuscate who is in control and who the target of protest should be, as shop owners tell workers that some abstract customer determined the piece rate. Castells and Carnoy (1996) call this reorganization "a disaggregation of labor in the labor process," and they note its deleterious effects on unionization.

It is not only the growth of the informal sector, including small contracting shops and homework, that has undermined unionization. The opening of trade with little attention to the enforcement of labor rights on an international level has also done so. The concept of fair trade, in which labor and environmental protections are incorporated, has lost out to the doctrine of free trade. Free trade is far from a simple elimination of tariffs. However, although agreements include complicated language requiring extensive changes in national laws to protect corporate rights through the enforcement of patents and intellectual-property claims, they do not effectively protect labor rights.

Unionists and others have tried for many years to win the insertion of labor-rights protections into international trade agreements, where they would have the force of action behind them. Activists have had the most success with inclusion in unilateral and bilateral trade agreements, although with limited results. The Caribbean Basin Initiative includes labor-rights protections, but the United States has never denied any country benefits based on violating such rights (Tsogas 2001). In 1984, Congress added a government's progress in protecting labor rights as an eligibility criteria for the Generalized System of Preferences, which gives developing countries preferential tariffs. Of eighty-six petitions submitted for review between 1985 and 1995, eleven resulted in a country's being removed or temporarily suspended from the GSP program (Tsogas 2001). Bilateral trade agreements with Jordan and Cambodia have also included labor-rights provisions. Cambodia's agreement is directed specifically at textiles and garments, as is a similar bilateral agreement with Vietnam that is still under negotiation. The Cambodian agreement has led to guarded optimism about improvements in labor conditions. However, all bilateral agreements become moot upon entrance to the World Trade Organization (Wells-Dang 2002). Although Vietnam and Cambodia have not yet been admitted, they are lobbying and preparing to do so. The effect of all these programs is dwindling as the reduction in tariffs and quotas are increasingly determined by superseding regional and global trade agreements (Tsogas 2001).

Although unionists and labor advocates have been able to creatively capitalize on small gains, they have not had much success in tying trade to labor-rights guarantees in these broader trade agreements. Congress refused to include labor rights in the North American Free Trade Agreement. A labor side accord was negotiated but has no sanctions or strong enforcement mechanism. Moreover, complaints must be brought through a laborious procedure. Still, unions and labor advocates have used the legal process as part of larger political and public-relations strategies that have had concrete outcomes in terms of policy changes, union recognition, and the development of cross-border cooperation among labor-oriented groups (Graubart 2002).

The WTO agreements to date include no trade sanctions tied to labor rights. During the long negotiations of the General Agreement on Tariffs and Trade, labor advocates unsuccessfully fought for the insertion of a "social clause" to protect workers' rights (Haworth and Hughes 2000). The same struggle has been repeated throughout the negotiations over the WTO, the new international-commerce agency that is charged with enforcing GATT. The WTO could actually result in the weakening of labor standards by disallowing any trade restrictions by individual signatories that do not conform to the general agreement.[5] At its 1996 meeting, the WTO issued a statement that included the following language: "We reject the use of labor standards for protectionist purposes, and agree that the comparative advantage of countries, particularly low-wage countries, must in no way be put into question" (as reprinted in Varley 1998: 37). Strong opposition from business interests in the industrialized world and the governments and elites of developing countries have defeated the inclusion of workers' rights protections in the WTO agreements, leaving the defense of such rights to the International Labour Organization, which has no enforcement mechanisms at its disposal.

In response, the ILO has proposed a number of measures that have not come to fruition. One is that membership in the organization should include ratification and enforcement of its core labor standards. The United States has ratified only two of the eight core conventions—one of two prohibiting types of forced labor and one on child labor. Another defunct proposal involved creating an international inspection apparatus that would ascertain whether a country was enforcing the core labor standards. If a country passed, it would be allowed to affix an ILO "global social label" to all goods manufactured there (Varley 1998). The ILO is a participating agency in the United Nations' Global Compact launched in 2000. This initiative promotes multinationals' adoption of labor, human-rights, and environmental principles through multisectorial dialogues and projects. While the first among the labor standards is that businesses "should uphold the freedom of association and the effective recognition of the right to collective bargaining," many labor activists have decried the program as another corporate-responsibility scheme with no power to oversee or enforce its principles (Broad 2002).[6]

Without international protections, unions have not fared well under globalization. Unionization in many countries is violently put down by governments as well as by business. In export-processing zones, which are often gated and secured by armed guards, unionization campaigns have almost universally led to firings and layoffs and often to physical abuse. In 1982, striking women in South Korea were beaten and arrested by police. The scene was repeated the same year in a free-trade zone in the Philippines when 10,000 workers protested conditions. The Philippine government responded by passing new anti-labor measures. There are other examples from Mexico to Sri Lanka (Fuentes and Ehrenreich 1983; Karl and Cheung 1993). The trend continues. In 1999, striking garment workers in Indonesia and Honduras were beaten; workers in El Salvador were threatened with death. Some unions do exist, but very few have collective-bargaining agreements, and most campaigns are aborted by firings and plant closings (Martens and Mitter 1994; Quinteros et al. 1998). Annette Fuentes and Barbara Ehrenreich (1983) have documented that governments interested in continuing to attract the presence of multinationals are heavily involved in repressing organizing drives.

Harley Shaiken describes how a controlled labor force is created in Mexican export industries through government control of official unions and repression of independent unions, as well as through other government policies to keep wages low in order to attract investment (Shaiken 1993, 1994). The situation also results in downward pressure on wages and a check on organizing in the United States. In the United States, the threat of job relocation is constant, and workers are illegally fired, laid off, and harassed for organizing (Appelbaum 1999, Delgado 1993; Human Rights Watch 2000).

Private monitoring enters this picture as another weak attempt to address the issue of labor rights without actually enforcing those rights. Private monitoring does not bolster workers' key rights to freedom of association and collective bargaining. In fact, it can undermine those rights. Companies have used their monitoring schemes for public-relations purposes in the struggle for public sympathy during unionization campaigns. GUESS?, for example, took out full-page newspaper advertisements slamming the union while proclaiming the relative advantages of monitoring. Companies have also used monitors to undermine workers' rights. Moreover, unions have accused NGO monitors in Central America of mediating problems, obscuring the need to unionize. Many unionists oppose outright or are highly skeptical of even alternative forms of monitoring that may infringe on their role in the employer–worker relationship, although I will argue in Chapter 7 that independent monitoring, as opposed to private monitoring, can in fact support workers' organizing.

Use of Vulnerable Labor

The garment industry has always relied on women and, to a great degree, immigrants as the mainstay of its labor force. However, with globalization, the garment industry combines the ideologies and material consequences of nativism, racism, and sexism ever more effectively to exploit predominantly disenfranchised Third World women. In the United States, most of the workers are immigrants. In Los Angeles, where the number of Latin American men working in the garment industry is actually growing, a large portion of the workers are undocumented. Abroad, most garment workers are newly proletarianized women who have come from rural or informal economies. In many countries, the workers are also extremely young. Even within the export-industry sector there is segmentation, with garments, as opposed to electronics, hiring the most vulnerable workers. Along the Mexican border, this has meant that older women with children, less education, and less time in the area have been employed in garment making (Fernandez-Kelly 1983; Tiano 1990).

Immanuel Wallerstein argues that racism—and, one could argue, patriarchy—reconciles two objectives: It minimizes the cost of labor while minimizing protest by naturalizing divisions in pay (Wallerstein 1991). Historically, the clothing industry has used racial- and ethnic-minority women to justify low wages and de-skilling. In Massachusetts, early textile-factory owners first recruited Anglo-Saxon country girls, who later organized to protest deteriorating conditions. Protest was undermined by the influx of Irish immigrants, who were divided from the Anglos in housing and job assignments and who had far more limited economic options (Dublin 1979).

In all industrialized countries today, garment factories hire immigrant women, combining sexism and racism to justify and enforce low wages. In the United States, Latinas predominate; in Canada, Filipinas; in Australia, Greek and Italian women; and in Britain, Bangladeshi women (Enloe 1993). Immigrants are often blamed for causing sweatshops. In a GAO survey of federal labor officials, the most common answer to the question of what were the major factors in the existence of sweatshops was immigrant workers (U.S. GAO 1988). However, many sociologists argue that immigrants do not create these opportunities but are in a position to take advantage of them, as well as to be taken advantage of by them (Portes 1989; Sassen 1998; Sassen-Koob 1989). Immigrants come because there is demand for their labor.

Heidi Hartman (1979) has theorized that, when the balance of power shifts toward capitalists and away from the organized (male) working class, capitalists gain the ability to undercut relatively privileged workers by using more vulnerable (female) labor. The globalization of production and the political imperatives that have accompanied it have caused such a shift. As described earlier, the breaking of the social contract involved the undermining of union strength. The ability of companies to switch from domestic production, where unions had great influence, to widespread use of offshore production meant that companies could search out the cheapest and most vulnerable labor abroad. Companies also relied on the most vulnerable labor at home, because domestic workers were forced to compete with those abroad—standards were lowered and protest was deterred by threats of plant closings.

In this section, "vulnerable workers" are defined as those constructed by society as disadvantaged in the labor market. The societal production of categories of gender, race, and citizenship all serve, and overlap, to create certain groups of workers as disadvantaged. Many theorists of race agree that racialization, the process by which groups of people are defined as distinct and placed in a hierarchy of status, is based on an intersection of ideology (beliefs, understandings, explanations) and structures (organizations, policies, practices). However, theorists differ in the weight given the economic arena. In their seminal work on the social construction of race, Michael Omi and Howard Winant (1986) posit that the labor market is one mechanism among many, including the patriarchal family and the democratic state, that both produce and reproduce people as racialized beings. Others, such as the sociologist Tomás Almaguer (1994), see economic competition as central to the racialization process. Robert Thomas, in his study of the lettuce industry, argues that "agribusiness firms, as well as their counterparts in other sectors of the economy, do not create the distinguishing statuses of gender, citizenship, or race, but rather seize upon and transform those characteristics to the organization's advantage" (Thomas 1985: 27). Thomas argues that different statuses are reinforced within the labor process but do not originate there.

The ideologies that render workers vulnerable and many of the social policies that enact such vulnerability are embedded in every sphere of life. These spheres are difficult to disentangle. Capitalists as a group, often organized within their sector, play an active role in the *political* formation of racial, citizenship, and gender meanings insofar as they influence the political process and lobby for specific policies. They also enforce labor practices (recruitment preferences, wage setting, task assignment, schedule requirements, and so on) that reenact difference in a variety of ways on a daily basis. I argue that monitoring is just such a practice.

For the case of garment workers, the focus here is on three interconnected aspects of the ways in which women and immigrants have been disadvantageously constructed: as supplemental wage earners, as docile, and as unorganizable. Society produces both women and immigrants as low-wage workers through legal constraints and ideological constructions (Phizacklea 1983). Society brands women and immigrants as supplemental wage earners, as unorganizable, and as docile, but it also enforces these constructs as norms through laws, institutions (including schools and families), and the economy. Moreover, these three constructs are mutually constitutive.

Neither women nor immigrants have been constructed as family wage earners. Marx pointed out that, for capitalism to survive, the labor force must be continuously replenished. Therefore, capitalists need to pay not only for the costs of producing labor (the basic necessities of a given worker) but also for reproducing workers (the costs involved in propagating, raising, and educating the next generation of workers) (Marx 1978 [1849]). However, women's reproductive labor is generally performed for free (without a wage) within a patriarchal family. So by paying a family wage to men, capitalists receive both production and reproduction through the spouse's unpaid work (Eisenstein 1979). A sector of capitalists is able to avoid such expenditures—that is, to pay a far lower wage by using labor whose reproduction costs are *supposedly* subsidized. Lower wages for women can be justified because women have not been culturally constructed as breadwinners; a male head of household is assumed to earn enough to cover reproductive costs. Immigrants are presumed to be supporting a family back home, where expenses are minimal compared with U.S. dollars. Even as families move to join immigrant workers, and women are becoming heads of households in unprecedented numbers, these ideologies continue to have material effects as seen in the persisting wage gaps between women and men and between native-born and immigrant workers.

These ideological constructions of women and immigrants as supplemental earners who are not responsible for reproductive costs are sometimes reinforced by state policies. Examples for women include sex-specific protective legislation and school holidays with no child-care coverage, which require women to have flexible jobs, thus excluding them from participation in family-wage jobs (Phizacklea 1983). Guest-worker programs, whereby individuals are admitted temporarily for specific employment, and California's Proposition 187, which tried to deny state-sponsored medical benefits and education to undocumented immigrants (and their children), reinforce the idea that reproduction is not to take place within the adopted country. If reproduction takes place in the home country instead, employers get a double bonus: They are spared the direct expense of paying a wage sufficient to support a family and of providing family medical care or family leave, and they enjoy lower taxes in a society that does not have to pay for education, medical care, and protective and social services for the family members of their workers.

Women actually carry the burden of this myth of subsidized reproduction in two ways. Not only are they paid lower wages in the marketplace, but they then return home at the end of this long, miserably paid day to do the housework for no pay at all (Sokoloff 1988). Many of these women are heads of households, forced to survive on an unrealistic wage and to work a double shift. This creates an unending circle in that women with home responsibilities are unable to get higher-paying jobs, which require more hours, more flexibility, and more permanent commitment than domestic duties allow.

Patriarchy combines with capitalism to oppress women not only by placing demands that physically restrict their earning capacity but also by materially hindering their ability to organize. The double day makes it impossible for many women to attend meetings, join unions, or even have the energy to *imagine* challenging the system (Louie 1992; Martinez and Quinteros 1997). The "unorganizability" of women then contributes to their continued low wages and exploitation in the place of employment and is therefore directly tied to their status as secondary earners. Thus, the constructions of supplemental-wage earners and unorganizability are mutually reinforcing for women.

For most garment workers, their status as immigrants compounds the difficulties presented by the double day. Government policies often enforce a certain level of docility on immigrants and make organizing extremely difficult. Many immigrants are placed in a position that gives them little choice but to accept the conditions of work. In 1998, the Immigration and Naturalization Service carried out Operation Buttonhole in Los Angeles, raiding a number of garment factories (Bacon 2000). The DOL had provided underlying information for these raids. Twenty immigrant and labor groups filed a formal complaint against the United States over DOL and INS collaboration generally because of its chilling effect on immigrant workers' rights and the government agencies were forced to partly change their policy, although some collaboration still occurs.[7] The DOL still provides the INS with information from its investigations although not from workers' complaints. Moreover, there are many examples of employers' calling in the INS during organizing drives, despite the INS's vow not to interfere in labor disputes.[8]

Finally, federal laws conflict. For instance, the 1986 Immigration Reform and Control Act penalizes employers who knowingly employ undocumented workers and requires them to check employees' documents. Under this law, undocumented workers may not be reinstated, despite a decision by the National Labor Relations Board that returning them to their jobs, with back pay, is the proper remedy for a retaliatory firing for union organizing. In many cases, a compromise has been struck whereby undocumented immigrants have been given back pay for the time between the illegal firing and the board decision but have not been reinstated. However, in 2002, the U.S. Supreme Court ruled in *Hoffman Plastics Compounds Inc. v. NLRB* that undocumented workers fired for unionization activities are not entitled to back pay, either. Thus, employers may now fire undocumented workers for organizing with no risk of any legal sanction. As the labor and immigration lawyer Mussafar Chishti wrote (even before the Supreme Court decision), IRCA has "become a highly useful tool in the hands of unscrupulous employers in their ability to suppress workers' rights, especially the right to organize" (Chishti 2000: 74).

Part of the perceived—and to some degree, real—problem with organizing in Los Angeles has been the high proportion of workers who are undocumented. Hector Delgado, whose study predates IRCA, points out that the willingness and ability of even undocumented workers to organize is differentiated along a number of axes, including geographical proximity of homeland, degree of adaptation, strength of social networks, labor-market placement, and absence of co-ethnic relationship with employers. Many external circumstances also determine the likelihood of organizing, including activities of the INS and the legal (labor and immigration) environment (Delgado 1993).

Perhaps the most important factor, however, is unions' commitment to organize or support the organization of these workers. Where this commitment has been strong, immigrant, including undocumented, workers have successfully organized.[9] As the century turns, the labor movement is realizing that, just as at the turn of the last century, immigrants are the best potential organizing base (Milkman 2000). Despite their social construction and the legal difficulties and other drawbacks mentioned, many immigrant workers possess social-network ties, activist backgrounds, and positive dispositions toward unions from their country of origin, all of which aid organizing efforts tremendously.

While the labor movement has begun to recognize the organizing potential of immigrant workers, immigrants' position has often been undermined by labor unions themselves. Until February 2000, the AFL-CIO supported IRCA and was among its leading proponents, believing it would "protect American workers against 'unfair' competition from abroad" (Zolberg 1990). Unions have been weakened by their own inability to adapt to a new globalized economy and, until recently, their inability to organize new immigrants (Castells and Carnoy 1996). The AFL-CIO's history and legacy of racism has not helped in attracting new immigrant members or in making a strong commitment to these workers (Brody 1993). Although the garment workers' union was founded by immigrants, it has remained Jewish at the top and has had little success organizing among Latinos in Los Angeles (Delgado 1993; Laslett 1993). Moreover, the AFL-CIO's long-standing protectionist stance and involvement in the oppression of progressive unions in the developing world has not helped its reputation among immigrants from the Third World (Barry and Preusch 1990). Since 1995 and the election of John Sweeney to head the AFL-CIO, the federation has changed its policies, purging the "cold warriors" from its ranks, disbanding the notorious American Institute for Free Labor Development, and reorganizing its international offices to promote worker solidarity. However, this comes after decades of allying itself with the military and dictatorships in Latin America and elsewhere (Scipes 2000).

Many unions at home and abroad have also not been successful at organizing women because of their internal dynamics and because of the way patriarchy works in the society at large. As stated, women who work a double day are often unable to attend meetings outside work. But unions have not aggressively addressed this problem. Historically, unionists have often seen women as akin to scabs rather than as fellow workers. In 1906, Samuel Gompers, head of the American Federation of Labor, wrote: "It is the so-called competition of the unorganized defenseless woman worker, the girl and the wife, that often tends to reduce the wages of the father and husband" (as quoted in Kessler-Harris 1982: 154). While such attitudes are no longer expressed in such blunt terms, they remain embedded in much of the labor movement. One reason more progress has not been made is that unions have been male-dominated and often not sensitive to women's issues (Anner 1998; Bick-ham-Mendez and Kopke 1998; Laslett and Tyler 1989; Martinez and Quinteros 1997; Mitter 1994; Waldinger 1985). This is in part due to a predominance of male leadership. In 1978, the membership of the ILGWU was 80 percent female, but only 7 percent of the officers and board members were women (Milkman 1985). By 1990, women's percentage of leadership positions had risen to 22 percent but still did not approach any reflection of their membership, which had risen to 83 percent (Cobble 1993). In addition, female leaders have often been marginalized (Laslett 1993; Laslett and Tyler 1989).

Difficulties in organizing also reinforce, and are reinforced by, the idea that women and immigrants are passive. Historically, when the clothing industry first chose women workers, capitalists cited family ideology and biological myths to justify the use of women and their low pay. In the 1830s, the textile mills in Lowell, Massachusetts, recruited the daughters of local farmers, noting that they only needed to supplement their families' income and that they had a "natural" ability at sewing and would thus be apt workers (Dublin 1979). It is not just that women knew how to sew from domestic production; the traits that made them good sewing-machine operators were precisely those that would keep them docile. Wendy Chapkis and Cynthia Enloe (1993: 2) point out that garment employers rationalize hiring women by referring to characteristics that epitomize vulnerability: "patience, tolerance for monotony, 'nimble fingers', attention to detail, little physical strength, no mechanical aptitude, no capacity to assert authority and a desire to be mothers and wives, not workers, first and foremost." Susan Tiano (1990) also discusses the use of ideology to justify women's employment in the Mexican garment industry. She posits that the cultural ambivalence about women working allows for low wages and bad conditions because it is assumed, despite the contrary reality, to be a temporary situation.

Karen Hossfeld (1990) compares gender logic and race logic, arguing that gender logic is internalized and can be much more easily used to justify low wages, bad job assignments, and so on. Race logic, however, is broadly deemed unacceptable and must be disguised as immigrant logic. So it is no longer acceptable to pay workers less because they are Latino, but it is all right to do so because they are newly arrived immigrants who perhaps expect less, need less because the family is at home, and/or are satisfied with less because their pay is still high compared with the home currency. Moreover, as immigrants, they are believed to be less likely not only to need more but also to demand more—that is, to be docile.

Immigrants are often thought to be exploited in ethnic enclaves that allow shop owners, particularly male shop owners, to rely on the loyalty of relatives and co-ethnics, who are often women. This loyalty implies tolerating bad conditions and not revealing violations (Portes and Manning 1986; Ross 1997). This model applies to much of the garment production in New York and San Francisco, where Chinese contractors invariably hire Chinese workers and Dominicans hire other Latinos (Waldinger 1986). However, the situation is far more complex in the Los Angeles garment industry, where minority-group factory owners of one ethnicity (often Korean) act as middlemen and buffers between the dominant-group–owned (white) manufacturers and the oppressed workers of another ethnicity, in this case generally Mexican and Central American (Bonacich and Appelbaum 2000; Fernandez-Kelly and Garcia 1989). This is often also the case in Central America, for example, where many of the contractors are Korean and Taiwanese working for U.S. transnational corporations.

The immigrant standing works differently for the middlemen, who generally have more access to resources, credit, information, and business experience than their workers do (Bonacich 1973; Portes 1986). Connections abroad to networks within the global system can also place a group of immigrants in a position of advantage—for example, Cubans in Miami (Stepick 1989). This is true of Korean garment contractors, who have an extensive network in Asia, Latin America, and Los Angeles (Bonacich and Appelbaum 2000; Lee and Song 1994; Light and Bonacich 1988; Petersen 1994; Quinteros et al. 1998). However, it should be noted that these middlemen, like the immigrant workers themselves, are often a form of cheap labor, putting in more time for less pay than native-born managers would (Light and Bonacich 1988).

In conclusion, the garment industry relies on a workforce made vulnerable by materially enforced ideologies of nativism, sexism, and racism, as well as by legal constraints and union indifference. Private monitoring does not challenge this system. Instead, it depends on and strengthens the construction of this workforce as vulnerable by treating the worker not as an agent but as a victim in need of protection. Under an alternative approach, monitoring could integrally involve workers in the process and focus on their right to organize, as will be seen in the final chapters. Monitoring could thus be a vehicle for empowerment. However, private monitoring can be seen as an institutionalization of vulnerability. Private monitoring entails the establishment of an entire industry and set of practices to protect workers without empowering them in any way. The system generates the threat of layoffs and firings with no guarantees of improvement. Worse, the workers are most often not even informed of monitoring, which was set up for their benefit. Private monitoring can thus be viewed as a new form of paternalism—one that does not even involve the consent of the worker. In the social-accountability scheme, the company is accountable to the consumer, the government, and the monitoring oversight body, but never to the worker.

THE SOCIAL CONTRACT VERSUS THE SOCIAL-ACCOUNTABILITY CONTRACT

It is commonly accepted that labor relations in the United States during the mid-twentieth century were characterized by a social contract that bound together government, employers, and workers, who were represented through their unions (Bluestone and Harrison 1982; Carnoy et al. 1981). Workers in the garment industry benefited from a relatively strong union. Membership in the ILGWU, which began to rise sharply in the 1930s, reached 400,000 in the late 1940s and continued above this level until the early 1970s, when it began its precipitous decline. While the decline mirrored a decline in jobs, it far outstripped the downward trend of employment. The union was weakened by deregulation, anti-union government policies, and the employers' constant threat to move production abroad.

In 1974, Richard Barnet and Ronald Muller predicted in *Global Reach* that government enforcement and strong unions could provide a "countervailing power" to multinational corporations (Barnet and Muller 1974). However, these two forces have only weakened in the intervening quarter-century. As Michael Piore writes of the domestic sweatshop, "The people who suffer these deplorable conditions are more accurately the victims of the reaction against unions and 'big government'" (Piore 1997: 142). By the 1980s, sweatshops were on the rise—a clear signal that the social contract had been shattered. The 1990s saw the emergence in its place of a new social-accountability contract in the form of monitoring.

In contrast to the tripartite social contract of the mid-1900s, the social-accountability contract involves workers in a minor and, more important, passive role. Workers have been left out of the formal contract altogether. Although the union staff of the social-contract era did not demographically represent workers, and it was not always sensitive to female workers' concerns, the union was elected by its members and accountable to them. Under the social-accountability contract, the manufacturer is made accountable *for* the workers. This shift is represented in Figure 7.

Today's agreements bring the government—or NGOs as alternative public institutions—together with manufacturers and contractors. In Los Angeles, manufacturers literally sign a monitoring agreement with the

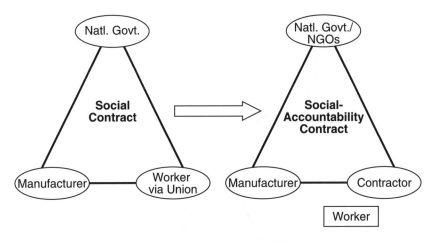

FIGURE 7. Shift from Social Contract to Social-Accountability Contract

DOL: the Augmented Compliance Program Agreement.[10] Each of the companies' contractors then has to sign on to the agreement. Not only are the workers not signatories, they generally are not even aware that such an agreement exists.

On the international level, the federal government played the role of prompting and facilitating an agreement while human-rights, labor, and consumer groups negotiated the accord. In 1998, the company and NGO members of the AIP signed the Fair Labor Association, an agreement to create an international monitoring system for the protection of workers. Contractors will have to agree to the monitoring before it takes place. The unions, representing the workers, refused to sign, taking the position that the agreement could only undermine the workers' struggle by covering up problems and codifying miserable conditions.[11]

The three signatories to the ACPA correspond directly to the three points of what intellectuals and activists in El Salvador refer to as the *"triangulo de poder."*[12] This "triangle of power" is meant to describe the structure of domination perpetrated through the maquila system. As in the United States, the three actors are the national government, the manufacturer (always a U.S. or European transnational corporation), and the contractor. I suggest that there is also a triangle of resistance putting pressure on each of these points: *local civil society,* which is pushing the state for legal and budgetary reform to strengthen labor-code enforcement or for stronger standards in the AIP process;[13] *workers,* who are organizing in the contracting facility; and *consumers and investors,* as well as the activists who try to motivate them, who are pressuring the manufacturers through boycotts, publicity, and other corporate-campaign strategies. These relationships are represented in Figure 8.

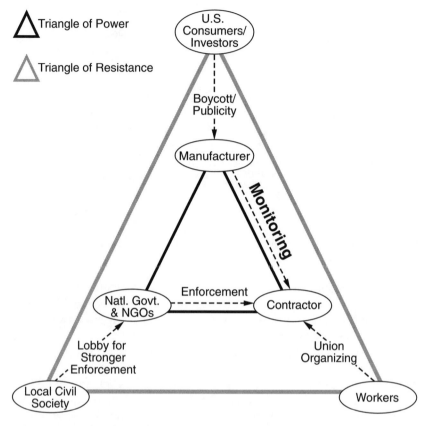

FIGURE 8. Triangles of Power and Resistance in the Garment Industry

Figure 8 not only delineates the players involved but also represents (with dashed arrows) the three strategies of combating sweatshops: enforcement, union organizing, and boycotts, publicity, and other corporate campaign tactics. To address sweatshop conditions, each strategy must have a practical impact on the shop floor (that is, an impact on the contractor). Enforcement involves the direct intervention of the government at the factory level through inspections and assessment of back wages and penalties. Organizing, when successful, results in collective bargaining—or, at least, negotiation—with the factory owner. Consumer and investor campaigns pressure the manufacturer, which most often responds by passing a code of conduct or by intervening at the factory level through monitoring.

In Figure 8, I have reoriented the inner triangle relative to Figure 7 to represent the power relations engendered by global capitalism. In Figure 8, manufacturers as well as consumers appear on top, because they wield the most power. Manufacturers negotiated the ACPA and AIP agreements—the former with the government, the latter with NGOs and the government's mediation. The U.S. government, while still able to force manufacturers into agreements through legal means, is hesitant to push too hard lest corporations flee. Using NGOs instead of the government to negotiate the international agreement further weakens this point in the triangle. Although they may have some "moral authority" and may be able to bring public and media attention to bear, NGOs lack enforcement powers and the ability to require manufacturers' cooperation, elements that are still within the government's purview in the domestic context. In the case of the AIP, it is clear that NGOs were out-negotiated in several areas in order to at least establish a "floor" and not lose the *voluntary* participation of the manufacturers altogether.[14]

In neither case did the contractors have a voice in the structure of the agreements or principles on which the monitoring is based. Contractors do not have much power vis-à-vis manufacturers, given the structure of the garment industry. However, to some extent they do have the ability to decide whether to work for manufacturers involved in monitoring, and some have refused. They are involved in the agreements to the extent that they accept them, and in many cases they have been able to affect the actual implementation of monitoring practices—for example, to insist that visits be announced, to turn in payroll records late, and to select the workers to be interviewed. Moreover, they retain a great deal of power vis-à-vis the workers, who have no influence over the practices of monitoring; who have not been privy to negotiations of the ACPA; and whose union felt excluded in the final stages of the AIP process and in the end decided not to sign on.[15]

This imbalance of power is also clear when one looks at the relative capacity of the different strategies of intervention. Enforcement, which relies on the power of local government, and organizing, which depends on the power of workers, are floundering while corporate campaigns and monitoring, which rely on publicity and consumer/investor power, are on the upsurge. With its near-scriptural tenets of deregulation and privatization, and with manufacturers' ability to easily cross borders beyond a government's control, globalization has undermined the ability of local governments to enforce their own laws. Workers' power has been greatly decreased in the global era by the reliance on vulnerable labor, undercutting of unions, mobility of capital, and inter-country wage competition. In contrast, the power of investors and consumers has been greatly increased in a world where global, consumer-driven, image-dependent companies vie for stock value. Thus, the decline of enforcement and unionization efforts, coupled with the buyer-driven nature of production, has led to the dominance of consumer and investor pressure. Monitoring caters to these actors.

The new preeminence of consumer-based strategies becomes a weakness in two ways: it can upset the potential synergy of different forms of resistance, and it creates an opportunity for manufacturers to obscure continuing problems by offering up monitoring as a "solution." The actors involved in resistance (consumers/investors, civil society, and workers) are not mutually exclusive; constituencies, in fact, overlap. And in the best scenario, the strategies would be coordinated and reinforcing. Media coverage, stockholder resolutions, and other corporate-campaign strategies help to establish in both the popular and corporations' imagination the principle of corporate responsibility, while lobbying can advance legislation to legally establish this concept, as in the case of a 1999 garment bill (AB 633) in California (see Chapter 4). Labor campaigns have long tried to support workers' organizing with consumer campaigns, as in the grape boycotts of the 1960s. However, such coordination has become extremely difficult to achieve with globalization. The GUESS? campaign of the mid-1990s, which involved both worker organizing and consumer—particularly student—protests and petitions, ended with the jeans maker simply moving production from Los Angeles to Mexico. In 1995, a U.S.-led consumer campaign against the Gap, which included prolific press coverage, rallies, and letter-writing drives, won independent monitoring, but a beleaguered and divided union on the ground in El Salvador failed to organize successfully. Both cases point to complex problems of communication and coordination, as well as to an enormous imbalance in power.

Pressuring the manufacturer for corporate accountability may at least be positively linked to enforcement and organizing. The manufacturers' response of monitoring, however, threatens to further destabilize these other two forms of intervention. As described earlier, private monitoring has been presented by industry proponents as an alternative to unionization and as a privatization of government enforcement.[16] The federal government itself describes monitoring as "an extension of the government" and a "partnership."[17] Further, manufacturers have been able to avoid certain aspects of enforcement, such as awaiting official DOL approval to move "hot goods," by signing a monitoring agreement.

Private monitoring offers manufacturers multiple benefits. First, monitoring has been a wedge to avoid enforcement and to help forestall legal reform for more serious forms of joint liability that would make manufacturers responsible for their suppliers' compliance with legal standards. At a forum for manufacturers and monitors in August 1998, Gerald Hall, district director of the DOL in Los Angeles, warned that if manufacturers did not take monitoring seriously and clean up the industry, legislation would be passed in Washington that would be "very negative." Senator Edward Kennedy (D-Mass.) and Representative William "Lacy" Clay (D-Mo.) introduced a federal bill in 1997 to create joint liability in the apparel industry: the "Stop Sweatshops" bill.[18] The Republicans tried to create a version that would exempt manufacturers from joint liability if they conducted monitoring of their contractors.[19]

Second, the manufacturers clearly use monitoring to mediate relations with consumers and investors as much as to clean up abhorrent conditions. Liz Claiborne and Kathy Lee Gifford, for example, both used their monitors' findings to publicly repudiate workers' reports of violations. Companies use monitoring not only to defend against specific accusations, but more generally as a form of advertisement and a way to placate disgruntled consumers and investors. Companies such as Nike, the Gap, and GUESS? send information to consumers, investors, those who have signed petitions against them, and the like, proclaiming their progressive labor practices based on their monitoring programs.[20] In response to a citizen-action request from Working Assets Long Distance (WALD; a socially responsible telephone company), Nike sent WALD customers a four-page letter defending it labor practices overseas and its charitable record. First on the list was that Nike "was the first company in the industry to establish and strictly monitor enforcement of a Code of Conduct for its contractors." A leaked Nike audit of a Vietnamese factory showed that Nike's "professional" audit was neither strict nor professional (O'Rourke 1997). The Gap takes a much more cautionary stance in its code, stating that the company "will continue to develop monitoring systems to assess and ensure compliance."[21] A letter to a concerned consumer, however, touts the Gap's monitoring program, which consists of "a global network of employees who are dedicated full time to monitoring factory compliance." GUESS? took out full-page ads in major newspapers promoting itself as a leader in the fight against sweatshops based on its monitoring program, even as the DOL continued to find its contractors in violation of the law. In the midst of a struggle with UNITE, GUESS? also advertised to consumers that its monitored shops were cleaner than unionized shops.

Finally, monitoring provides companies with a proactive as well as a reactive tool. The head of the largest monitoring firm in Los Angeles explained that, for international audits, his company gives three grades to factories: high risk, medium risk, and low risk. When asked what the risk was, his response was bad publicity.[22] A monitor at the same firm explained that he considered armed guards a plus in terms of a factory's rating, because guards keep out the muckrakers.[23]

Moreover, many of those who are developing monitoring, including the government, clearly view it as a service to consumers. This is exemplified in the words of Eileen Kaufman, director of Social Accountability International, a monitoring oversight body based in New York: "Basically I consider my daughter an end user. She goes to a store; she doesn't want to buy anything made by anybody younger than she is. How can she know?"[24] When asked how the AIP's idea for monitoring arose, a top DOL official responded: "The president asked the group to come up with a way to ensure that when consumers buy goods they are not made under sweatshop conditions and a system to inform consumers of this."[25] As Kaufman stated: "What we all want to do is improve the factories, and we think that consumers are a way to improve the factories. And we *want* consumers to be a way to improve the factories."[26] While the implication is that workers will be protected if consumers care about their welfare, this is an entirely different strategy from empowering workers themselves.

The DOL program in Los Angeles clearly had workers' welfare in mind, but it did not leverage workers' power at all. There was no requirement to inform workers of the program. Nor was the program combined with any effort to protect unionization rights. GUESS? used monitoring to undermine the unionization drive at its factories. Companies have not been legally challenged, even when monitoring is clearly inadequate. Rather, there has been an attempt to leverage consumer power to discipline the companies. The DOL has gone to retailers and directly to consumers to put pressure on manufacturers. The DOL pressures retailers to require monitoring programs among manufacturers who wish to sell to them. The DOL also established the Trendsetters List, which included almost exclusively companies that were monitoring or on the AIP. The list, often referred to as the "Good Guys of Fashion" list, was posted on the Internet as part of the DOL's consumer-education campaign.

In recent years, "successful" labor campaigns in the garment industry in terms of yielding concrete outcomes have generally been tied to the consumer/investor-pressure strategy. Asian Immigrant Women's Advocate against Jessica McClintock, the National Labor Committee Against Gap, Global Exchange, Press for Change, and United Students Against Sweatshops against Nike are some of the campaigns that are widely considered somewhat successful.[27] AIWA forced McClintock to pay the back wages of garment workers in San Francisco, whose immediate bosses owed them thousands of dollars. The Gap consented to independent monitoring by NGOs in El Salvador. Nike agreed to raise wages for workers in Indonesia, allow some outside audits of its factories, and disclose the names and addresses of contractors that sew university products for the company. All of these campaigns relied on publicity and public outcry and only minimally, if at all, on union organizing. Meanwhile, organizing campaigns among workers in garment factories around the world are being crushed (Armbruster-Sandoval 2000; BSR et al. 2000; Fuentes and Ehrenreich 1983; Frundt 1999; ILO 2000; Quinteros et al. 1998; Varley 1998).

Conclusion

In short, monitoring is an outgrowth of public outcry about sweatshops in Los Angeles and internationally, not an outgrowth of workers' organizing. Private monitoring is, in fact, a new form of paternalism in labor relations, one that plays into and reenacts the vulnerability, not the strength, of garment workers. As Secretary of Labor Alexis Herman wrote, "Sweatshops reflect too vividly how we feel as a nation about the weakest among us" (as quoted in Leibhold and Rubenstein 1999: 36). Private monitoring reflects this vision of garment workers—in Los Angeles, primarily Latina immigrants—as weak.

Private monitoring is directly linked to the globalization of production and the accompanying neoliberal policies. This constellation of practices and ideologies renders workers increasingly vulnerable. What garment workers need are policies that play to their potential strength, not policies that institutionalize their vulnerability. Not only is private monitoring paternalistic, but statistics (detailed in the next chapter) show that its effectiveness is quite limited. More significantly, it may well substitute for, cover up, or obviate workers' own organizing.

In contrast, independent monitoring recognizes garment workers' potential strengths in monitoring their conditions and organizing on their own behalf. Independent monitoring, or "verification," as is being developed by labor activists, students, and unionists in the United States and producing regions is grounded in the idea that workers must be brought back into the contract. Monitoring turned on its head—with the worker at the center—may accomplish this. Most notably, this model is being developed in the Worker Rights Consortium, organized to implement university codes of conduct in factories producing collegiate apparel. Chapter 7 will analyze the struggle between the model of private monitoring described here and detailed in the next two chapters and independent monitoring.

3   Private Monitoring in Practice

IT IS IMPORTANT to understand the details of the monitoring process because it is the practice on the ground that belies the manufacturers' claims that monitoring is the answer to the industry's problems of abuse. Practices on the ground reveal that monitoring is not a guarantee of "sweat-free" labor by any means. It is, rather, a haphazard process, as this chapter will show.

The details also reveal how current power dynamics are institutionalized in the private monitoring process. Manufacturers hire monitors and determine what activities they will carry out and what the follow-up will be. Despite the fact that monitoring was meant as a way to control flagrant abuses by the manufacturers, manufacturers are in control of monitoring. As monitoring firms say, "The manufacturer is the client." Workers, who are supposedly the beneficiaries, remain powerless. They are not protected if they reveal violations; they are not informed of their rights; and they are often not even aware that the monitoring is being conducted.

It is not surprising that monitoring's structure reinscribes the relationships of capitalism. Monitoring in Los Angeles is a commercial enterprise, a multimillion-dollar industry. This chapter will begin with a discussion of who monitors—that is, which companies have monitoring programs and who actually conducts the monitoring in these programs. This leads to a delineation of the structure of payment between the company requiring the services and the monitors.

The majority of the chapter is devoted to covering monitoring practices and their ramifications. Actual practices will be compared with U.S. Department of Labor guidelines and requirements, focusing on a number of different areas. Although actual observations of monitoring visits were limited,[1] the conclusions are also drawn from a wealth of interviews and documentary data. I compare practices observed with information about monitoring received through interviews, monitoring companies' internal protocols, and public documents; training materials from the DOL and California's DLSE; legal agreements; and statistical data. I also conducted a short survey of monitoring companies. Primary data from Los Angeles were for the most part collected during fieldwork in 1998. The reader should understand that the field of monitoring is developing and changing even as this book is being written. Although I have attempted to keep up to date and have included new data from the DOL's 2000 survey and follow-up conversations with various DOL officials, much of the description is based on the state of the program in 1998, and some information may no longer be accurate. However, I would also posit that the monitoring program in Los Angeles reached its peak (in terms of number of participants and effectiveness) in 1998, and using data from that year gives a view of the program at the height of its capacity. Moreover, in 1998 the program was still focused on securing legal agreements that had more potential for enforcement than the current practice of simply issuing confirming letters when a company voluntarily agrees to monitor.

The chapter will finish with an assessment of the effectiveness of monitoring, as defined by a reduction in violations, based on the DOL's survey data.

WHO MONITORS?

To understand monitoring, one must have an idea of who is actually doing the monitoring and for whom. The domestic monitoring program originated in Los Angeles, the largest garment-manufacturing area in the country. According to a list from the DOL in Los Angeles, between 1992 and 1998 sixty-three firms had signed the Augmented Compliance Program Agreement, or the "Long Form," with the DOL to monitor their contractors. After 1998, the DOL signed on very few manufacturers, and several of those who had signed on had gone out of business or otherwise removed themselves from the program. Thus, in late 2000 there were only forty-eight current signers on the DOL list. By 2003, the garment enforcement coordinator reported to me, only thirty-four manufacturers were still on the Long Form.[2] All of those firms were in the Los Angeles area, with the exception of two in San Francisco and one in McLean, Virginia. In 2002, the DOL switched its focus to the M-CAP, under which it encourages rather than coerces manufacturers to undertake monitoring. Under M-CAP in Los Angeles, the DOL attempts to contact a broad range of manufacturers (not in response to specific instances of violations) and inform them of monitoring and its benefits. Manufacturers who agree to monitor—about ten confirmed in 2002—do so voluntarily and without a formal agreement. Although the DOL sends a letter of understanding and asks the manufacturers to provide periodic reports, these manufacturers are not legally bound to the requirements of the ACPA (which later became the FCPA) in the way that signatories are.[3]

Although staff at the Los Angeles DOL founded the monitoring program, and Los Angeles is the site of this study, it should be mentioned that the New York DOL also used the agreement widely. The New York office of the DOL signed on about forty-three firms in New York and New Jersey between 1994, when it first used the agreement, and 1998. In the following few years, the program expanded significantly, with forty-one signers more between 1999 and 2002, the large majority of those in 1999.[4] As in Los Angeles, many of these agreements are no longer in force.

In New York the program was less strict than in Los Angeles, with some companies allowed to write their own forms rather than sign the standard agreement.[5] It is unclear how many firms outside California and the New York area ever signed, but there were very few.[6]

While the original program emphasized gaining formal legal agreements, Long Form signers have been a minority among the hundreds of firms in Los Angeles (and elsewhere) that monitor.[7] Most companies monitor with no agreement with the DOL, preferring to avoid government contacts, which they feel give the impression of previous wrongdoing. Even if a company has not signed the ACPA or FCPA, the fact that it is monitoring is taken into consideration if the DOL finds violations at a contractor's shop. The DOL is less likely to contact the retailer, for example, and if it does, it will inform the retailer that the company has taken proactive measures.

The Los Angeles DOL reports that there is no count or list of how many manufacturers may be monitoring or of who they are. According to my survey and interviews with Los Angeles compliance firms—consulting companies that offer monitoring services—their manufacturing clients totaled approximately 350 in 1998. However, some manufacturers use more than one compliance firm. At the same time, the 350 figure does not include manufacturers who rely solely on in-house monitors—that is, their own employees. Although 350 is a significant number, it is less than one-fifth of the 2,000 manufacturers that the DOL estimated to be in the Los Angeles area at the time.[8] According to surveys of Los Angeles apparel companies done by the sociologist Judi Kessler in 1997 and 2000, "virtually all large manufacturers have monitoring programs," as do many smaller firms (Kessler 2002: 88).

Table 2 shows the cumulative results of a survey I conducted in October 1998. In Los Angeles, monitoring is dominated by compliance firms that specialize in monitoring labor conditions in garment factories. Four of the six compliance firms in Los Angeles provided information in response to the survey. These figures represent the total number of clients contracting the four firms but do not reflect whether those companies hired the monitors for domestic or international monitoring. Although retailers and some large manufacturers conduct significant international monitoring, most companies contracting monitoring services with Los Angeles compliance firms are conducting all or part of their monitoring in the United States.

As can be seen in Table 2, manufacturers make up the bulk of the firms with domestic monitoring programs. Spurred by negative media exposés that link retailers to labor abuses, and by attempts of litigators and lawmakers to hold retailers accountable for the production of their private-label clothing, a small number of retailers have begun to monitor. To increase their control over the process and avoid being monitored by a number of different manufacturers, a growing number of contractors

TABLE 2. Number of Clients of Four Los Angeles Monitoring Firms by
Client Business Type

	1994	1996	1998
Manufacturers	168	237	324
Retailers	0	11	33
Contractors	35	51	159
TOTAL	203	299	516

Source: Figures are derived from a survey conducted by the author in October 1998.

choose to monitor themselves rather than or in addition to being monitored by the manufacturer.

Manufacturers (and other entities) hire a variety of companies and
organizations to carry out the monitoring and report back to them. In Los
Angeles, and in the rest of the United States, all monitoring is conducted
as part of a business enterprise, either by employees of the manufacturers
themselves (known as internal monitors) or by employees of separate, specialized firms (known as external monitors). In Los Angeles, the market is
dominated by compliance firms, which are now proliferating abroad.
Accounting firms have been minimally involved but are likely to be doing
more monitoring in Los Angeles, as are certification agencies. All of these
operations are run on a for-profit basis. The contradictions of such commercial institutions profiting from the protection of workers' rights will
be discussed in detail in the next chapter. A few local NGO monitoring
projects involving religious and human-rights organizations exist abroad;
none, however, have been established in the United States to monitor
domestic production. Because accounting firms, certification agencies, and
NGOs monitor primarily abroad, they will be discussed in Chapter 5, as
will the monitoring bodies that conduct or coordinate monitoring globally.

Internal Monitors

Many manufacturers began "monitoring" by using their own quality-
control staff, who frequently are already in the factories, to check for
labor-law compliance. Although many still do this, especially abroad, it
has been widely recognized that quality-control staff have neither the
expertise nor the incentive to conduct thorough monitoring. The priority of the quality-control person is to get high-quality garments on time
and within the estimated budget. Rectifying labor-law violations, which
entails additional expenditures as well as time, clearly interferes with this
goal (at least in the short term).

Many manufacturers have now hired specific personnel to act exclusively as internal monitors. Some manufacturers find it cheaper to hire their
own monitor than to pay compliance firms for each individual visit. Internal monitors are in charge of all compliance for a company's contractors,

either supervising outside services or conducting their own audits. Many of the internal monitors are former employees of the monitoring firms and tend to use the same sort of system.

Some large companies combine internal monitors with outside services. For instance, GUESS? has an internal monitor who coordinates her efforts with the services of an outside firm. She sometimes accompanies the firm's monitors on visits. More often, she takes the firm's reports and then speaks directly with the plant owner. She also makes visits on her own when problems arise. The Gap has a compliance department that coordinates the services of outside monitors with audits conducted by its own "compliance officers."

Although the DOL states in all of its materials and agreements that the monitor may be an employee of the firm or an outside person, it promotes the use of outside monitors. Gerald Hall, district director of the DOL in Los Angeles, stated at a monitoring forum that the DOL does not recommend one over the other; it recommends both to provide a check on the system. Rolene Otero, another district director who created and first ran the monitoring program, explained that when the DOL finds violations in shops that are monitored by a manufacturer's personnel, it urges the manufacturer to use an outside agency.[9] An outside monitor is assumed to be more independent and therefore more effective.[10]

Compliance Firms

In Los Angeles, the majority of monitoring is conducted by compliance firms. These are companies that have grown up specifically to do labor-law compliance in the garment industry (although some have now branched out to audit production of toys, shoes, and other products). In 1998, there were four major firms in the Los Angeles area: Cal-Safety Compliance Corporation, Apparel Resources Inc., Labor Law, and Garment Compliance Consultants. There were also two smaller, one-person operations. I interviewed the directors of the top five firms and had formal interviews or extended conversations with several of their monitors.[11]

The largest of these firms is Cal-Safety, which began offering services as a consultant on compliance with health and safety regulations and now monitors for labor-standards compliance.[12] The owner is Carol Pender, and Bill Bernstrom, a former DOL investigator who coordinated the Los Angeles Apparel Task Force, is the executive director. Apparel Resources, located in Orange County, is owned and run by Randy Youngblood, who worked for many years as a production consultant in the apparel industry. Labor Law is generally thought to be the third in the big three but actually has fewer clients than Garment Compliance Consultants. Jesse Atilano, a former DLSE investigator, is the CEO and owner of Labor Law. His firm specializes in advising contractors on how to defend themselves against workers' claims and DOL investigations, as newspaper articles framed on the company's wall proclaim. Stephen

TABLE 3. Number of Visits Conducted by Four Los Angeles Monitoring Firms by Area

	1994	1996	1998
Los Angeles	7,885	9,420	10,240
Other areas of the United States	1,515	2,080	3,115
Abroad	505	1,515	3,044
TOTAL	9,905	13,015	16,399

Source: Figures are derived from a survey conducted by the author in October 1998.

Esmond, the son of a garment contractor, runs Garment Compliance Consultants. The fifth-largest firm is run by Elizabeth Moreno, who is also its only full-time employee. Moreno, a former employee of Cal-Safety, specializes in working directly for contractors in an effort to empower them in this process.

Monitoring is a booming business. Cal-Safety had revenue of $4.5 million in 1996. The firm has grown considerably: By 1998, it had approximately 100 employees and did almost 30 percent of its audits abroad. By 2002, Cal-Safety had offices in Mexico, Turkey, Bangladesh, and India and claimed on its website to conduct audits in sixty-five countries. International audits are much more expensive and more lucrative than domestic audits for the compliance firms. In 1998, local audits in Los Angeles ranged between $150 and $375, with $300–$350 per visit the most common price. International audits by compliance firms cost about $1,000.[13] Large accounting firms and certification agencies charge far more.[14]

To give a sense of the breadth and growth of the compliance industry, Table 3 shows the combined activities of four of the six compliance firms based in Los Angeles—the number of audits conducted in Los Angeles, in the rest of the United States, and internationally from 1994 to 1998. The fastest-growing sector is monitoring abroad, although most of this growth is due to an expansion of international monitoring by one firm, Cal-Safety. The number of audits conducted in the United States outside Los Angeles doubled between 1994 and 1998.[15] This growth was accounted for by two firms: Cal-Safety and Apparel Resources. Cal-Safety had not expanded its business in Los Angeles over the four-year period. The increase in auditing in Los Angeles came about because of two newly formed compliance firms and the growth of Apparel Resources, which was conducting the largest number of audits in the area by 1998.

The compliance firms generally hire untrained staff, often young college graduates or students as part-time employees. Some require that new employees speak a second language but ask for no specific skills beyond that. Although they are capable of doing simple audits, they do not have any specialized knowledge in accounting, health and safety, or interviewing techniques (see Chapter 4). Several of the companies have senior staff with expertise as former government investigators or trained accountants.

All monitoring by compliance firms is done on a checklist basis. The firms do not look at systems of operation or procedures. If, for example, there are apparently no minors in the factory on the day of the visit, the factory will pass on that score. No attention is paid to procedures the company might be employing to ensure that minors have not been hired and will not be hired in the future.

Accounting Firms

Accounting firms are mainly involved in international monitoring. However, several accounting firms did some monitoring in Los Angeles when the program began. They already worked as financial auditors for many garment manufacturers and began offering an additional service, which they viewed as a sort of expanded audit. But according to two of those firms, when the compliance companies sprang up, the accounting firms could no longer compete for customers. The accounting firms hire trained staff, certified public accountants, and business-school graduates. It was not worthwhile for the accounting firms to compete for domestic monitoring jobs at the prices the compliance firms were offering.[16]

The staff of accounting firms are highly trained in calculation and bookkeeping, which may facilitate addressing wage and hour issues. They claim to look beyond surface appearances at systems of operation (for example, the procedures a company has in place). However, they have no professional training in other areas, such as health and safety, labor law, worker interviews, and human-rights issues. Moreover, most of the accounting firms' business involves helping large corporations manage their resources and maximize profit. It can be argued that their operating principles do not prioritize the needs of workers and are often antithetical to them.

STRUCTURE OF PAYMENT

It is important to look not only at who is monitoring but also at who is paying for that monitoring, both immediately and ultimately. The structure of payment has implications for the "independence" of the monitors, the systems of reporting, and the coordination of monitoring activities by different manufacturers in the same factory. In Los Angeles, manufacturers or contractors pay for the monitoring services. In terms of international monitoring, groups have made attempts to avert direct conflict of interests by creating intermediary bodies that oversee the monitoring process or fund private monitoring with foundation money and grants.

Manufacturer Pays

In Los Angeles, the manufacturer almost always makes the actual payment for the monitoring service. If the manufacturer hires an internal monitor, it pays his or her salary. If it hires an external firm, it writes the check for those services. However, in the latter case it is very common for the manufacturer to charge back some or all of these expenses to the contractor—that is, to deduct the money from what it owes the contractor. Because retailers set the prices they pay the manufacturer, manufacturers can avoid monitoring costs only by passing the costs down the chain, not up.

Large manufacturers often have an agreement that they will pay for all audits that the contractor passes and charge back the contractor for all audits that it fails. If a contractor passes, it is not visited again for a specified period of time—in most cases, three months. If the contractor fails, a visit is scheduled within a shorter period of time. Some manufacturers will pay for these quarterly visits but charge back any extra visits that are required because a contractor has failed an inspection. Other manufacturers, especially small manufacturers, charge back half or all of the quarterly visits to the contractor.

The DOL's intention, as described to me by the creator of the monitoring program, was for the manufacturer to pay these costs.[17] However, there is no language in the ACPA that requires the manufacturer to absorb the expenses.

The system of charge-backs can be excessively burdensome to the contractor, which usually works for more than one manufacturer and is being charged back for monitoring visits on behalf of each manufacturer. Monitoring companies rarely combine their own reports (much less with those of any other firm). So if a monitoring firm needs to visit a contractor for more than one manufacturer, it generally does not consolidate the visit—or, at least, it does not consolidate the charges. The monitoring companies claim that the manufacturers do not want to share information and reports and that they must create separate reports for each manufacturer, thereby justifying the repetitive charges. Manufacturers contradict this justification by saying they would be happy to share expenses and that the information is not secret, because all manufacturers know who else is in the shops they use since their quality-control staff are in the shops regularly and see all other work there.[18] Several sources reported to me that, although monitors charge manufacturers for their own visits, in some cases they simply change the name on the report. In any case, the contractor is subjected to charge-backs for several reports and possibly subjected to the disruption of several visits.[19]

Contractor Pays

Other monitoring arrangements have been proposed or exist in which contractors pay directly for the monitoring services and are provided with a passing certificate that they can then show to any prospective manufacturer. Contractors have to continue to be audited at specified intervals—annually, for example—and are de-certified if they fail subsequent audits or are found to be in violation of labor standards in the interim (through government investigation or additional audits triggered by registered complaints).

The Garment Contractors' Association of Southern California made a proposal to the DOL in 1996 that would allow its members who were in good standing and who had had no violations for three years, according to DOL and state DLSE records, to become "certified contractors." The contractor would be awarded certification when it passed an audit by an approved monitoring company. The contractor would arrange and pay for such an audit from a company on a list of monitors approved by the GCA and the DOL. According to the GCA's executive director, the DOL rejected the proposal because officials in Washington felt that it would undermine monitoring's purpose of creating responsibility on the part of the manufacturer. Without the DOL's support in terms of approving a list of auditors or guaranteeing that such a certificate would be accepted by the department in lieu of a manufacturer's arranging for the monitoring, the GCA decided not to go forward.[20]

The GCA arrangement would have avoided the problems of overlapping (in visits and charges). It also addressed another contractor concern: autonomy. Contractors feel that having manufacturers send someone to look at their records is unfair interference in their business practices. The contractor would certainly not have a similar right to access the manufacturer's accounts. Moreover, contractors complain that the monitors often act like policemen and treat the contractors disrespectfully. Some contractors feel that, if they must participate in this process, they should have the right to own the report that they often in effect pay for. Many contractors would also rather be in the position to hire a monitor to provide compliance assistance than have the manufacturer hire the monitor to scrutinize and possibly punish the contractor.[21]

Contractors are increasingly hiring monitors directly. One small monitoring firm in Los Angeles specializes in serving contractors directly and encourages them to take a more forceful stand on the issue. In 1998, the firm had about sixty contractor clients. Other monitoring firms also sell consulting services directly to contractors and include clean contractors in a referral service that they offer to manufacturers. Internationally, two of the three U.S.-based monitoring systems (described in Chapter 5) use contractor-level certification.

Although contractor-level certification makes sense in many ways, it is also open to problems of direct conflicts of interest. The director of a Los Angeles monitoring firm described such a model as follows: "They are looking for a slam-dunk, and that isn't it. If the contractor owns the report, if it's a bad report, they are not going to send it out. They are going to get another one."[22] If the monitor is being paid directly by the contractor, it clearly would be in danger of losing a client if it failed the factory; conversely, the contractor could just look for a monitor who would pass the factory. The system would have to depend on accepted standards of monitoring and oversight to be credible, and as will be shown shortly, no such mechanisms are in effect in Los Angeles.

Intermediary Bodies and Grants

Whereas in Los Angeles all monitoring is paid for by the manufacturer or the contractor, elsewhere there are proposals for structures that involve payment to an intermediary body that would hire the monitors, review the reports, and oversee the corrective actions. These models allow for some measure of "independence" on the part of the monitor, who would not be hired directly by the interested party, and provide more transparency.

In San Francisco, Manufacturing Excellence Corporation and the Northern California Chinese Garment Contractors Association have designed an Independent Monitoring Component as part of their Made by the Bay program (which also includes technical assistance and marketing training). The IMC would carry out all audits and report to the consortium of contractors rather than to its individual members. There are provisions for contractors to be dropped from the program for repeated violations or refusal to pay owed back wages. The model also stipulates that the IMC will report regularly to the DOL and that all results and findings of the IMC will be a matter of public record.[23]

The Clean Clothes Campaign is a coalition of trade unions, consumer organizations, women's groups, and solidarity and development organizations that began in the Netherlands in 1990 and now has local branches throughout Western Europe. In 1997, the CCC outlined a system for independent monitoring that it calls a "Foundation Model." The foundation, or monitoring body, responsible for monitoring would represent equally NGOs, trade unions, producers, and retailers. Each manufacturer or retailer would sign a contract with the monitoring body that included payments. The monitoring body would guide the companies on how to implement their codes at the factory level and would then hire monitors to do external audits. These monitors would report to the monitoring body, which would advise companies on actions that must be taken. The advice would be binding; if it was not followed, the contract would be considered broken. Information would be made public if corrective actions were not taken.[24] The Fair Labor Association, discussed at length in Chapter 7, recently switched from direct payment by manufacturers to an intermediary-body model to avoid conflicts and gain credibility.

VARIETY OF MONITORING PRACTICES AND STANDARDS

It is not only the relationships involved but also the objective quality of the monitoring that determines its effectiveness. For monitoring to be even minimally effective, the monitors must first gather reliable information. Then the manufacturer, or the monitor in its stead, must follow up on violations found. Monitoring practices have implications not only for the thoroughness of the findings but also for the role and involvement of workers in the process. In addition, the variety of practices indicates not just that there are inconsistencies on the part of monitors, but also that there is a great deal of flexibility available to manufacturers to determine and control their own programs.

The following sections are based on DOL data and a limited number of observations of actual monitoring practices; a general level of suspicion within the compliance industry hindered a more thoroughgoing observation process. While the executive directors at each company granted me generous interviews and some provided me with their standard monitoring forms, I was denied access to significant observation of the monitoring process. I requested permission from the four monitoring companies I interviewed in person (the four leading companies) to be allowed to accompany them on visits for a week or two to understand monitoring. Three companies agreed that I could accompany them, but for only one day each. The head of the fourth company simply refused. In the end I was allowed to observe only two companies conduct audits. Specific examples are therefore taken from a limited number of observations: six audits done on three different days by two firms (plus two aborted audits, one with a third firm, in which the contractor denied us entrance). The monitors were, however, the most experienced field staff in their offices and did represent to me that the procedures I witnessed were standard.

Although I cannot verify that all of the following examples are evidence of patterns of practice, they do indicate important weaknesses in the system. Moreover, the statistics given, which are based on my analysis of the raw data from the DOL's survey, confirm that these weaknesses are widespread. The DOL's analysis showed that only 28 percent of firms in 1998 and 29 percent in 2000 were being effectively monitored. Furthermore, the DOL data show widespread violations even in effectively monitored shops (44%).

By creating a database with the raw data from the 1998 surveys that the DOL conducted of Los Angeles garment factories, I can present specific breakdowns of monitors' performance for each component of monitoring. While the DOL surveyed seventy shops, it collected separate monitoring information on each manufacturer that had clothing in each shop. Thus, the raw data actually provide information on 176 cases. Of these 176 cases, 88 represent instances in which manufacturers were conducting at least one component of monitoring and form the universe of the statistics on monitoring. Of these 88, 21 instances involved ACPA signatories. I report also on four additional cases in which the manufacturer was an ACPA signatory but did not, in fact, monitor the contractor.[25]

Table 4 gives a sense of the monitoring components that are being practiced. The monitoring points, as laid out by the DOL, are as follows: making unannounced visits; conducting interviews of employees; reviewing payroll; reviewing time cards; providing compliance information; advising of compliance problems; and recommending corrective action. The information was gathered by DOL inspectors, who asked each contractor whether the manufacturers they currently worked for took any of the seven actions. The inspectors then recorded this information separately for

TABLE 4. Specific Components of Monitoring Actually Performed in Los Angeles Garment Factories (%)

	All cases of monitoring	Cases involving ACPA signatories
Unannounced visits conducted	61	40
Employee interviews conducted	73	80
Payroll checked	78	72
Time cards checked	87	80
Compliance information provided	81	80
Contractor advised of compliance problems	45	48
Corrective action recommended	40	44
Price negotiation allowed	49	40

Source: Figures are derived from the author's analysis of raw data from a 1998 Department of Labor survey. Eighty-eight cases of monitoring are reported here. Twenty-five cases involving ACPA signatories are reported (of these, only 21 performed monitoring and are thus included also in the "All cases" column).

each manufacturer. The inspectors also asked whether each manufacturer allowed price negotiation. Although price negotiation is not in the monitoring guidelines, the ACPA specifies that if the contractor informs the manufacturer of the inadequacy of a contract price, the manufacturer should respond (see Chapter 4). Thus, Table 4 lays out the percentage of all firms that monitored and of ACPA signatories that actually conducted each of the seven components and that allowed price negotiations. The table also illustrates the inconsistency of practices within the whole monitoring group—even among ACPA signatories, who are required by legal contract to conduct all seven components and to consider price feasibility.

What follows is a review of monitoring requirements and practices. It is broken down into the various elements and issues that make up monitoring in Los Angeles. It is important to keep in mind that monitoring is a private enterprise. Compliance firms offer a variety of services, and the manufacturer is viewed as a client who has the prerogative to choose the services it desires.

Factory Visits

Compliance firms audit factories as directed by the manufacturer. Although every three months is the norm, manufacturers that have not signed an agreement with the government sometimes choose to have factories monitored less frequently—every six months or even once a year. If violations are found, the frequency is increased. However, unless a company has signed an agreement, there are no rules about the frequency of visits. Even for those that have signed, the frequency of the audits actually conducted is ultimately determined by the manufacturer.

The standard on visits was set by the DOL in the ACPA. For those that sign, the agreement requires audits every three months for one year, as long as the shop passes inspection. If no problems are found, the shop can be moved to every six months, provided that (1) a tamper-proof time clock is used for punching in and out in the factory, (2) an independent payroll service is used, and (3) the DOL is informed of and approves the 180-day status.

When a problem is suspected or found, audits move from minimum intensity to intermediate intensity, or once a month. If a violation is found while a factory is on intermediate-intensity audits, the facility is supposed to be moved to high-intensity monitoring, to occur once per work week. The factory is also supposed to be moved to high-intensity monitoring if the DOL informs the manufacturer of willful or repeated violations on the factory's part. Each status continues until the factory passes two consecutive inspections and has no uncorrected violations for 180 days on minimum wage, overtime, and child labor and no uncorrected violations for ninety days on simple record-keeping.

Although the legal agreement is clear on the frequency of visits, actual practice varies. Extra visits involve an additional charge that must be pre-approved by the manufacturer, or "customer." According to several monitoring firms, manufacturers often decide not to spend the money or delay in approving the recommendation. I observed a ninety-day audit at which the monitor reviewed all payroll for the previous three months. This is a lengthy procedure and is used only as a follow-up after serious problems have been found. The monitor told me that the factory had been visited ten times, and problems had been found every time. Back wages had been found more than six months earlier that had never been paid. However, the factory had never been visited weekly. The monitoring firm had recommended a ninety-day audit months before it was approved. The manufacturer in this case was an ACPA signatory. It was not until shortly before the ninety-day audit that the manufacturer had stopped sending work to the factory.

Monitoring audits are relatively short. General audits tend to last one hour to two and a half hours, depending on the amount of bookkeeping to be reviewed, whereas ninety-day audits can be lengthier and follow-up audits are often briefer. Some firms use teams of two inspectors; others send one inspector on each audit. The inspections I witnessed were conducted by one person and lasted no more than two hours. The factory-floor inspection and employee interviews lasted thirty to forty-five minutes. At Cal-Safety, two inspectors go out together, and inspections are scheduled every three hours. This includes time to commute to a new site and to take a lunch or rest break. DOL investigations take twenty hours, according to District Director Gerald Hall.

Unannounced visits were one of the two most powerful monitoring components, according to statistical analysis of the 2000 DOL survey data by Boston University researchers.[26] However, despite legal stipulations and government urging, a minority of audits appear to be unannounced. The ACPA requires unannounced visits, and the DOL recommends them in all of its materials and workshops. One monitor with many years of experience told me: "If you want to clean up the garment industry, you would do all unannounced visits. . . . On announced visits, you find less. It would be like Child Protective Services telling you they are coming. The kid will be well dressed, all bathed with [its] nose wiped. Everything will look great."[27] In reality, the manufacturer can request announced or unannounced visits. The firm that conducts the most audits in the Los Angeles area, Apparel Resources, does almost all announced visits. In fact, the firm's owner said, "We reserve unannounced audits as the pinnacle of distrust of a contractor."[28] Apparel Resources justifies this by claiming that its surveillance counts as unannounced visits. Cal-Safety usually does announced visits, although it is now doing more unannounced visits than it had been,[29] perhaps because the DOL insisted on this point when it released the 1998 survey statistics. Apparel Resources and Cal-Safety conduct 85–90 percent of the audits in Los Angeles. A smaller firm used to do only unannounced visits but now does announced visits at the insistence of its clients. A fourth firm generally uses its surveillance as a time to schedule the audit. When it does an "unannounced" visit, it tells the factory which week it will take place so the books are on hand.

Data from the DOL's 1998 survey confirm that a large percentage of monitoring is announced even when required by legal agreement to be unannounced. In the DOL survey, only 61 percent of the cases involved unannounced visits. Moreover, in only 40 percent of the cases did ACPA signatories conduct unannounced visits. In actuality, the rate is probably far lower. Because surveillance—which is unannounced—often includes entering the shop, talking to the manager, and counting time cards and workers, contractors most likely responded affirmatively to the question "Are there unannounced visits?" even when the full audit was scheduled ahead of time. Therefore, these figures could include cases of unannounced surveillance even when the audit is announced.

Manufacturers contend that they request announced visits because unannounced visits cause too much disruption in the contractor's production schedules and because it is more costly to do unannounced visits. If the manager or owner of the factory is not present and no one else can show the books, the auditor must return at an extra charge. Even when the owner or manager is present, it is very possible that he or she will not have payroll records available because the records are kept at an accountant's office. I observed a day of auditing in which none of the four shops visited had payroll records. That particular compliance firm, which does almost exclusively unannounced audits, has a policy that the company can send over the records to the compliance firm within three business days. Another firm I observed gave the contractor twenty-four or forty-eight hours to send the records. Although these policies mitigate the expense of return visits, they also undermine the effectiveness of an un-announced visit by giving the contractor time to modify the books.

Surveillance

Surveillance differs depending on the firm. For some, surveillance involves sitting outside the factory in a car and watching whether people are work-ing beyond regular hours, perhaps trying to get a head count through the window and checking whether material is going in or out of the factory in order to detect homework or further subcontracting. This is, as one firm's director put it, "undetected observation." Other companies go into the shop on a Saturday, introduce themselves, and count heads and time cards. They see whether the two numbers coincide and then return for an audit in about two weeks to check whether the payroll accurately reflects the number of people who had been working that Saturday.

Surveillance is a separate service, usually billed for apart from visits (ranging from $85 to $150 extra). However, some companies fudge the difference by counting unannounced visits as surveillance or surveillance as unannounced visits. In other words, a company may do surveillance (which is unannounced in nature) and make appointments for its visits and still claim to fulfill the DOL's recommendation of unannounced visits. Conversely, it may make unannounced visits and claim that this counts as surveillance according to the DOL's requirements in the ACPA. Although surveillance is not one of the seven components of effective monitoring out-lined by the DOL (perhaps leaving room for the manipulations cited ear-lier), the ACPA is clear that surveillance is required by its signatories even as part of minimum-intensity monitoring. Further, the ACPA specifies that surveillance must be done in the early morning and late afternoon and on weekends. Two different instances of surveillance for each audit are in-cluded as a requirement for effective monitoring in the DOL's training mate-rials. In their presentations to me, firms indicated that normal surveillance was done once before or after work or on a Saturday, although stepped-up surveillance could result from suspicion or findings of violations.

One of the internal monitors told me that surveillance was the key to monitoring. He said that he does surveillance of the contractors almost weekly and then double-checks his observations against the payroll records. In fact, he felt that surveillance was much more reliable than employee testimony. With thorough surveillance, he claimed, one can collect hard evidence of off-the-clock work, whereas employees will not always reveal such practices, as will be discussed.

Record Checking

Compliance firms check various records during an audit. They check the state registration, which they then verify with state authorities. They check for workers' compensation insurance and often ask the contractor to sign a waiver that allows the insurance company to notify the compliance firm when the insurance expires. They also look for public-health licenses, city licenses, W-4s, I-9s (verification of workers' immigration status), and general liability insurance for fire and theft.

The focus of the record checking is on time cards and payroll records, as well as on piece-rate tickets when those are available. Monitors use these documents to check the workers' hourly wages, whether they are being paid overtime correctly, and whether they are being paid for all the time they have clocked in. They also scrutinize the time cards for uniformity to make sure that they are not all being punched in by the supervisor or owner. In addition, monitors cross-check time-card information against testimony given by workers in the employee interviews (for example, whether they work on Saturdays, the number of hours they work during the week). Again, as they do during surveillance, monitors count heads and time cards to make sure they correspond during each audit.

The amount of payroll examined again varies. Although the ACPA states that all records since the preceding visit must be checked, this seems a rarity. One company does ninety-day audits, but this is considered an extreme measure, reserved for clear violators. Cal-Safety requires companies to keep thirty days' worth of payroll on the premises. With announced visits, monitoring firms usually request the most recent payroll and, if different, the one that covers the period in which a surveillance visit was conducted. As stated earlier, at least two of the three major firms allow records to be turned in within a short period. This practice gives factory owners the opportunity to doctor their books, rendering a clean bill of health dubious.

Some monitoring firms check the general ledger or the company's bank statements to make sure that no one is being paid off the payroll record. However, there is more resistance from the contractors to showing general ledgers and bank statements than payroll records, and some firms are more insistent than others.

No compliance firm reviews contracts and prices, a common practice in both state and federal investigations. Monitors believe contracts to be the proprietary business of their client. Cal-Safety does ask the monitor to assess whether the "work in process [is] in balance with # of employees & machinery."[30] However, it is questionable whether young investigators inexperienced in apparel production could make such an assessment. State investigators told me that the only way to know whether people are working more than the time cards reflect is to calculate out from the contracts. The surest way to catch hidden violations is to figure whether correct payment according to the production records, plus rent, expenses, and minimal profit, could possibly be covered by the prices listed in the contracts. According to a former investigator with twenty-five years' experience, "Books can look right if you don't focus in on productivity."[31]

Moreover, even in just checking the books there appear to be significant lapses. According to the DOL survey, in 87 percent of the monitoring cases time cards were checked, but in only 78 percent was payroll checked. For the cases in which ACPA signatories were involved, 80 percent checked time cards but only 72 percent checked payroll records. Checking time cards alone reveals only whether someone is working off the clock at that moment; if time cards are not double-checked against payroll, much of their value as indicators of compliance or violations is lost. When looking at the 2000 DOL survey data, the Boston University researchers found payroll checking to have one of the two most significant correlations to compliance (the other factor being unannounced factory visits).

Calculation and Payment of Back Wages

The DOL includes computation and payment of back wages as the "final aspect of monitoring" in its training materials. However, except for ACPA signatories, the calculation and payment of back wages is optional for most manufacturers. One of the monitoring firms always calculates back wages, but it is still up to the manufacturer to do something with that information. Cal-Safety charges an additional fee for back-wage calculation. The company's director, Bill Bernstrom, told me that only a handful of his clients have this done (presumably, that is outside of those required to do so by the ACPA).

Bernstrom estimated that 60–70 percent of the manufacturers who cover back wages themselves charge them back to the contractor. If a manufacturer is on the ACPA and the amount of the back wages exceeds $2,000, it must write a check to the DOL, which distributes the money. Of the manufacturers who pay and are not on the ACPA, about half choose to write a check to the DOL so that they have no direct (possibly construed as legal) relationship with the workers. The other half prefer to pay directly to avoid contact with the DOL.

The ACPA requires that back wages be calculated for all employees for a thirteen-week period. This is because the "hot goods" provision of the FLSA specifies a ninety-day period as the time in which the goods in question can be assumed to be linked to the nonpayment of a worker. The worker actually has the right to two years of unpaid back wages and three years if the violation was intentional under state law. However, because the monitors are only seeking to protect the manufacturers for the time they may be liable, they check only for the ninety days.

In fact, back wages tend to be calculated not for all employees but in a much more random fashion. One monitor I observed calculated for only the four or so employees he interviewed. Another calculated for ten employees per pay period—those interviewed and another group selected at random. Even during the thorough ninety-day audit, back wages were calculated for everyone during the first few time periods and then for a rotating random sample for the earlier payrolls.

Manufacturers pay back wages because once owed money has been paid, the DOL cannot object to the shipment of goods because any found violations have already been remediated. However, as mentioned, most manufacturers pressure the contractor into paying the back wages or deduct back wages they pay from the amount of money they owe the contractor.

Employee Interviews

The interviews are perhaps the most controversial of all the monitoring components. Some argue that employee interviews are almost useless, because workers are subject to threats and intimidation.[32] Others argue that employees have a vested interest in keeping information on off-the-book payments hidden.[33] However, most monitors I spoke with view the employee interviews as the key to any inspection, because the employees almost always know when they are being cheated. Although all agree that employees hold key information, they also agree that workers are afraid to talk and that contractors often tell them what to say.

The difficulty in speaking is exacerbated by the interview situation. Cal-Safety's brochure states that the employee "must be confidentially interviewed. The interview process must be conducted randomly in an environment free from reprisal or intimidation." However, several Cal-Safety monitors reported to me that the interviews are conducted on the factory floor or in an office in the factory. A former Cal-Safety monitor said, "There is no privacy in the conversations. The employer always knew who was being interviewed."[34]

The interviews I witnessed with other firms were neither private nor probing. One interviewer conducted all interviews on the shop floor at the workstations while the manager wandered about the floor continuing his business. Another interviewer held interviews in the manager's office without the manager present but allowed the manager to choose who was interviewed and send the employees in one by one. The interviews were cursory and rote. The monitors followed the forms and did not try to delve into problems they had detected. Although some workers seemed at ease, others were uninterested or nervous and anxious. One firm asked the employees to sign their interview forms, which seemed to further intimidate the workers. No assurances were made to the employees about the confidentiality of the information. Even if the information was to remain anonymous, the workers would not have known that.

It is sometimes possible to call monitors anonymously, but it is unlikely that workers will do so when most are at best ignorant and at worst fearful of the monitors. Cal-Safety, for example, has a toll-free telephone number and receives an estimated 100 calls per year. GUESS?'s internal monitoring program also runs a toll-free number, but when interviewed in 1998 the director of compliance said she had not received any calls of complaint in the previous year.[35]

I was provided with interview questionnaires from the three main firms. They all cover the following areas: how long the worker has been at the company; the hours she or he works during the week; whether she or he works on weekends, what hours, and how often; whether she or he takes work home; whether she or he is paid in cash or check and whether she or he gets a check stub; when she or he gets paid; and who punches her or his time card. Some of the questionnaires are more thorough, asking similar questions not only about the interviewee but also about co-workers. The Cal-Safety questionnaire asks the monitor to assess whether the employee appeared truthful, coached, or fearful.

There is a general feeling that having monitors of the same ethnicity helps put workers at ease. For example, the Latino monitor I observed used slang and started all conversations with the male employees by talking about the World Cup soccer championship that was in progress. Several workers smiled at this and answered congenially. Randy Rankin of PricewaterhouseCoopers, which monitors throughout the world, told me that the company always hires locally because it feels that co-ethnic monitors have more rapport with the workers. It is not clear whether this is the case, but the monitors I observed in Los Angeles had the same impression. A white male monitor said that, despite his ability to speak Spanish to Latino workers, "The employees are afraid of me. Veronica [a Latina monitor] just says hello to them and they spill their guts." If this is true, Los Angeles presents a complicated situation, because workers have immigrated from a variety of countries.

All firms claimed that interviews were conducted in the employees' language and that professional interpreters were hired when necessary. However, the practice was different in the few cases I observed. Both of the men I observed spoke Spanish and English but no other language. In one case, a manager was asked to translate for a worker who spoke Vietnamese. In another, the manufacturer sent a Thai designer to translate during the interviews with Thai workers. In this case, the woman translating had much lengthier interchanges with the workers than represented by the brief translations. However, the monitor, while acknowledging this to me, did not follow up with the translator by asking what else had been said. In this instance, the owners of the contracting shop began pleading their case to the designer, who tried to intervene on their behalf, asking what could be done so they could pass. This seemed to undermine the sense of the translator's impartiality. I was told by one monitor that the company often looks for someone at a nearby business who speaks the same language and pays that person $20 to translate, bringing into question the professional nature of the translations.

The number of employees interviewed varies from firm to firm. The ACPA guidelines call for interviewing at least 5 percent of the employees but no fewer than three people for minimum-intensity monitoring; 10 percent and at least five people for intermediate-intensity monitoring; and 15 percent and at least ten people for high-intensity monitoring. All companies claim to meet or exceed these standards. However, one of the monitors I observed did four interviews whether the shop was on minimum or higher intensity, although the clients were not necessarily ACPA signatories. On another observance of an intermediate-intensity audit for an ACPA signatory, a monitor asked the manager to send in five employees, but when she said they were busy and asked whether three would do, he accepted. The internal monitor at another ACPA signatory manufacturer reported to me that he rarely conducted employee interviews and instead did weekly surveillance. Having worked at a monitoring firm previously he had found interviews to be unreliable and unrevealing.

The DOL data again confirm highly inconsistent practices. In more than one-quarter of the monitoring cases, and for 20 percent of the ACPA signatory cases, *no* employee interviews were conducted.

Contractor Advising

The DOL puts considerable emphasis on interaction with the contractor in its recommendations about the monitoring visits. Three of the DOL's seven components of effective monitoring revolve around contractor advising: (1) providing compliance information, (2) advising of compliance problems, and (3) recommending corrective action. The ACPA requires an initial and a close-out conference with the contractor on each monitoring visit. The first should include a review of the Employer Compliance Program, which is laid out in a pamphlet of that name to be given to each contractor working for an ACPA signatory, and to ask whether the ECP is being complied with and whether any previous problems have been corrected. The close-out conference should note all problems and corrective action to be taken and elicit a commitment from the contractor to take such steps.

According to DOL survey data, most monitoring firms provide compliance information, but many fewer advise of problems, and even fewer recommend corrective action. Of the monitoring cases, 81 percent of firms provided information, only 45 percent disclosed problems, and only 40 percent recommended corrective action. Even among the ACPA signers, fewer than half performed these required components. For ACPA signers, although contractors were provided with information in 80 percent of cases, they were advised of problems in only 48 percent of cases, and corrective action was recommended in just 44 percent of cases.

During my observations, no monitor reviewed the ECP with the contractor. One audit was a first-time visit to the contractor of an ACPA signatory, and no review of the ECP or overview of the law was done. The monitor only advised the contractor of the laws he appeared to be violating.

Monitors began the visit by introducing themselves to the owner or manager and reviewing what the audit would consist of. At that point, the owner would either agree to or refuse the audit. I was present on two occasions when the manager refused to be audited. In one, the monitor called the manufacturer contact from the facility but could not get hold of him and left. In the second, the contract-shop owner said the shop was very busy and, besides, the monitors had been there only a month earlier. She asked the monitor to return the next week and make an appointment first. He said he would return but could not make an appointment. The monitor said he was accommodating because he remembered that he had recently monitored that shop and had been mistakenly assigned to it or assigned to it for another manufacturer. A monitor also told me about going into a shop and being threatened by the owner with a pair of scissors. He reported this to the manufacturer, GUESS?, which reprimanded the contractor but did not drop the shop. The executive director of Cal-Safety said that it was common to be refused entrance and that it happened in about one-third of all first-time audits.[36]

Two of the three main monitoring companies do conduct close-out conferences. They provide a sheet explaining what needs to be fixed and ask the contractor to sign it. The third company, which conducts almost half of all of the audits in Los Angeles, provides only a request for any records needed to complete the audit. It does not conduct close-out conferences, the monitor told me, because it does not believe that doing so is safe. He said that a contractor had once demanded a passing report, threatening him with a gun. However, not holding close-out conferences seemed to be part of the philosophy of the firm, because it also did not provide the contractor with a corrective-action-recommendation report. It sent this report to the client, the manufacturer, which then had to follow up with the contractor. The monitoring company claimed that the report is the property of the manufacturer, which, after all, had paid for it.

Child Labor

Auditors told me that they checked for child labor by making sure they included in their interviews the youngest-looking workers in the factory. They asked them their age and could follow up by asking their date of birth. There was no further record check. It seems that the only instances of child labor the monitors could really catch were those of very young workers who were obviously under the legal limit. One monitoring firm also asked whether any employees brought their children to work as part of the standard questionnaire.

OSHA

Most compliance firms include a minimal inspection for violations of the Occupational Safety and Health Act as part of their audits. This includes looking for frayed or hanging wires or obvious electrical hazards and checking whether the required space is cleared around the electrical box. Inspections also included checking whether exits are clearly marked and unblocked; that the appropriate number of fire extinguishers is present and that they have not expired; that the machines' pulley guards are on; and that an evacuation plan is posted. Monitors also asked whether a stocked first-aid kit was on the premises. They checked whether there was an eating area and, if there was, whether it was clean. I did not see anyone check bathroom conditions. I was also told about inspectors checking for bio-hazard containers for sewing-needle disposal to reduce the risk of AIDS infection in case an employee was stuck by a needle. I did not see anyone actually check for this, though.

Some facets of the OSHA compliance inspection are done as much to ensure the safety of the goods as the safety of the workers. For example, on one inspection the auditor asked whether the sprinkler system had an automatic turn-off. The manager replied that the system was disconnected and did not run. The auditor said that was fine. I later asked him about this. It turned out that the concern was not the adequacy of a response to a fire but whether the sprinklers could accidentally go off and damage the clothing.

Collective-Bargaining Rights

No monitoring firm I interviewed considered collective-bargaining rights or freedom of association within the purview of its audits in the United States, although the Cal-Safety literature states, "Freedom of association and forced labor must be addressed at every inspection." No firm includes interview questions on this subject in its employee-interview questionnaires. When asked about this issue, the heads of the monitoring firms responded that, for U.S. audits, they stick to the areas covered by the FLSA: minimum wage, overtime, record keeping, homework, and child-labor regulations. However, as indicated earlier and advertised in their literature, they do (at least superficially) check for compliance with health and safety and immigration law, as well as for compliance with state regulations regarding registration and workers' compensation insurance. But they do not investigate for violations of the National Labor Relations Act.

Auditors did report that when they monitored abroad, depending on the code of conduct of the particular manufacturer, they sometimes checked for violations of unionization rights. However, among the auditors there seemed to be at best ignorance about union issues and at worst a negative view. Several auditors told me that unions were not an issue in the United States or not an issue on the West Coast. One auditor told me that in El Salvador factories were clean and workers were well paid and that "unions just mess things up."[37]

Monitoring firms may help foment such a view. One monitoring firm also offers services to defend employers at the National Labor Relations Board on unfair labor-practices issues. At Cal-Safety, a large GUESS? ad attacking the garment workers' union was posted on the wall in the hallway near the coffee machine. This paid advertisement voices the message that monitoring is a substitute for unionization. This is a widely held belief in the apparel industry, summarized to me by a leading proponent for monitoring, the industry attorney Richard Reinis:

Through self-policing, my monitoring, the workers are able to improve their standard of living—increase their wage level without organizing, in effect. . . . So what's happened here is that through people like Cal-Safety, hired by . . . socially responsible [manufacturers], minimum wage and over-time is guaranteed to be paid and the workers don't need to organize; they don't need to pay dues to Jay Mazur [president of UNITE] in order to obtain the benefit because they have stronger forces than even the union in order to compel payment in accordance with the law.[38]

This argument assumes that wage issues are the only basis for organizing and that workers only want or need the minimum required by the law.

EFFECTIVENESS OF MONITORING IN LOS ANGELES

For the DOL and many others, the bottom line is not where, when, and how monitors conduct audits but how effective monitoring is in changing patterns of compliance within the industry. To determine rates of compliance, the DOL has conducted four studies of approximately seventy garment shops each in Los Angeles over an eight-year period. The first survey did not include information on monitoring; the following three did, with the final two including detailed questions on the thoroughness of monitoring.

Table 5 summarizes the DOL's analyses of these surveys. All of the figures are taken from the DOL's published survey results.[39] In compiling the table, I noted that one of the figures for 2000 was irreconcilable with other data in the table. When I contacted the current district director, Don Wiley, to obtain more accurate figures, he explained that there is considerable confusion over the numbers. Three different entities have been "massaging" the data, and the DOL therefore has several different sets of numbers. He provided a second set of numbers for the final two columns of the 2000 data, which I will refer to in the following description.[40] However, I have compiled the published figures because they are the only officially released numbers (and were republished in 2001), there is no clear sense of the *most* accurate data, and I have not been able to document any alternative figures.

The DOL's survey data show that monitoring seems to significantly raise the rates of compliance in the industry. Table 5 shows that monitored shops had lower rates of violations and, in 1996 and 1998, smaller violations (see back wages owed) than nonmonitored shops. Figure 9 graphically illustrates the difference. In 2000, DOL statistics indicate that the rate of compliance in monitored shops was at least twice as high as in nonmonitored shops, although the back-wages-owed violations in monitored shops appear to be more severe than in nonmonitored shops.[41] Figure 9 also depicts a decline in the effectiveness of monitoring between 1996 and 1998, from 58 percent to 40 percent. There appears to be a similarly sharp decline between 1998 and 2000, from 40 percent to 27 percent. However, according to information I received verbally from

TABLE 5. Results of Department of Labor Surveys of Garment Industry in the Los Angeles Area, 1994–2000

	1994 Overall	1996 Overall	1996 Nonmonitored	1996 Monitored[a]	1998 Overall	1998 Nonmonitored	1998 Monitored[b]	1998 Effectively monitored[c]	2000 Overall	2000 Nonmonitored	2000 Monitored[b]	2000 Effectively monitored[c]
Overall compliance[d] (%)	22	39	22	58	39	20	40	56	33	11	27[e]	44
Minimum wage compliance (%)	39	57	36	73	52	33	56	72	46	11	55	61
Overtime compliance (%)	22	45	25	61	46	40	48	56	40	21	36	44
Average back wages per shop[f] ($)	7,284	3,235	4,872	1,972	3,631	5,324	2,955	1,413	4,062	3,924	4,502	2,819
% of shops surveyed	100	100	52	48	100	23	77	28	100	30	70	29

Note: These are *published* results from the DOL. The figures in the final two columns for 2000 are in question (see text).

[a] Contractors were simply asked whether they had been monitored by the manufacturer.

[b] Contractors were asked whether any manufacturer had carried out at least one of seven monitoring components at their shop: review of payroll, review of time cards, interviews of employees, providing compliance information, advising of compliance problems, recommending corrective action, and making unannounced visits.

[c] Contractors were asked whether any manufacturer had carried out at least six of the seven monitoring components at their shop.

[d] Overall compliance refers to compliance in the five areas covered by the FLSA: child labor, homework, record keeping, minimum wage, and overtime payments.

[e] This figure is clearly incorrect—that is, it is impossible in relation to the other figures. The overall average cannot be 33 percent if it is composed of the non-monitored group at 11 percent and the monitored group at 27 percent. In 2001, it was verbally reported to me by the DOL's district director that this figure is in fact 44 percent, but I have not been able to document the new figure. Moreover, in 2003 I was told by the DOL's regional director that 27 percent was correct.

[f] Back wages are the amount that employees are owed for nonpayment of minimum wage and overtime and are an indication of the extent of the violations. It should be noted that the amount listed covers only a ninety-day investigation period conducted by the U.S. DOL. Under California state law, workers are entitled to up to two years of back-wage payments.

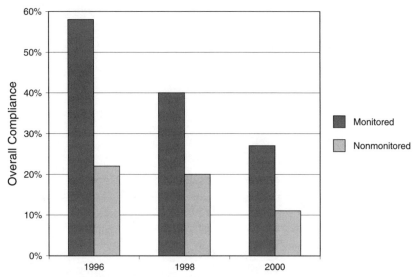

FIGURE 9. Rates of Compliance in Monitored versus Nonmonitored Shops in the Garment Industry, Los Angeles, 1996–2000.
Source: Department of Labor.

Wiley, the 27 percent figure should actually be 44 percent, which would indicate a slight recovery. The decline between 1996 and 1998 may be partially accounted for by the changed nature of the survey. In 1996, investigators asked whether the manufacturer made unannounced visits to the factory to check payroll and did confidential employee interviews. An affirmative answer put the contractor in the monitoring category. In 1998 and 2000, the criteria to be include in the monitored category were much lower: The manufacturer had to have conducted only one of the seven monitoring components.[41] It may also be that, with a proliferation of monitoring and the consequent hiring of new monitors and emergence of new firms, the quality of the monitoring declined.

However, we should also be cautious about assuming a singular causal link between monitoring and compliance. Although a small portion of manufacturers are monitoring because they have been found in violation, a much larger group is self-selecting—that is, monitoring voluntarily. One can assume that this larger group is somewhat cautious because it is *choosing* to monitor (for whatever reason—to avoid bad publicity, to avoid contact with the DOL, or simply to be responsible). The same reasons may move companies in that group to work with better shops. That is to say, it is probably not entirely an effect of the monitoring that monitored factories have better compliance. Rather, there is most likely also a correlation between the manufacturers' monitoring and their using better shops—or, more likely still, the factories manufacturers choose to monitor are their longer-term, better factories (as discussed in Chapter 4).

The data on how a factory is monitored support this hypothesis. In the 1996 survey, the DOL asked shops simply whether they were being monitored. However, in the 1998 and 2000 surveys, investigators asked specifically whether each of the seven components of monitoring was being conducted. The 1998 and 2000 "monitored shops" columns include shops that were being monitored in at least one of the seven component areas, whereas the "effectively monitored" columns cover only shops that were being monitored in at least six of the seven areas. In 1998, there was a significantly higher rate of compliance in effectively monitored shops than in the overall monitored group (56% versus 40%).[43] However, the data from 2000 may contradict this pattern. While the official data repeat this pattern, the figures reported to me by Wiley indicate that effectively monitored shops had substantially lower rates of compliance than the overall monitored category (29% versus 44%). Wiley also revealed that the rate of compliance for firms being moderately monitored (a middle range that the DOL analyzed but for which it did not release results) were higher than those in the effectively monitored category. So the most recent data indicate that the thoroughness with which a company is monitored may not be particularly influential in determining compliance. Rather, it is simply whether the factory is monitored that matters. Again, this may lead us to look at the correlation between monitoring and choosing better factories, or choosing better factories to monitor, at least for some manufacturers. If monitoring caused compliance, one would expect thoroughness of monitoring to have a measurable effect.

The crucial point is that even in the higher of the monitored categories, *more than half the shops are still out of compliance.*[44] This is starkly illustrated in Figure 10. This has very serious ramifications for garment workers who toil long hours and do not earn even the minimum they are entitled to. Calculating out from average back wages owed,

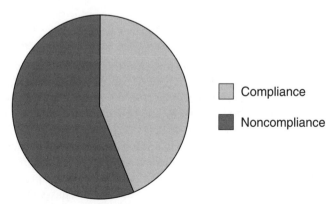

FIGURE 10. Percentage of Effectively Monitored Shops in Compliance in the Garment Industry, Los Angeles, 2000.
Source: Department of Labor.

garment workers in Los Angeles in *monitored* shops were cheated out of approximately $63 million in 2000 alone.[45] This can hardly be viewed as effective enforcement.

In 1996, the DOL garnered much praise for its monitoring program. For instance, it won the Ford Foundation and Kennedy School of Government's Innovations in Government award. However, by 2000 observers and the DOL were less sanguine. The rate of compliance rose 17 percent between 1994 and 1996, in part due to the proliferation of monitoring during that period. More companies signed on to the ACPA in 1995 than in any other year.[46] Between 1996 and 1998, rates of monitoring continued to rise, with both a significant increase in ACPA signatories and a surge in "voluntary" monitoring. However, although the percentage of monitored shops increased dramatically between 1996 and 1998 (from 48% to 77% of those surveyed), the overall compliance rate did not improve. And in 2000, the overall rate of compliance actually dropped, even though the percentage of shops being monitored remained relatively high (70%). Figure 11 illustrates the steady (1996–98) and declining (1998–2000) trend in compliance, despite increasing and continuing high rates of monitoring. It would appear that monitoring has not been refined and has not grown in effectiveness; rather, its effect has plateaued and slightly declined.[47] One factor in this may be that, as monitors and state and federal officials all agree, contractors become accustomed to monitoring and better at hiding violations from the monitors.

Although monitoring may have played a role in substantial improvements in compliance rates between 1994 and 1996, it seems to have reached the limits of its effectiveness possibly by 1998, and certainly by 2000. As T. Michael Kerr, wage and hour administrator at the DOL, wrote in the press release that accompanied the 2000 statistics:

> The Department continues to believe that monitoring of contractor shops by manufacturers can be an important factor in improving compliance. However, monitoring is only one part of what must be a much more comprehensive solution to the very pervasive compliance problem in this industry, and our survey findings indicate the quality of monitoring is suspect.[48]

At a meeting to release the 2000 statistics, the DOL announced that it would be moving toward other strategies, including suing manufacturers for ill-gotten profits that stemmed from the shipment of "hot goods." By 2001, it was doing so.[49] However, in 2002 the DOL decided to renew its efforts toward monitoring in Los Angeles, although it did not conduct a survey and this revitalization is based entirely on voluntary participation, meaning that there are no legal requirements to standardize or improve procedures. While part of the problem is the inconsistent practices just described, it is clear that there are more fundamental flaws in the monitoring approach. Even in the most thoroughly monitored shops, violations continue at extraordinarily high rates.

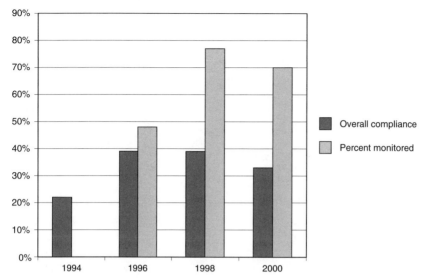

FIGURE 11. Rates of Overall Compliance and Monitoring in the Garment Industry, Los Angeles, 1994–2000.
Source: Department of Labor.

CONCLUSION

Monitoring practices not only are inconsistent, but they reinforce the inequality of power among manufacturers, contractors, and workers. Manufacturers retain control; contractors scramble to hide violations; and workers remain powerless.

How and where interviews are conducted during monitoring partly determine workers' ability to participate. All interviews are conducted on site, and the manager is or can be aware of who is being interviewed. Workers are not offered confidentiality, protection, or even information. Private monitoring as conducted in Los Angeles condemns workers to a role of ignorance, passivity, and fearfulness. In this arena, the practice of monitoring is reinforced by its scope. Monitoring covers violations of the FLSA and, to a much smaller degree, OSHA and IRCA. It does not cover rights to freedom of association or collective bargaining under the NLRA—rights that might actually give workers some measure of power. In fact, monitoring has been touted as a substitute for unionization.

Also, the nature of visits determines to a large degree the ability of contractors to hide violations. Making announced visits, allowing submission of records at a later date, and conducting surface "checklist" inspections all contribute to a lax system that gives contractors the opportunity to appear to be in compliance without changing their day-to-day practices. Further, contractors are not given enough information. In more than half the cases, they are not informed of the problems found and corrective actions that must be taken. The contractors do not own, or sometimes even have access to, the information about their shops, even though they often pay (through charge-backs) for its gathering.

Finally, the fact that monitors do not strictly follow standards means that manufacturers can really determine their own monitoring program and control the process. Compliance monitoring is a fee-for-service industry, and monitors offer made-to-order programs. Manufacturers choose whether visits are announced, surveillance is conducted, and follow-up is done—even whether back wages are calculated. The manufacturers own both the process and the information gathered through it. Moreover, they determine the results of the process: whether violations are ignored and whether workers even receive the wages owed them. This situation will only intensify with the switch from pursuing legally binding agreements with incorporated standards to voluntary participation.

Monitoring practices address violations without addressing the power imbalance among workers, contractors, and manufacturers. As a result, the same imbalance is replicated within monitoring, which becomes part of the system rather than a check on it. The next chapter discusses the ways in which monitoring fails to challenge the abusive structure of the industry. It will also analyze both the causes of the erratic practices of monitoring and the underlying defects in its logic.

4 Weaknesses and Conflicts in Private Monitoring

PRIVATE MONITORING, as it is currently being conducted in Los Angeles, is erratic and often ineffective. Government guidelines are only sporadically followed; manufacturers can tailor monitoring to their own priorities and budget; and monitors often miss important violations. In this chapter, I discuss some of the institutional and structural causes of monitoring's inconsistencies, both in its implementation and in its logic. These underlying weaknesses include problems with training, oversight, and reporting systems, and conflicts of interest.

It is not the incompetence of individual monitors that results in failure to detect or correct violations; rather, it is private monitoring as a system. Private monitoring has become another commercial enterprise, with monitoring firms seeking to expand business and raise profits. Monitoring was conceived as a remedy to the abuses against workers resulting from the government's inability to regulate the garment industry, a highly competitive sector of free-market capitalism. Yet monitoring itself is now another element in the field of unregulated competitive free-market capitalism. As such, it is not a process that prioritizes the needs of workers. This basic contradiction is the essential flaw in the logic of private monitoring.

The system is constructed to protect the manufacturers from liability, whether by cleaning up violations or by hiding them. This is glaringly clear in international monitoring. As mentioned in Chapter 2, the largest auditing firm in Los Angeles gives factories abroad ratings based on publicity risk. While avoiding negative publicity is the single driving force for monitoring abroad, it is also an important aspect of monitoring in the United States. Manufacturers do not monitor only because they have been compelled to do so by the DOL. Many more monitor "voluntarily" to avoid ending up on the DOL's website or the nightly news. The government has actively supported this concealment aspect of monitoring by allowing monitoring reports to be confidential and not building any transparency into the process. The contradiction within monitoring of being supposedly designed both to protect companies and to benefit workers becomes clear as we explore the many conflicts of interest within the system.

The first section of this chapter will address the minimal amount of training and oversight involved in monitoring, which has contributed to inconsistent practices on the ground. It will also cover the hidden nature of monitoring reports, which undermines monitoring's credibility. The subsequent section will delineate the multitude of conflicts of interest inherent in the system. The final section will explore monitoring's relationship to some of the major issues central to eliminating sweatshops: pricing structures, disclosure of chain-of-production information, stabilizing the industry, and joint liability between the manufacturer and the contractor.

I will conclude by underscoring the principal defect of monitoring: the failure to involve workers in this process in any meaningful way. Monitoring has become a means of dealing with workers through a system of "protections," not empowerment. As will be shown, private monitoring is a means by which manufacturers protect themselves from liability while retaining control of power and profits.

Lack of Training and Oversight

Private monitoring has often been portrayed as an extension of the federal government's limited capacity to enforce labor laws, given the insufficient number of investigators. The government has in fact relied on monitors to help combat the sweatshop crisis and advertised the monitoring program as proof of its concerted efforts. Yet monitors with little training have not proved to be reliable investigators. Furthermore, the government has only minimally overseen the program and has helped to hide its deficiencies by refusing to make public reports showing monitoring results.

Minimal Qualifications and Training of Employees

Labor-violation investigation requires not only accounting skills but also knowledge of the industry and an ability to gain the trust of workers. Investigators working for the State of California are trained for several months before they conduct investigations, and it takes two years to train a federal investigator.[1] There are many schemes to cheat workers; workers at the Garment Workers Justice Center came up with twenty-five ways that their employers had cheated them. Many of these schemes would not be apparent from a review of the pay records. Detecting violations takes experience and training, yet monitors tend to be young and inexperienced, with little training. "Confessions of a Sweatshop Monitor" (reprinted in Appendix 1) gives a personal account of monitoring abroad for a Los Angeles firm. The article chronicles the problems of qualifications and training.

Monitoring field investigators have minimal qualifications. While the director at each of the five compliance firms I interviewed had substantial experience either in investigation or in the garment industry, the in-field monitors had generally acquired all their experience on the job. Most compliance firms prefer that new hires have a bachelor's degree, although at least one firm used college students as part-time investigators. A second language is the most critical skill required. Cal-Safety, which is the largest firm and does much of its business abroad, recruits former Peace Corps volunteers and Mormon missionaries because of their language skills and overseas experience. Firms prefer someone with accounting or investigative background, but most of the auditors I met had taken the job soon out of college. There is some hiring between firms, so that several auditors I spoke to had worked at another compliance firm. In fact, the largest firm is reported to have a high rate of turnover.[2]

Most training is on the job. The director of Cal-Safety reported that new hires spend a week in the office learning labor law, the forms they will use, and data entry for those forms. They are then sent out for a few days with a mentor. When the director determines that there are enough new hires to justify a training session, he organizes one. It should be noted that Cal-Safety, unlike several of the other firms, generally sends monitors out in pairs, even after the training period. Another firm said it sent monitors out to accompany an experienced auditor for two or three months before they went out on their own.

Firms have training materials to teach monitors the laws and regulations and legal books available for reference. The director of Cal-Safety was developing an extensive training manual. Firms also provide monitors with check-off sheets and interview questionnaires to guide each audit.

Firms also rely on the DOL for formal training. The DOL "trainings" are actually two-hour sessions meant mainly for manufacturers. I attended one of these trainings, which covered the law, why manufacturers should monitor, and some basic principles of monitoring. Only about half an hour of the two-hour session was devoted to the specifics of how to monitor. DOL representatives reviewed the seven components of effective monitoring and went over a list of common schemes to cheat workers. They did not describe how to uncover any of those schemes; neither did they teach actual monitoring skills or techniques, except the calculation of correct overtime wages from piece-rate information. I attended another training that Gerald Hall described as "unique" because it was the first time the DOL had specifically invited monitoring firms and internal monitors. Hall said of this larger forum, "We have never set up a meeting from that perspective."[3] Even with this targeted approach, Cal-Safety had sent only about 5 of its 100 employees to the session.

Moreover, a state investigator pointed out that the government investigators might not want to teach monitors *all* the techniques. Joe Razo, a senior deputy labor commissioner of the DLSE, told me that it was an awkward position for government enforcement officials because, on the one hand, they want the monitors to be effective in helping to detect and correct violations, but on the other, the DLSE does not want to teach the monitors too many specifics about investigating because the same monitors can act as consultants for contractors defending themselves against DLSE charges of violations.[4] Even if monitors do not act as consultants, it is clear that monitoring allows contractors to learn how to correct or to hide violations—it can be almost a practice run for a government investigation. This conflict militates against thorough training.

Insufficient Oversight

Monitoring firms face little oversight. There are no formal checks on who the monitors are, what they do, or how they do it. There is no registration process (as there is for garment contractors and manufacturers). In 1998, the DOL did not have a complete list of monitoring firms. In fact, the head of the DOL program asked me to let the department know if I found out about small companies of which it was not aware.

There are no requirements to open a monitoring firm. "Any consultant can start a compliance firm," a top investigator at the DLSE said.[5] Two companies are even headed by individuals who were under suspicion of unethical practices when they left their previous posts with governmental investigative agencies. In addition, firms may have other areas of business that create direct conflicts of interest with monitoring. These will be discussed in detail later.

There are no acknowledged and accepted standards for monitoring as there are for accounting and industrial hygiene, for example. "Like CPAs, let's establish some criteria for auditing firms," Randy Youngblood of Apparel Resources suggested. "We are more or less holding ourselves to the DOL standards and hoping our bases are covered."[6] The ACPA lays out some required procedures for its signatories in terms of numbers and frequency of visits, record review, employee interviews, and close-out conferences. The DOL has also put forward its seven components of monitoring. (These are somewhat unclear, however. Advising of compliance problems and recommending corrective action could also be considered to be providing compliance information, but they are meant to be three separate components. Also, as suggested earlier, the list of components does not make clear that unannounced visits are separate from surveillance.) The DOL's monitoring guide includes three and one-half pages on how to monitor. Although brief, this document does offer some guidelines, which include "using trained individuals with experience in the garment industry"; conducting unannounced visits; doing surveillance; "look[ing] at all the work orders that are currently 'in house.' . . . It may be necessary to count the goods"; and holding confidential employee interviews in which the worker is asked whether he or she has been coached. As noted earlier, these guidelines are either ignored or only partly and sporadically followed.

Despite the inconsistencies in monitoring practices, Gerald Hall, the head of the DOL monitoring program in 1998, rejected the notion of regulating the monitoring industry. He stated that the DOL did not need another program to oversee and that another layer of bureaucracy was unnecessary. He asserted that the free market would work things out:

There are people saying [that monitoring firms] should be licensed and regulated and so forth.... That's silliness.... The competition there works
wonderfully. It's the best example of free enterprise.... What we found was,
if monitoring companies were not doing a good job, [manufacturers] fired
them because they didn't want their name on the report; they didn't want
the liabilities.... So the way a monitoring company becomes better and better was that, I'm paying you so that the department doesn't find violations
in my contractor shops and if I don't get that, then I'm not going to pay
you anymore. I'm going to find someone else.[7]

The irony of this is stark, since it is the free-market competition among
manufacturers and contractors that leads to the violations in the first place.

Hall's explanation relies on the assumption that if monitoring companies are doing a bad job, the contracting shops will be found in violation and the manufacturers will look for a more thorough monitoring
company. However, as industry attorney Richard Reinis said, "there is not
much of a threat" of being investigated by the government.[8] Given the
ratio of investigators to garment shops, the risk of a government investigation is low.[9] In fact, this ratio was one of the impetuses for creating the
monitoring program. As a former DOL investigator conceded, the contractors' "chances of being hit are almost nil."[10]

In practice, thoroughness is only one—and probably not the most
important—consideration in choosing a monitoring firm. Cal-Safety has
received a great deal of publicity for missing violations, yet it continues
to be the largest firm in the Los Angeles area. Manufacturers also weigh
such considerations as price, attitude, treatment of the contractors, and
hype of the firm. Manufacturers who reported that they had switched or
considered switching firms said they had done so because they felt one
firm was rude to the contractors or because they felt that the firm was
creating reasons for extra visits or double charging for reports. Manufacturers did not mention the DOL or DLSE finding violations as a reason for switching. According to the general manager of a manufacturer
that sells to Wal-Mart, when he decided to switch from Cal-Safety, the
monitoring firm responded with threats. The manager recounted that
Cal-Safety's owner called him and claimed that Wal-Mart, for whom she
personally also worked, would not accept another monitoring company's
reports. The manufacturer later discovered that this was not true, but it
demonstrates that there are a variety of reasons and relationships that may
be considered in choosing a firm.[11]

Clearly, monitoring firms do not catch every violation, and they will
be the first to tell you this. They do not have the resources or time to put
into an investigation that the government does. However, there have been
cases of gross violations missed by monitors that highlight the existence
of weaknesses in the system. In 1994, Cal-Safety inspected a front shop,
D&R, that was transferring work to the El Monte sweatshops and did
not uncover the fact that large amounts of work were being sent out of

the shop;[12] in November 1996, the GUESS? contractor Jeans Plus was given a clean inspection report and then found by the DOL to owe $80,000 in back wages;[13] and in the fall of 1998, Cal-Safety gave Trinity Knitworks a clean report even though the company failed to provide full records, whereas state investigators turned up massive violations.[14] Even if these cases were due to the failings of individual investigators, they point to the need for more standardized and regulated monitoring. I went to a factory with the lead monitor for one company who failed the shop. I then spoke to another company's lead monitor who had passed the same shop only the week before.

Moreover, even when violations are found, they can be ignored over and over. Monitoring companies reported that they find violations on 75–80 percent of their initial visits and on approximately half of their follow-up visits. Several manufacturers and monitors told me that a three-strikes-and-you're-out policy is common—that is, a manufacturer will drop a contractor after three failed inspections. However, I was also told that manufacturers often have a group of contractors that they will continue to work with, despite bad reports. There is no mechanism for disqualifying a contractor. The monitors simply recommend more frequent visits.

According to the DOL, high-intensity monitoring was meant to be a deterrent to continued use of a contractor.[15] High-intensity monitoring would be so costly that the manufacturer would drop the contractor rather than pay for weekly visits. However, the system is so lax that high-intensity monitoring is not actually done weekly. The report is sent out; the manufacturer must respond and give approval for another visit, which is then scheduled. This process takes some time. As described earlier, I observed an audit for an ACPA signatory of a factory in which serious violations had been found repeatedly and weekly audits had never been done. It is clear that, because there is no oversight—even for the ACPA signers, who have guidelines—the system functions not according to the steps that *should* be taken but the steps the manufacturer wants to take and pay for.

Table 6 demonstrates the erratic nature of private monitoring in Los Angeles. The table is based on an original analysis of the raw data produced by the 1998 DOL survey. It shows the number of monitoring points conducted for all those that were monitoring and for the ACPA signatories. It also indicates at the bottom the percentage of firms that covered all seven monitoring points and allowed price negotiation. The seven points are all required by the ACPA, and price negotiation is required when the contractor notifies the manufacturer of unprofitability. The question of whether the contractor was able to negotiate does not exactly mirror that requirement, but it is an indication of the manufacturer's flexibility on pricing. While the first group includes *all* those who monitor, most of whom have no relationship with the DOL, the second group is supposedly subject to the requirements of the DOL program. It is clear

TABLE 6. Number of Monitoring Components Actually Performed in Los Angeles
Garment Factories (%)

Number of components performed	All cases of monitoring	Cases involving ACPA signatories[a]
0	0	16
1	12.5	4
2	2.3	0
3	12.5	4
4	12.5	16
5	21.6	16
6	17	24
7[b]	21.6	20
All seven, plus price negotiation allowed	8	4

Source: Figures are derived from the author's analysis of raw data from a 1998 Department of Labor survey. Eighty-eight cases of monitoring are reported here. Twenty-five
cases involving ACPA signatories are reported (of these, only 21 performed monitoring
and are thus included also in the "All cases" column).

[a] The ACPA signatory group includes all of the manufacturers that signed an agreement,
regardless of whether they did any monitoring. In several cases (4 of 25) no monitoring
was done, thus significantly lowering the overall statistics for this group. If one were to
exclude the four who did not monitor, the ACPA signatories who monitor do slightly
better than the "All cases" group. However, because *all* ACPA signatories are required
to monitor, the table as it appears accurately reflects their overall performance.

[b] Of the nineteen manufacturers that performed all seven components, seven (37%)
appeared on a survey of a single shop. Because the surveyor checked every box for every
manufacturer, it is likely that this contractor did not distinguish among different manufacturers' programs, which may significantly skew the statistics upward. This shop included
one out of five of those ACPA signatories that conducted all seven components.

that despite the DOL's efforts to provide guidelines, and even to legally
require certain manufacturers to follow them, monitoring is inconsistent,
at best, and nonexistent, at worst.

These statistics also reveal that ACPA signatories monitor no more consistently than the general group of those who monitor. The DOL's survey
data reveal that, of twenty-five instances in which ACPA signatory manufacturers showed up randomly in the survey, 16 percent had not monitored at all, 80 percent had not performed all of the required monitoring
components, and only one had complied with all monitoring requirements and allowed negotiations over price. Why aren't ACPA signatories
more serious about monitoring? It may be that once a company signs the
ACPA it feels protected by the agreement or that the ACPA group includes
more chronic violators, since those were the companies that were compelled to sign.

In any case, in 1998 the DOL was aware of numerous cases of manufacturers' not following up on monitoring reports or not following ACPA
guidelines. Yet it had never sued a company for breaking the agreement,

nor had it taken any other legal action against it. The DOL adopted a strategy of spending its resources on recruiting or compelling firms to sign on to the ACPA rather than on ensuring that those who were on the agreement complied.

However, as it became clear that monitoring was not a solution to the problem of continuing violators, the DOL began to abandon this strategy. After 1998, it signed on only three more firms. Although it still did not sue any companies for failure to comply, it did begin to suspend companies from the agreement. By 2001, seventeen of the sixty-six that had signed were no longer on the agreement. Many of those companies had withdrawn because they no longer had production in Los Angeles, were no longer in business, or no longer found it beneficial to be on the agreement. But several had been punitively removed so that the DOL could once again object to their shipment of goods.[16] By 2003, only thirty-four manufacturers were on the agreement, and the DOL had switched its focus to voluntary participation.[17]

Problems with Reporting Systems and Transparency

For each audit, monitoring firms issue reports to the manufacturer. The reports are completely confidential, and there is no way for an interested party—a researcher, a concerned consumer, or whomever—to check the status of a company's monitoring program. It is a completely internal system. Therefore, when factories are found in violation by the government, it is not clear whether the monitor missed the violations or the manufacturers were informed of the violations but failed to follow up on them. With hidden reports, the manufacturer and the monitor can continue to blame each other for uncorrected violations in any specific instance.

It is clear that fault occurs on both ends: violations are missed, as described earlier, and reports are not followed up on. Evidence from a lawsuit brought against GUESS? by workers in its contracting shops shows that manufacturers do not always follow up when violations are reported. In 1997, UNITE and the *New York Times,* each of which had access to more than 1,500 pages of monitoring reports done for GUESS?, alleged that violations had been reported and ignored for years.[18] At one shop, reports done over a five-year period repeatedly indicated serious violations, yet nothing was done. Meanwhile, GUESS? advertised itself as the leader in monitoring with the most effective program.

Manufacturers who have signed the ACPA are required by the agreement to report the results of their monitoring biannually to the government. However, the DOL keeps these reports secret and will not release them even under Freedom of Information Act requests. It is therefore impossible to know whether a company's claims about the effectiveness of its monitoring program are true. This "confidentiality" opens the door to companies' making false claims that their products are "sweat-free."

It is not even clear how much the government itself reviews these biennial reports. The creator of the program, Rolene Otero, described the reporting system:

> We never had any idea how much work that would create for us. And it has. And we've been overwhelmed. Sixty-five or so companies on those agreements all send in six-month reports, so we've got volumes of paper. I've been out of the program for the last year and a half, so I'm not sure what they are doing with them. For a long period of time, [the reports] just sat on a shelf, and if they didn't turn them in we hardly even called them up until months later.[19]

Although the DOL has in the past spot-checked the reports and done some follow-up investigations, this is very sporadic. As Gerald Hall, the district director in charge in 1998, explained: "They can make it up, to be real honest, because you know I can't check it all the time. . . . We randomly see things, and we randomly run into things, anyway. So there is a certain amount of randomness."[20] He also stated that some companies do not turn in the reports.

A lack of transparency undermines the potential for public confidence in the program. Not only do consumers have no way to check reports, but more important, workers and their advocates have no incentive to report violations through this hidden system.

CONFLICTS OF INTEREST

The effectiveness of monitoring is compromised not only by weaknesses in the implementation process; it is compromised more fundamentally by an inconsistent logic manifested in the conflicts of interest embedded in the system. Every party involved in the monitoring system has interests that militate against open and thorough investigations. Manufacturers have an interest in keeping the prices they give contractors low; contractors must appear to comply with the law without necessarily having the resources to do so; workers may be fired or lose income if the contractor is found in violation; and monitors are not neutral but working for the manufacturer and, in some cases, strongly tied to the contractor community, as well.

Manufacturers

The manufacturers are the ones who initiate the monitoring and are in most cases the direct employer of the monitoring company. The manufacturers want the contracting shops to be cleaned up but only to the extent that contractors can do so without raising prices. As Richard Reinis, founder of the Compliance Alliance—a group of monitoring manufacturers—put it: "In effect, you have a monitor going into shops being paid by a manufacturer whose interest is getting work out of these shops at the right price. And every time Cal-Safety calls up and says a shop is in violation, [the manufacturer gets] angry. Conflicts really need to be worked out. . . . The conflicts are very real."[21] For the manufacturer, there is a direct conflict between wanting to clean up labor-law violations at the contractor level and profiting from them, insofar as violations lower costs. It is widely recognized that manufacturers do not calculate what they pay based on the legal price of labor. In the intensely competitive global garment industry, manufacturers look for the best quality at the lowest price. Because manufacturers contribute to violations by paying low contract prices, monitoring by those same manufacturers is by nature contradictory. As many have phrased it, private monitoring is like "the fox guarding the chicken coop."[22] Even monitoring proponents acknowledge this conflict. Reinis responds: "At least the fox is concerned now. Before he was indifferent."[23]

The time-sensitive nature of garment production—particularly women's wear, which predominates in Los Angeles—creates a further conflict. Short seasons require quick turnaround, and manufacturers' sales to retailers depend on their ability to deliver in a timely fashion. Monitoring itself slows down production because it takes time during work hours. Finding serious violations could theoretically mean a disruption in production with more audits and, possibly, cutting off the contract. Yet manufacturers need their clothes done on time. They are extremely reluctant to pull clothes out of a shop in mid-production if they are informed that there is a problem. As Razo explained: "Who is paying [the monitoring firm's] wages? The manufacturer is, and they ask them to turn their head when it is crunch time and they need to get production out."[24] Manufacturers also want high-quality work and are reluctant to stop working with a contractor that does timely high-quality work despite bad reports from the compliance firm. Compliance firms reported that there are contractors they go back to again and again, giving failing reports each time. Yet the manufacturer does not want to drop the contractor.

This conflict is intensified when the monitors are quality-control staff or when the production manager is in charge of receiving and reviewing the monitoring reports, which has usually been the case. Quality-control staff and production managers' first obligation is to get high-quality work on time and within the budget allocated. A further complication is the practice of contractors' giving kickbacks to production managers, which occurs in the industry.[25] Such payments can further tie the production staff to certain contractors, making them reluctant to cut off work. Although some companies have recognized this conflict and switched the monitoring duties to a different department, others feel that it is important that monitoring oversight be part of the production manager's duties because production managers have the closest relationship to the contractors and the contractors are more likely to listen to them than to anyone else.

Manufacturers are also unlikely to want monitors to look for NLRA issues because they are usually involved in opposing unionization efforts (either directly or by dropping the contractor). A representative of several manufacturers told me that monitoring is a way to avoid unionization because it eradicates the violations that lead workers to unionize.[26] There is a fundamental contradiction between monitoring's conceptualization as a process to protect workers' rights and an avenue to avoid the exercise of such rights.

Contractors

For contractors, monitoring creates more of an irony than a conflict of interest. Contractors claim that violations in their shops come about because of their inability to cover their overhead, pay their workers, and make modest profits, given the low prices manufacturers pay them. This situation is only compounded by monitoring, which interrupts production, costing contractors additional time and money and adding yet another expense when the manufacturer deducts the costs from the contractor's payments. As Joe Rodriguez, director of the GCA, pointed out:

> [Monitoring] created a new industry, new breed of millionaires compensated out of industry funds. It diverts a lot of money, which could have gone to improving wages, benefits, and conditions. Instead, new millionaires and new jobs in monitoring are created in an era when we as an industry are an endangered species, when we have to think of ways of surviving in the global economy with NAFTA and GATT.[27]

For contractors, monitoring actually siphons off funds that could be used to comply with labor law in a situation in which prices are already depressed by global competition.

Although monitoring does help educate new contractors and others unfamiliar with the laws, it does not address this dilemma. A representative of a large group of contractors anonymously testified that monitoring "makes the contractor a better window dresser." Contractors explain that they are being asked to appear to have no violations without receiving the resources to make real changes.

Bill Bernstrom of Cal-Safety told me that when the DOL's monitoring program started in 1992, violations were blatant. With monitoring, he said, contractors have become "slicker and slicker."[28] Officials from both the DOL and the DLSE said that, although monitoring had cleaned up a lot of violations, remaining violations are harder to detect.[29] Contractors use monitoring visits to learn the laws and how to follow them, but some also learn how to hide violations.

Workers

Workers, whom monitoring is meant to benefit, are kept from participating openly in the process. As noted in Chapter 3, most workers do not know who the monitors are. Workers I interviewed had seen, and some had even spoken to, people in their shops but did not know whether they were from the state, a monitoring firm, the manufacturer, or somewhere else. When workers did know who the monitors were, they often feared that all the workers could be laid off if violations were revealed because the manufacturer might pull the work from the shop. This threat, which is real, was most often made to these workers by the contractor. One worker described how, in his factory, "They have a meeting before and say that [the manufacturer] will take the work away from us and say, 'Then you will not have work.'"[30] Moreover, workers told me they believed that if they revealed violations and the employer found out, they would be fired.

Razo said that workers had complained about being fired after signed forms had been shown to employers. Even if most forms are kept confidential, workers, lawyers, monitors, and state officials reported that workers have been fired for talking to monitors.[31] Monitors said all they could do with such complaints is include them in the report to the manufacturer. Although the state labor code protects workers from retaliation for filing complaints about violations with government agencies, Razo said that this offers little protection to workers fired for complaining to private monitors. Those workers are basically "helpless," he said, and suggested that there should be legislation specifically including monitors in such retaliation provisions. However, he also said that retaliatory-firing cases are very difficult to win, because the employer can always use other excuses for having fired the person.[32]

In 1999, a state judge decided in favor of a family of fired workers, perhaps setting new legal precedent in this arena. Graciela Ceja; her husband, Samuel Guerra; and their daughter Lorena worked in a sewing factory in downtown Los Angeles for less than minimum wage. In September 1998, a monitor from Cal-Safety went to the factory. The owner told the workers to leave the premises or they would be fired. Outside the factory, the auditor approached the family and asked about their working conditions. Believing the monitor to be a government inspector, Graciela and Samuel revealed the violations of minimum-wage and overtime laws in the shop. The owner told the couple that whoever had spoken to the monitor would be fired; a few days later, they were laid off. The family sought legal help. An advocate called the monitoring firm, but it responded that it could do nothing. As Julie Su, an attorney with the Asian Pacific Legal Center, describes:

> They tried calling the monitor afterwards. I tried calling for them as well but never got through. [A staff member] at UNITE finally spoke with the monitor on behalf of the workers and told the monitor what had happened and asked what the monitor was going to do to protect the workers, since their firing was a direct result of his visit. The monitor said there was absolutely nothing he could do and it wasn't his problem.[33]

The couple took their case to the state labor commissioner and sued the contractor for retaliatory firing. After seven months, the case was decided in the couple's favor, and the judge ordered the contractor to pay the workers' salary from the time of the firing until the decision to reinstate them—more than $7,000 each. The daughter, who had filed after the thirty-day deadline, was ineligible for compensation. However, the contractor declared bankruptcy, and the couple did not receive the $14,000 owed.

Having failed to recoup any money from the retaliatory-firing case, the three workers went to federal court in November 1999. They sued the manufacturers that had hired the contractor (BCBG, Francine Bower, and John Paul Richard) for back wages owed from violations of minimum-wage and overtime laws during the year and a half that the family had worked at the contracting shop. One of the companies argued that the money should not be its responsibility *because* it had done its duty by hiring a monitor, even though Cal-Safety testified that it had given the factory failed reports. The lawyers were able to prove that the manufacturer had been sufficiently involved in the employment relationship to establish "joint employment." Two years after their firings, the family was granted $134,000 in back wages. Guerra later explained why he felt that the manufacturer should have been liable:

> Manufacturers do know what's going on inside the factories, but they choose to ignore the facts. They come into the factories and won't even make eye contact with or greet the workers. But we're right there, and there's no way they can walk by us and not see the conditions we work in. They're choosing not to see.[34]

In the end, the workers gained recompense through legal action against the manufacturers on joint employer status, an increasingly successful tactic used by legal advocates in Los Angeles. Although the retaliatory-firing claim was upheld, no compensation came from that court action.

While the Ceja-Guerra's success in winning remediation is unusual, their experience with the monitoring visit itself was not. It seemed, both in the audits I observed and from talking to garment workers and their advocates, that workers most often do not know who the monitors are. They do not know whether the people coming into the factory are private monitors, government inspectors, or employees of the manufacturer. This is not well clarified by the monitors. No meetings are held to explain what the monitors are doing. In the audits I observed, monitors simply introduced themselves as working for "the one who sends the work" and reassured the workers that they were not government agents. In so doing, the monitors sought to allay workers' fears of the INS and thus encourage them to speak out. However, Bernstrom, who was a DOL investigator for many years prior to running Cal-Safety, said that he thought workers were more likely to be candid with government officials because the government had the ability to ensure they would receive back wages. Others I spoke to gave different reasons for believing that workers revealed more to government investigators: that the government was more intimidating; that workers felt they would get in trouble for lying to the government; and that the government had the resources and prerogative to interview people at home, where they felt freer to talk.

Because not all monitoring firms calculate back wages, and those that do do not necessarily calculate them for all workers, there is little incentive to reveal the truth. There may be hope that the employer will change its practices on minimum-wage or overtime pay, but the possibility of losing work temporarily or permanently looms larger. A monitoring firm does not guarantee any direct financial benefit for revealing violations. Back-wage remediation depends on the particular client manufacturer.

Workers may also have material incentives *not* to participate honestly in this process. For example, many workers prefer to be paid in cash off the books (even if it represents less than they should be paid under overtime laws). They, of course, save money in taxes this way. Moreover, given their meager earnings, some workers find it necessary to supplement their income with government benefits for which they need to show less than their true earnings. Moreover, if the workers are undocumented, they will not be docked unrecoverable deductions, especially social security taxes. Undocumented workers have a difficult time filing for tax refunds, and undocumented children do not qualify them for the Earned Income Tax Credit. Also, if a contractor comes into compliance, it might be cheaper to hire more workers than pay overtime premiums. In this scenario, the worker who had been earning overtime, albeit at straight-time wages, would lose this income.

Monitoring Firms

The monitoring firms have their own conflicts of interest. They have to do with working directly for the manufacturer and increasing their business in terms of number of visits and other areas of service.

The manufacturer is both client and employer of the monitoring firm. Although monitoring firms may want to maintain certain standards, they must please their clients to stay in business. Depending on the commitment a manufacturer has to correcting violations at its contractors, satisfying manufacturers may require very thorough monitoring or minimal monitoring, at a lower price. Without regulation, free-market monitoring to some degree creates made-to-order monitoring. For example, the director of one monitoring firm told me that the company had a policy of doing only unannounced visits but was now doing some announced visits because the manufacturers insisted.[35]

The manufacturer's status as direct client interferes with effective monitoring in other ways. The heads of the monitoring firms told me that they do not involve themselves in the pricing issue. They represent the manufacturer and do not feel it is their job to interfere with that entity's business negotiations. As described in Chapter 3, the monitors do a less thorough job in uncovering violations than they could, given their perceived inability to look at the actual contracts and determine whether income corresponds to wages being paid and whether garments ordered correspond to garments present in the factory.

I was also told by several manufacturers that monitoring firms create reasons to return to shops to charge for more visits. One manufacturer complained that, instead of following up on problems found in an earlier visit, Cal-Safety monitors looked for new problems.[36] On the other side, one long-time monitor told me about monitors' receiving kickbacks from the contractors for clean reports.

Some of the monitoring firms offer other services that can cause conflicts of interest. One firm, Labor Law, not only monitors contractors but is also a legal consultant to contractors. At one minute, the firm may be trying to find violations, and at the next, protecting the contractor from accusations of violations by the DOL or DLSE.

All parties agree that the monitor's job is to find violations of the rights of the *employees*. To do so, monitors must maintain at the least a neutral position vis-à-vis the workers, if not be their advocates. Labor Law offers services to defend employers from workers' wage and hour complaints, workers' compensation claims, and in front of the Labor Board (presumably the NLRB). Labor Law's sales packet states:

> A typical scenario nowadays is as follow: *John Doe, employee, has not been reporting to work on time. On a particular day, after written warnings, the employer receives a phone call from John Doe saying that he is ill and will be late. The employer is naturally upset and tells John Doe that he no longer has a job. John Doe goes to the Unemployment Office, files for benefits and will file a wrongful termination action against the employer and will win that also. Then, if John Doe is still up to it, he will file an action with Labor Commission alleging he started work 2 times, 5 minutes before his regular start time and was not paid properly.* This scenario is all too common in labor during this period in time. All the while, the employer, not only has to pay a few thousand dollars attorney fees, but will also live with the fact that someone got something for nothing.[37]

It seems questionable that a firm that portrays workers as liars and cheats in one area of its business can take seriously employee testimony against the contractor in another. As discussed earlier, when employees do talk, the information given can be the key to an investigation. The DOL's monitoring guide ends with this point: "This [employee interviews] is where even the best schemes unravel. Look carefully at any employee statement that suggests a violation, even if the other statements indicate compliance." The DOL suggests here that, to be effective, monitors must see workers as credible.

The conflict between representing both the contractor and the employees can have other serious consequences. For instance, the monitors interview employees and, at Labor Law (and Cal-Safety), have the employees sign interview sheets. Although a monitor may want to find all violations during a particular audit, if that same monitor is later called on to assist in defending the contractor, a signed sheet from the employee testifying that there are no violations can be useful. Apparel Resources is an employee-leasing company and could be found jointly liable for any violations found by government investigators.

When a monitor is internal and works directly for the manufacturer, the conflicts may be even greater. For instance, the GUESS? staffperson in charge of the monitoring program visited shops and asked workers to sign "opt-out forms" giving up their right to be included in a lawsuit other workers had brought against GUESS? for violations that included non-payment of the minimum wage and overtime. Workers were intimidated into signing the forms, which, the judge later found, many did not even understand. Although internal monitors may not have some of the other conflicts of interest described earlier, they are clearly not neutral parties who can look out for the rights of the workers if those rights come into conflict with the interests of their own company.

FAILURE TO CHALLENGE CURRENT PRACTICES

Private monitoring does not challenge the key structural aspects of the industry that facilitate exploitation. The garment industry relies on mobility of production and secrecy of its supply chains to keep down the price of labor. The industry also uses the subcontracting system to protect itself legally from any liability for violations in its production facilities. Monitoring does not involve increasing the prices paid to the contractor and ultimately to the workers. It does not lift the veil of secrecy. It has only marginally limited the mobility of the industry. And it does not reinforce the legal relationship between the manufacturer and production workers. This section will cover monitoring's relationship to these practices by looking at pricing, disclosure, mobility, and joint liability.

Pricing Problems

Government officials recognize that the contract price paid by the manufacturer to the contractor in large part dictates the ability of the contractor to comply with minimum-wage and overtime regulations. Those prices are often completely detached from the legal cost of labor. A stark indicator of this disjuncture occurred in California when the minimum wage rose 35 percent between 1996 and 1998. Notably, manufacturer prices to the contractors did not rise during this period.[38] Workers testified that, ironically, they were forced to work harder and faster to sew enough pieces at the old rate to make the new hourly minimum. The DOL created the monitoring program precisely because it recognized that manufacturers, through their enforcement of low contract prices (and thereby lower piece rates), were responsible for many of the violations. Yet the monitoring program has failed to affect pricing.

The monitoring program addresses the issue of pricing but only on the level of formalities. The original version of the ACPA contained a lengthy section titled "Pre-Contract Review; Feasibility of Price Terms," which required that the manufacturer discuss with the contractor the economic feasibility of the proposed price to signing the contract and on the basis of a time and cost study that the *manufacturer* had conducted.[39] This clause was modified with new formulations of the agreement. In the 1998 version of the FCPA, it is titled "Required Notices of Unprofitability." The clause reads: "If Contractor will be unable to make a profit on its work on any purchase while complying with the Act [FLSA] and this ECP, Contractor will immediately notify the FIRM [Manufacturer] in writing."[40] This section goes on to state that the *contractor* should perform a time and cost study and calculate the necessary change in price to produce the item legally. If the manufacturer does not agree in writing to the new price, the contractor should notify the DOL. The new language thus shifts the burden of bringing up pricing and conducting a time and cost study to the contractor and the timing of negotiations to after the fact. This shift in responsibility and timing significantly undermines the attempt to enforce fair pricing on manufacturers. Contractors, in all practicality, will not be able to take the steps specified; thus, noncompliance will remain their fault, not the manufacturers'.

According to contractors' representatives, many contractors are not aware of this clause. It is unclear how often the contractors receive this information from the manufacturers and whether they understand it. The DOL has published two documents directed at contractors as part of its monitoring program. The first is the ECP, which the ACPA signatory manufacturers are supposed to give to contractors to obtain their written agreement to be monitored. This form is excerpted from the ACPA, including the unprofitability clause, and has a line for the contractor's signature. The ECP is written in formal legal language and had not been translated from English in 1998. Even for a native English speaker, the document is not accessible, and most contractors do not speak English as their native language.[41] By contrast, the DOL had translated into Chinese, Vietnamese, Korean, and Spanish a second document, "Apparel Contractor Guide to Compliance," which is written in comprehensible prose. Although this document explains the major requirements of the FLSA and what monitoring is, it mentions nothing about pricing.

Even if contractors are aware of the clause, they do not feel that they have the leverage to demand higher prices. The GCA's Rodriguez attributes this to two factors: contractors are often newcomers, and there is intense competition among contractors. Many contractors are immigrants who may have limited English skills and diverse cultural forms of negotiation. Moreover, according to data from the DOL's 1998 survey, more than half of the sewing factories in Los Angeles have been in business for less than two years. In some cases, production managers who are seasoned negotiators have an advantage over entrepreneurs unfamiliar with or inexperienced in U.S. price negotiations. Most important, all contractors, even experienced ones, have little bargaining power when competing against cheap imports and an oversupply of contractors in Los Angeles that includes hundreds of unregistered shops.

Furthermore, pressing the issue could threaten future business with a customer and others. The DOL has also been slow to support contractors in this area. As District Director Otero explained, "We never devised a mechanism by which contractors could come to us, but a few have. . . . It's pretty rare, though, [and] usually blackballs them—certainly from any more work with that manufacturer, and probably with anyone who knows about it."[42] Early on, Otero was advised by the DOL's lawyers in Washington, D.C., to steer clear of the issue, and she herself felt that it was a "quagmire." She argued that it is difficult to determine a fair price when shops have different levels of efficiency and modernization.[43] However, the DOL did become more interested in exploring the pricing issue. In the 1998 survey of contractor shops, it included pricing information for the first time. It hoped to analyze whether low pricing had a direct effect on the number and kinds of violations. However, as the department admits, its questions were so poorly designed that it did not obtain useful data. The DOL asked only about the type of item produced (jeans jacket, T-shirt, etc.) and the price per piece. Without any information about the labor involved in sewing the item (number of seams, number of buttons, trim) the DOL was unable to analyze the data it had collected.

The DOL appeared increasingly committed to forcing the pricing issue. In August 1998, the department held the first forum for monitors, in which both the DOL and DLSE presented information and monitoring firms and manufacturers were encouraged to ask questions. In this forum, the DOL emphasized pricing for the first time. District Director Hall instructed monitors to talk to manufacturers about pricing, warning, "We are never going to get compliance without dealing with this issue."

Hall explained to the audience that the DOL had been "afraid" to bring up pricing, but a February 1998 court decision had emboldened it to do so. In New York, the U.S. secretary of labor had brought a case against Fashion Headquarters, a manufacturer that had repeatedly ignored the DOL's requests not to ship goods that the department had found to be produced in violation of the FLSA. The federal district judge ordered the company not only to monitor all of its contractors but also to review with the contractors, before entering into a contract with them, "the economic feasibility of the proposed price in terms of the requirements of the minimum wage and overtime provisions of the FLSA."[44]

In its 2000 survey in Los Angeles the DOL included three questions about contractors' ability to negotiate: their ability to bid on a contract; their ability to renegotiate the contract price if conditions changed; and their

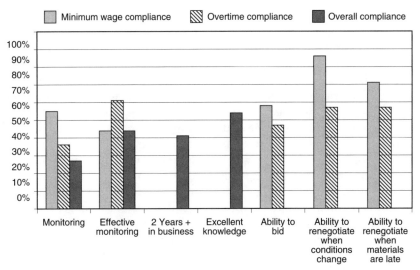

FIGURE 12. Various Factors and Their Correlation to Compliance in the Garment Industry, Los Angeles, 2000.
Source: Figures are derived from a DOL-supplied data packet: "Apparel Industry: Southern California Survey 2000" (August 2000).

ability to renegotiate if the material was late. Figure 12 illustrates that pricing, reflected in the contractor's ability to negotiate with the manufacturer, is actually the most important factor in compliance for which the DOL tested. The other factors were contractors' knowledge of the laws, time in business, and monitoring. Although the DOL did not release statistics on every aspect of these factors' correlations with the different measures of compliance (minimum wage, overtime, and overall compliance), the data are enough to indicate that contractors' ability to negotiate—and, particularly, to renegotiate when circumstances change—is the most important factor in compliance, more important than the most effective monitoring.

The DOL data from 1998 also confirm that monitoring has not affected pricing—at least, on the level of the contractor's having the ability to negotiate (which was, as described, one of the aims of the ACPA). In the 1998 survey, the DOL did ask contractors whether they had been able to negotiate prices with the manufacturer over the previous six months. Although it is in no way clear that these negotiations resulted in a fair price, the possibility of negotiation lays a foundation for pricing discussions and flexibility. Contractors said they could negotiate prices in 47.2 percent of the total 176 cases and in 49 percent of the cases in which there was monitoring. However, ACPA signatories were less likely to negotiate prices: Only 40 percent of contractors said they could negotiate with ACPA signatories. In only one of these cases had the manufacturer performed all seven monitoring components, and in two of the cases the manufacturer had conducted no monitoring. The absence of a link between negotiations and monitoring indicates that monitoring has not in any way strengthened the contractor's ability to negotiate.

In 1998, the DOL planned to take more concrete actions to address the pricing issue, including lawsuits, exploring pricing guidelines, and researching pricing practices. In late 1998, the DOL won a consent judgment against a Los Angeles sewing contractor, requiring the contractor to pay workers hourly wages rather than piece rates.[45] The DOL also expanded its questions relating to pricing on the 2000 survey. However, it is doubtful that the DOL will be able to enforce fair pricing negotiations through the monitoring system. The manufacturers are the monitors' direct clients, and monitors will have a hard time evaluating them neutrally on their business negotiations, if they feel they can get involved at all. Moreover, as the DOL moves away from formal agreements, it has less leverage to push the pricing issue through monitoring.

Lack of Disclosure

The secrecy of chain-of-production information in the garment industry serves the manufacturer in numerous ways. It prevents consumers from obtaining concrete knowledge about the production of specific garments. It prevents workers from finding out who else is producing for a given manufacturer and organizing together against abuses and exploitation. And it undermines the monitoring process itself.

One problem with the monitoring system as it now operates is that there is no way to verify whether a manufacturer is monitoring all factories or just a portion of its production facilities. This occurs because reports are hidden and the names and locations of manufacturers' contractors are a closely held secret. Even if the reports were public, manufacturers could still appear to have a strong monitoring program but in fact be simultaneously using unmonitored facilities that do not appear in the reports. Omissions might be detected because workers (probably through their advocates) could check for their facility on the reports, but workers do not always know whom they are producing for. Full disclosure of reports and production-chain information would allow anyone, including the DOL, to check whether a company was monitoring all of its production.

There is evidence that manufacturers do have hidden contractors. Of the sixteen manufacturers that appear in multiple factories in the DOL's 1998 survey, all but one conducted monitoring in at least one factory. Of these fifteen, eight, or 53 percent, conducted monitoring in one shop and *not* in another. In the shop where these eight manufacturers did conduct monitoring, they averaged 4.12 of the 7 monitoring points—that is, there was clearly a monitoring *program,* not just a single component. Yet in these eight cases, the manufacturer conducted *no* monitoring in the other shop in which it had garments.

It is clear that manufacturers do not always give monitors complete lists of their contractors. Monitors reported that they sometimes enter a facility for one manufacturer and see garments for another client that had not informed them that it worked with that facility. "They have good shops and ones we're not supposed to know about," one monitor said.[46] Government investigators confirmed that they find shops that are not being monitored doing work for manufacturers that have agreements with the DOL to monitor all their subcontractors.[47] The executive director of a contractors' association described this process: "The manufacturers play around the monitoring game. Each manufacturer has contractors to keep on a list of good contractors for regular work and demand full compliance. But on quick turnaround, they give it to someone else and hope for the best."[48] In this way, manufacturers build a stable of steadier, monitored contractors and use others, often unmonitored, more sporadically. Thus, the correlation between monitoring and compliance may be due to whom is being monitored—the "good contractors"—and not the monitoring itself.

Manufacturers have claimed that they cannot release the names of their contractors because that would undermine their competitiveness. The government has supported this position in its denial of Freedom of Information Act requests for documents that include such information. Factories that produce high-quality work on time are a company's competitive advantage; thus, the information about them should be kept secret, the argument goes. The fact is that manufacturers already know some of this information. Competitors often subcontract to the same facilities (for example, Nike and Adidas use the same shops in Central America to make their clothes). Moreover, contractors willingly give out this information, because working for a big-name company is a form of advertisement. As the economist Harley Shaiken has argued, "If keeping secret one's suppliers was an important competitive advantage, why don't the electronics or auto industry do so?"[49]

Although the government accepts garment companies' claims to confidentiality, legal experts in the field have argued that factory location does not meet the standards set for trade secrets. According to those experts, location could be considered a "trade secret" only if the company treated it as confidential information in all of its business dealings. This means that all employees of the company and anyone entering the factory on behalf of the company would have to be contractually bound, or asked to agree, to keep it a secret. And they could not reveal it to any government body unless that office also agreed to confidentiality.[50]

Neither workers nor suppliers are sworn to secrecy. The government posts the addresses of violating shops along with the manufacturer's name on the Internet. Students in the anti-sweatshop movement managed to demonstrate the fallacy of these arguments by forcing manufacturers of collegiate apparel to disclose their factory location. Pressured by the movement, Nike announced that it would disclose its collegiate-apparel-production facilities, and many others followed suit, posting the addresses on the web.

Manufacturers have been hiding behind the claims of "competitive secrets" and "proprietary information" to avoid disclosure and to artificially depress workers' wages. If such information were to be made public, *and* the manufacturers' scenario of finding out and bidding up one another's contractors were to occur, what would this mean? Such openness would actually allow a more genuine functioning of free markets. If the workers' productivity level deserves higher wages, the workers should be able to compete for such wages openly. Secrecy serves to hide productive factories, cutting off their access to free and open competition and consequently undermining workers' capacity to demand the wages they deserve. Manufacturers, who are championing free-market competition, are in fact distorting the process and rendering market mechanisms ineffective. To reward productivity and focus resources on suppliers who are doing a good job, information must be available.

Disclosure of reports and factory information is thus important for a variety of reasons. Disclosure would ensure *full* monitoring; it would allow consumers to check the veracity of a manufacturer's claims; it would help workers locate the manufacturers for which they were producing, if they did not already have that information, and inform the manufacturers of problems; and it would give workers a better chance at fair competition. Although disclosure could thereby contribute to eradicating violations, it is not incorporated into the private monitoring system. Quite the opposite is true: confidentiality is a pillar of private monitoring.

Failure to Address Mobility

Private monitoring has had contradictory effects on manufacturers' mobility. Although the expense of monitoring has created more stable relationships in some cases, it has undermined stability in others. Moreover, the program has not addressed the question directly. Private monitoring as conducted in Los Angeles does nothing to prevent companies from moving from factory to factory in the pursuit of lower wages, to avoid a unionization drive, or to run away from a problem in a given factory to avoid bad publicity. In fact, to some extent it creates incentives to switch factories.

As problems are found in a factory, it becomes increasingly expensive to stay with that factory because of the increased frequency of audits. The DOL envisioned that weekly monitoring, which occurs when a contractor has failed an audit during intermediate-level monitoring, would be so prohibitively expensive as to cause the manufacturer to drop the contractor. The idea is to promote the use of good contractors rather than bad ones.

This policy assumes that it is the contractors who cause violations rather than the pricing policies, production scheduling, and other factors imposed by the manufacturers.

Moreover, many apparel companies are moving production to other areas of the country to avoid the scrutiny of the monitoring program, which has been focused on Los Angeles. Even if the DOL were to expand its efforts, companies are also moving abroad—entirely beyond the department's reach.

At the same time, the expense of monitoring has reportedly had a marginal effect on consolidating the number of contractors with whom some manufacturers work. Some manufacturers have tried to build more stable relationships with contractors who have passed inspection. However, there is more evidence of this abroad than domestically. The Investor Responsibility Research Center reported that manufacturers such as Liz Claiborne, Levi Strauss, and the Gap had reduced the number of contractors they work with to have more control over conditions (Varley 1998). The expense of added audits appears to have deterred mobility somewhat. The DOL prompted the creation of a voluntary replica of the private monitoring system on an international scale without directly addressing the question of mobility. However, the contractor base of FLA members has stabilized to some degree; the executive director attributed this to the exigencies of private monitoring as well as to the increasing difficulty of quality control.[51] Private monitoring makes the manufacturers aware (sometimes for the first time) of their production chains, and a thorough system requires continuous reporting of new contractors. Unfortunately, the DOL program in Los Angeles does not place such a burden on the manufacturers, which often monitor only the long-term portion of their contractors.

Most companies continue to use a large and changing number of factories. Moreover, at least internationally, manufacturers tend to hold a minority position in clothing factories for undisclosed business reasons.[52] That is, they will use several or many factories in a given country but only a fraction of the production capacity of any given factory. This practice makes it impossible for the contractor to depend too heavily on any manufacturer, giving the manufacturers flexibility and, perhaps most important, relieving them of responsibility. Manufacturers also use this minority position to claim that they do not have sufficient leverage to make contractors change their practices.

Short-term relationships also make it less likely that contractors will comply with monitoring recommendations, because there is no guarantee of continued orders even if they do. Such guarantees could strengthen the process considerably. The monitoring system itself *could* promote such guarantees and reward active intervention on the part of manufacturers rather than cutting and running. Workers are doubly punished when work is simply moved—first, by the exploitation they have suffered, and second, by the loss of their jobs when the exploitation is uncovered.

Ambiguous Joint Liability

The DOL originally envisioned monitoring as a means to create a measure of joint liability between the manufacturer and the contractor for labor-law compliance. According to John Nangle, the DOL's solicitor general in Los Angeles, "Historically there had been a reluctance to go from fining at the contractor level to the next person upstream."[53] However, with rampant abuses and an inability to reduce the numbers of labor-law violations by focusing on the contractor level—given the ease with which contractors can disappear, file for bankruptcy, or change names—the DOL decided to move up the chain.

Until 2000, manufacturers were not legally responsible for most of what occurs in their contracting shops. California state investigators had legal reach to the manufacturers only when the contracting shop was unregistered. The California Garment Registration Bill was passed in 1980, after compromises restricted the joint-liability provisions to manufacturers that contracted with unregistered shops. In the early 1990s, the California legislature passed across-the-board joint-liability bills for the garment industry three times, but each bill was vetoed by a Republican governor. In the fall of 1999, an anti-sweatshop bill was finally signed into law by a Democratic governor. Although this bill originally included strong joint-liability language, the phrasing was changed in negotiations with the industry. Assembly Bill (AB) 633 offers workers instead a "wage guarantee" whereby manufacturers and retailers that act like manufacturers become "guarantors" liable for remediation of wage and hour violations. Still, advocates hailed the bill as the "toughest sweatshop law of its kind in the country" when it was passed.[54]

Passing legislation was only a first step. Implementing and enforcing the legislation has proved a long, slow process. The wage-guarantee section of the law went into effect in January 2000. By March 2001, only 382 claims had been filed, probably representing "well under one percent of those who have potential claims," according to a UCLA study. The study found that 108 of the cases had settled for a fraction of what the workers were probably owed. In the great majority of cases, no guarantor was identified. Workers often do not know which label they produce for; contractors are afraid to tell for fear of being labeled squealers and blackballed; and the DLSE has failed to issue subpoenas to obtain the information. The DLSE was also unable to recover *any* money at all from identified guarantors in the cases in which it issued an order against them (Blasi 2001). Part of the problem has been understaffing at the DLSE—a problem that should have been addressed by hires financed through the higher fees included in the bill. These fees and many other provisions of

AB 633 did not go into effect until three years after the bill's adoption because of ongoing negotiations with the industry and the issuance of various sets of regulations, the last of which an industry journal called "more industry friendly."[55] The results of the full implementation of AB 633 in October 2002 have yet to be seen.

One effect of AB 633 has been manufacturers' changing their production practices to take advantage of a loophole in the legislation. By requiring contractors to purchase the cloth, manufacturers can attempt to avoid the legal designation of manufacturer because they no longer own the fabric during production but become a buyer of the goods. Companies have devised complicated financing schemes to provide their contractors the capital they need to operate in this fashion. Retailers with private-label goods use evasionary tactics.

However, this scheme and other complex arrangements may not stand up to legal scrutiny. In January 2003, the California state labor commissioner awarded $240,000 in back pay to four garment workers who, for three years, had toiled in dim lighting for more than seventy hours a week with no overtime compensation. In the first ruling of its kind, the retailer— Wet Seal, which was making private-label goods and thereby acting as a manufacturer—was found liable for $90,000 of the total. After appealing the ruling, Wet Seal finally settled the case in January 2004, agreeing to pay the $90,000 *not* because they were legally liable (which they continued to deny) but because "it was the right thing to do," according to chief executive Peter Whitford.[56] Although advocates hope this victory will set a new precedent in terms of retailer liability, it is not clear whether the workers will see any of the $150,000 still owed them by the other entities involved. The manufacturer, Rad Clothing (which incidentally is represented by Jesse Atilano, CEO of the monitoring firm Labor Law), and the contractor, DT Sewing, have both closed down and disappeared.[57]

California is at least attempting to create a measure of legal joint liability. The U.S. Congress never even voted on a proposed national bill. The only federal legislation approaching joint liability is the circuitous "hot goods" provision of the FLSA. This provision allows the DOL in effect to hold the "hot" garments hostage until they are made "unhot" through the remediation of the violation, which generally involves the payment of back wages. Unlike California's state investigators, the DOL does not have the authority to confiscate the clothing unless that authority is granted by a court in a lengthy procedure. Instead, the DOL officially objects to the shipment of goods until remediation occurs. This is not a foolproof system. The DOL suspects that manufacturers sometimes ship despite its objections. If the department suspects this has happened repeatedly, it may take the manufacturer to court. Although companies have been found jointly liable in court, litigation is lengthy and expensive. Moreover, the provision applies only to goods destined for interstate commerce. Instead, the DOL has used the provision to force companies to sign monitoring agreements.

Finally, under "hot goods" the DOL is able to collect back wages from the manufacturer only for the previous ninety days, even though the worker may be owed for years of violations. Any violations that occurred more than ninety days earlier are unrecoverable under this provision, because the goods are assumed to already have reached the retailer, which is protected from liability by the "good faith" clause mentioned earlier. Without legislation and the ability to litigate large numbers of cases, the DOL has had to rely on the "hot goods" provisions to create a measure of liability, despite its limitations.

Although the DOL did want the monitoring program to create liability in terms of violations of the FLSA and its ability to recover back wages for workers, it did not want to go so far as to make the manufacturers "joint employers." Otero said that the two things the DOL wanted to stay away from were pricing and joint employment. Joint employment could make manufacturers jointly responsible for all claims against the contractor, including workers' compensation, discrimination, and wrongful termination.

Monitoring has in fact been an effort to stave off more serious forms of joint liability. Manufacturers have argued against the necessity of federal and state legislation by simply pointing to their monitoring efforts. The industry testified to this effect at the hearings for AB 633 and in discussions brought up the unsuccessful federal "Stop Sweatshops" bill. In negotiations at both levels, as well as in individual lawsuits, manufacturers have contended that if a company is monitoring, it should be absolved of further responsibility.

Individual lawsuits are another realm in which advocates have struggled to establish the concept of joint liability. Although lawyers have won impressive victories—for example, in the case of the seventy-two Thai immigrants enslaved in El Monte—the process is extremely resource-intensive. A legal debate over whether monitoring exonerates companies from joint liability or helps establish it has arisen in several of these cases. In *Figueroa v. Guess?, Inc.*, plaintiffs argued that, through monitoring, the manufacturer was or should have been aware of violations and that this knowledge, coupled with the manufacturer's role in structuring pricing and turnaround time in such a way as to make violations inevitable, established liability. In fact, evidence from the case shows that GUESS? received report after report from monitors detailing problems at the contracting shops and ignored the information. Rejecting GUESS?'s motion to dismiss the suit, the judge ruled that the plaintiff's argument was legally adequate for proceeding to trial.[58]

In a more recent case, *Xue Zhen Zhao v. Bebe Stores, Inc.*, plaintiffs' lawyers asserted that monitors not only repeatedly reported problems with payment but also identified when workers had been overpaid. The lawyers argued that through monitoring the manufacturer not only would know about violations but also could control labor costs and that monitoring should therefore be seen as one indicator of joint control. However, in a preliminary ruling (the case has yet to go to trial) the judge found that it would be "bad public policy" to use monitoring as a factor in establishing joint liability because it would discourage the practice. Julie Su, who has pioneered these joint-liability cases, explained:

> We essentially argued that the court's position was wrong, and that absolving companies from responsibility because they monitored was a perversion of the DOL's position—in other words, companies could then simply set up ineffective monitors and/or ignore what the monitors said, then hide behind the shield of having implemented monitoring, however shoddy, to avoid liability.[59]

This scenario would certainly undermine the DOL's intent. However, the DOL seems divided in its approach.

Industry representatives and the DOL have argued that if monitoring is considered a factor in liability, no one will continue to monitor, and the program will disintegrate.[60] However, legislation and enforcement that effectively imposes joint liability on all manufacturers, regardless of monitoring activities, could strengthen monitoring. The risk of joint liability might compel manufacturers to conduct serious and thorough monitoring.

The DOL and others fear that sweeping joint-liability legislation would drive production out of the United States. After all, the contracting system provides a way to avoid such liability. If that insulation were stripped away for production in the United States, joint-liability opponents claim, manufacturers would move all of their production abroad.

Joint-liability proponents, by contrast, argue that a lot of the work is moving anyway (because of relative labor costs, NAFTA and other trade agreements, and improved transportation and communication technology). Advocates argue that potential job flight is not a reason to allow the work that remains in the United States to be done in violation of the law. Furthermore, demand remains for quick turnaround and small-batch production that only a local industry can fill. Joint liability will be one factor in manufacturers' decisions on where to produce, but it will not override other economic realities.

CONCLUSION

The DOL created monitoring as a way to address the stubborn persistence of sweatshop violations even in the face of focused government enforcement efforts. The government felt that bringing manufacturers into a "partnership"[61] would increase available resources to fight the problem.

One DOL official publicly referred to monitoring as "an extension of the government."[62] Reinis has characterized monitoring as "a privatization of a government function. Monitoring is simply the private sector taking over a function that is much too large for the government."[63] Unfortunately, as we have seen, the government and manufacturers do not have the same priorities.

Despite the obvious conflicts of interest involved, the government is trusting the manufacturers to a large degree. The DOL is relying on monitoring to improve the industry, promoting the expansion of monitoring, and advertising monitoring as a government-sponsored effort. Yet it has not taken active responsibility for monitoring. The DOL acts as an adviser to monitors rather than a regulator. It allows bad monitoring to continue without sanction. The government is thereby promoting a system of misleading appearances in which a company can be praised for making an effort without changing, in any significant way, its system of production.

As described, monitoring involves a web of contradictions. Most fundamentally, the manufacturer, which profits from the workers' exploitation, is charged with eradicating that exploitation. The manufacturer is both the profiteer and the protector. It is precisely this paternalistic relationship that makes monitoring an attractive form of labor relations for manufacturers. It is a form in which they control—to some degree—both the abuse of workers' rights and the defense of those rights.

Workers are neither empowered nor truly protected by this system. The most workers can gain are the meager wages they were already due, and in return they can easily lose work or their jobs. Workers are not offered any meaningful change: no more control of their hours or work pace, no more job security, not even fair compensation.

Even given the contradictions and limits of the system, monitoring could offer workers education about their rights and a better chance at remediation. But it does not. It is the mandate of the DOL to defend the rights of workers. However, this is a difficult task when workers are ignorant or suspicious, or even fearful, of the processes created to serve them. Worker education and protections are not integrated into monitoring. Monitors could inform workers, in group meetings held on factory or work premises and during work hours, of who they, the monitors, are; why they are there; and what will happen with the information they collect. They could inform workers of their rights and tell them how to register complaints about violations of those rights, both with the monitors and with government agencies. Yet they give vague introductions, ask perfunctory questions, and say nothing about what could result from their audit. Moreover, the implementation of monitoring does not include establishing strong protection for workers who do reveal violations.

Monitoring should seek to change the practices of the industry and empower the workers, who observe what goes on in the factories every day, to speak out on their own behalf. Monitoring could force changes in the pricing structure, create more stability in manufacturer–contractor relations and thus more job stability for workers, and require an end to secrecy. Most important, monitoring could guarantee the rights of workers to organize and consistently "monitor" on their own behalf.

However, monitoring skirts the fundamental issue of how profits are allocated along the chain of production, leaving the worker squeezed at the bottom. It is true that, to the extent that the contractor is unaware or negligent, monitoring is an effective tool in educating and simultaneously pressuring the contractor to follow the rules. The 1998 DOL survey showed that contractors that knew the law had a better rate of compliance, and that contractors who were more thoroughly monitored had higher rates of self-reported knowledge. Monitoring is also a risk factor that may deter contractors who simply want to make extra profit. However, to the extent that violations occur because the contractor is not receiving enough to pay its workers, monitoring can have little effect without more seriously addressing the issue of pricing. As the 2000 survey showed, the ability to negotiate is more highly correlated with compliance than either employer knowledge or monitoring. Although the DOL showed an interest in exploring the pricing issue further in 1998, the ACPA's history shows a weakening rather than a strengthening of the department's position on pricing as *part of* the monitoring process.

The DOL is cautious in part because it is accused of running businesses, and jobs, out of the country. Businesses have in fact gone elsewhere because of the DOL's focus on monitoring in Los Angeles. One manufacturer who makes private-label goods for retailers reported to me that Macy's had just told her that it did not want any more of its private label produced in Los Angeles. She went on to say that she had been told that this directive came from Federated Department Stores, the owner of Macy's and many other major department stores.[64] At the monitoring forum I attended, a representative of Quiksilver, a popular maker of active wear, complained about the difficulty of doing unannounced inspections because it had to pay for monitors to go back several times when the records were not there. When he got an unsympathetic response from the DOL, he threw up his hands and said, "We're just going to move to Mexico." In 1998, Kessler found in her survey of Los Angeles manufacturers that "a number" cited monitoring as a factor in the decision to source from Mexico, and "four cited increased enforcement as the primary reason for shifting production." One of her respondents warned, "California is a police state. Monitoring is essential, but they [the government] just need to back off a bit, ease off a bit, to keep manufacturing in business" (Kessler 2002: 89). The stridently pro-business Bush administration has taken such sentiments to heart, employing a "compliance assistance" model that puts more emphasis on education and much less on enforcement. For all intents and purposes, the Bush administration is thus eliminating the only strength of the monitoring program—that it had the threat of law behind it—by switching to informal agreements in which the partnership is not enhanced by the possibility of punishment, however remote.

The new, more informal DOL "letters of understanding" parallel the development of voluntary monitoring abroad. While moving production offshore evades DOL requirements to monitor, a consumer movement is growing to pressure companies to monitor abroad, as well. Many companies have latched on to such voluntary monitoring as a way to appear progressive—a way that, as Los Angeles shows, does not necessarily require paying higher prices for labor or empowering workers. The next chapter will deal with the rise and effectiveness of international monitoring, where many of the same problems and contradictions have emerged.

5 The Development of International Monitoring

AN ANALYSIS of monitoring in Los Angeles is valuable not only for understanding the effects that the policy has had locally, but also because the model of private monitoring is being implemented internationally with the enforcement of company-adopted codes of conduct and of collective codes drafted by international monitoring organizations. Codes of conduct and monitoring are rapidly proliferating worldwide, even as this book is written. Such codes are now being implemented through a variety of international monitoring systems—most of them relying on the services of commercial monitoring firms. Although the standard differs from Los Angeles in that international monitoring is a matter of assessing compliance with a "voluntary code" rather than a national law, the concept of linking responsibility for labor conditions to a brand-name company through monitoring is the same. The Los Angeles program is also beginning to look more like the international situation as the government moves away from forcing companies into formal agreements and toward persuading companies that they should voluntarily adopt a monitoring strategy as a tool to "reduce their risk" and "enhance their marketing."[1]

Prior to 1992, companies operating in Los Angeles and globally did not agree that they were responsible for the conditions in their contracting factories. While the DOL program in Los Angeles addressed this disjuncture, negative publicity, and the activists who generated it, exposed companies' lack of responsibility on an international level. The resulting outcry forced companies to establish codes of conduct for their contracting operations. In 1991, a reporter asked Nike's general manager in Indonesia, John Woodman, about labor conditions in Nike's contract factories. Woodman responded, "It's not within our scope to investigate." He expanded that he knew of labor problems in six factories but did not know what they were about, adding: "I don't know that I need to know" (as quoted in Barnet and Cavanagh 1994). Woodman's reactions were indicative of the industry as a whole. In fact, in the face of exposés of horrendous conditions, companies' first line of defense has often been outright denial that any abuses occurred. When this fails, they follow with an "It's not us; we're not the employers" argument and its corollary, "It's not us; we didn't even know this was going on." However, because of unrelenting public pressure, many companies have arrived at an acknowledgment of some level of accountability.

In 1992, Nike adopted a "Memorandum of Understanding and Code of Conduct for Indonesian Business Partners" in response to negative publicity. Levi Strauss adopted a comprehensive code covering all of its suppliers worldwide (Schoenberger 2000; Shaw 1999). Since 1992, hundreds of companies have followed suit. The adoption of codes was eventually followed by implementation efforts in the form of monitoring, primarily by commercial firms but in a few cases by independent NGOs.

Although Levi Strauss is credited with being the first *apparel* company to adopt a comprehensive code of conduct applicable to its international contractors, codes of conduct governing U.S. companies' activities in foreign countries are not new. Since the 1970s concern about the behavior of multinational corporations has been growing, and efforts have been made in many areas to rein in abuses through the use of voluntary codes. This chapter opens with a brief history of these codes to contextualize the current proliferation of codes in the apparel industry. An overview of the global apparel industry follows, giving an idea of the expanse of the industry and the types of problems that these efforts are attempting to regulate. Then I will look at the structure of monitoring at the international level, including a description of the firms and NGOs conducting monitoring and the coordinating bodies that have emerged to oversee such monitoring.

As they do in Los Angeles, companies by and large implement monitoring of contractors outside the United States by either sending in their own employees to monitor contracting facilities or hiring an outside private firm to do so. Companies generally do this on their own, although a growing number are associating themselves with one of the coordinating bodies. A handful of companies have also agreed to alternative monitoring projects in which a local NGO undertakes to monitor, generally a single factory. The development of NGO monitoring and the controversy that has arisen over the merits of "independent" versus private monitoring will be the focus of Chapter 7. This chapter and the next will provide a framework for this debate by covering the development of codes of conduct, the scope of global apparel industry and the abuses that prevail, and the current understanding of the efforts to monitor the industry.

A HISTORY OF CODES OF CONDUCT

As noted, codes of conduct for multinational corporations operating abroad are not new. Although they proliferated in the apparel industry in the 1990s, codes emerged in a number of different contexts in the last quarter of the twentieth century. While the mid-1970s saw the promulgation of several multilateral codes, subsequent years were marked by the establishment of private codes focusing on specific countries or industries. There were large variations not only in the foci of the codes, but also in the actors involved in setting the standards and in the extent to which the codes were implemented and enforced.

In the 1970s, various multilateral organizations attempted to establish codes of conduct to restrict the excesses of growing multinational corporations. The first code of this type was negotiated under the United Nations Commission on Transnational Corporations, established in 1974. Observers attribute the United Nations' action to pressure from developing countries that had banded together a decade earlier in the Group of 77 to lobby for their own interests independent of the Soviet bloc and the United States–led industrialized countries. The Group of 77 objected to the involvement of multinational corporations in the national politics of countries in which the corporations had investments (Cavanagh 1997; Compa and Hinchcliffe 1995).[2] A second code was elaborated in 1976 under the auspices of the Organization for Economic Cooperation and Development, composed primarily of the U.S. and European governments. Both the United Nations' "Code of Conduct on Transnational Corporations" and the OECD's "Guidelines for Multinational Enterprises" dealt with labor conditions, environmental and safety issues, and limiting corporations' involvement in local politics. Unfortunately, President Ronald Reagan's antipathy to the United Nations' effort eventually blocked negotiations. The OECD's code was implemented but without any enforcement mechanism. In 1977, the International Labour Organization adopted a code entitled "Tripartite Declaration of Principles Concerning Multinational Enterprises and Social Policy." Although it was more detailed in its standards, the ILO's code, like the OECD's code, failed to incorporate sanctions. Moreover, pushed by International Monetary Fund and World Bank policies, developing countries that had been instrumental in promoting such codes began to view multinational corporations less as unwanted intruders than as coveted investors.

The late 1970s and the 1980s saw a proliferation of codes passed outside the realm of intergovernmental institutions. The best-known codes— and, by some observers' estimation, the most successful—were those targeting apartheid (Varley 1998). Between 1977 and 1985, five codes were created to dictate standards for companies with operations in South Africa. The Sullivan Principles underlay the most developed program. Drafted in 1977 by African American civil-rights activists and twelve multinational corporations, the Sullivan Principles eventually dealt not only with working conditions for black employees but also with community development, employers' obligations to political detainees, and pressing for an end to apartheid. The program also included third-party auditing and public reporting of company ratings.[3] Other codes at that time included the 1984 MacBride Principles for equal treatment of religious-minority workers in Northern Ireland; the 1989 Ceres Principles (originally the Valdez principles) focusing on companies' commitment to environmental safety and sustainable development; and the Slepak Principles for the Soviet Union

(1988) and the Miller Principles for China (1991), both of which focused on the use of forced labor. With the exception of the Ceres Principles, these codes did not attract many signatories (Cavanagh 1997; Compa and Hinchcliffe 1995; Varley 1998).

In the 1990s, apparel manufacturers began to adopt company codes to protect themselves from growing criticism about the labor conditions in their contracting factories abroad. Levi Strauss adopted the first broad code of conduct, which applied to all of its international contractors, in March 1992. Levi Strauss had long been at the forefront of corporate responsibility, racially integrating its factories in the U.S. South in the 1950s, adopting principles against bribery and political intervention in the 1970s, and refraining from investments in South Africa until Nelson Mandela's election to the presidency in 1994 (Schoenberger 2000). Levi Strauss was motivated not only by an internal commitment to ethical business (bolstered by its family-owned tradition and the independence that provided) but also by outside pressure. In 1991 and 1992, companies that included Levi Strauss, Toys "Я" Us, Dow Chemical, and Sears were accused of using prison labor in the manufacturing of their products in China. Negative publicity about virtual slave labor in a Levi Strauss–contracted facility in Saipan provided additional pressure.

Levi Strauss's "Business Partner Terms of Engagement" dealt not with single issues such as child and forced labor, as some previous company commitments had. Instead, it dealt with principles in a range of areas, including environment, health and safety, working hours, wages, child labor, forced labor, discrimination, and disciplinary practices. Freedom of association was given only a mention, and the right to collective bargaining was omitted. Uniquely, Levi Strauss's code included Country Assessment Guidelines that speak not to the conditions of a particular factory but to the legal, human-rights, and political restraints in a given country that may prevent compliance, with the result that production in the entire country should supposedly be avoided. However, this provision was weakened by revisions in 1996, and in 1998 Levi Strauss reversed its five-year-old decision to gradually withdraw from China.

Following Levi Strauss's move in 1992, many individual companies soon adopted their own codes of conduct. In 1995, President Bill Clinton released his Model Business Principles, encouraging "all businesses to adopt and implement voluntary codes of conduct for doing business around the world" (reprinted in Varley 1998: 9). The president laid out a set of basic standards to serve as a common denominator for code content. However, company codes continued to vary considerably in scope. Most company codes did not deal with labor standards at all, and those that did left out key elements of the president's model (Sajhau 1997; Varley 1998). Although companies in industries ranging from chemicals to toys adopted codes, it was the apparel industry that became the focus of the White House's campaign and of public scrutiny.

THE DISTRIBUTION OF THE GLOBAL
APPAREL INDUSTRY

The apparel industry became the focus of the movement urging codes for several reasons. Its image-dependent nature made it particularly vulnerable to publicity attacks (Klein 1999). Apparel also became a target because of the sheer size of the industry and the enormous shifts in the preceding two decades that had resulted in job loss in the United States and incredible expansion of the export sector of the industry globally. With such a global and mobile industry, local mechanisms of redress—such as enforcement based on national laws and unionization—had become ineffective. To understand the pressing need for new mechanisms to address labor conditions, it is useful to have a clear sense of the breadth of the industry and the conditions abroad.

Clothing is an enormous industry that accounted for 22 percent of the worldwide trade in consumer goods in 1997.[4] Textile and clothing together made up more than two-fifths of all exports of consumer goods. Production of and trade in clothing has increased dramatically in the past two decades. The entire world production of clothing in 1998 (both domestic use and trade) was $336 billion, an increase of 36 percent from 1980. The value of clothing produced for export in 1997 was $177 billion, a 335 percent increase from 1980. Thus, the percentage increase in the value of clothing *made for export* was nearly ten times that of the increase in the value of production generally. Through the late 1990s and early 2000s, the trend continued at a breakneck pace. Between 1997 and 2001, apparel imports to the United States alone rose 34 percent, to more than $67 billion.[5]

In addition, major geographical shifts took place in the location of production. Between 1980 and 1995, production in Asia and the Americas increased 177 percent and 67 percent, respectively, while production in Europe fell 13 percent. By 1998, Asian production accounted for more than half the industry. The rise in Asian production was even more dramatic in footwear, with a 424 percent increase between 1980 and 1995. Although production has also increased in other areas, the relative amount of production there remains small. In 1995, Africa and Oceania accounted for just over 3 percent of clothing production and just under 3 percent of footwear production. Employment figures reflect these shifts. Of the 11,222,000 people *formally* employed in the clothing sector in 1998 (this total does not include the informal sector, which accounts for a large percentage of the workers), 62 percent were employed in Asia, 21.3 percent in Europe, and 11.4 percent in the Americas.

Within these regions there has generally been a shift from more developed to less developed countries. The employment in the clothing sector in such countries as Bangladesh, China, Indonesia, Mexico, and Thailand increased considerably between 1980 and 1995. Turkey, Italy, and Portugal were the only countries with increases in garment employment that are not considered "less-developed countries." Likewise, the principal countries that experienced decreases in employment, with the exception of Brazil, were industrialized areas such as France, Germany, Hong Kong, Japan, Poland, the United Kingdom, and the United States. Although trends can be identified over the past twenty years, the fact is that all employment in the production end of the industry is incredibly unstable. As a researcher at the ILO wrote, "Jobs created in any one country cannot be regarded as long-term gain. . . . Centres of development, production and trade are constantly shifting and taking jobs with them" (ILO 2000: sec. 1.2.3).

In 2005, with the phasing out of the Multi-Fiber Arrangement quotas, more significant shifts from developed to developing countries are expected. Researchers also predict shifts among developing countries, with the percentage of worldwide production increasing in Asia and decreasing in Mexico and the Caribbean (Diao and Somwaru 2001). China is expected to receive the biggest influx of new production.

The distribution of production is influenced, among other factors, by proximity to markets, trade restrictions, ready supply of material, and labor costs. However, as transportation technology advances and trade restrictions are liberalized, labor costs play a relatively more important role. The disparity in wage levels and other associated labor costs is striking. In the United States, the labor costs in apparel were officially $9.53 per hour in 1995, whereas they averaged only $1.25 in Latin American countries. Similarly, in Asia, labor costs in Japan were $16.45 per hour versus an average of $2.78 elsewhere (ILO 2000). In 1998, when wages and fringe benefits in the United States were $10.12 in the apparel industry, they were $0.43 in China, $0.39 in India, $0.22 in Vietnam, and $0.16 in Indonesia (Bair and Gereffi 2002).

As quotas are phased out, not only may wages be driven down even further by an intensification of competition, but conditions may worsen, as well. There is an expectation that subcontracting and homework will grow and that companies will flee to areas where workers' rights are least protected (Hale 2000). The MFA's phaseout has already been used to justify a weakening of workers' existing protections. In Sri Lanka, a high-ranking government official called for the overtime legislation to be changed from 100 allowed hours a year to 100 hours a month so the country can remain internationally competitive when the MFA quotas are removed (Dent 2002). Even now, without the phaseout, conditions are often miserable.

CONTROLLING COSTS AND WORKERS

The garment industry super-exploits workers by avoiding even the low labor costs that are legally required. Reports from around the world reveal not only that there is regular non-payment of the legal minimum and overtime premiums, but also that workers are further cheated through the deduction of "fines" or penalties for refusal to work overtime, for failing to finish a quota, for being out sick, and for other perceived violations. Workers' checks are sometimes also reduced by deductions for transportation, food (usually insufficient), and lodging (often overcrowded and unsanitary). Employers generally save money by failing to provide a safe and healthy workplace, including machine guards, potable water, ergonomic seating, clean bathrooms, and clear and functioning fire exits and extinguishers. Workers are also subjected to chemical exposure and unhealthy levels of particles in the air they breathe.

Employers also keep costs down by evading the payment of required social-security and health benefits. Moreover, employers are reluctant to let workers interrupt their productive activity, thus causing or worsening workers' health problems. It is not uncommon for employers to restrict workers' access to toilets or deny permission to leave work to visit a doctor, which has led to instances of serious medical problems, miscarriage, and even death. In many countries, employers avoid maternity benefits by forcing women to take pre-employment or regular pregnancy tests and discriminate on this basis by firing or not hiring pregnant women, often in contravention of protective legislation. There are cases of pregnant women being beaten and of women being injected with hormonal contraceptives under threat of firing, or forced to take birth-control pills, sometimes being told that the pills are vitamins (Pearson and Seyfang 2002; Varley 1998).[6]

The garment industry pushes down costs not only by locating in the lowest-cost countries but also by utilizing the workers in those countries with the least bargaining power: women, immigrants, children, and forced labor. Globally, women predominate, accounting for 74 percent of workers, although there is variation by country. Female workers not only face more barriers to organizing (see Chapter 2); they are also more vulnerable to common societal abuses of pay discrimination, physical mistreatment, and sexual harassment, which abound in the garment industry. There are innumerable reports of supervisors' yelling at, swearing at, hitting, and groping workers and scattered reports of much graver physical abuse. Also, the ubiquitous policy of forced overtime has grave consequences for women who are responsible for child care and may be endangered by nighttime travel. In the well-publicized case of Ciudad Juarez on the U.S.–Mexican border, the 300 women who have disappeared or been murdered in the past decade include many maquila workers returning home at irregular hours after working overtime.[7]

Immigrant workers are also the mainstay of the industry in most industrialized and newly industrialized countries. These women often have fewer rights or are afraid of or are threatened with deportation if they attempt to exercise their rights. In China, the industry relies heavily on internal migrants. Employers often confiscate workers' travel documents (passports for international migrants or identity cards or resident permits in China), and workers are unable to travel freely or find other jobs.

Child labor is a significant problem internationally. According to the ILO, of the 250 million children age five to fourteen working worldwide, a "high proportion of these children work in the manufacturing sector and in particular in the TCF [textile, clothing, and footwear] industries" (ILO 2000: sec. 2.1). Children are often involved in industrial homework, which has increased considerably with the globalization of the industry and intensified competition. Monitoring is almost impossible in situations involving homework.

Monitoring is also difficult when so much of the industry operates through clandestine shops. Underground shops have proliferated even in some industrialized countries in which the formal economy (although in decline) predominates. It is estimated that in the Netherlands more workers are involved in the underground garment industry than in formally registered work sites (ILO 2000). In Los Angeles, researchers estimate, a quarter to a third of sewing-machine operators work in unregistered shops (Bonacich and Appelbaum 2000).

Labor costs can be slashed by using forced labor. Debt peonage and prison labor have been found from California to China. Recent lawsuits have brought to light what U.S. Attorney General John Ashcroft describes as "nothing less than modern-day slavery."[8] In 1867, the United States passed the Anti-Peonage Act, prohibiting "voluntary or involuntary servitude" to abolish the practice of indentured servitude. At the dawn of the twenty-first century, the new "indentured servants" include tens of thousands of workers from Bangladesh, China, the Philippines, and Thailand who in the 1990s paid fees of up to $7,000 to be transported to supposedly well-paid garment jobs in the United States and ended up behind barbed-wire fences in Saipan, a U.S. territory in the western Pacific. Many worked seventy-hour weeks in unhealthy and dangerous conditions, paid high prices for horrendous living quarters and unhygienic food, were regularly cheated out of overtime pay, and spent years trying to pay back their debt.[9] Seventy-two Thai immigrants suffered similar conditions in a guarded compound in El Monte, California (Su 1997), and an FBI investigator testified that a factory owner in American Samoa had "defrauded, failed to pay and at times deprived of food, beat and physically restrained these workers to force them to work".[10] Dozens of companies, from JCPenney to Wal-Mart to the Gap, sold clothes made in these factories but bearing "Made in the USA" labels. In these few cases, lawsuits have brought some compensation for the women, but in many other, less well-publicized cases elsewhere in the world, the situation has gone unaddressed.

Even in Saipan, which is subject to U.S. laws and courts, a full decade passed between the time reports of forced labor surfaced in 1992 and the situation was rectified. Three lawsuits filed in 1999 have brought not only monetary recompense to the workers but also extensive monitoring to the island. Some three years after the lawsuits were filed on behalf of more than 30,000 workers, the case was settled with an agreement for twenty-six brand-name companies to fund a multimillion-dollar monitoring program in Saipan. The program, to be instituted by the ILO and overseen by three retired judges, will be the most comprehensive anywhere. Unfortunately, it may not last long. Many industry analysts believe that with the MFA's phaseout in 2005, the garment industry in Saipan will be abandoned, as there will be no more quota-exemption benefits from producing in a U.S. territory. Ironically, a decade after the Saipan scandal forced Levi Strauss to adopt a code of conduct, the company is the only one that refused to settle the Saipan lawsuit. In defending this stance, the company has said that it has its own monitoring program, which was among the first in the world—although it apparently was not terribly effective.[11]

Like homework, the various forms of forced labor not only reduce labor costs but are also a means of thwarting unionization, thereby ensuring that costs remain low. In the case of Saipan, workers were required to sign "shadow contracts" that prohibited them from unionizing and from attending religious services, marrying, and quitting. In America Samoa, where employers own both the factories and the migrants' living quarters, owners simply turned off the electricity in stifling buildings when workers struck for unpaid wages.[12]

Direct repression of organizing efforts is a common practice. The International Confederation of Free Trade Unions releases an annual report documenting the repression of trade unionists around the world. In 2001, 223 workers were reported killed or "disappeared" for their union activities. Four thousand workers involved—or alleged to be involved—in organizing were arrested, and one thousand more were injured, largely through beatings and some through torture. Moreover, reported cases of union leaders being fired for their efforts reached 10,000 in 2001 alone. These figures do not include unreported cases or the thousands more who are not fired but are regularly intimidated by employers through a variety of other means, including discrimination in pay and promotion, threats, house visits, surveillance, bribes, and even detention in factory cells (ICTFU 2002). Blacklisting of labor activists is another common practice that further intimidates workers and keeps them from becoming involved.

The United States is no exception to the anti-union atmosphere that prevails. According to an in-depth investigation by Human Rights Watch in the United States, workers who attempt to unionize are often "spied on, harassed, pressured, threatened, fired, deported or otherwise victimized in reprisal for their exercise of the fight to freedom of association" (HRW 2000: 2). A report on seven countries, including the United States, by the organization Business for Social Responsibility and others also concluded that reports of anti-union practices on the part of employers were widespread (BSR et al. 2000).

The numbers of repressive incidents indicate not only the intensity of repression but also the continued efforts by workers to organize in the face of such repression. Even in China, where independent union organizing is illegal, protest is rampant. According to the *Washington Post,* official Labor Ministry statistics in China placed the number of labor disputes in 1999 at more than 120,000, and in 2002, reports of protest and repression there abounded.[13]

Workers in the apparel industry are part of this pattern of widespread protest and abuse (Armbruster-Sandoval 2000; BSR et al. 2000; Fuentes and Ehrenreich 1983; Quinteros et al. 1998; Varley 1998; Yimprasert and Candland 2000). In 1998 in Guatemala, Phillips–Van Heusen closed the only factory of the more than 200 export-processing plants in the country that had an independent union (ILO 2000).[14] In 2001 alone, the ICFTU reported garment workers fired for union organizing in Burma, Cambodia, Kenya, Lesotho, Malaysia, Mexico, Nicaragua, and South Africa; activists from Kenya, Mexico, and Thailand were arrested, and cases were documented of unionists' being beaten in Iran and Thailand (ICFTU 2002).

While employers around the globe usually take the primary role in repressing organizing efforts, government regulations and practices also thwart unionization. As discussed earlier, local governments sometimes participate in repressing workers' rights to attract foreign investment. In a few countries, such as Bangladesh, Namibia, Pakistan, and Panama, union activity is prohibited or restricted in export-processing zones as a matter of law (ILO 2000). In other countries, including China and Mexico, the only unions allowed in the export-processing zones are official unions that are traditionally allied with the government. Those unions have taken a non-adversarial role vis-à-vis employers, professing a commitment to the government's development plan, which requires continued investment.[15] In El Salvador, the government participates in a system of repression through lack of enforcement of labor laws, actually providing companies with information on those who have unionized and, at times, using police to disband strikers.

The story of Aleida Ramirez, a worker I interviewed in El Salvador in 1998, clearly demonstrates the way in which the three points of the triangle of power discussed in Chapter 2—the manufacturer, the contractor, and the national government—work together in a system of domination that perpetuates sweatshops. Ramirez and hundreds of other Salvadoran women worked long into the night sewing T-shirts for Hanes at a factory in one of the country's many export-processing zones. Working extra hours at Maqdisal was neither voluntary nor compensated according to the law. The owners continually raised the production quotas and, consequently, the pressure on the workers. Supervisors yelled at workers and restricted their access to the bathroom. With a small core of activists, workers organized and formed a union. The union officially registered with the Ministry of Labor by filing an application with the names of the requisite eleven members, including the seven board members, although without membership of the majority of the workers, the union was unable to bargain collectively.

When Hanes dropped its contract with Maqdisal, the owner, Ana Rivas, began to negotiate with Russell, another U.S. company that makes basic items such as T-shirts. Rivas told workers that Russell would agree to a contract only if there was no union in the factory. The week before Russell sent its first order to the factory, Rivas fired the seven leaders. This was on July 12, 1998, two days after the Ministry of Labor had delivered the list of the seven union board members to the factory owner, according to normal ministry practice.[16]

Ramirez and four of her co-unionists filed for severance pay. Under Salvadoran law they were entitled to a month's pay for each year worked. It is also customary to pay union leaders their salary for the year that their position should have lasted. In fact, it is illegal to fire union leaders during this period, but the government interprets payment for the year as fulfilling this obligation. In response, Rivas denied that the five had worked at her company and falsified her records to reflect the claim. After long, drawn-out administrative and then court proceedings, three of the workers were able to prove they had worked at the factory and were owed severance pay. However, Rivas then argued that she did not have enough money to pay the remediation. A year later the workers were still trying to collect their money, blacklisted and unable to find employment. According to the workers, the owner was living in the Bahamas, and her factory was running at full capacity making Russell's shirts, some of which are sold with college logos.[17] The actions of Russell, Rivas, and the government combined to deny workers their right to organize.

This is a story that repeats itself regularly in the maquila industry of El Salvador and, in its general sense, elsewhere in the world. Even the most thorough monitoring could not correct the violations, which—as this chapter describes—are universal. In China, the largest exporter of clothing to the United States, workers are sometimes required to work up to fourteen hours a day, seven days a week. Workers' overtime hours are almost always underpaid. It is common practice to withhold several weeks of pay so workers will not leave their jobs. Windows are barred and gates locked during work hours. Industrial accidents are common, with tens of thousands of fingers a year being amputated. And many employers fail to pay into the state social-security-insurance system (BSR et al. 2000; Kwan 2000; Varley 1998). According to a reporter who visited a factory owned by the largest shoe-assembly contractor in the world, Yue Yuen, "Slogans everywhere exhort workers: `Work diligently because life is hard and short (The spirit of Yue Yuen).'"[18] Yet the head of the American Chamber of Commerce in China declared about conditions there, "I don't see any contradiction with our members' codes of conduct. . . . We're upholding the highest standards, and we're living by them."[19]

Companies such as Nike, New Balance, Disney, and Wal-Mart regularly send private monitors to China and continue to advertise their good business practices. In May 2000, the National Labor Committee, a small nonprofit organization based in New York, released a report accusing apparel firms of using factories with horrendous working conditions and auditors of failing to detect egregious violations. The NLC's *Made in China* included specific allegations about a Chinese factory in which workers were beaten, their identity papers were confiscated, and they lived virtually as indentured servants, owing the company for food and board.

The factory made Kathie Lee Gifford handbags that were sold at Wal-Mart. The store chain and Gifford immediately put out a press release that dismissed the report as "lies" and claimed that they had never had "any relationship with a company or factory by this name." A three-week investigation by *Business Week* not only corroborated the allegations but revealed that Gifford bags were made at the factory until December 1999 and that Wal-Mart and Gifford had sent two different monitors (Cal-Safety and PricewaterhouseCoopers) five times during that year. During the investigation, *Business Week* was unable to discern which violations had been caught by auditors but then denied by Wal-Mart (as PricewaterhouseCoopers claimed) and which had never been detected (as Wal-Mart claimed), because each party cited confidentiality agreements with the other that forbade them from revealing details of monitoring reports. *Business Week* concluded that the conditions of the workers it had uncovered "stands in stark contrast to the reassurances that Wal-Mart, Payless, and other U.S. companies give American consumers that their goods aren't produced under sweatshop conditions."[20]

FORMS OF CODE IMPLEMENTATION

The National Labor Committee campaigns, as well as the research of other activists and academics, turned attention not only toward the question of whether companies had adopted codes of conduct. More important, it turned attention toward whether and how companies were implementing such codes. It was clear that most companies were simply promulgating codes and attaching them to their contracts without active enforcement (U.S. DOL 1996; Varley 1998). Since 1995, when the National Labor Committee launched a campaign to expose the superficial nature of attaching codes to contracts as a supposed regulatory mechanism, a growing number of firms have begun to actually implement codes through monitoring. As was described for Los Angeles, a variety of "implementation" methods are currently being used at the international level. The most prevalent form of code implementation internationally still appears to be requiring contractors to sign a guarantee of compliance in the contract. For companies that go further and actually monitor, it is most common to use company-hired monitors—either a commercial firm or a company's own employees. Some companies have set up large compliance departments to monitor their contractors and to coordinate outside efforts. A few companies are engaging local NGOs to conduct monitoring. Many companies are now using monitors under the auspices of one of the various oversight organizations that have emerged in the past five years to systematize and coordinate monitoring.

International Monitoring Systems

Several monitoring organizations have been established to coordinate or oversee monitoring. Each organization has its own code of conduct and monitoring system that specifies such things as who may conduct the monitoring, who pays for it, what the protocols are, and who receives the certification of approval. These systems entail varying degrees of company control, involvement of non-industry players, disclosure requirements, and independence of monitors. Although many companies monitor outside these programs, a growing number are participating in them.

The monitoring organizations based in the United States are the Fair Labor Association, developed out of the Apparel Industry Partnership presidential task force; Social Accountability International, created by the Council on Economic Priorities; and the Worldwide Responsible Apparel Production program, launched by the American Apparel Manufacturers' Association. These organizations accredit monitors, and those seeking certification choose from the list of acceptable social auditors. The oversight organization may also conduct its own audits of factories in response to complaints (SAI and FLA) or as a follow-up measure based on "risk" (WRAP). In the case of WRAP and SAI, companies contract directly with the monitors. This was also true of the FLA until mid-2002, when the FLA made significant changes in its program that included centralizing the contracting and payment of monitors through the FLA itself. These developments will be discussed in Chapter 6, along with the fourth organization, the WRC, which was established by students, unionists, and anti-sweatshop activists. The WRC does not oversee or coordinate monitoring activities. Instead, it conducts its own monitoring, or "verification" of workers' complaints using WRC staff and U.S. and local labor experts, often lawyers, academics, and human-rights workers.

The various monitoring organizations are using three different types of programs. WRAP and SAI have developed factory-certification plans. The FLA certifies brand names, not factories, and the WRC does not certify at all. Under the factory-certification model, the factory itself is responsible for retaining a monitor and achieving certification. The obligation of the brand-name company is focused on committing to use certified factories and encouraging the factories it uses to go through the monitoring process. Under the SAI model, the brand-name company can become an SAI "Signatory Company" by also certifying factories that it owns and operates (as opposed to those it contracts with) and showing progress toward using an increasing percentage of certified factories. Some labor advocates, including Neil Kearney, general secretary of the International Textile, Garment, and Leather Workers Federation, argue that this scheme is more thorough because it will eventually cover 100 percent of factories used, whereas under the brand-name-certification plan only a small percentage of the brand's factories have to be externally monitored each year to remain in good standing. Others point to grave conflicts of interest because the contractor directly hires the monitor for its own certification.

Notably, the factory-certification model undermines the concept of manufacturer responsibility that monitoring was originally created to ensure. The American Apparel Manufacturers Association touts the fact that "factory certification places primary responsibility for improving workplace conditions on those who own and operate sewn products manufacturing facilities."[21] The system places the major onus—and, more important, all financial costs of monitoring and of improvement—on the factory owners. This process is expensive. Under WRAP, a factory pays a $750 fee each year plus the cost of monitoring, which ranges from $1,500 to $3,000 or more for the initial visit (MSN 2002a).[22] A 10 percent fee is automatically charged to cover any unannounced follow-up visits WRAP might order during the certification period.

Although they share the factory-level approach, WRAP and SAI are quite different in terms of the involvement of non-industry players and in the level of their standards. WRAP was developed and is supported exclusively by private industry. In 1998, the American Apparel Manufacturers Association launched WRAP as an industry alternative to the programs then being developed through negotiations among labor, human-rights groups, and industry in the settings of President Clinton's Apparel Industry Partnership and the Council for Economic Priorities. The association hired PricewaterhouseCoopers, Clarke and Weinstock (a public-policy firm), and Sandler and Travis Trade Advisory Services (a customs firm) to develop WRAP.[23] The code, adopted by the American Apparel Manufacturers Association in 1998, has now been endorsed by trade and manufacturers' associations in fourteen countries. Besides the American Apparel Manufacturers Association (which is now the American Apparel and Footwear Association) in the United States, business groups in Costa Rica, the Dominican Republic, El Salvador, Haiti, Honduras, Hong Kong, Jamaica, Mexico, Nicaragua, the Philippines, South Africa, Sri Lanka, and Turkey are "participating organizations" that endorse the code and promote certification among their members. Government representatives in several countries, including the Dominican Republic, El Salvador, and Nicaragua, have publicly supported the program, which, unlike other programs, harbors no intentions of pressuring governments to raise standards or improve enforcement efforts.

Many of the "participating organizations" are associations of factory owners. Factory owners like the plan, despite the expense incurred, because they own the process. Contractors, as was shown in the case of Los Angeles, do not like being visited multiple times by various monitors sent in by different manufacturers. As a Salvadoran manager said, factory managers often do not like the attitude of the monitors, whom they see as acting like police and arrogantly insisting that management comply with their immediate demands, regardless of the managers' own schedule.[24] Under the WRAP (and SAI) program, the factory owner arranges the visits and is the client of the monitor. The process is more one of consultation aimed at improvements than of policing for violations. Moreover, factory management owns the report, which it can choose to show, or not show, to any brand-name company that might order from the factory. Because the global contracting system is based on ever changing relationships, the contractor may see more benefit in owning the certification that can be used with a variety of clients than in making improvements to satisfy a temporary customer.

More attractive still to the factory owner, and to many brand-name companies, is the WRAP code itself, which sets much lower standards than the SAI, FLA, and WRC codes.[25] With respect to labor conditions, the WRAP code basically requires the manufacturer to comply only with local laws—for example, wages must comply with the local legal minimum and hours with the local legal maximum. The code apparently does go beyond local law by stipulating that workers should be given every seventh day off, but it then provides an escape clause by adding, "except as required to meet urgent business needs." On child labor, the code specifies fourteen as the acceptable working age rather than fifteen, the ILO standard, except in specified circumstances. Under the freedom-of-association section, the original code stated: "Apparel manufacturers will recognize and respect the right of employees to exercise their lawful rights to freedom of association, including joining or not joining any association."[26] This is by far the weakest unionization-rights clause of these collective codes. Collective bargaining was omitted, and under the clause manufacturers are required to recognize freedom of association rights only where such rights are "lawful." Thus, in areas where such rights are restricted by countries' or export-processing zones' policies, no such requirement applies. Collective-bargaining rights were later added to the code, and language that referred to joining *or not joining* any association was removed to bring the section closer to internationally accepted principles; however, "where such rights are lawful" remains in the code, and the "not joining" language has been retained in the *Self-Assessment and Monitoring Handbook* (MSN 2002a). Also, the WRAP code is alone among the monitoring organization codes in including sections on customs compliance and drug interdiction, which signals its development around industry's rather than workers' concerns.

In addition, the WRAP system has no built-in transparency. There is no public disclosure of monitoring reports or even of certified factories. If lists of certified factories are not made public, workers and their advocates cannot refute any certification. Thus, there is no check on the system. WRAP does not even disclose the countries in which certified factories are located. If workers do become aware that their factory is certified, it is unclear how they can challenge that certification. WRAP was recently criticized by anti-sweatshop activists who report that violations have surfaced at certified factories in Thailand and Honduras. Yet there is still "a lack of any mechanisms for registering complaints" (MSN 2003).

WRAP's "Independent Certification Board" has some supposed labor representatives, along with such large corporations as Sara Lee, Vanity Fair, and Kellwood (a Wal-Mart private label). But these representatives are not in line with current labor politics in the United States. The members of the board and of the staff are old "Cold Warriors" from labor's anti-communist days. Lawrence Doherty, WRAP's executive director, served for eleven years on the Latin American staff of the American Institute for Free Labor Development, an organization known for allying itself with military dictatorships, undermining democratic unions in the region, and maintaining close ties to the CIA. Doherty's father, William Doherty, was the executive director of the AIFLD for thirty years. WRAP's chairman, Jack Otero, was also closely associated with the AIFLD in its anti-Castro work and served as president of the Labor Council on Latin American Advancement. He holds very conservative positions on foreign policy and on immigrant workers in the United States. WRAP's vice-chairman, Otto Reich, was nominated by George W. Bush to be assistant secretary of state for Western Hemisphere affairs and has been described by the *Boston Globe* as "a Cuban-American with an enduring enmity for Fidel Castro—and a penchant for likening Castro's communist regime to that of the Nazis."[27] Reich has been a lobbyist for liquor and tobacco companies and was involved in the Iran–Contra scandal. When Reich was recruited into the Bush administration, he was replaced as vice-chairman by Charles Masten. Although Masten has serious labor experience as inspector general at the DOL from 1991 to 1999, that post followed nearly twenty years with the FBI.

WRAP is now the most popular of all the programs in terms of the number of audits being conducted. As of early 2003, 330 factories in 32 countries had been certified, earning WRAP's "good factory seal of approval." More than 1,000 factories in 68 countries have registered to certify. Although monitors do not appear to exist yet for all these countries, the process begins with a ramp-up period in which factories are expected to do self-assessment and carry out improvements. The manager of a Honduran factory involved in these preparations told me that the company was spending a great deal of money on improvements, none of which affected the wages or hours of the workers.

Unlike WRAP, which is completely industry-controlled, SAI and FLA are multi-stakeholder initiatives. The FLA is the result of long and complex negotiations within the apparel industry task force described in the next chapter. SAI is a creation of the Council on Economic Priorities, a research institute for corporate social responsibility. The council launched the CEPAA, or CEP Accreditation Agency (now SAI), in 1997 in response to a request by the brand-name companies involved in the organization.[28] SAI conducted broad consultations on its standard, Social Accountability 8000, and monitoring protocols with labor and human-rights groups throughout Europe and the United States. SAI is a broader initiative than the other monitoring organizations. Its board includes not only members from European and U.S. companies but also from firms in a variety of industries, including apparel, agriculture, and toys.[29]

SAI is clearly far more concerned with workers' rights than WRAP. Two union representatives serve on its board, including Kearney of the ITGLWF and a former president of the Amalgamated Clothing and Textile Workers Union. The SA8000 code is stronger than the FLA and WRAP codes. It is based on ILO standards and goes beyond them to includes language requiring a living wage and the facilitation of "parallel means of association and bargaining" in countries where these rights are legally restricted.[30] The latter requirement is aimed at China. SAI has also initiated a joint program with the ITGLWF to form study circles with 6,000 workers in Latin America and Asia to discuss codes of conduct.

SAI has higher standards on disclosure than WRAP (although lower than those of the WRC and FLA, which require some level of public release of factory lists and reports). Although it does not disclose reports, SAI lists all certified factories on its website. At the end of 2002, it had listed the names and addresses of 190 certified facilities in 31 countries. Apparel was the largest sector by far, with 43 apparel and 18 textile plants, together accounting for nearly a third of all facilities. The chemical industry followed, at 7 percent of the total. Public disclosure of certifications is crucial to any real complaint process because it allows workers—or, more likely, their advocates—to check which factories have been certified and challenge that status if violations are present. In September 2000, a Hong Kong NGO filed a complaint that charged an SAI-certified factory in China with violating the SA8000 standard. The Hong Kong Christian Industrial Committee asserted that factory management had violated many provisions, including those on payment of minimum wage, overtime pay, length of overtime, required days off, and illegal fines levied on workers. The factory was removed from the certified list.

The incident tested SAI's complaint mechanism. It also revealed much graver problems with the process. The China director of Det Norske Veritas of Norway, the certifying monitor in this case, told the *South China Morning Post*:

> You have in southern China all the factors working against the auditors[:]
> . . . the multinationals, which want low labour costs; the factory managers,
> who don't like us because of fines for non-conformity; . . . the local Chi-
> nese Government. . . which wants this business and does not want it threat-
> ened. . . . Right now, in labour-intensive industries in southern China, [the]
> SA8000 standard cannot be enforced effectively. . . . The factories always
> find a way around the auditors. (as quoted in MSN 2001)

Although it participates in the certification process, the monitor admits
that it is impossible to guarantee the results of an audit in Chinese factories. Yet China is the site of the largest number of SA8000-certified factories, with one-fifth of the total (see Appendix 1 for a personal account
of auditing in China).

Certification of compliance is certainly a problematic endeavor.
Although China is unique in some ways, the interests described by the
auditor are true around the world, as are the difficulties of the auditing
process. Based on written policies, on-site interviews with workers, and
appearances on the day of the inspection, SAI- and WRAP-accredited
auditors across the globe "certify" factories as being in compliance. As
Bill Bernstrom of Cal-Safety wrote about the WRAP program in a leading industry journal (*before* Cal-Safety joined the program as an accredited monitor):

> Of greater concern to me is the "certification" process. . . . I have a great
> deal of experience with labor compliance (nearly 20 years with the U.S.
> Department of Labor and three years with an international compliance
> monitoring company). I can unequivocally state that the findings of an
> inspection are only as good as the day of the inspection. To "certify" a fac-
> tory as being in compliance for any period is nonsense.[31]

Yet these programs do certify factories (largely using Cal-Safety). Brand-
name companies can use these "seals of approval" to assure consumers
of their good practices while conditions for workers may in fact change
very little. In this sense, the FLA plan, which is based on a very limited
number of similarly short external audits, may be no better.

The Maquila Solidarity Network, which is represented on the advisory
board of SAI, is ambivalent about the potential outcome of the program.
While acknowledging the potential of certifications to be simply a "publicity stunt," as Alice Kwan of the Hong Kong Christian Industrial Committee put it, MSN holds out hope for the process. MSN points out that
the trainings on health and safety and workers' rights that are a part of
SAI-sponsored audits (but not of WRAP) may improve workers' ability
to negotiate their conditions with factory management. If so, then the
process will have contributed to the creation of a "parallel means" of providing freedom of association, as required by the SA8000 standard, in an
atmosphere in which these rights are virtually nonexistent. However, the
outcome is yet to be seen (MSN 2001; Yanz and Jeffcott 2001).

Each organization has its own accreditation system. To date, both WRAP and SAI rely exclusively on private monitors. WRAP accredits monitors to work in specific countries; so far, it has accredited ten private firms to conduct audits in forty-nine countries (MSN 2003).[32] SAI does not do country-specific accreditation; thus, its nine accredited monitors can conduct audits worldwide. The FLA has certified fourteen companies and organizations to monitor in twenty-seven countries.[33] Because of differing accreditation procedures and requirements, a monitoring firm may conduct audits in a particular country under one system but not under another system. For instance, Cal-Safety is accredited under the FLA only in the United States; under WRAP, it is accredited in thirty-two countries, and under SAI, it is accredited worldwide.

SAI has made overtures to NGO monitors, offering them free entrance to their training sessions and encouraging them to apply for accreditation, but it has had no success to date. This failure is due in part to SAI's high accreditation fees and lengthy and bureaucratic application process and in part to the fact that SA8000 audits focus on management systems—not something with which NGOs are familiar. Monitoring for both WRAP and SAI has been criticized for emphasizing management-side information, although SAI argues that focusing on process by requiring managers to present written policies for a variety of issues gives them a better sense of how the factory operates than would the typical checklist. SAI requires monitors to consult with local NGOs and unions as part of its auditing process. However, local NGOs are then put in the position of giving free consultation to monitors who are being paid handsomely. Even when auditors such as PricewaterhouseCoopers have offered to pay local groups for consulting, they have refused to give the groups any editorial control in the reporting process.[34] In most cases, NGOs who are consulted do not see the final report.

There is potential for private and NGO monitors to work together. Some European initiatives have tested a joint approach in which private firms do the financial audit of the factory and an NGO conducts the interviews with workers. Verité, a nonprofit private firm in the United States, has also had success in hiring local NGO staff and affiliates to assist with worker interviews. This "hybrid" method has been highly touted by the Europeans and may be used by U.S. groups in the future. The British Ethical Trading Initiative has set up local-level multi-stakeholder structures involving NGOs, unions, and companies. The Swedish branch of the Clean Clothes Campaign (CCC) also centrally involves local NGOs and unions in the monitoring process. The NGOs and unions act as information gatherers prior to the commercial audit, providing vital information from worker interviews and other sources to the monitors (Ascoly et al. 2001).

Between 1998 and 2000, five European initiatives were launched to verify compliance with collective codes of conduct through monitoring projects. These multi-stakeholder groups are the Ethical Trading Initiative in

England and the CCC affiliates in France, the Netherlands, Sweden, and Switzerland. These projects are taking a slower and more exploratory approach based on testing monitoring structures and mechanisms through pilots. They have also involved more cooperation and consultation with groups in garment-producing countries than have U.S. initiatives (MSN 2003). Although the initiatives are mainly using private monitors, some involve local NGOs and contemplate pooling corporate resources to centrally hire the monitors (O'Rourke 2003).

International Monitors

A number of important retailers and brand-name manufacturers are monitoring using the programs outlined in the preceding section. However, most manufacturers who engage in international monitoring do so completely outside these systems (MSN 2003). In either case, some type of internal process is used. The systems include contractors carrying out self-assessment in the case of factory certifications through WRAP and SAI, and manufacturers conducting "internal monitoring" of their contractors in the case of the FLA's brand-name certification. This is combined with the hiring of an outside or "external" auditor in the case of WRAP and SAI and the possibility of an external audit ordered by the FLA for its members' contractors. For brands not involved in these systems, the internal process may be the extent of their implementation or they may independently hire an auditor.

The internal monitoring of brand-name manufacturers often involves giving contractors with existing contracts a timeline to come into compliance and evaluating potential contractors for compliance before entering into new contracts. As occurs in Los Angeles, the brand-name company then assigns the task of following up on compliance to staff members. While these are sometimes simply quality-control or purchasing staff, it is becoming more common for the large firms to hire specially trained employees. Firms such as Nike and the Gap have developed specialized compliance departments with large staffs. The Gap has 115 compliance officers monitoring its nearly 4,000-factory supplier chain. Nike combines the work of its seventy in-house monitors with visits by outside auditing and consulting firms (O'Rourke 2003).

External monitoring was originally dominated by large accounting firms. When international monitoring took off in the late 1990s, accounting firms quickly got involved in the business. Large accounting firms touted the advantage of established offices in many parts of the world and local staff familiar with the language and customs of the workers. Three main accounting firms conducted primarily international audits: PricewaterhouseCoopers, KPMG, and Ernst and Young. PricewaterhouseCoopers, the accounting firm with the highest level of participation in monitoring, set up a separate division offering "social accounting" services. Growth in this area was astounding. PricewaterhouseCoopers, which reported that it had done no audits in 1996, conducted an estimated 6,000 audits in 1998.[35] Its clients tended to be big companies with large profits, such as Disney and Nike.

By 2002, most of the big accounting firms were no longer very active in monitoring. Ernst and Young appears to have abandoned the practice, as have other firms. KPMG seems to be minimally involved still, offering services under its "sustainability" program but not participating in any of the global monitoring programs discussed earlier. This may have come about—at least, in part—because the accounting firms have been scaling back in the wake of Enron and subsequent scandals, as well as of growing skepticism about their neutrality.

PricewaterhouseCoopers spun off its social-accounting services in May 2001, with two of the company's partners forming Global Social Compliance. Although Global Social Compliance can claim its status as an independent corporation, it brought its clientele and directors from PricewaterhouseCoopers and it contracts with the accounting firm's auditors across the globe to conduct its audits. Global Social Compliance continues to play a major role in the social-accounting field. According to Gertie Knox, the chief operating officer, Global Social Compliance (and its previous PricewaterhouseCoopers incarnation) conducted 25,000 audits between 1996 and 2001. It is possible that accounting firms will start conducting more audits in the United States because they are heavily involved in developing WRAP. Interestingly, Global Social Compliance has culled rhetoric from the anti-sweatshop movement. Its website (which looks newly developed) has only a short screen about its monitoring program and is primarily devoted to the company's collaboration with NGO partners, a clear effort to gain credibility within an environment that reflects increasing wariness of its integrity. Global Social Compliance was finally accredited by the FLA to monitor in China only, after it was originally rejected.

Certification companies are also conducting audits abroad and in the United States under the auspices of SAI. They are mostly agencies involved in the International Standards Organization system, such as DNV of Norway, International Certification Services of Switzerland, and Bureau Veritas Quality International of France.[36] The latter two are also accredited by the FLA. These companies previously audited for compliance with internationally recognized environmental and production-quality standards (ISO 14000 and ISO 9000, respectively) and have expanded their services to include certification of compliance with labor standards. They are familiar with doing factory audits and specialize in reviewing systems of operation. They have expertise in environmental areas and in production standards, which gives them insight into whether things are as they appear (for example, whether the amount of work contracted could be accomplished by the machines and workers present or whether homework or further subcontracting must be going on). However, they are not trained accountants; neither do they have experience with labor issues and workers' concerns.

Specialized monitoring firms like those in Los Angeles are expanding, and new ones are emerging. In 1998, Cal-Safety was doing a considerable business in international monitoring, and Apparel Resources was conducting audits in Mexico. Cal-Safety merged with another company, Specialized Technology Resources, in 1999 and is now one of the leading monitors internationally; it is accredited by SAI, WRAP, and the FLA. Like Cal-Safety, the A & L Group of New York began monitoring under the DOL program and has now expanded to monitoring in Asia and Latin America. Consulting firms have sprung up in Bangladesh (LIFT-Standards), India (T-Group Solutions), and Vietnam (Global Standards/ Toan Tin) to do labor monitoring specifically in those countries, and this trend can be expected to continue. All three of those firms have been accredited by the FLA.[37]

A variety of specialty firms now conduct labor-standards monitoring. They include product-testing, customs, and forensic and investigation firms. Product-testing groups such as Intertek Testing Services, Merchandise Testing Laboratories, and Underwriters Laboratories, which specialize in product-safety and -quality testing, all now offer monitoring services.[38] Forensic and investigation firms such as the FLA-accredited Cotecna in Switzerland are also entering the business, as are customs firms such as Sandler and Travis. With the formation of coordinating bodies that accredit in the area of labor monitoring, the number and type of firms entering this business have increased dramatically.[39] The FLA, and to a lesser extent SAI, have tried to encourage the participation of locally based NGOs, although with little success.

Much of the debate around monitoring has been over whether it should be conducted by "external" commercial monitors, from the various types of business enterprises, or by local NGOs with a proven commitment to labor or human rights. A growing number of independent monitoring projects are now operating in Central America. At present, each is limited to a small number of factories. The first NGO monitoring group began in El Salvador. The Grupo de Monitoreo Independiente de El Salvador , or GMIES, has been monitoring the Mandarin International (now Charter) factory, which produces for the Gap, since 1996. Its monitoring originally focused on correct payment of wages, visible conditions, social-security payments, reinstatement of fired employees, and right to association but has expanded to include the full gamut of code provisions. GMIES works with an industrial hygienist, a chemist, and a water-quality laboratory to cover the technical areas of health and safety. In 2001, GMIES expanded its work to include more Gap factories and a Liz Claiborne contractor. The FLA recently accredited GMIES.

Three other Central American independent monitoring projects followed the emergence of GMIES. Equipo de Monitoreo Independiente de

Honduras was set up through the same channels as the Salvadoran group; it also came together to monitor a single factory producing for the Gap under an agreement between the factory owner and the National Labor Committee. However, that effort was disbanded after the plant was unionized and in the aftermath of Hurricane Mitch, which demanded the available resources of the member organizations. In 2002, Equipo de Monitoreo Independente de Honduras began operations again and is monitoring three other Gap factories. In 2002, the Gap also began working with a newly formed organization in Nicaragua, Profesionales por la Auditoria Empresarial, on a pilot monitoring project.

In 1997, a group of professionals with experience in labor rights in Guatemala established the Commission for the Verification of Codes of Conduct, or COVERCO, in response to professed interest in independent monitoring by Liz Claiborne. In 1999, COVERCO began monitoring a complex of two factory units producing for Liz Claiborne that employed 550 workers. The group has continued to monitor the factories, which now employ nearly 1,200 workers, on a regular basis. In 2000, COVERCO began to monitor two factories for the Gap that have a combined work force of more than 3,000 employees. COVERCO has also done labor-standards monitoring in other contexts, including an initial study of conditions in the coffee industry for Starbucks. COVERCO is accredited by the FLA.

The Central American projects are collaborating in an effort to strengthen their work and to potentially offer manufacturers more comprehensive services. The groups meet to discuss relations with manufacturers, developments in the U.S. monitoring programs (SAI, FLA, WRAP, and WRC), conflicts with unions, monitoring methodologies, and other issues. In 2001, GMIES, COVERCO, Equipo de Monitoreo Independente de Honduras, the Maria Elena Cuadra Movement of Working and Unemployed Women from Nicaragua (now joined by PASE), the Research Center for Feminist Action in the Dominican Republic, and the Central American Labor Research and Education Center from Costa Rica formed the Regional Initiative for Social Responsibility and Jobs with Dignity to continue to work in coordination. The Central American groups hope to thus have a stronger presence in the development of international monitoring.

Two NGOs in Asia that existed for other purposes recently launched monitoring projects under the auspices of the FLA: Phulki in Bangladesh and Kenan Institute Asia in Thailand. Phulki was founded in 1991 to aid female factory workers and their children and communities. It has set up child-care centers as well as shelters and potable-water projects. Kenan Institute Asia was founded in 1996 by the University of North Carolina Business School's Kenan Institute of Private Enterprise. The Thai institute is funded by US-AID and seeks to promote sustainable development through private enterprise and closer cooperation between the United States and Asia. Neither of these NGOs specializes in the protection of workers' rights. Kenan Institute Asia is a pro-business entity whose mission includes facilitating the creation of smoother global networks for export production. And although Phulki advocates for female workers, it is not accredited to monitor freedom-of-association rights. Acknowledging the complexities of this area, Phulki in fact exempted itself from accreditation for monitoring this essential part of the code. No explanation has been given as to how a factory monitored by Phulki can be found in compliance if such a major issue is omitted.

The nonprofit monitoring entity that has conducted the largest number of audits is Verité, which is based in the United States. Verité has conducted 700 audits in sixty-one countries. Founded in 1995, Verité receives part of its funding from foundations and donors and carries out some research activities. Although Verité has its own standards, which are higher than those generally found in company codes, it actually operates in many respects like any commercial firm. Verité charges standard fees, maintains the confidentiality of reports for clients, and conducts one-time or short-term audits, often temporarily hiring local employees or bringing in staff from the United States. Although it advertises itself as the only nonprofit with a global monitoring program, Verité actually occupies a liminal space between commercial firm and local NGO. It was the first organization accredited to monitor for the FLA but pulled out recently, reportedly because of new requirements to publicly publish reports that conflict with the organization's commitment to client confidentiality.

"Independent monitoring" by NGOs has also been used on a one-time basis to verify or evaluate specific situations. The factory producing for Phillips–Van Heusen in Guatemala mentioned earlier was "monitored" on a short-term basis by Human Rights Watch during a labor dispute. Levi Strauss contracted with Oxfam and two NGOs in the Dominican Republic to evaluate the implementation of its codes of conduct in the Dominican Republic and has conducted similar studies elsewhere. Reebok conducted a project of this nature in Indonesia. Many other short-term and long-term independent monitoring projects are being developed at the writing of this book, most under the auspices of the WRC and of NGOs involved in the FLA.

NGOs, like all monitors, have strengths and weaknesses. Like many of the commercial firms, local NGOs do not necessarily have employees trained in health and safety or other technical areas. At the same time, some of the NGOs have the trust of the workers, expertise in investigating violations of human rights and freedom of association, and credibility with the larger society. This credibility is not assured, however. There are often local conflicts among NGOs and between unions and NGOs, sometimes attributable to turf wars over activities and to competition for international funding. Moreover, companies may find or create a "pet" NGO. In 1999, Nike donated $7.7 million to the International Youth Foundation to establish the Global Alliance for Workers and Communities jointly with the World Bank and the Gap. Although the Global Alliance at present focuses on assessing workers' needs and on worker training, sweatshop activists have expressed concern that its reports could slide into monitoring or be used to refute monitoring reports. In fact, Nike responded to a report produced by Oxfam Community Aid Abroad Australia documenting problems with freedom of association and working conditions in its Indonesian factories by citing its work with "an independent entity, the Global Alliance."[40]

Financial independence from corporations is an important, though not definitive, criterion of credibility. For its first five years of operation GMIES received no company funds but had to apply each year for funding from North American and European unions and NGOs.[41] Although it still receives grants for office expenses and for the salaries of its full-time staff, GMIES began charging companies for the expenses involved in the actual monitoring visits. GMIES needed more financial stability and felt that corporations should logically bear the financial burden for monitoring that has arisen as a response to conditions caused by their own business practices.[42] Although organizations such as COVERCO and GMIES have on the whole managed to produce critical reports even though they receive money from the name-brand corporations, concerns have been raised about the effect payment may have on their independence and about whether their continued services might be in danger if other, less critical NGOs were to emerge. The pool of NGO monitors is expanding.

One member of the FLA, the International Labor Rights Fund, received substantial funding to provide training to enable more NGOs to seek certification as monitors. The ILRF has carried out a number of training sessions with NGOs and union staff in Indonesia, Taiwan, and Central America, but none of the participants has yet sought accreditation. The ILRF attributes this to several factors. Many NGOs do not want to take funding from corporations because they feel it can compromise their position; this concern may be addressed by new FLA policy whereby the FLA rather than the companies contracts with monitors. However, the accreditation process also requires a burdensome amount of paperwork. Unless NGOs are receiving requests for their services, it is unlikely they will choose to go through this bureaucratic process.[43] To date, most NGO monitoring has taken place outside of these monitoring systems.

CONCLUSION

The garment industry is a huge, growing, and often shifting industry with rampant violations of many laws pertaining to the health, compensation, unionization rights, and even basic human rights of workers, such as freedom of movement and physical safety. Garment production is often one of the first steps in a country's entrance into the global economy and has become emblematic of the excesses of the new global system and the increasing disregard for workers' rights. Codes of conduct have arisen as an international response to the vacuum left by the lack of local and multilateral responses to this situation. Transnational companies have adopted codes in response to exposés and pressure by labor-rights activists, who also have insisted that written promises are not enough. This in turn has led to compliance monitoring.

Just as it has in Los Angeles, the move toward monitoring internationally has spawned an entire new industry. A variety of companies and organizations have either retooled themselves or been formed specifically to participate. These entities include Los Angeles firms that have expanded their services, multinational accounting firms, European certification agencies, locally based NGOs, and more. The field of monitoring has developed to such a degree that it has not only dozens of direct providers offering their services, but also several coordinating organizations with different levels of standards, independence, and responsibility. Some of these organizations are moving toward certification of factories or brands as being in compliance, implying "sweat-free" production. As will be seen in the next chapter, the certification enterprise is problematic, because studies show that monitoring has not ensured the absence of violations.

6 Examining International Codes of Conduct and Monitoring Efforts

A CENTRAL QUESTION for consideration is: What impact have codes of conduct and international monitoring actually had? Several researchers have systematically analyzed the content of codes, but no one has systematically evaluated the relationship between international monitoring and compliance. Studies such as the U.S. Department of Labor's investigatory surveys of Los Angeles garment shops have not been conducted on an international level; such studies would in fact be very difficult to carry out under the present circumstances. There is no international body with the authority to demand entry into offshore factories to do inspections. Although it is unable to conduct factory *investigations*, the DOL did conduct a survey of various apparel companies regarding their policies on codes of conduct and monitoring in relation to the use of child labor and a series of factory visits in 1996. It concluded:

> These policies usually prohibit the use of child labor, and often establish guidelines for the monitoring of foreign manufacturers and disciplinary action for violations. The actual implementation of these policies, however, varies from company to company and from country to country. Awareness of the policies among foreign manufacturers, workers and trade unions seems to be limited at best. Similarly, monitoring by U.S. importers is not consistent, even within the same country. (U.S. DOL 1996: 93)

Awareness and consistency has increased since 1996, but the continued unevenness and lack of transparency in monitoring efforts makes it difficult to assess the results. However, studies have been conducted that describe or evaluate the general state of international codes and their implementation as well as specific instances. This literature offers a considerable amount of piecemeal evidence about international monitoring practices and their effectiveness.

In this chapter, I will review sixty reports, papers, and articles published from 1996 to 2003. The literature on codes of conduct and monitoring to date falls into five broad categories. The first group of studies is based on cross-country or cross-company comparisons. These studies use social-science methodologies of surveys, in-depth interviews, and comparative data analysis. A second group of reports is based on in-depth investigations of a specific company's factory or on factories in specific countries. These include reports produced by companies themselves, by local NGOs hired to evaluate code implementation, and company critics. The third category of documents consists of reports by NGO and multi-stakeholder monitoring projects. A fourth set of documents offers recommendations gathered through meetings and consultations with NGOs and workers in producing regions. These reports provide anecdotal evidence of code compliance and enforcement as well as lessons from the workers' own perspectives on codes of conduct. The final group comprises a broad range of critiques, commentaries, and proposals that address the issue of codes from a conceptual perspective rather than on the basis of analyzing original research. This category includes many documents; a selected sampling from some of the most active and vocal groups participating in the international debate on codes and monitoring is reviewed here.

Many of the findings from Los Angeles are applicable to the wider context of international code monitoring. Four areas of weakness found in Los Angeles that have been repeated on the international level will be highlighted. Reports reviewed here reveal an overwhelming consensus on the superficiality of code implementation; the lack of worker knowledge and participation; the failure to protect rights to freely associate and bargain collectively; and the deficiencies in the process and outcome of private commercial monitoring. An additional issue addressed by a minority of these international studies is the effectiveness of independent monitoring.

The most common theme repeated throughout these reports is the workers' lack of knowledge about company codes of conduct that are applicable to their own workplaces. Most workers are ignorant of the codes; most contractors fail to post codes, and when they do the codes often are not in the workers' language or the workers are intimidated from reading them. When workers do read the codes, they often do not understand the content or the implications for their working conditions or actions.

Moreover, many of the studies note the lack of monitoring or the lack of thorough monitoring. The findings indicate that most companies monitor only internally or simply demand contractual affirmation of compliance. It should be noted that, although these studies were all conducted within the past several years, the field is growing so rapidly that many more companies now hire external monitors than was common even a few years ago.

As to effectiveness, only a few reports document actual monitoring efforts and link them to factory conditions. These reports provide conflicting evidence on the impact of code implementation. Similarly, reports of consultation with unions and workers themselves reveal that code implementation in some factories has led to concrete improvements but not to full compliance, while in other factories there have been no improvements. In the studies that reported improvements, the most common concrete examples were improvements in the physical conditions in the plants (ergonomically correct equipment, potable water, ventilation, bathroom access), in a reduction of physical and verbal harassment, and in the correct payment of minimally required wages and benefits. Only in rare cases has implementation led to higher wages or respect for the right to organize. Several of the reports find grave deficiencies with the process of private external monitoring in terms of ability to detect violations. Similarly, reports on independent monitoring, while more positive in terms of improvements, bring out conflicts with unions and questions of capacity.

CROSS-COMPANY AND CROSS-COUNTRY COMPARISONS

In 1996, the DOL conducted its the most in-depth study, looking at both company codes of conduct in the apparel industry and changes in labor conditions (U.S. DOL 1996). The DOL study was limited to evaluating one labor standard: the elimination of child labor. The DOL surveyed forty-two of the top apparel firms and found that thirty-six had some policy, often a code of conduct, governing child labor in their contracting facilities. Only a small group indicated that an attempt had been made to communicate the code to workers by requiring the contractors to post the codes.

The DOL also visited seventy plants that produced apparel for the U.S. market in six countries. From these site visits it drew several conclusions. Many companies "monitor" only by including in the supply contract a requirement that the factory comply with the code. Many companies send quality-control staff to the factories, some of whom review labor conditions as well as product quality. And a smaller group actually monitors for code compliance. The most frequent and thorough monitoring is more likely to happen in plants that are owned by or contract directly with a large U.S. company and less likely to happen if the contracting is done through intermediaries or with small U.S. importers. Monitoring is least likely to occur in *sub*contracting and homework situations. The DOL also found that, although about two-thirds of managers knew about the codes, very few workers were aware of their existence, and codes were posted in only twenty-one of the seventy factories. However, the DOL did conclude that codes had had a positive effect in reducing child labor. Although the department did not link any particular codes to the results at any particular factory, it found that anecdotal evidence showed a drop in child labor and that codes were one of several factors responsible for this change.

A study by the Investor Responsibility Research Center analyzed the codes of conduct of 121 companies collected through a survey of 580 companies (Varley 1998). Forty-six of these dealt with labor standards, and of these 36 were apparel companies. The least common elements of the codes were the right to organize and bargain collectively and the right to overtime pay, each mentioned in 12 of the 121 codes. These results are confirmed by economist Rhys Jenkins, who analyzed a database of codes collected by the OECD. Freedom-of-association and collective-bargaining rights were the least mentioned of the core ILO standards, which also include prohibitions on child labor, forced labor, and discrimination and harassment. These unionization rights were mentioned in only 24 percent of the 101 company codes and 13 percent of the 30 business-association codes. By contrast, 95 percent of multi-stakeholder codes in the database (such as FLA, SAI, WRC, and others) included these rights (Jenkins 2002). Jean-Paul Sajhau, a researcher with the ILO, found this disregard of freedom-of-association rights to be true at apparel companies, as well. Sajhau compared the contents of 10 codes of major apparel manufacturers and retailers with the ILO conventions. Once again he found that, although some conventions such as child labor and nondiscrimination are widespread, only a small number of codes mention the rights to organize and to bargain collectively (Sajhau 1997).

Codes are also unlikely to include specific language on monitoring. In the OECD database, only about a quarter of codes mention monitoring, and fewer than 10 percent specify the use of external monitoring. Multi-stakeholder codes again are the most likely to mention monitoring (55%) and to specify that it should be conducted externally (15%) or by the the multi-stakeholder organization itself (15%). Jenkins also summarized the results of a 1999 survey by Ans Kolk and colleagues that confirm these findings. In that survey of 132 codes, 41 percent do not mention monitoring and 44 percent more require only internal monitoring. External monitoring is rarely included, with fewer than 10 percent of company codes and 5 percent of business associations specifying its use (Jenkins 2002).

The analysis of codes content has been quite thorough. Their information on monitoring, however, is more scattered. Based on interviews with brand name companies and various sectors in several producing countries, the IRRC provided an overview of different types of monitoring and the perspective of companies and activists on them. However, the IRRC researchers did not attempt to assess the results of code implementation. They did conclude that manufacturers tend to give monitoring duties to quality-control or auditing staff and that retailers tend to require compliance as a contractual obligation. They also stated that independent monitoring is new and "almost entirely untested," although they did call the project in El Salvador "a success." Sajhau noted the dearth of information on implementation but confirmed the IRRC findings: "It would appear based on the piecemeal information available, that most enterprises entrust their local buying agents or quality control representatives with the task of monitoring respect for the code of conduct" (Sajhau 1997: n.p.). Although he did not assess the effectiveness of such monitoring, Sajhau did state that such staff are untrained and that many companies require only written affirmation of compliance and do not monitor at all (Sajhau 1997).

Two studies commissioned by universities that had adopted codes for their licensed goods show that contractual obligation did *not* result in compliance. Both studies, based on factory investigations, found widespread violations in factories covered by university and licensee codes. In the first study, apparel licensees themselves selected one factory site in each of five countries. The plants were therefore likely to be model factories rather than representative of the most common conditions. Yet noncompliance was rampant. In its findings on the initial factory visits, the auditor, Verité, reported that only two of the five factories had posted codes of conduct and that none had posted local laws, as required. Verité also found widespread violations of the codes in the areas of wages, overtime compensation, discrimination, harassment, and health and safety. It found evidence that workers had been fired for union organizing at two factories and that at four of the five factories workers were either unaware of their right to form a union or believed unions were prohibited (Verité 2000).[1] In the second study, the Independent University Initiative looked at two factories in each of seven countries chosen by researchers rather than companies. It found violations in the same areas—hours and overtime compensation, rights to freedom of association and collective bargaining, wages, discrimination, and health and safety (BSR et al. 2000).

The Independent University Initiative study, whose methodology was broader in scope,[2] aimed to explore not only whether university codes were being complied with, but also what the barriers to compliance were. In this regard, the report has several noteworthy findings. Although the report commends efforts some companies have made to monitor, it also confirms other studies' finding of low levels of worker awareness of codes and monitoring efforts. The study concludes that this lack of worker and informed management participation contributes to noncompliance, along with larger factors such as local economic conditions, failure of government enforcement efforts, cultural attitudes, and the "diffuse nature of apparel production." The report recommends that universities attempt to consolidate licensed apparel production, work to educate and empower workers, and promote transparency, among other measures.

A report by Peter Utting of the United Nations Non-Governmental Liaison Service also found that implementation of codes was "often very weak," even in multi-stakeholder initiatives, and confirmed some of the underlying causes. Utting found that workers were often unaware of codes; codes often were not posted in the workers' language or at all; management was untrained in implementation; and workers were unaware of how to file complaints. Utting added that multinationals often leave the economic burden of compliance to suppliers with small profit margins to draw on, further weakening the process of implementation. In looking at the multi-stakeholder oversight bodies, Utting points to problems in low numbers of participants, quality control of monitoring, and lack of attention to the realities of developing countries (Utting 2002).

In a more recent overview of monitoring efforts, Dara O'Rourke of the Massachusetts Institute of Technology stated that it is not yet possible to evaluate the effectiveness of various programs because the numbers of factories monitored under them has not reached a critical mass. However, he noted that internal monitoring has improved conditions in many Nike factories and that NGO monitors have made further gains in terms of key health and safety conditions in at least one factory. He also commented on the dangers involved in monitoring by firms such as PricewaterhouseCoopers, which offer certification of compliance based on superficial audits. To strengthen the various multi-stakeholder and NGO systems, O'Rourke has called for a much higher degree of transparency, avoidance of conflicts of interest, capacity-building for Southern NGOs, and a more central role for workers. While noting the various strengths and weaknesses of different models, O'Rourke pointed to the possible "complementarity and inter-operability" between the three basic models of external monitoring: "Factory monitoring identifies willing factories and gives managers information to support change. Supply chain monitoring helps move standards down out-sourced chains of production, and provide brands with information to better manage their suppliers. Independent investigations help to expose the worst actors, provide information to workers and create incentives for brand to prevent problems in their contractors" (2003: 24). Further, he advocated connecting the initiatives that focus on these different levels—factory certification, brand certification, and independent verification—to create a more holistic approach (O'Rourke 2003).

RESEARCH-BASED REPORTS ON IMPLEMENTATION BY SPECIFIC COMPANIES

Company-based reports have reiterated many of the findings on how low worker knowledge and involvement, inconsistent monitoring, and industry structure all contribute to ineffective code implementation. An article on the experience of the Pentland Group (parent company of Speedo, Kickers, Lacoste, and other brands) advises that strong business relationships between brand and factory, with large and regular orders, is a key to implementation. Moreover, Pentland points out that implementation is most difficult in small factories and where workers are most vulnerable—young, female, and migrant (Roberts 2002).

The link between long-term business relationships and compliance surfaced in a study of Levi Strauss, as well. In 1998, Levi Strauss and Company contracted with four NGOs in the Dominican Republic to evaluate and improve its internal process of code implementation and monitoring (Oxfam et al. 1998). The NGO team of eleven people used interviews, factory-floor observations, and record analyses to conduct their investigation over a four-month period. They concluded that the code has had a positive impact on working conditions. This was largely attributed to the fact that managers identified with the code of conduct and generally accepted Levi Strauss's opinion that quality depends on a positively motivated workforce.[3] Manager buy-in is probably related to the fact that all four of the factories had worked for Levi Strauss for at least eight years, and two for eleven years.

Unlike management, workers had poor knowledge of the code and its implementation and little involvement in the latter. The investigation team also found weaknesses in internal monitoring, including a need for better health and safety evaluation, more systematic interviewing of workers, and guidelines to standardize data collection. This project was the first in a series of similar initiatives by Levi Strauss in producing regions.

Magali Piñeda, executive director of one of the Dominican NGOs, published her own assessment of the process (Piñeda 2000). Piñeda was positive about Levi Strauss's internal monitoring program, although she said that it should be combined with an independent check that involves credible participants—that is, local experts who are committed to workers' and human rights. She found that Levi Strauss's contracting factories compared favorably to others in the export-processing zones in terms of the physical plant and services offered to the workers, including medical and dental care, food-buying cooperatives, transportation, and scholarships for workers' children. Few complaints had been registered about these factories with the Ministry of Labor; the rate of turnover was low; and workers showed satisfaction with the conditions in confidential interviews.

However, Piñeda also found that local contractors (rather than Levi Strauss) paid the costs for improving conditions, offering services, and complying with codes. These investments were made without any guarantee of long-term contracts with Levi Strauss (although given the lengths of the business relationships, one would assume that the managers expected the relationships to continue.) In noting this common dynamic, Piñeda brought two questions to the fore: How sustainable are these improvements? And is the cost recouped by increasing the pace of work? She notes that, to date, setting reasonable production quotas has not generally been an area covered by codes or monitoring.

Researchers with the Thai Labor Committee, half a world away from the Dominican Republic, echo this concern about stability. In a report based on more than two years of research, Junya Yimprasert and Christopher Candland assessed the effects of codes in Thai factories producing footwear and sports apparel for Reebok, Nike, and Adidas. Yimprasert and Candland found widespread violations of these companies' codes of conduct, primarily related to problems with underpayment, excessive overtime, interference with unionization rights, and health and safety issues. They concluded that some improvements had been made in the footwear industry, particularly with regard to health and safety, but that codes had failed to improve conditions in the apparel industry. They attributed this difference to the fact that manufacturer–producer relationships are far more unstable in apparel than in footwear. Apparel factories are often small, they work on short contracts, and they work for many manufacturers at once. This lack of guarantees of long-term work makes it hard for manufacturers to have much leverage with factory owners and for factory owners to have much incentive to change. Furthermore, Yimprasert and Candland found evidence that contractors recouped expenses for improvements made to come into compliance by cutting benefits to workers and instituting more stringent quota systems.

Yimprasert and Candland also emphasized the lack of worker knowledge about codes. They noted that even in the case of Nike's code—which was given to every worker on a laminated card—it was so broad as to be meaningless to workers. For instance, there was no specific information about what minimum wages and maximum hours were. Moreover, there was no contact information to register a complaint—the code contained only a statement to contact managers or their representatives (Yimprasert and Candland 2000).

In 1999, Reebok contracted with a social science research and consulting firm in Indonesia to study the implementation of its code of conduct in two footwear factories, which employ more than 10,000 workers (IHS 1999). Insan Hitawasana Sejahtera used a three-pronged approach: surveying workers, observing in the factory, and conducting in-depth interviews with workers. Its report attributed many problems found to a lack of worker knowledge, inconsistent enforcement, and a lack of technical expertise on the part of the contractor. Insan Hitawasana Sejahtera made several specific recommendations to improve conditions, including using new chairs, foot rests, and protective gear. The report also made recommendations about how to improve the code-implementation process, including involving the workers in evaluating the code and procedures for its implementation, protecting their unionization rights, and making company policies and procedures transparent to workers.

Insan Hitawasana Sejahtera further recommended a continuing program of internal as well as independent monitoring. However, the organization's staff spent 1,400 hours conducting the study, running air-quality tests, doing follow-up visits, and writing the report, at a cost of $35,000 to Reebok. The factories spent $250,000 to implement recommendations. Because of the level of expense involved, Insan Hitawasana Sejahtera recognized that this is not a replicable model for factory improvement. The organization also noted that many contractors would not be able to afford improvements.

Another company-commissioned study was conducted by the Global Alliance for Workers and Communities for Nike (see Chapter 5). This study again shows that, even in monitored factories, violations abound. Global Alliance worked with local groups to produce studies in Thailand, Vietnam, and Indonesia. Although the organization focused its studies on "workers' perceptions" and did not give definitive findings about factory conditions, it did report survey results that indicated widespread code violations. According to one study, which was conducted in Indonesia, based on on-site interviews of 4,000 workers, and publicly released, problems were reported in various areas, including verbal mistreatment, physical abuse, denial of legally mandated leaves, and forced and excessive overtime. Although only 4 percent of workers reported a base salary below minimum wage, more than half reported salaries that were "low and not sufficient" (CSDS 2001).

A 2000 report by Alice Kwan of the Hong Kong Christian Industrial Committee focused on nine Nike and Adidas factories in China but without these companies' consent or participation. Again, the research demonstrated that, despite both companies' codes of conduct and implementation processes, serious violations were rampant. Noncompliance included withholding workers' wages to ensure low turnover, illegal fines, forced overtime, incorrect compensation of overtime, nonprovision of social-security coverage, and nonexistence of independent trade unions. Kwan also reported that workers were unaware of the codes of conduct and that, although outsiders and foreigners visited the factories regularly, none spoke to the workers about the conditions in their workplaces (Kwan 2000).

Two investigative delegations of U.S. religious leaders, academics, and socially responsible investment activists have also produced reports about code of conduct compliance. The Interfaith Center on Corporate Responsibility conducted visits to Reebok and Nike factories in Indonesia, Vietnam, and China. It concluded that codes of conduct had improved some specific conditions in the plants, such as health and safety, lighting, ventilation, and calculation of wages paid and overtime. However, many problems remained, and specific recommendations were made by country and by factory. Overall recommendations included paying a sustainable wage, permitting union organizing inside factories, and implementing independent monitoring projects using local NGOs (ICCR 1998).

In February 1998, the National Interfaith Committee for Worker Justice sponsored a delegation to Tehuacán, Mexico, to investigate the conditions in four jeans factories, all of which produced for GUESS?, as well as other companies. The resulting report documents the delegation's findings of forced overtime, unpaid overtime, minors (thirteen year olds) working, verbal abuse, and violations of minimum-wage laws, among other problems, despite external monitoring (NICWJ 1998).

GUESS?'s compliance coordinator, Irma Melawani, had accompanied a hired compliance firm on an audit of contracting factories in that region only weeks before. In an interview in August 1998, Melawani told me that the compliance firm had not found any of the violations discussed in the NICWJ report. She said the firm had found only "minor things," such as a lack of toilet paper, blocked aisles, non-use of protective gloves, and permitting open shoes. With regard to the child-labor question, she said this was hard to determine, because people can look younger than they are. But she also acknowledged that not all of the personnel files were complete.

Melawani also noted that she and the compliance-firm auditors had returned to Tehuacán two or three months later, in April: "We went back to ensure [these issues] had been corrected, and they were." When asked whether she meant that the documentation was complete, she answered, "Well, no. The documentation is a very difficult thing. It's a long process to work on [because getting birth certificates takes a long time in Mexico]." When asked whether GUESS? would require this by the next visit in September, she simply said, "We'll check on that again, and we'll see how the process is going."[4] There seemed to be a lot of leeway in terms of what is generally considered a crucial issue: the possibility of child labor. GUESS? refused to release copies of company-commissioned audits, so a thorough comparison was not possible.

However, the discrepancies between the claims made by the NICWJ delegation and the GUESS? compliance officer may be due in part to the fact that the delegation relied heavily on off-site employee interviews for its information. GUESS? did not conduct such interviews. Instead, GUESS?'s monitor reviewed company records and spoke to employees on the factory premises. Recognizing that contact with workers outside the factory, facilitated by local groups, was essential to gathering honest testimonies, the delegation recommended the use of locally based NGOs to carry out more effective implementation of codes.

Off-site interviews were a crucial methodology for MIT's O'Rourke, an industrial-hygiene specialist who produced a report in 1997 critiquing the effectiveness of monitoring by accounting firms.[5] O'Rourke analyzed a leaked audit by the accounting firm Ernst and Young of the Tae Kwan Vina factory, Nike's most technologically advanced plant in Vietnam. O'Rourke compared the Ernst and Young audit report to his own findings from three walk-through audits of the plant, interviews with managers, and interviews with workers outside the factory. O'Rourke found that Ernst and Young missed numerous violations of Nike's code, including failure to pay properly, forced overtime, strikebreaking, and physical and verbal abuse of workers. Moreover, O'Rourke criticized Ernst and Young's conclusion that the factory was in compliance with Nike's code despite the many violations the firm had found and reported. Those included violation of maximum overtime laws, management control of the union, unprotected chemical exposure, and poor treatment of workers.

O'Rourke highlighted the shortcomings of commercial audits, which generally rely on information provided by management, lack confidential worker interviews, lack rigorous methodology in health and safety testing, and involve numerous other problems. His conclusions raise serious questions about manufacturer-commissioned monitoring. Because all such reports are confidential (unless leaked), Nike was able to claim that its factories were in compliance without revealing that violations had been found. Moreover, Nike publicized that it was "doing a good job" according to the estimation of former U.N. Ambassador Andrew Young, whom Nike hired to evaluate its factories partly based on a review of the Ernst and Young report (O'Rourke 1997).

O'Rourke released a second critique of private monitoring in October 2000 (O'Rourke 2000). That report, "Monitoring the Monitors: A Critique of PricewaterhouseCoopers' Labor Monitoring," was based on O'Rourke's participation in the Independent University Initiative. As part of the project team, O'Rourke accompanied PricewaterhouseCoopers on audits in China and Korea and evaluated a third audit from a factory in Indonesia. O'Rourke pointed out that PricewaterhouseCoopers is the leading monitor in the world and that the firm's staff knew that they were being observed on these audits. Therefore, the monitoring O'Rourke observed not only was very possibly the most developed in terms of practices, but it was also conducted by one of the most experienced private firms in the field. Yet the audits and resulting reports were insufficient to detect and to describe violations. According to O'Rourke, "The factory inspection reports [PricewaterhouseCoopers] produced did not convey an accurate picture of the conditions in these factories. The reports are so condensed that they miss major issues and paint a false impression of a factory's compliance with local laws. This analysis shows that [PricewaterhouseCoopers's] monitoring methods are significantly flawed" (2000: 1). O'Rourke charged that the reports did not adequately convey the firm's findings and that the findings themselves were deficient. The auditors failed to detect hazardous chemical use, among other serious health and safety violations, barriers to freedom of association and collective bargaining, violations of overtime and wage laws, and time cards that appeared to be falsified.

A main point in O'Rourke's detailed analysis is the differential treatment of workers and managers in the monitoring process. Managers are sent questionnaires in advance to prepare them for the audit. They are also offered some guarantees of confidentiality and are the main source of information. Auditors meet with managers at the beginning and end of audits, and the managers participate throughout the process. Workers, however, are not informed in any systematic way of the meaning or purpose of the audit. No meetings are held with the workers, and only the workers who are interviewed are informed of the audit. Workers are either selected by management or selected at random by auditors, and management is asked to bring them and their personnel files to the meeting room. As in Los Angeles, managers obviously know who is being interviewed. Workers do not speak to auditors outside this context, nor are they given the opportunity to show any documentation of their own, since they are not told in advance of the audit or the interview.

Moreover, O'Rourke explained that, in choosing half of the interviewees, the auditors selected the youngest-looking workers.[6] Although their intent appeared to be to ferret out child labor, the result was that they interviewed the factories' least experienced workers, those who were the least likely to have long-term information and the most likely to be intimidated and unwilling to speak out. In addition, the other half of the interviewees, who were selected by the managers, were probably the most loyal to the company and therefore also unlikely to speak out.

As for labor rights, PricewaterhouseCoopers failed to detect a single instance of violation of freedom of association and collective-bargaining rights in the audits conducted in any of the seven countries. In both audits witnessed by O'Rourke, the interviewer skipped over the questions regarding collective bargaining and in one also omitted all questions on freedom of association in the worker interviews. Moreover, O'Rourke noted that the questions were superficial and inadequate to evaluate this issue. The auditors failed to distinguish among independent, company-controlled, and government-controlled unions in all cases. In China, the PricewaterhouseCoopers auditors did not even record the fact that managers admitted that the company controlled the union.

REPORTS FROM NGO AND MULTI-STAKEHOLDER PROJECTS

Private monitoring reports have generally been kept confidential. Monitoring in Central America, in contrast, has resulted in a number of public reports. Reports by and about COVERCO in Guatemala, GMIES in El Salvador, and EMI in Honduras document violations and point to progress made toward compliance through the implementation process. Improvements include correct payment of wages and health benefits, relief from forced overtime, a significant decline in harassment, free bathroom access, and other advances in health and safety. Most significantly, the return of fired unionists and the ability of unions to register and remain active in plants in each of the three countries is noted, although the plant in Honduras—where workers had gained a collective-bargaining agreement and a pay raise—was later closed (Anner 1998; COVERCO 1999, 2000, 2001; GMIES 1997a, 1997b, 2002; Koepke 2000; Molina 2000). These cases will all be covered in more detail in the following chapter.

In June 2003, the Fair Labor Association published an extensive report on its monitoring efforts and the remediation that resulted from those audits. This report was the result of changes at the FLA (discussed in the next chapter) that led to a much greater degree of transparency. The report, which covers August 2001 to August 2002, and its accompanying Tracking Charts give a lot of detailed information about violations in particular factories and trends found in terms of each code provision, as

well as remediation efforts taken by contractors and brand-name participants in the FLA. The report clearly documents concrete improvements
and ongoing efforts in many areas. The report also provides analysis on
issues that complicate compliance. For instance, in discussing the lack of
worker awareness of codes and rights the report notes that high turnover,
low literacy rates, and large percentages of migrant workers aggravate
efforts to create an informed workplace. The report also states that violations of freedom of association rights present "the greatest challenge to
the FLA system" because such infractions are difficult both to detect and
to remedy once identified. However, the report does detail an innovative
approach by Reebok to facilitate democratic elections of union representatives in two large factories in China (FLA 2003).

In Europe two multi-stakeholder organizations have begun implementing pilot monitoring projects. The United Kingdom's Ethical Trading Initiative is a government-sponsored group of companies, unions, and
NGOs that has elaborated the ETI Base Code for international production, not limited to apparel. The Clean Clothes Campaign, which originated in Holland and now has branches in ten European countries, has
worked with what are now called "global union federations" (formerly
international trade secretariats)[7] to develop the "Code of Labour Practices for the Apparel Industry including Sportswear." Both organizations
have recruited company signatories and are in the stage of developing
monitoring programs.

In 1999, the ETI issued two reports on its early progress. The first was
an investigation of the signatory companies' implementation process; the
second covered the progress of three pilot projects. Based on interviews
with core company executives at twelve firms, researchers found that
only seven had adopted codes and that only one included all the elements
of the ETI Base Code, collective-bargaining rights and a commitment to
regular employment being most often excluded (Burgess and Lane 1999).
They also found that most companies plan to monitor through the visits
of their quality-control staff. The assessment of the pilot projects found
that in no country was the ETI Base Code translated into local languages,
and many employees were not able to scrutinize it. The organization also
assessed monitoring by independent local groups and commercial agencies, concluding that there was a tradeoff between credibility of the former and technique of the latter (Burgess and Burns 1999).

In 2001, the Amsterdam-based Centre for Research on Multinational
Corporations, or SOMO, published two papers based on the experiences
of ETI and CCC projects. Its findings included the need for code harmo-
nization, international standards in the field of social auditing, the inclusion of cost and fair pricing as part of monitoring, and ongoing pressure
on factory owners who are often reluctant to respond to demands. The
last point reiterates the necessity of strengthening business relationships

between brand and supplier. A central finding was that labor-rights education campaigns for suppliers, buyers, retailers, and especially workers
are crucial. In fact, many NGOs in producing countries felt that mass-
education campaigns were a mandatory precursor to workers' participating in monitoring. SOMO also criticized the limited attention multi-
stakeholder initiatives have given to complaint mechanisms, as opposed
to social audits, which are dominated by corporate firms. NGOs and
unions have an advantage in terms of the strong role they can play in complaint mechanisms. Unfortunately, they have instead been drawn into the
social-auditing field to participate in the dialogue. Moreover, complaint
mechanisms are key because no system can really cover all factories.

   SOMO also emphasized the need for local participation. It found that
local organizations trusted by workers were most effective in doing
worker interviews and that there should be some local "ownership" of
the process. ETI found setting up local tripartite groups of unions, NGOs,
and local companies "essential" to successful compliance. Swedish CCC
pilot projects in India and Bangladesh showed that using local NGOs to
do preliminary studies of the factories, including worker interviews, which
then fed into audits by commercial firms was an effective combination.
They also highlighted the importance of unannounced visits. Finally, while
these projects noted improvements in factory conditions, they found living wage and freedom of association to be the hardest standards to implement (Ascoly et al. 2001).

REPORTS FROM CONSULTATIONS WITH NGOS AND
WORKERS FROM PRODUCING COUNTRIES

The four NGO partners of ETI, the British nonprofit group Women Working Worldwide, Labor Rights in China, the American Friends Service
Committee, and the Maquila Solidarity Network have all carried out
consultations with labor and women's NGOs or workers in producing
countries. Reports from all of these consultations concluded that the most
important process for the improvement of workers' conditions was not
codes but the ability to organize and bargain collectively, and they emphasized the necessity for codes to bolster these rights and the danger of
codes or monitoring supplanting organizing. Another conclusion common
to all of these reports was that workers are generally unaware of codes
and that they should be informed of codes and involved in code implementation (Green 1998; LARIC 1999a; MSN 2002b; Prieto and Bendell
2002; WWW 1998, 1999).

   In May 2000, the American Friends Service Committee held a roundtable in Hong Kong of NGOs working in the area of labor in Asia, at
which participants also came to the above conclusions (see AFSC 2000).
The committee expanded on the first point by noting that the most impor-

tant right to monitor was that of freedom of association and collective bargaining: In a factory with a union, workers can negotiate for better conditions and wages, but in a factory with some improved conditions no further rights are guaranteed. Some participants argued that codes "prove most useful where union organizing is difficult or dangerous," and examples from Guatemala, Nicaragua, and the Philippines were offered. Participants also discussed their doubts about the possibility of knowing whether codes were being implemented along the entire chain of production, with homework and subcontracting often overlooked. They warned of the resulting specter of "ethical trade by unethical sources" (AFSC 2000).

Women Working Worldwide has done the most extensive work, consulting with women in six Asian and six Latin American countries and then holding two regional workshops. Women workers reported that in the few cases in which codes were posted, they were either not translated or pinned to the wall with no explanation. There were mixed reports on the effectiveness of the codes. The WWW recounted that workers in Pakistan were very surprised by codes of specific companies for whom they produced, as their conditions did not match those prescribed by the codes. In the Dominican Republic, it was reported that the factories with codes, while not fully complying with the standards, are generally still better than those without. Workers also felt that monitors must be either workers, if they are unionized, or local NGOs who enjoy the trust of the workers and credibility in the local community (WWW 1998, 1999).

The WWW's 2001 final report was positive about the potential for a process of worker education arising from codes where NGOs are able to capitalize on this tool but was much less sanguine about monitoring. The report generally found current monitoring efforts to be ineffective and to exclude workers from participation. The exception was a report from Bangladesh noting that where monitors have visited factories there have been improvements in terms of hours, break times, and management attitudes toward workers. Again, codes were found to be least effective in situations of subcontracting and homework, which are rampant in certain regions. Also, workers from various places confirmed that the costs of improvements tend to be absorbed by local factories and eventually by workers (WWW 2001). Linda Shaw and Angela Hale of the WWW concluded in a recent article that it is not simply that workers should be better informed about codes, but that codes should arise out of a consultative process with workers. This would transform codes from top-down "corporate-responsibility" measures to bottom-up mechanisms that truly represent the most pressing concerns of workers. In this way, codes could also be integrated into other, broader strategies of empowerment. Otherwise, codes may be just the "emperor's new clothes"—with nothing really there (Shaw and Hale 2002).

A paper published in December 2002 by the New Academy of Business was based on five focus groups that included about seventy-five female garment and plantation workers in Nicaragua. This study again confirms that most female workers do not know about codes and that codes are sometimes posted in foreign languages or in areas where the women cannot read them. The workers also recommended that visits be unannounced: "When a delegation from the transnational is about to arrive, the employers put everything in order, everything is clean, they do not shout at us, or demand that we work harder and harder. . . . The employers behave completely different" (as quoted in Prieto and Bendell 2002: 9). The workers insisted that monitoring should not be intermittent but continual and that interviews should be conducted off-site and by people whom workers trust. The authors conclude, "The evidence from this study is that codes as they stand are of little or no benefit to the supposed beneficiaries" (Prieto and Bendell 2002: 11). However, they do go on to say that if workers were brought into the process in terms of formulating codes, influencing the focus of investigations, and participating in monitoring, workers could benefit.

Another set of articles consists of transcriptions of interviews with and speeches by labor leaders in producing countries who give anecdotal evidence about their experiences with codes of conduct. In such an interview, the Indonesian unionist Emelia Yanti Mala Dewi Siahaan says that she worked for Levi Strauss for eight years and never knew about its code. She says the same is true for other companies, with the exception of Nike (Siahaan 2000). She gives both positive and negative examples in which workers tried to use the code to elicit cooperation from management over a contentious issue. In a speech, the Bangladeshi union leader Amirul Haque Amin attests to the lack of code compliance in local factories and testifies that when a supplier was called on to respect the code, he responded that it was only a piece of paper (Amin 2000). An interview with the Haitian labor activist Jannick Etienne again emphasizes the importance of using local, trusted NGOs to monitor, noting that this is particularly true in a country with a history of political repression and fear (Etienne 2000).

Kelly Dent of the Transnational Information Exchange—Asia, a regional labor-network based in Sri Lanka, also presented a mixed review of codes in a recent article. Although she acknowledges that particular campaigns around codes have benefited "factories, regions or groups of workers," she says, "there are millions of workers worldwide who have not benefited" (Dent 2002: 139) Specifically, she says that using codes to defend the right to freedom of association has not yet been successful in Sri Lanka, where more than 1,000 workers covered by codes were fired for union organizing in 2000 alone. She also warns of the "misuse and manipulation" of codes, giving an example in which a proposed weakening of Sri

Lankan labor legislation was justified on the basis that the country would need to compete better when the MFA was phased out and that the changes were necessary to conform with codes of brand-name companies producing in the country. At this point, almost all Sri Lankan factories are out of code compliance because codes incorporate local laws that in this case include a statute restricting overtime to 100 hours a year (Dent 2002).

CRITIQUES, COMMENTARIES, AND PROPOSALS ABOUT CODE MONITORING

Many NGOs involved in the anti-sweatshop movement have theorized about corporate codes and their potential to improve factory conditions. The directors of the Canadian MSN and the directors of the ILRF have written comprehensive and significant pieces. Both of these organizations have been centrally involved in the debate and have participated in workshops and interviewed numerous activists from producing regions involved in monitoring projects.

Both groups concluded that codes have strong potential to contribute toward improving labor conditions. The MSN noted the need to combine codes with government regulation in a manner that is mutually reinforcing. The ILRF concluded that, although codes have improved conditions, they have not led to workers' empowerment but could do so if the rights to freedom of association and collective bargaining were adopted and enforced through the process.

The MSN'S review also cautioned about the potential conflict that exists between code monitoring and unionization, as exemplified in the El Salvador project (Jeffcott and Yanz 2000; Yanz et al. 1999). The ILRF also uses the Salvadoran project to highlight the dangers of monitoring, stating that the independent monitoring group there took on a role of "grievance handling" and unintentionally obviated the need for a union (Harvey et al. 1998). Stephen Coats, director of the U.S./Guatemala Education Project, wrote an article in a series published by the Campaign for Labor Rights on the monitoring debate within the anti-sweatshop community. He focused on the relationship between NGO monitors and unions, warning that monitors must clearly define their roles so as to not usurp the work of unionists and that they must work to build good relationships with labor unions. Using the example of the Phillips–Van Heusen factory in Guatemala, Coats advocated for an emergency network of credible third-party monitors to investigate specific complaints, especially those concerning labor disputes (Coats 1998).

In the same series, Jeff Ballinger, director of Press for Change, broadened the definition of monitoring by including in it a focus on worker surveys. He posited that in Indonesia such surveys served to legitimize workers' individual complaints and empower workers to see their problems as collective. Moreover, such information gathering belied companies' claims and set the groundwork for forcing companies into discussions with workers (Ballinger 1998).

In 1999, in a critique of monitoring as it has developed, Charles Sabel, Dara O'Rourke, and Archon Fung proposed a drastically different model of "Ratcheting Labor Standards." Within this paradigm companies would be forced to disclose information regarding labor conditions in their factories; this information would be publicly available in a comparative format; and a system to verify or refute such information would be constructed. This proposal, like other programs, would rely on companies' adopting a code of conduct and hiring certified monitors. However, a "super-monitor" or umpire would monitor the monitors and ensure that information was in fact comparable. The principal mechanism for enforcement would be "upward" competition based on a ranking or grading system (Sabel et al. 1999). This proposal became the center of an issue of the *Boston Review*, where it was published along with a variety of responses (Fung et al. 2001). The model was criticized on the basis that it de-emphasizes the rights and role of unions (Broad 2001; Moberg 2001); that it would have unintended effects on displaced children and other regional workers (Bardhan 2001; Basu 2001); and that it is unrealistic (Levinson 2001; Standing 2001).

A final group of documents involves critiques of specific systems of monitoring by anti-sweatshop activists. The National Labor Committee has published several pieces criticizing companies for using factories that were out of compliance with their codes. In 1999, the NLC put out a report critiquing the implementation of Liz Claiborne's code in the Do All factory in El Salvador, noting many violations of the code (NLC 1999). The report specifically criticized PricewaterhouseCoopers' model of monitoring, pointing to the shortness of the visits, the fact that interviews with workers are not confidential, and the secrecy in which monitoring reports are kept.

Criticisms have also been aimed at the multi-stakeholder initiatives. The strongest commentary may have been a piece written by Labor Rights in China after attending a training seminar for SA8000 monitors (LARIC 1999b). LARIC described a situation in which neither the trainer nor the trainees had experience in labor or human rights, yet the participants were certified as capable of verifying conditions for workers. LARIC also criticized the minimal nature of the training, especially considering the amount of discretion monitors are then given in applying the standards.

The multi-stakeholder initiatives continue to have serious problems. In January 2003, the MSN summed up the progress in these initiatives as follows:

> In 2002, the limitations and unresolved issues plaguing these emerging non-governmental regulatory systems became more apparent. As competing

multi-stakeholder initiatives moved into the implementation stage, questions arose about the quality of workplace audits, particularly those carried out by commercial compliance verification firms, the limited capacity or lack of interest among Southern NGOs in compliance verification, the lack of transparency in corporate reporting, inadequate systems for worker and third-party complaints, multiple codes with varying standards, duplication in factory audits, and slow progress in achieving real improvements in working conditions and labour practices. (MSN 2003)

Clearly many of the problems detected by the various reports over the past few years continue to pervade international monitoring, even in the newer systems that have been created with checks and balances in mind.

CONCLUSION

Much of the foregoing information is summed up in an evaluation of codes given by Rohini Hensman, a labor-rights researcher from India:

> After attending several ETI meetings . . . last year, and coming back feeling annoyed and frustrated from all of them, it was tempting to feel that codes are useless as a tool, they are merely a public relations exercise from the standpoint of companies and a distraction from the standpoint of workers, and it is a waste of time to continue working on them. However, when we think how prevalent international subcontracting chains have become, that companies and middlemen at each level are making profits at the expense of workers right down at the bottom, and that codes are so far the only mechanism that has been suggested for putting pressure on retailers at the top, then it seems silly to give up. Instead what we need to do is to admit that they are a very unsatisfactory tool at the moment, and try to re-shape them so that they work better in the future. The biggest problem with codes, as we all know, is ensuring they are implemented. (as quoted in WWW 2001: 12)

Despite the plethora of evidence that codes have not resulted in widespread changes, there is also general agreement that codes hold the potential to be used as a *tool* for change. Codes have the most potential when worker-friendly entities are able to use them as a means of educating workers about their rights and the structure of the industry in which they find themselves. Codes offer an opening for this dialogue. Not incidentally, the hype around codes has also opened up funding sources for such worker and NGO training. However, Hensman's ambivalence comes from reasonable fears that codes can actually undermine government enforcement by providing an alternative focus to worker empowerment, because "the assumption can be made that once codes exist they are implemented and therefore there is no need for unions" (as quoted in WWW 2001: 10).

Various lessons about implementation can be derived from this review. The most important is that workers need to be more involved in the process. Codes are a façade if workers cannot use them as a tool to improve their work sites. Codes must be translated, posted, and made accessible so that workers can both see and understand them. Better still, workers should be involved in the creation of codes to ensure that their primary concerns are included. As shown, codes often fail to include core labor standards, much less specific concerns of female workers such as safe transportation, freedom from sexual harassment, and free access to toilet facilities. Moreover, workers should be trained and involved in reporting on the implementation of codes.

There is also a preponderance of opinion that monitoring should be raised to a higher standard. Accepted practices should include off-site and confidential interviews, unannounced visits, strong complaint mechanisms, local NGO involvement, and a process that does not emphasize management information but gives the words of workers (who may not have or be able to produce the same type of documentation) equal weight. There is also a consensus among workers'-rights advocates that freedom of association and collective-bargaining rights not only must be included in the codes but must also be focal points of monitoring efforts so that improvements can be guaranteed by workers themselves.

It is also clear that for monitoring to be sustainable, business relationships between contractors and brands need to be strengthened. Longer-term contracts would provide suppliers with incentives to make improvements. Universities and multi-stakeholder initiatives could reward the implementation of longer-term contracts. Moreover, improvements should not be strictly the responsibility of the factory owners. They should be considered part of the brand-name company's expenses, as well. In fact, fair pricing should also be a part of the codes and monitoring process so that compliance is a realistic expectation. Fair pricing should be based on reasonable quotas, another vital area entirely ignored to date by codes.

Finally, independent monitoring offers a promising alternative to many of the problems found in private monitoring. Although several questions have been raised here about capacity and about conflicts with unions in terms of roles, independent NGO monitoring has also proved to facilitate the involvement of workers and to better protect unionization rights. Independent monitoring is a newer phenomenon than private monitoring, and its emergence and the struggle for its adoption is the subject of the next chapter.

7 The Struggle for Independent Monitoring

As the preceding chapters have documented, private monitoring has not significantly ameliorated the exploitation of apparel workers in Los Angeles or globally. This is in part because private monitoring is controlled by manufacturers and is not structured to involve workers. Workers are rarely aware of codes of conduct and are intimidated from complaining during interviews that take place at their work sites. Moreover, monitors hired by the workers' bosses, or their bosses' bosses, face serious challenges in terms of gaining workers' trust and credibility more broadly. Private monitoring to date has been more successful at improving conditions (such as availability of potable water, hygiene of bathrooms, levels of harassment, correct payment of minimum wage, and reduction in forced overtime) than at guaranteeing respect for workers' basic rights to organize. Thus, workers have not achieved an avenue to defend their own interests on a day-to-day basis or raise wages beyond the legal minimum, which is below subsistence levels in most countries.

However, the codes movement and monitoring should not be dismissed. Codes of conduct created or agreed to by companies are a public statement of intent. Workers and their advocates can use these as a tool to hold companies accountable. What is needed is a more credible form of verification and a means by which workers can participate in the process. Independent monitoring—whereby local NGOs, or international NGOs working with local advocates, investigate code violations in part by building long-term relationships with workers who are integral to the monitoring process—offers a necessary check on a system that is otherwise controlled by the companies themselves. Several of these projects were introduced in Chapter 5.

This chapter posits that developing models of "independent" NGO monitoring (particularly that promoted by the WRC) should not be understood simply as an alternative form of monitoring, but rather as an inversion of private monitoring. By concentrating on *rights* rather than conditions and creating a system triggered by the *worker* rather than the manufacturer, independent monitoring turns private monitoring on its head. Independent monitoring has not only resulted in some impressive gains for workers of late, with collective-bargaining agreements in environments where they are quite rare. It has also changed the nature of the debate about monitoring. The existence of monitoring programs in which industry plays no governing role; workers are interviewed off-site; visits are conducted by labor experts; and the focus is remediation, not certification has highlighted the inadequacies of a completely unregulated industry and has pushed other monitoring initiatives to reform.

How have advocates been able to develop such a model in an area dominated by ideas of self-regulation? This chapter will focus on the political agitation that led to the legitimation of independent monitoring. Independent monitoring began as the idea of a small NGO in New York that was attempting to support a union-organizing drive in El Salvador. With the growth of international private monitoring and its institutionalization in the Fair Labor Association, the concept of independent monitoring was taken up and reshaped by students and other activists in the United States. However, even among labor advocates there has been no consensus over the appropriateness of independent monitoring.

The chapter will begin with a history of the original campaign for independent monitoring, laying out the economic and political developments that led to the conflict over a Salvadoran factory. The project established a precedent and resulted in the reinstatement of fired unionists and improvement in conditions, although it did not result in a collective-bargaining agreement or wage hikes. As this was the pioneer project, implementation also involved tracking unknown territory. Other unions were suspicious of NGOs' involvement in the protection of labor rights, and the unclear definition of roles made many question the whole concept. But even as these difficulties arose, the existence of independent monitoring represented a new understanding of the codes movement and presented new opportunities to activists. It was this potential, rather than the messy details of the specific outcome, that made independent monitoring the center of continued debate.

The debate over independent monitoring took place largely within the confines of universities. Unionists and NGOs had unsuccessfully raised the issue during the AIP negotiations. Without the direct presence of corporations, students were able to raise the issue on their own campuses. Because of the explosion of student activism over the sweatshop issue, universities had become concerned with the production of products bearing their college logos. Hundreds of universities passed codes of conduct and began to look for a means to implement them. The FLA originally set itself up as the logical mechanism, to the chagrin of student activists, who claimed that the FLA was controlled by industry. Students and allies formed the Worker Rights Consortium as an alternative. The WRC model was built on verification of complaints rather than certification of compliance. The latter portion of this chapter will be devoted to the development of the FLA and the WRC and their divergent structures and practices, as well as the significant changes that have taken place within the FLA.

THE MAQUILA INDUSTRY IN EL SALVADOR

El Salvador was a natural site for the first corporate campaign about apparel manufacturers' international responsibility for two reasons. First, the Salvadoran maquila sector had grown tremendously within just a few years and had become a center of debate in that society. Second, and perhaps more significant, a large network of groups interested in El Salvador already existed in the United States, formed during the Central American solidarity movement of the 1980s and early 1990s.

From 1980 to 1992, a civil war between the government and the Faribundo Martí Liberation Army raged in El Salvador, claiming more than 75,000 lives and pushing more than 1.5 million people into exile in a country of just over 6 million. As part of its Cold War strategy, the U.S. government supported the Salvadoran government to the tune of $4 billion during ten years of war.[1] The U.S. complemented its support of low-intensity warfare with an aggressive campaign in the region to build up capitalist economies oriented toward the United States. However, during the height of the war, economic development was frustrated by sabotage, insecurity, and instability. When the right-wing ARENA party came to power in 1989, it began instituting a plan of structural adjustment that included export-oriented development, although it was not able to fully implement its plan until the signing of the peace accords.

When the Salvadoran civil war ended, the country had only one free-trade zone, in which 6,500 workers were employed. In the next two years, four more zones opened, and employment in the industry exploded. By 1998, there were 80,000 workers in the export-processing plants, accounting for more than one-third of the industrial workers in the San Salvador metropolitan area. U.S. government funding was essential to this growth because it provided the needed infrastructure to expand manufacturing activities.[2]

The Salvadoran government has also been integrally involved in attracting investors. It offers investors many benefits, as do governments of many developing nations caught in the neoliberal economic order described in Chapter 2. Maquila operations, which involve the importation of unassembled parts—in the case of garments, cloth—and the exportation of finished products, are exempt from import, export, and income taxes and from sales tax on services and taxes on rent (Quinteros et al. 1998). The Salvadoran Foundation for Economic and Social Development, which is almost entirely supported by US-AID, places advertisements in U.S. trade journals publicizing the most important attraction: easily available, cheap, and docile labor. The ad, which features a young woman, says "You can hire her for 57 cents an hour. Rosa is more than just colorful. She and her co-workers are known for their industriousness, reliability and quick learning. They make El Salvador one of the best buys" (as reprinted in Kernaghan 1997). In a later version of the ad, "Rosa" was available for only 33 cents an hour.

For the Rosas of El Salvador, industriousness and reliability are not the quaint indigenous traits the ad purports, but attributes enforced by factory discipline, high unemployment, and the government, which keeps workers in line through bureaucratic channels as well as through security-force interventions in labor disputes.

Maquilas in El Salvador are located in two areas: *zonas francas* (free-trade zones) and *recintos fiscales*. *Zonas francas* are "extraterritorial geographic spaces"; *recinto fiscal* is a legal designation accorded to qualifying factories located outside the free-trade zones that also produce for export and are given many of the same benefits. Factories in the free-trade zones are much larger, averaging 400 workers, and are most often operated by foreigners—principally from Korea, Taiwan, and the United States. Nearly all of the *recintos fiscales* are owned and operated by Salvadorans (Quinteros et al. 1998). The great majority of all production is for U.S. labels, and the merchandise is bound for the U.S. market.[3] More than 80 percent of the workers are women younger than thirty-five. Most are younger than twenty-five, and two-thirds are mothers.[4]

In 1997, the research institute Center for the Study of Work, or CENTRA, in El Salvador surveyed 750 workers from 37 factories. The results showed a number of widespread violations in the maquilas. Forced overtime was rampant: More than 45 percent of the workers said they never had a choice as to whether to work overtime, and 18 percent more reported that they only sometimes had a choice. High production quotas and very little rest time were other commonly reported problems. In addition, 44 percent of the women and 28 percent of the men reported earning less than minimum wage (Quinteros et al. 1998). Even if workers were paid properly, the minimum did not provide for basic subsistence. In 1999, the minimum industrial wage was $144 (U.S.) per month. A basic basket of *food* (not including rent, medical expenses, child care, etc.) in the urban area was estimated to be $547 dollars per month for a family of five (Molina and Quinteros 2000).

The maquila sector generates the largest number of officially registered worker complaints. The chief inspector at the Salvadoran Ministry of Labor estimated that in 1999, approximately 30 percent of all complaints were from the maquila sector, and that in 1995 and 1996 that figure was as high as 70 percent.[5] The chief inspector emphasized that this is true even though most workers do not complain unless they have already been fired or have left their jobs. Moreover, in 1997, as part of a "modernization plan," the ministry moved its offices from San Salvador's downtown area to the exclusive and hard-to-reach neighborhood of Escalón, making it difficult for workers to pursue complaints.

As is the case with the U.S. DOL, the Ministry of Labor in El Salvador is ineffective in enforcing local labor laws, largely due to a lack of resources. In 1999, the minister of labor had only nineteen inspectors for the entire country.[6] Inspectors are not given vehicles; they must travel to distant work sites using public transportation or their own cars, paying for the gas themselves.[7]

There is also a question about the ministry's political will to enforce laws and protect workers' rights to organize. [8] As a matter of long-established practice, the ministry forwards the approval of a registered union to the factory owner; the form includes the names of all union leaders, which the ministry requires to complete the registration. Furthermore, the ministry regularly interprets the statute stipulating that union leaders "cannot be fired, transferred nor downgraded in their conditions of work, nor disciplinarily suspended" during their year-long tenure as allowing firms to prohibit workers from coming to work as long as they pay the workers.[9] The ministry, in fact, has sometimes paid wages to barred unionists for the companies (Anner 1998).[10] It has also failed to combat blacklisting and has at times contributed to the practice.[11]

With such rapid growth and high rates of violations, maquilas became a focus of union-organizing efforts, as well as of general public debate inside the country. Organizing campaigns strove for higher wages and better conditions but were often sparked by resentment over abusive or disrespectful treatment on the part of managers. However, organizing campaigns generally ended in firings and lay-offs. CENTRA documented twenty-eight efforts to unionize maquilas between 1993 and 1998, twenty-five of which resulted in firings or plant closures and none of which resulted in a collective-bargaining agreement (Quinteros et al. 1998). In a particularly active organizing period from 1994 to 1995, more than 4,000 workers were fired or lost their jobs when plants closed in response to organizing drives.[12] In 1999, CENTRA reported that there were only three active unions in the apparel maquilas, two of which were at the same factory, Mandarin International. Mandarin had been the focus of an international campaign that resulted in the first independent monitoring project in the garment industry.

THE GAP CAMPAIGN AND THE BIRTH OF INDEPENDENT MONITORING

On December 15, 1995, the National Labor Committee, a three-person nonprofit group based in New York, signed an unprecedented agreement with the Gap, an enormous multinational corporation with production located in more than forty countries and annual sales exceeding $3.5 billion.[13] A year-long struggle by workers at the Mandarin International plant in El Salvador and a solidarity campaign by unionists, religious groups, and human-rights organizations in the United States led to the accord.[14] However, the consumer and investor pressure and publicity generated by these groups, rather than the workers' actions, were the key to the Gap's agreeing to independent monitoring of labor conditions in its contracting factories.

The campaign was coordinated by the NLC, which had a decade of experience in organizing labor and religious communities around human-rights issues in El Salvador, particularly with regard to unionists.[15] The NLC was successful in the Gap campaign in great part because it came to the campaign with ties not only to Salvadoran groups but also to U.S. networks that it had built up over years of solidarity work. The NLC was able to draw on this support in its strategy of publicity and consumer and investor pressure.

In 1995, the NLC received a call from a union federation in El Salvador that was seeking support for fired unionists at a Taiwanese-owned maquila producing primarily for the Gap.[16] Female workers at Mandarin International complained about frequent yelling by supervisors, punishments that included being hit on the head and sweeping all day in the sun, bathroom visits that were denied or limited to three minutes, wrenching pressure from production quotas, and overtime that at times extended to twenty-three-hour days. In response to union organizing, management began firing workers. After visiting Mandarin, the NLC's director, Charles Kernaghan, appeared on the Canadian public-radio program "As It Happens" (which is widely distributed in the United States) describing the rampant abuses he and his co-worker had found at the plant. According to Kernaghan, the Gap called the radio station within an hour of the program's airing, threatening to sue.[17] Rather than backing down, the NLC launched a full-scale publicity campaign around the case. However, while the labor dispute in El Salvador had arisen as a protest over mistreatment and unpaid overtime and benefits, the U.S. campaign focused to a great extent on child labor. Kernaghan felt that violations of labor rights, which are hardly respected in the United States, would not attract the public's sympathy in the same way that child labor would. In fact, major U.S. newspapers have covered the sweatshop issue largely as a problem of child labor (Anner 2000).[18]

In June 1995, the NLC arranged a speaking tour in the United States for Judith Viera and Claudia Molina, two teenage workers from Mandarin. By this time, Mandarin had fired 200 workers for organizing with the Union of Mandarin International Workers, or SETMI.[19] The tour was also sponsored by UNITE, and Viera and Molina's opening appearance was at the first convention of the newly merged union.[20] Later in the tour, during a rally at the Gap's headquarters in San Francisco, Stan Raggio, a company vice-president, agreed to meet with Kernaghan and the two workers. Raggio defended his company by pointing to its code of conduct and monitoring efforts. However, the workers had never heard of the code and, the monitoring had not improved the situation. Continuing pressure from a growing solidarity campaign of students, unionists, and religious activists protesting across the country eventually led the Gap to make a public statement in which it denied that Mandarin had violated the company's code based on seven months of intensive and detailed monitoring.[21]

During the solidarity campaign in the United States, a parallel campaign was being waged in El Salvador by religious, women's, human-rights, and workers' organizations. The conflict at Mandarin had received a lot of attention in the Salvadoran press. At one point, SETMI seemed poised to become the first union with a collective-bargaining agreement in the free-trade zones. As organizing intensified, unionists used more radical forms of protest. Unionists blocked the entrance to the free-trade zone, carried out "sit-down" work stoppages, and occupied the factory. During these incidents, workers were physically removed from the factory, beaten, arrested, and threatened with guns and knives. Colonel Amaya Garcia, a former military officer who was Mandarin's head of personnel, directed the reprisals. The company also locked workers out, told workers it was going to close the factory, and fired workers en masse.[22] The legislature stepped in to try to negotiate an accord.

In response to the Gap's public denial of violations in the factory, a group of twenty-three prominent civil-society leaders in El Salvador sent the company an open letter challenging the Gap's findings and offering to provide evidence of alleged problems. Members of the legislature, university professors, and church representatives, among other human-rights activists, signed the letter, dated October 13. This group later formalized its association in the Coordinating Committee for the Dignification of Employment in the Maquilas. The coalition undertook several activities focused on the sector. It distributed educational leaflets outside the free-trade zones, held a forum to raise public debate on the issue, and lobbied for reforms to the Law of the Free Trade Zones.[23]

In November 1995, after Viera and Molina's well-publicized tour, concurrent actions at Gap stores around the United States, and the letter from Salvadoran activists, the Gap conceded that there were labor violations at Mandarin and declared its intention to suspend further orders from the plant. The NLC and other organizers who had joined the campaign pressured the Gap to return production to the plant. They wanted to establish that companies should negotiate ways to deal with labor violators rather than wash their hands of the incidents. They also knew that international solidarity would be viewed as a burden rather than a support if solidarity efforts led to plant closures.[24]

Forcing the multinational to keep production in the country to some degree undermined the charge that local unions and workers themselves were dupes of U.S. unionists who only wanted to see jobs returned to the United States. During the Mandarin dispute, such accusations culminated in high Salvadoran government officials' publicly denouncing the signatories of the October letter to the Gap as "traitors," calling for the death penalty to be imposed on those who were Salvadoran nationals and deportation for those who were foreigners (Anner 1998). The accusation of manipulation is so ingrained in the debate that competing Salvadoran unions also accused each other of simply acting at the behest of U.S. unions.

Meanwhile, Mandarin was setting up a company union within the plant. Mandarin's owner, David Wang, had hired the lead inspector from the Ministry of Labor in charge of writing the decision on the Mandarin case. One of her first actions as personnel director for Mandarin was to form the Employees Association of Mandarin International. ATEMISA offered workers a food-buying cooperative with company-paid staff and a loan program, among other benefits. ATEMISA's leaders became the company's strongest defenders. In a group interview in 1996, five ATEMISA members praised the company and declared that all of the problems were caused by SETMI workers. As is the case with many company unions, management was able to shift much of the conflict between itself and the workers to tensions between the ATEMISA and SETMI.[25]

The Gap campaign and the Mandarin struggle resulted in two agreements: one signed in New York in December 1995, and the second signed in San Salvador in March 1996. The first agreement was signed by the Gap, the NLC, and two New York ministers. It stated that Mandarin would meet with unionists; that the Gap fervently hoped that the unionists would be reinstated; that the Gap would agree to independent monitoring; and that it would renew its contract with Mandarin when it was confident that workers' rights, as defined by the Gap code, would be protected.

Meanwhile, in El Salvador the SETMI leaders were receiving death threats. In interviews in the summer of 1996, one leader recounted that she had received eleven threatening telephone calls, starting in mid-November.[26] Another leader described how two men had come to her house in a type of vehicle traditionally used by death squads in El Salvador.[27] Terrorized, the unionists resigned with severance pay the week after the New York agreement was signed. The Ministry of Labor then took the position that the union was legally dead.

In January 1996, negotiations over the second agreement began in San Salvador, but they principally involved non-Salvadorans. Several U.S. citizens who worked in El Salvador in religious, academic, and labor-related capacities served as negotiators with Wang and with the Canadian head of a Hong Kong-based company that acted as a kind of buying agent for the Gap.[28] In the end, the SETMI unionists were brought in to sign the agreement, along with the directors of ATEMISA and representatives of the four Salvadoran organizations that would make up the monitoring group—the CENTRA, the Archdiocese of San Salvador, Tutela Legal (Legal Trust) of the Archdiocese, and the Institute of Human Rights of the Jesuit-run University of Central America. This agreement focused on the return of six union leaders, the return of all other workers who had left or been fired in 1995–96, and the responsibility of the monitoring group to investigate compliance with the agreement, Salvadoran law, and the Gap's code. The agreement also specified that the signatories promised to "maintain the peace and harmony between workers" and "maintain the existing peace between the employer and employee,"[29] a mandate that would later become the basis of union resentment of the project. Finally, the agreement called on the monitoring group to solicit the Gap or other companies to contract with Mandarin to ensure the success of the agreement.

The implementation process then began. A coalition of the four religious and academic groups listed above formed GMIES. The monitors, who had expertise in the area of labor rights, began by focusing on the return of fired workers. They checked employee lists regularly to make sure that no worker had been hired who was not prioritized under the terms of the agreement. Monitors also visited the plant floor on a weekly—and often more frequent—basis to check on conditions. Monitors used both announced and unannounced visits. Monitors spoke with individual workers and conducted periodic surveys of the workforce. They met with workers outside of the factory, gave workers a telephone number through which they received complaints, and provided a complaint box within the factory. They met regularly with the administration, unionists, and the company-association representatives to air complaints and resolve problems. They also reported their findings to the Independent Monitoring Working Group, which included the Gap; the Interfaith Center on Corporate Responsibility; Business for Social Responsibility; and, for a time, the National Labor Committee, as well as to the public (Molina and Quinteros 2000).[30]

The GMIES reports (Anner 1998) and my research (including three visits inside the factory) confirm that the situation at the factory has greatly improved since monitoring began. The workers have potable water; bathroom visits are not limited; ventilation in the factory has been improved; all social-security payments are being met by the owner; and there are no longer complaints about physical abuse by management. Fired strikers have been reinstated and remain active as a union within the factory. The union, which was renamed STECHAR after Mandarin changed its name to Charter in 2000, is growing. Some complaints are still being made about verbal mistreatment and high production quotas. Also, although workers are now paid according to the law, their wages have barely increased in the six years since monitoring began.[31] And the union has never managed to win a collective-bargaining agreement or demand wage increases.[32]

Although this case did not result in a union victory, it did show that independent monitoring can provide a much higher level of scrutiny of the factory than private monitoring. This scrutiny contributed to the factory's continued lack of violations. GMIES provided the first proof that a local NGO could carry out a different kind of monitoring. GMIES gained workers' confidence and provided enough access that workers could present problems as they arose.

NGO MONITORS AND UNIONS: WARY ALLIES

Workers had so much access to GMIES, in fact, that they complained only to monitors, and the union's staff began to feel felt that the monitors were usurping their role. In July 1999, Jiovanni Fuentes, an organizer with the Federation of Independent Associations and Unions of El Salvador, explained: "Until just recently, the unions had a bad image of GMIES. But by being in contact we all understood each other better, we could suggest things, coordinate better. . . . We felt they were substituting for the union. Now we see they are the only one who can go inside the factory."[33] Although unions have certainly grown less hostile, it is still not completely clear what the division of labor should be. The monitors also still seem to act as somewhat of a buffer in the factory. In 1999, I asked the management of the factory, ATEMISA leaders, and SETMI leaders what in their view independent monitoring was supposed to accomplish. The answers were revealing:

> Pedro Mancillas, corporate director, Mandarin: "To maintain a climate of tranquility. . . . GMIES has worked in the sense that there is no longer a confrontational work atmosphere, more than anything, between the workers. The center of the conflict is between the two groups of workers, and the administration is in the middle. We've achieved a balance."[34]

> Secretary-general, ATEMISA: "They help us to all be at peace."[35]

> Secretary-general, SETMI: "They verify that the workers have the right to demand their rights. They are an arbiter between the three parties: SETMI, ATEMISA and the management."[36]

Although all three groups—management, ATEMISA, and SETMI—saw the monitors as peacemakers, as the original agreement mandated, only SETMI members believed monitors to be present principally to give workers a space to demand their rights.

GMIES is still working through this conundrum. Although GMIES's staff feels that it has a mandate to inform management about complaints received, some have seen its attempts to resolve these problems with management as obviating workers' need for a union. Moreover, in 2002 GMIES was again criticized for interfering with unionization when it failed to verify that a factory had closed to rid itself of a union (MSN 2003).[37] GMIES counters accusations of anti-unionism by pointing out that, in 2001, two of the three unions in export-processing zones were still in factories that were independently monitored (Quinteros 2001).

Independent monitors in Honduras also encountered tensions with local unions over the definition of their respective roles. The Honduran independent monitoring team EMI also arose from an international campaign over the firing of unionizing workers. In 1997, religious, human-rights, and women's groups joined together to monitor KIMI, a Korean-owned company in La Lima.[38] Again, monitors helped ensure the return of fired unionists to the factory but also came into conflict with the union. Once the union was established, monitors withdrew from the factory. Some portray the collective-bargaining agreement that workers won, including a 10 percent raise in pay, as a clear sign of the success of independent monitoring (albeit a short-lived success, as the factory closed within two years and moved to a non-union location in Guatemala). Other observers are much less sanguine about even the initial experience, pointing to the ongoing tension between unions and NGO monitors, whom one commentator called "wary allies" (Compa 2001).

Some observers attribute conflict between the monitor and the union in part to the open criticism of EMI by the AFL-CIO's Solidarity Center, which supported the local union (Koepke 2000). This charge resonates with the claims of GMIES staff, who have come into the gravest conflict with local unions and activists who are tied to organizing campaigns sponsored by the U.S. labor movement, which itself is somewhat divided over the concept of independent monitoring.[39] In fact, a lot of local unionists find the whole monitoring debate to be a Northern conflict that has little relevance to their work.[40]

Learning from the example of GMIES and the experience of monitors in Honduras, COVERCO in Guatemala has developed a clearer concept of roles. COVERCO is often referred to as a model for having defined a "non-substitutive role" in which it is careful not to usurp the role of either unions or government regulators. COVERCO explains to workers that monitors are not advocates, and while its monitors note grievances, they also encourage workers to take complaints directly to management or to file grievances with the appropriate government office. Rather than advocating and mediating, the COVERCO monitors report the results of their observances and investigations to the company and eventually to the public.

During the summer of 2001, unions took shape and attained legal status at each of the factories COVERCO had monitored for Liz Claiborne, demonstrating that, as in El Salvador, independent monitoring can provide space for workers' organizing. These were the only two registered unions active in the Guatemalan apparel sector. Although COVERCO was careful not to intervene actively, it did produce a special report on the violations that occurred in the organizational process (COVERCO 2001). As happened in El Salvador, management's reaction to the formation of a union was not only to intimidate union supporters and potential supporters but also to promote the formation of a company association with company-sponsored benefits. In both cases, management encouraged workers to oppose the unions, at points violently, and forced workers who supported the union to resign. However, in Guatemala the workers' unions were recognized as legal entities while the company unions were not. As Jonathan Rosenblum, who helped develop the COVERCO project on behalf of the ILRF, explained:

> The test of independent monitoring is whether civil-society organizations have impacts not only at the level of the improvement of working conditions in the factory, but whether they can make regulatory machinery act in the protection of workers' rights—whether the Ministry of Labor receives a case, responds to it in an appropriate time frame and in accordance with the law, and the labor courts do the same thing. In this case, the courts responded appropriately. I attribute that to COVERCO's vigorous role in monitoring those factories.[41]

Unlike private monitoring, independent monitoring often seeks to reinforce national systems of regulation. Although the recognition of the unions and nonrecognition of the company union were victories, COVERCO, like other NGOs, is facing a difficult balancing act. Unionists have recently criticized COVERCO for failing to verify and report some of the workers' allegations,[42] and the companies have contended that COVERCO participated in organizing unions at Choi Shin and CIMA textiles (COVERCO 2001).

Despite these conflicts, independent monitoring has been more successful than private monitoring at guaranteeing a space in the factory for unionists and a place for workers to voice concerns. Mandarin continues to be audited by other monitors, the Gap's compliance officers, and private monitors sent by other brand-name companies.[43] One SETMI leader described her perspective on a private firm that had monitored the plant: "This monitoring does not have any benefit for the worker, because if they only visit the company's administration and talk to them, they give the impression that they are on their side. It would be different if they came to the workers and it was the workers who really expressed the problems that the workers live through."[44] Pedro Mancillas, the manager of Mandarin, confirmed that monitors from Cal-Safety only sometimes interview workers and that workers "don't understand who they are."[45] Private monitors also seem to lack an understanding of the history of labor conflict at the factory. A Cal-Safety monitor interviewed in 1998 had audited the factory and had no idea that it had been the site of the most contentious labor dispute in the free-trade zones or that it was being independently monitored.[46]

The Gap's acceptance of the concept of independent monitoring was a groundbreaking step toward manufacturer responsibility for worldwide conditions of production.[47] Companies realized that they had to move beyond codes to implementation and were challenged to do so in a credible fashion. There are certainly limitations to the El Salvador project: it was imposed from the North; it has had only mixed results for organizing;[48] and its relationship with the union movement has not been fully worked out. That said, conditions in the factory have vastly improved; SETMI continues to exist (although it does not bargain); and workers seem to feel free to express their concerns. The project demonstrated that an alternative could be created, even under extremely constrained circumstances. The existence of a truly independent monitoring project changed the nature of the debate. As Kernaghan put it, "Even in a successful campaign, it's sad to say this, but sometimes the improvements on the ground for the workers are much less than you'd like them to be. However, it moves the entire process to defend human rights forward, and certainly this case did. Certainly, this case put independent monitoring on the map."[49] Even after it was on the map, independent monitoring still did not receive widespread attention in the United States for a few years. Faced with the challenge to implement codes, companies latched on to the private monitoring model and sent auditors to thousands of factories around the world, while independent monitoring expanded one factory at a time. Furthermore, until 2001—when GMIES began the controversial practice of accepting company fees—there was no stability built into the Salvadoran monitoring project in terms of funding. GMIES had to apply each year for funding from organizations in Europe and North America.[50]

However, this initial campaign paved the way for other international campaigns, such as those focusing on Kathie Lee Gifford and Disney, that brought enormous public attention to the phenomenon of exploited maquila workers around the world sewing for huge multinationals that seemed indifferent to their plight. That publicity eventually led to the formation of the president's AIP task force. This task force in turn became a battleground over the institutionalization of independent monitoring concepts developed in El Salvador versus private monitoring practices originating in Los Angeles.

The AIP and the Emergence of International Monitoring

In 1996, the Clinton administration called together the AIP task force, which was composed of manufacturers, NGOs and unions. The DOL played the role of convener, facilitator, and, at times, "cheerleader."[51] Spearheaded by former Secretary of Labor Robert Reich, the initiative rode a wave of public outcry around two cases. First, seventy-two Thai workers had been found in virtual enslavement in El Monte, California, sewing garments for such well-known companies as Mervyn's, Montgomery Ward, and Miller's Outpost. Shortly after, Kathie Lee Gifford was reduced to tears in front of a nation of viewers as she lamented the use of child labor (unknown to her) in the making of her Wal-Mart line of clothing, which sported tags advertising that a portion of each purchase would be donated to children's organizations.

Reich, under whose tutelage the monitoring program in Los Angeles had been launched, seized the opportunity to push the issue of offshore sweatshops. Reich personally tried to recruit the top executives at the nation's best-known apparel firms to attend a summit on the problem of sweatshops at Marymount University in Arlington, Virginia, on July 16, 1996.[52] Although many companies declined, a number were present among the 300 attendees. The Fashion Industry Forum resulted in a call for the formation of a presidential task force.

The Gap campaign had marked the beginning of both the concept of independent monitoring and companies' realization that they would be forced to monitor offshore facilities, not just promulgate codes. The combination of these two ideas may have convinced some companies that they should be involved in developing a monitoring plan that they felt was amenable to their interests. Manufacturers were probably also motivated to participate by the possibility of national legislation and the specter of public hearings on the sweatshop issue,[53] not to mention the relentless negative press over the issue.[54]

The task force, announced in August 1996, varied in membership over the more than two years of negotiations. Although eight manufacturers were involved throughout most of the process of negotiations, no major retailers participated.[55] The two unions selected to participate were UNITE and the Retail, Wholesale, and Department Store Union, neither of which participated in the final stages. The NGOs that were involved for the majority of the process were the National Consumers League, the Interfaith Center on Corporate Responsibility, the International Labor Rights Fund, Business for Social Responsibility, the Lawyers' Committee for Human Rights, and the Robert F. Kennedy Memorial Center for Human Rights.

The AIP began its work by forging a standard code of conduct. According to Michael Posner, director of the LCHR and a driving force in the AIP process, "80 percent of the code was dealt with within a couple of months." The biggest sticking points were the language on freedom of association and wages.[56] On April 19, 1997, the AIP issued its code, which required, among other things, that workers be at least fifteen years old, in most circumstances, and that workers not be required to work more than sixty hours per week, "except under extraordinary business circumstances." Workers could work an undetermined number of voluntary hours. Some members argued that when workers are paid below a living wage and are thereby forced to work overtime to survive, it is questionable how voluntary "voluntary" overtime is. The language on wages in the AIP Workplace Code of Conduct, like that on hours, reflected the internal conflict of the group: "Employers recognize that wages are essential to meeting employees' basic needs. Employers shall pay employees, as a floor, at least the minimum wage required by local law or the prevailing industry wage, whichever is higher, and shall provide legally mandated benefits."[57] Although the unions and NGOs managed to get a reference to their demand for a living wage included, the companies were *required* to pay nothing more than they had previously. The language on unionization rights was basic, simply guaranteeing the right to freedom of association and collective bargaining, although the NGOs and unions hoped this would be fleshed out in the next stage of negotiations.

The AIP then moved on to the even more complicated and contentious issue of an implementation process. As Roberta Karp, the Liz Claiborne representative and AIP co-chair, described this stage: "Every single issue was in conflict. It was a long, tortured process."[58] The task force soon became the site of an ideological struggle over the meaning of "independent monitoring." All agreed that there had to be some check on the obvious conflicts of interest involved in internal monitoring. However, there were many debates over whether an apparel company hiring an outside monitoring firm could be characterized as conducting "independent" audits. Nike's website summarized the company's argument at the time (the summary has since been removed from the site):

> Is an auditor like PwC [PricewaterhouseCoopers] truly an "independent monitor?" Companies like PwC have one invaluable asset: integrity. The Securities and Exchange Commission requires financial audits of publicly-traded companies precisely because those auditors live or die by their independent judgments of company financial statements. The independent financial auditor is trusted to judge company performance for shareholders, securities brokers and financial regulators by governments all over the world.

Companies argued that accounting firms—with their recognized standards and codes of ethics—were well positioned to be trusted judges of company performance.

The unions and NGOs argued that all monitors should be local NGOs who had credibility with the local society and were trusted by the workers. NGO groups usually conduct long-term monitoring, in which they build ongoing connections to workers in local factories. These monitors tout the fact that their efforts are either ongoing or intensive, stressing that they occur over a period of months rather than being based on visits of a few hours or, at the most, days, as is the case with commercial firms. Such visits provide a view of factory conditions that more accurately reflects the conditions experienced by workers on a daily basis rather than a snapshot of conditions often staged by factory management for the visit.

The NGO–union bloc also questioned PricewaterhouseCoopers' integrity and independence: Firms that offered "social-accounting" services often provided financial auditing or consulting for the same companies they monitored. Moreover, as apparel companies would directly pay the accounting firms, those firms face all of the same conflicts of interest that domestic monitoring firms confronted. Epistemologically, accounting firms approach problems from a business perspective. Thus, they are not only untrained in workers' rights and interviewing workers, but they also have a bias in favor of business inculcated by years of business education and practice.

It was not until after the agreement was signed that Pricewaterhouse-Coopers' reputation was officially challenged. In January 2000, the Security and Exchange Commission found the firm to be in violation of its regulations that no auditor should have a financial stake in the companies being audited. The SEC found more than 8,000 violations of this rule, which was meant to ensure independent review.[59] In 2001, the Enron scandal, as well as the WorldCom scandal and the others that followed, led to more serious questioning of the presumed "integrity" of accounting firms. Although these events influenced the lack of full success in the accreditation of Global Social Compliance, PricewaterhouseCoopers' reincarnation, they happened long after negotiations over the FLA format took place.

In the spring of 1998, UNITE began to back away from its commitment to the process. Internal conflicts within the newly merged union made decision-making difficult. Many in the union felt that their involvement in the AIP process had been a mistake. By the time the problems with implementation became clear, most people in UNITE felt that the union was losing ground. Its chief representative to the AIP, Alan Howard, explained:

> We accepted a monitoring model that was very conventional, very consistent with the way industry and business function, which is the CPA (certified public accountant) model. . . . The idea is that we are going to certify these monitors, and we're going to lay down certain rules for how they can function, and that's going to make sure that the monitoring gets done in an independent way. We probably should have challenged at that point, the model, but we didn't. What we did instead was, we accepted the model, and I would say we were only half-conscious of accepting the model and of the implications. But we accepted that model with the idea that, OK, we're going to take this model and we're going to build in all kinds of safeguards and make it rigorous.[60]

At that point, UNITE's resolve was to modify rather than subvert the concept of private monitoring. However, it had become clear that the union–NGO side was going to lose out on a principal modification of conventional monitoring—using an intermediary body to select and retain the monitors. The unions and NGOs argued that monitors should not be selected or paid directly by the companies. The association should at least select and hire the monitors. Having companies choose and pay monitors directly gravely compromised the neutral position of the monitor as well as the credibility of the process, they argued. The companies in the AIP defended their right to select the monitors, contract directly with them, and maintain proprietorship over the reports.

Furthermore, the provisions of the code, which had at the time of their adoption appeared to be a floor, would be virtually carved in stone by the second accord, which stipulated that any modification had to gain the vote of two-thirds of the companies, as well as two-thirds of the NGOs. On June 12, 1998, the NGO and union members sent a final proposal to the companies. They never received a formal response.

After negotiations broke down, a subset of companies and NGOs began meeting "informally" without the unions. The ICCR (the only faith-based NGO) refused to join informal discussions away from the table.[61] The remaining NGOs capitulated on the issue of who would hire monitors but insisted on a format they felt would bring some measure of accountability. An organization named the Fair Labor Association would be set up to oversee and coordinate monitoring. While the companies could choose and contract with the monitors, they could choose only from a list of FLA-approved entities. The companies could suggest which factories would be monitored each year, and, the FLA charter stated, "There shall be a general presumption in favor of the Participating Company's suggested list," but the FLA would have the final say in selection.[62] And all monitoring reports would remain secret, but the FLA would issue an annual summary of each company's performance.

The unions and the religious NGO refused to sign the FLA agreement, which was released to the public on November 2, 1998 (Election Day). UNITE had received a copy of the agreement only the day before and had been given no opportunity to offer modifications. In effect, the union had to take it or leave it. UNITE left it, with a ringing critique.[63] The union claimed that it had been excluded in the final stages of the process. Other participants countered that UNITE had purposely made proposals that it knew would never be accepted in order to extract itself from the process without having to walk away. UNITE had certainly been under strong pressure from the Clinton administration to make this public–private partnership a success.[64] Accusations of protectionism surfaced, as well, claiming that UNITE acted out of self-interest because the process would allow consumers to feel better about buying goods made outside the United States (Sweeney 2000).

Although they were not as critical of the final agreement as UNITE, the RWDSU and ICCR also declined to sign. The RWDSU released a joint statement with UNITE and the AFL-CIO that simply stated, "The labor movement has concluded that signing on to an agreement with the participating companies at this time is not possible."[65] In fact, the out-going president of the RWDSU, Lenore Miller, urged the ILRF to continue its participation, and she later rejoined the FLA as an individual member of its advisory council.

Not only UNITE but also many anti-sweatshop activists felt that the compromises made were too great. The FLA's board was to be made up of six NGOs and six companies, plus a neutral chair. To become a participating member, a company would need only majority approval. However, two-thirds of each side would need to approve any decertification, making it necessary for four companies to vote another company out. In fact, any important change would require a "super-majority" vote, virtually congealing what was touted as a preliminary arrangement with room for improvement. Information on factory locations and evaluations was considered confidential. Although the agreement required companies to internally monitor all factories each year, external monitoring was to be infrequent and mainly announced. Companies were required to hire a firm to externally audit 30 percent of their factories in the initial period and 5–15 percent thereafter. Although the factories are not "certified" as such, a manufacturer is considered—and can advertise itself as—in good standing if its factories appear to be in compliance for as little as one day each (an average of once a decade). In addition, the complaint mechanism was long and drawn-out. Moreover, workers were only passive participants, as potential interviewees, and local NGOs needed only to be consulted, not included, in the monitoring process. Finally, companies' monitoring costs for the initial three years were to be subsidized by taxpayer and foundation money.

UNITE argued that not only was the structure of the FLA flawed, but also the agreement undermined basic principles set forth in the initial code. For instance, in terms of the recognition of the need for a living wage, the new agreement simply called for the DOL to study the issue. Although there was a mandate to consider "the implications, if any" to the code, no process to do so was established, and, of course, any change to the code would now have to be approved by a majority of companies. There was no language detailing how freedom-of-association rights were to be guaranteed in countries that did not prescribe such rights by law or routinely suppressed them. Although some language from the NGO–union bloc's June proposal had been adopted in the final charter, the language was altered. Instead of prohibiting employers from "cooperation" with repressive state authorities, the provision barred companies from "affirmatively seek[ing]" assistance in repression. As Howard quipped, "This presumably means that they can let the army in the door, but better not pick up the phone to invite them in" (Howard 1999: 42).

The sharp debate over the FLA caused a large rift in the anti-sweatshop movement.[66] The controversy led to a series of meetings in Boston, New York, and Washington, D.C., to discuss questions of strategy and alliance among anti-sweatshop groups. The unionists and many anti-sweatshop activists felt that the participating NGOs had sold them out by agreeing to an accord that was too weak. Some questioned the role the human-rights NGOs were taking in the process. Although unions must answer to their workers and businesses must answer to stockholders, NGOs are not organically responsible to a particular constituency. As Lora Jo Foo, who chairs the board of Sweatshop Watch, explained, "Human-rights groups are not accountable to anyone; they are only accountable to their own conscience, and that is not good enough."[67] Others took a more conspiratorial view. Corporate Watch detailed all the corporate connections and funding of the participating NGOs in an article bestowing upon the FLA its "Sweatwash Award" (a takeoff on the group's yearly Greenwash awards, given to companies with bogus environmental policies). Although no such connections were mentioned for the ILRF, it, as the only truly labor-focused NGO, was hardest hit by the controversy. All of the AFL-CIO members on the ILRF's board resigned, and the organization's executive director, Pharis Harvey, lamented: "There is something toxic in the air."[68]

THE STUDENT MOVEMENT AND THE FLA

The FLA agreement met with resounding criticism from the anti-sweatshop movement in the United States. Moreover, the FLA was originally able to enroll only eight companies, all of which had been involved in the negotiations. The association was faltering badly before it had even begun. However, it found its flock not in apparel companies, its intended members, but in universities. The Clinton administration came to the FLA's rescue by recruiting universities, which had been under pressure from students to ensure that their licensed products were sweat-free and had begun passing their own codes of conduct. Many were now wrestling with the question of implementation.

In the spring of 1998, students at Duke University in Durham, North Carolina, negotiated with their administration to pass a code of conduct governing the production policies of the university's 700 licensees. Duke was the first university to adopt a code, and many others followed suit, often in response to student protests. In July 1998, students formed a nationwide organization, United Students against Sweatshops. A number of the campus leaders had been interns with unions (including UNITE) through the AFL-CIO's Union Summer. UNITE was very supportive of USAS, offering advice and logistical resources such as conference calls.

Government officials also joined the code crusade. In May 1998, Democratic Congressman George Miller of California introduced a resolution in the House of Representatives encouraging all U.S. colleges and universities to adopt a code of conduct for their licensed products and to guarantee "independent external monitoring" of the codes. The Congressman recounted violations at the BJ&B factory in the Dominican Republic, which produced college-branded caps that sold for $20, of which the university received $1.50 and the worker who stitched the cap together received $0.08. The university, which also profited from this business, had a moral obligation to address the situation, he argued, and the resolution was adopted. Miller also credited the students with "leading the way," adding, "It is time for Congress to acknowledge that they are headed in the right direction."[69] Within days, the California legislature passed a similar resolution,[70] which prompted the University of California system to proactively adopt a code. However, students returning from summer break were dismayed that the UC code failed to meet the minimum standard set forth in the Duke code, as was called for in the legislature's resolution. Students organized throughout the ten-campus system to demand revisions, such as the inclusion of a collective-bargaining clause and attention to women's rights. This culminated in a protest outside the UC president's office in Oakland in March 1999. The university agreed to set up a committee to recommend such changes that would include students and faculty. Such consultative committees were established at schools across the country.

By the spring of 1999, USAS had activists on more than sixty campuses. Frustrated with the slow pace of university committees or unable to move their universities through bureaucratic channels, many students chose other routes. Students at some schools moved from fashion shows and leafleting to civil disobedience. Starting in January 1999, students at Duke held a sit-in that touched off a wave of similar actions around the country. Students at six universities from North Carolina to Wisconsin and Arizona engaged in sit-ins against their administrations. Students at Harvard, Berkeley, Middlebury, and many other schools won concessions from their universities through less drastic means. The student anti-sweatshop movement became a national phenomenon. The *New York Times* reported: "In the biggest surge of campus activism in nearly two decades student protests have burst onto the scene with rallies, teach-ins and sit-ins. . . . The protests are the biggest wave of campus activism since the anti-apartheid movement in the early 1980s."[71] These protests resulted in universities' adopting or strengthening codes that required such things as women's rights, living wages, and full public disclosure of factory locations. Students also began negotiating with their administrators to keep them from joining the FLA.

However, students faced a serious challenge as government and business wooed universities to the FLA. In October 1998, capitalizing on student activism, the DOL and the Smithsonian Institution, which was presenting a historical exhibit on sweatshops, held the No Sweat University forum in Washington, D.C., to encourage universities to adopt codes and join the AIP process of looking toward implementation. On March 15, 1999, the *New York Times* reported that seventeen universities had joined the newly formed FLA. The American Council on Education sent a letter to 1,800 schools urging them to join, and the DOL continued its recruitment efforts, sending out materials and answering questions for prospective university members. [72] In June 1999, the DOL hosted an inaugural meeting for the college and university participants in Washington, D.C. The president sent a greeting message praising the schools' participation. By the end of the school year, more than 100 universities had signed on.

Big business also urged universities to join the FLA. Nike, an FLA charter member that has exclusive multimillion-dollar agreements with many universities to outfit athletes in exchange for free advertising on uniforms and in stadiums,[73] had called on its sponsored universities to affiliate in March. In exchange, Nike offered public disclosure of the names and locations of the contracting facilities that produced its collegiate apparel on the condition that its competitors also committed to disclosure. Disclosure was a point students and the larger anti-sweatshop movement had been fighting for. In 1999, the NLC coordinated the "People's Right to Know" Campaign, culminating in a day of conscience on December 9 with actions in more than forty cities. Companies had claimed that disclosure was impossible, however, because factories' names and locations were trade secrets and revealing them would undermine the companies' competitive position. Nike's offer was an abrupt reversal. While some heralded it as a breakthrough, others condemned it as a bribe to bring the university code movement into a forum Nike could to some extent control.

Universities did not just buckle under pressure from business and government. Many administrators felt that the FLA would relieve them of having to deal with the messy business of implementation for their newly passed codes. Here was a formulated solution. For the FLA, the universities' membership not only began a new momentum; it also legitimized the organization. As Michael Posner, the Lawyers' Committee for Human Rights representative and a central figure in the formation of the FLA, explained about university participation: "This is a great boost for the Fair Labor Association. They're intellectual centers. Their participation in this process will strengthen the association and broaden the discussion."[74] The universities gave the FLA a certain moral authority. Moreover, although goods carrying college logos account for only $2.5 billion in the $45 billion U.S. apparel market, universities would force their licensees into the program. Many of these licensees, such as Russell, Champion, and Adidas, are large corporations with production that goes far beyond collegiatewear. The hope was that these companies would agree not only to monitor college goods but also to join as participating companies. In fact, most of the growth in the number of participating companies (there are now thirteen) is due to university pressure on licensees. Moreover, more than 1,000 licensees have joined not as participating companies but in a lesser capacity (although the majority of these are not apparel companies).[75] For universities and the FLA, it seemed to be a win–win association.

However, many student activists were outraged. After all, they had been the ones to raise the issue of sweatshop production of collegiate goods on their campuses and now their input was being ignored. Students affiliated with USAS who had protested for higher standards in their codes now turned their attention to fighting the stampede toward the FLA. They argued that the FLA was a corporate-controlled institution and that students and their universities would not be able to hold the FLA accountable. While students were having some success negotiating with their own universities, often after long hours or days of sit-ins, protests, and rallies, they would be reduced to one vote among many in the FLA, which had offered the University Caucus one seat on the board. At one point, the FLA offered USAS its own seat on the board, and after a long internal discussion over whether the students could "change things from the inside," USAS rejected the offer on the grounds that its presence would legitimate the FLA with no guarantee of reforming it.

Instead, students took a two-pronged approach to their schools' involvement. Those students whose schools had already affiliated with the FLA demanded that the universities pull out in six months if the FLA did not conform to a set of principles that included university selection of monitors and factories to be monitored, public disclosure of monitoring reports and complaints, prompt investigation of complaints, and the exclusive use of unannounced visits. Students at nonaffiliated universities fought to keep their colleges out of the association.

DEVELOPING AN ALTERNATIVE: THE FORMATION OF THE WRC

USAS activists soon found themselves in an awkward position. After all, students had been the ones to call on universities to adopt codes of conduct. Now students were demanding that universities *not* join a monitoring organization that offered to help implement those codes without suggesting any alternative. USAS members began strategizing with anti-sweatshop activists, academics, and unionists about alternative implementation methods—methods that might shift some power back to the workers. Discussions that took place in small groups and through conference calls for several months led to a two-day meeting in Washington, D.C., in July 1999, preceding a national USAS conference. Students and their allies continued to formulate a new model and in October released a document laying out their model code and framework for a new organization to be called the Worker Rights Consortium.

The WRC proposal took an approach to monitoring that was entirely different from the FLA's. In fact, the proposal emphasized that the mission of the new organization would be "verification" rather than monitoring. The WRC would focus not on certifying companies or factories—which, the proposal argued, was an impossible task given the size and breadth of global production chains—but on verifying workers' complaints. The WRC would be in the business not of giving seals of approval for compliance but of identifying and working to rectify noncompliance. To maintain complete independence, the governing board would include *no* corporations, only representatives of three constituencies: students, university administrators, and labor experts (including academics, unionists, and advocates). Finally, the organization would promote worker empowerment by aiming to "build capacity and open up the space for workers and their allies to advocate on their own behalf."[76] With an alternative model in hand, but no actual organization, students faced the daunting task of convincing administrators to join an entity still in formation.

By the time the WRC held its founding convention in April 2000, forty-four universities had already signed on. A weary administrator representing the ten-campus University of California system, the largest research-university system in the country, arrived on an overnight flight to announce that the system's universities had decided to join the previous evening (according to students, in response to the threat of protests at Berkeley).[77] In fact, many universities joined to appease students who were holding protests, sit-ins, and hunger strikes. USAS, which continued to grow, with new chapters sprouting up almost weekly, had established a national office in the summer of 1999 and planned its campaigns largely through e-mail and conference calls.[78] In the spring of 2000, students coordinated a second round of sit-ins demanding that schools drop out of the FLA or join the WRC. Students at the universities of Michigan and Wisconsin held simultaneous sit-ins, resulting in the schools' membership in the WRC, the first major licensing schools to join. At the University of Pennsylvania, students sat in for more than a week and held a nationally supported fast that lasted forty-eight hours; the university dropped out of the FLA in response.[79] The sit-in at the University of Arizona lasted for ten days, and for eleven days, Purdue students held a hunger strike. Sit-ins continued throughout the spring, with students taking over offices or outdoor areas at state universities in Oregon, Iowa, Kentucky, and New York–Albany and at Tulane and Macalester, among others. At a few campuses, university administrators resorted to sending in the police, who threw tear gas and made dozens of arrests. Some students used other means to get their point across, such as the dozen students at Syracuse University who bicycled through campus "100% garment-free" (Featherstone and USAS 2002).

As students continued to protest, the WRC's ranks grew, and the organization evolved. Students, professors, and administrators joined labor experts from such groups as Sweatshop Watch, People of Faith Network, Press for Change, and UNITE to form working groups that continued to develop the organization and its policies. WRC organizers began their work by pushing universities to implement the section of the code requiring licensees to disclose factory locations. The resulting requests revealed that many large licensees had no idea where all their production was located, as they used intermediaries and subcontracting arrangements.

Collection of disclosure data turned out to be an ongoing process that in and of itself forced companies to grapple with—and, in some cases, streamline—their production systems. In December 2000, the WRC hired an executive director, Scott Nova. By January, the WRC was receiving considerable attention for its first investigation (at a Nike contractor in Puebla, Mexico), which many saw as a test of this new conceptualization of monitoring.

With the formation of the WRC, the tension between supporters of private monitoring and an alternative model had accelerated. In response to the University of Oregon's decision to join the WRC, Nike's CEO, Philip Knight, canceled a promised $30 million donation to the university. [80] Knight, a graduate and long-time supporter of the University of Oregon, also released a press statement admonishing, "With this move the University inserted itself into the new global economy where I make my living. And inserted itself on the wrong side."[81] A few weeks before the Oregon incident, Nike had cut its sponsorship of the ice-hockey team at Brown University, the first school to sign on to the WRC. Coming only days before the WRC's founding conference, Nike's rebuke of Brown was viewed as a warning call to other universities. Nike's actions were part of an ongoing rivalry between the FLA, of which Nike was a founding member, and the WRC for university membership, and more broadly over the concept of monitoring.

Knight's criticism of the WRC centered on the fact that licensees had no decision-making power over the development of the program. Knight insisted that monitoring must arise out of a negotiation among stakeholders.[82] Student activists stood firm that universities needed an independent means of verification in which apparel companies had no influence. The WRC was fashioned to act as a "watchdog" organization. According to this arrangement, companies were responsible for doing their own monitoring, but universities required an independent mechanism to address identified problems. The WRC paradigm attempted to re-center workers in the process by relying principally on programs of worker education and complaint mechanisms to trigger investigations. The students hoped that a strong emphasis on the right to organize as a fundamental standard might bring attention to the repression of workers' rights. A basic premise was that protected workers could best monitor their own work sites.

Debates were held publicly and within the confines of committee rooms at universities around the country. While USAS representatives and sympathetic faculty defended the WRC model, FLA supporters (largely university administrators) argued that the association was a far more developed and viable model. The WRC, it was said, would only alienate companies, which were, after all, the universities' business partners and needed to be part of the process.[83]

Criticism surfaced within the anti-sweatshop movement, as well. Some charged that the WRC was adopting a "gotcha" model of monitoring and that its punitive style might keep companies from cooperating, thus barring monitors from obtaining access to factories (MSN 2003; O'Rourke 2003).[84] Critics also claimed that the WRC would have a very limited scope not only because it is restricted to factories that produce collegiatewear but also because it included no systematic monitoring plan. Although it contemplated proactive monitoring, the WRC had neither outlined nor implemented such visits. By focusing solely on the workers' complaint mechanism, the WRC might drive production into areas where workers were too repressed to complain.

INTERNATIONAL MONITORING IN PRACTICE: THE CASE OF KUKDONG

Despite the limitations noted, the WRC has in practice pushed the envelope on what monitoring should entail: thorough investigations, off-site worker interviews, and pressure on local government to enforce the law. The WRC quickly established a reputation for its brand of monitoring in its first investigation at a maquiladora in Puebla, Mexico. Kukdong International (now named Mexmode) is a Korean-owned sewing factory that produced mainly Nike and Reebok garments carrying the logos of Purdue University, Georgetown University, the University of Michigan, the University of California, Berkeley, and many other universities. As part of its own monitoring program, Nike had sent PricewaterhouseCoopers to monitor the factory in the fall of 2000 and failed to uncover any major problems, including in the area of freedom of association. However, as several subsequent reports would show, there were numerous problems, including underpayment of wages, provision of rancid food, verbal and physical abuse, child labor, nonprovision of legally mandated maternity and sick leaves, and the presence of an "official" union never chosen by the workers.

On January 3, 2001, five workers were fired at Kukdong. The workers had protested conditions in the factory, particularly the issue of rotten food in the cafeteria and the fact that the official union was not representing their complaints. The official union, known as the Confederación Revolucionario de Obreros y Campesinos, had signed a collective-bargaining agreement with the management of Kukdong in December 1999, before the factory had opened for production and without going through the necessary legal channels. The imposition of a union that will supposedly represent and negotiate for workers without their consent, while common in Mexico, violates both international and Mexican laws. Workers were unaware of the existence of the union until it announced itself six months later and began requiring weekly dues. CROC is tied to the Partido Revolucionario Institucional, which ruled Mexico from 1931 to 2000 and is still in power in many local states, including Puebla. In fact, it controls the local Conciliation and Arbitration Board that resolves labor disputes.

On January 9, 2001, more than 800 of the 900-person workforce at the plant began a work stoppage to protest the firings and to demand a new union. As many as 600 workers continued the action by setting up camp between the factory building and the outside gates. On January 11, riot police and members of CROC violently dispersed the workers. More than a dozen workers ended up in the hospital. A struggle then ensued to ensure workers' reinstatement. On January 13, Kukdong's management signed an agreement with the Conciliation and Arbitration Board to allow all workers to return to their jobs without discrimination. Despite this agreement, many workers who attempted to return faced harassment. The retaliation included being forced to sign loyalty pledges to CROC; being hired as new workers and thereby losing seniority and accrued benefits; being threatened with greater workloads; and being refused reinstatement outright.

Within days of the work stoppage, both the FLA affiliates (although not the FLA directly) and the WRC had become involved in the situation. Nike hired an FLA-accredited monitor, Verité, to do an audit. The ILRF, an FLA board member, also arranged for the Mexico City labor lawyer Arturo Alcalde, a prominent advocate of Mexican independent unions, to investigate the situation. Meanwhile, the WRC was receiving complaints from workers and sending its own delegation composed of U.S. and Mexican labor-law experts.

On January 18, Amanda Tucker, a Nike representative, told the University of California's Advisory Group on Monitoring and Enforcement Issues that the factory was unconditionally reinstating the fired workers. Tucker made these statements even as Alcalde's investigations were showing otherwise. Furthermore, Tucker dismissed the charges of rancid food. She explained that the factory was giving the workers steak when they were used to beans and rice and that it was a question not of rotten food but of cultural difference.[85] Nike had also received and refused a request from the WRC for assistance in gaining access to the factory. Tucker explained that Nike denied the petition for cooperation because of its inhospitable relationship with the WRC. As witnessed at this meeting, the Nike representative's first line of attack was to deny the charges of violations at the plant. Nike later changed its position on the violations of reinstatement, the rancid food, and facilitating access to the factory. This switch was no doubt due to the pressure exerted by WRC schools, Alcalde's report, the press, and the public.

The WRC investigation and the one conducted by Nike's contracted monitor, Verité, differed more in their approach than in their findings on the facts of the situation. Both reports found rampant violations at the factory in the areas of wages, abusive treatment, and freedom of association. However, while Verité planned a standard audit, the WRC insisted that there would be immediate and irreparable damage if workers were not allowed back into the factory right away, as Kukdong had promised the local government. Workers would be forced to find other jobs to survive, allowing the company to crush the organizing campaign. By denying or even delaying workers' return to the factory, the company was actually prohibiting workers from freely associating. In response to the WRC's complaints, Verité sent an observer specifically to check whether workers were being allowed to return to the factory. However, the observer was not supposed to release information to anyone except Verité and Nike. The WRC objected that human-rights observers would keep information hidden. The purpose of the observers was to pressure management to let the workers back in, and this would not be accomplished by guarding the results. Verité eventually agreed to have its observer issue public daily reports over e-mail.[86] However, this was an exception under pressure, completely outside Verité's policy as a paid monitor and outside of the FLA protocol under which all such information is kept confidential.[87]

In the end, both reports were made public: the WRC's as standard practice; Verité's because of the enormous attention given the case and the public pressure on Nike to report its monitors' findings and the company's intentions.[88] In both its preliminary and final reports, the WRC focused heavily on the right to organize. Verité's report is much more general and includes only a few pages on the subject. Moreover, although the WRC did not issue its final report until June, it issued a preliminary report immediately on January 24, the day after its investigation, with timely recommendations to universities. Universities put more pressure on Nike, and Nike in turn put pressure on Kukdong, eventually resulting in the return of the majority of the workers to the plant. The WRC continued to follow the case with local investigators and frequent updates to universities, which pressured Nike to remediate and, just as significant, to return orders to the factory after its withdrawal. Verité did not conduct its audit until February 5 and did not issue a report until March 14.[89] This report alone, without earlier action by Nike, might have improved conditions for the remaining workers, but it would not have ensured the reinstatement of fired union supporters, which came more than two months after the initial incident. Moreover, without pressure to remain in the factory, any victory would have been nullified by factory closure. A standard monitoring approach most likely would not have led to the eventual recognition of the union, marking a milestone in Mexico's labor relations, as an independent union gained a collective-bargaining agreement for the first time in an export-garment factory. In 2002, the union successfully bargained for significant wage improvements.

The FLA and the WRC:
Divergence and Convergence

The emphasis placed on workers' rights rather than on conditions, and the attention to the action needed to protect those rights, marks an important distinction between the premises of private and independent monitoring. In its report to the president dated April 14, 1997, the AIP expressed its purpose this way: "The Partnership's commitment to work together to form, during a six-month transition period, a nonprofit association that would have the following functions *intended to provide the public with confidence about compliance with the Code*" (italics added). The report goes on to list six functions, the last of which is "to serve as a source of information to consumers about the Code and about companies that comply with the Code." None of the functions mention workers. Like the model in Los Angeles, the FLA was originally constructed to rely on consumers' caring about workers' conditions rather than on the actions or desires of workers themselves. However, the confidentiality clauses with regard to disclosure of information about both factory locations and monitoring reports limited even this strategy. Moreover, in the FLA's model, unionization rights were just one of many possible code violations. In fact, one of the first three FLA-accredited monitors exempted itself from investigating the freedom-of-association clause, and there has been no explanation of how this gap is to be filled. Thus, it appeared that a company could use this monitor and simply skip that provision in the code.

The WRC, by contrast, was built on the concept of empowering rather than simply protecting workers. According to WRC protocols, a decision about initiating any specific investigation will be based on the desires of the affected workers. While the Central American independent monitoring projects' investigations are initiated by agreements with the brand-name companies, the WRC's investigations are generally initiated based on an advocate's or workers' complaints. To date, this protocol, along with the fact that the AFL-CIO is on the WRC board, has helped the WRC avoid the conflicts described earlier. Also, Nova explains that, while many code elements are of equal import, freedom of association plays a unique role as the "right to organize is the mechanism for achieving respect for the whole code."[90] Freedom of association was a primary part of each of the underlying complaints in the five investigations carried out in the first two years of the WRC's operations (in the Dominican Republic, El Salvador, Indonesia, Mexico, and the United States). Local workers (not from the factory in question) or their advocates must be included on any investigative team, according to WRC protocols. A central criterion for WRC decisions about where to initiate long-term projects is also the potential for worker empowerment in the site. Although there is no language in the WRC bylaws addressing the role of consumers, students have taken active roles in most of the cases, pressuring their universities to mediate with the brand-name companies and sometimes pressuring those companies directly. In addition, the university members, which license the goods, are expected to hold the licensees accountable.

Disappointment with the FLA's monitoring model led the ILRF, the last labor group on the association's governing board, to decide to withdraw and remain only on the advisory board.[91] The ILRF simultaneously decided to associate itself with the WRC by joining its advisory council, overcoming some previous antagonisms. According to Terry Collingsworth, the new executive director or the ILRF, "The FLA was so concerned about offering companies an 'acceptable' monitoring regime to attract more companies that it was willing to sacrifice some pretty fundamental points."[92] In a letter to the FLA dated October 4, 2001, the ILRF expressed its grave concern over such issues as companies' selecting and paying for monitors, the infrequency and brevity of the audits, the lack of protection for complaining workers, and the voting structure of the organization. The ILRF also complained about its weak negotiating position vis-à-vis the companies: "Several of the NGOs on the [FLA] board, including the ILRF, are relatively small and have spent countless hours in marathon negotiations with large multinationals that can far better afford to dedicate staff and resources to a lengthy process, and that may have an interest in delay."[93] Although the former executive director of the ILRF remains on the FLA's board, he does so as an individual, further weakening the NGOs' position.[94] However, the ILRF's withdrawal led to a shakeup within the organization that resulted in the board's adopting some long-standing NGO proposals.

The ILRF's critique and withdrawal added to the dissatisfaction some FLA members had felt with their executive director, who was replaced in January 2002 by Auret van Heerden, who had been the monitoring director. Van Heerden, who had worked at the ILO for ten years, brought a a seriousness about workers' rights and a consensus-building style to the organization. Van Heerden explained that, as the FLA moved into a new stage, ideological positions had to be set aside to address the practicalities involved in implementation.[95] The FLA began a process of significant reforms. Corporate board members were drawn along by the new leadership and pushed forward by the ongoing advocacy of the NGO members and of the specter of the public dismay over corporate scandals. The success of an independent WRC advancing an alternative concept of monitoring also added pressure.

The existence of the WRC, the activism of students on their campuses, and continued negotiations within the FLA had already forced the organization to change in certain respects. Early in its formation, the FLA had adopted language on women's rights in its benchmarks, and it included language on worker education in its monitoring guidelines. Affiliated universities agreed to require public disclosure of factory locations, but companies did not do likewise. The FLA had also begun to use NGOs as one source of monitors, largely because of the efforts of the ILRF, which received substantial grants from universities to develop that capacity among NGOs.[96] In October 2001, the FLA decided to implement a policy of only unannounced visits, the first significant change to its monitoring practices. The FLA also made information and reports public on certain cases—not coincidentally, those that also involved the WRC (Kukdong, BJ&B, and PT Dada).

However, it was not until 2002 that many of the changes that students had been calling for for years were finally implemented. The board, which now included three university representatives, agreed to a major shift by deciding that the FLA itself, not the companies, would select and pay the monitors. Companies would also have less influence over the selection of the factories to be audited. Moreover, disclosure was considerably expanded. Summary monitoring reports would be publicly released. The reports would include the name of the member company, the name of the monitor, the country or region in which the factory was located, the points of noncompliance, and the progress of remediation.

Although these changes are significant and promising, it should be noted that certain compromises were made. The companies could no longer select monitors, but more private monitors were accredited, and the number of factories to be monitored was dramatically reduced (MSN 2002). Although a "random-sample model" of factory audits replaced a less stringent system that included company suggestions, the number of factories to be externally monitored decreased. Rather than 30 percent of factories being subjected to external monitoring in the initial implementation period and an average of 10 percent each succeeding year, only 10 percent of a company's factories are externally monitored in the initial period and 5 percent thereafter (although the company is still required to internally monitor all of its facilities). This decrease was also a response to a drop in federal funding that was supposed to defray the monitoring costs. Finally, in terms of disclosure, monitoring summaries are to be made available but not factory names, which some critics believe undermines the value of publicly displaying reports because without the factory names challenges will be difficult. Also, while van Heerden continues to lead the organization, as of December 2003 he is based in Europe and holds the title of president and CEO. The FLA has hired a new executive director, Rut Tufts, to oversee everyday operations. Tufts worked for thirty-one years in different aspects of business administration at the University of North Carolina. He has been deeply involved in the development of codes of conduct and monitoring for the universities and has served on both the FLA and WRC boards. While sympathetic to workers, he does not have the same kind of expertise in workers' rights and consensus building as van Heerden, and it remains to be seen whether he can have the same strong influence on the FLA's board.

Still, as of this writing, the FLA has publicly acknowledged that workers' empowerment is a central facet of code enforcement and has moved toward a model that mitigates companies' control of their enforcement process.[97] There has also been an increase in cooperation between the FLA and the WRC. In several recent cases, the organizations have worked in complementary rather than conflictive ways. At BJ&B in the Dominican Republic, the WRC was first alerted to problems and able to gather information from workers and their advocates, and the FLA was able to work closely with the brand-name companies to gain access and press for remediation. Van Heerden characterized the connection this way: "The WRC has great connections on the ground and an early-warning system that is invaluable at times. There is an obvious synergy emerging. They can uncover problems. We can get the brands to get us both into the factory."[98] In 2003, the WRC proposed that the two organizations jointly appoint "an 'ombudsman' in El Salvador to review and resolve individual complaints of anti-union discrimination at factories supplying university licensees."[99] The FLA approved the concept and in late 2003 an ombudsman was hired to investigate complaints in El Salvador, Guatemala, and Honduras. Unfortunately, the companies have not yet agreed to act on the ombudsman's findings, as proposed, but instead want to be able to follow up findings with their own investigations. Such a procedure would undermine the agility of the system, essentially leading to the ombudsman triggering the complaint mechanism of the FLA rather than having the ability to function as an appointed investigator. Still, if the project can combine the WRC's ability to engage workers who have complaints and the FLA's potential to get companies to respond by using their leverage with local contractors, the project could have a broad and dramatic impact on freedom of association rights in Central America.

Certainly, both organizations serve a purpose. With the recent changes, companies that join the FLA are able to monitor themselves in a more credible fashion. Unfortunately, the FLA presents itself as "an independent monitoring system,"[100] even though companies play a large role in governance, and most of its audits are conducted by private firms whose primary clients are corporations. By joining the FLA, universities force their licensees into what a United Nations researcher has called "co-regulation," in which the control of companies is tempered (Utting 2002). But the FLA is not an appropriate venue for universities to seek *independent* oversight of their codes. The WRC offers this watchdog function and in so doing pushes FLA members to abide by their own standards. In fact, USAS has now taken a less oppositional stance, insisting that schools join the WRC but not opposing additional membership in the FLA. In fact, as of February 2003, sixty-two universities—or more than half of the WRC's 112 affiliates and more than one-third of the FLA's 177 members—were dual members.[101]

However, many school administrators continue to argue that FLA membership is sufficient, highlighting the danger still posed by a widespread belief among universities and certainly companies that private monitoring can substitute for independent monitoring. Unfortunately, if and when consumers begin to find labels on clothes advertising that a participating member of the FLA has produced the garment, they will be unlikely to know the difference, either.

CONCLUSION

The emergence of independent monitoring is a crucial development in the movement for corporate accountability. Through the efforts of anti-sweatshop activists, companies came to recognize that it was not enough to adopt codes of conduct with no implementation mechanism. Activists also challenged the validity of implementation mechanisms that were controlled by companies by offering viable alternatives, first through NGO monitoring groups in Central America and then through the formation of the WRC.

The independence of the WRC has allowed it to take principled positions on such issues as disclosure, lack of financial relationship between monitor and company, and worker empowerment as a stated goal. These positions, albeit some in modified forms, are now being adopted by the FLA and may eventually help raise standards more broadly in the field of monitoring, which to date is wracked by inconsistencies. As Scott Nova said about the ramifications of the WRC's work:

> It has an impact on the thinking, the responsiveness, and the conscience level of the buyers and the chains they are a part of and on the geographical area where the factories are located in terms of other workers' expectations . . . also on students and the university. They see that the university's role can be significant and even decisive. . . . We have also had a significant impact on the field of monitoring, a field which is standardless. Any organization can advertise itself as a monitoring organization; any report can be put forward as monitoring. What conflicts of interest need to be avoided? What do reports need to cover? There are no such standards. WRC is helping to begin to set reasonable standards in terms of methodology, thoroughness of interviews, [and] depth and nuance of reports.[102]

Although the WRC is limited in the number of investigations it can carry out, those investigations can have a ripple effect on the attitudes and actions of workers, contractors, and manufacturers. Moreover, independent monitoring has the potential to raise the bar on standards.

More significantly, independent monitoring inverts private monitoring by bringing workers back to the center of the picture, rather than pushing them to the margins. Independent monitoring focuses on workers' voices through attention to their complaints. It also ensures that their perspective is centrally represented by mandating inclusion of local workers or their advocates on all investigation teams. Moreover, independent monitoring can support workers' organizing. As Nova points out, the potential effect of successes gained through WRC intervention—and through independent monitoring more generally—is not only to improve monitoring but also to raise the expectations of workers in other factories. Independent union victories, wage gains, and government agencies' acting to protect workers' rights enter the realm of realistic possibilities. In 2002, three of four active unions in the Salvadoran apparel sector and both of the unions in the Guatemalan apparel sector were in independently monitored factories. Unlike in Kukdong, these unions had not gained collective-bargaining agreements and thus were unable to demand wage increases, although their legal recognition is an important step.[103]

In addition, by providing open and timely information, the WRC's investigations allow actors at the point of consumption to take an active role of support in protests occurring at the point of production. At Kukdong, as at New Era in New York and BJ&B in the Dominican Republic, students at campuses across the country closely followed union negotiations and gave support by pressuring their universities, the brand-name companies, and even government officials at key junctures. The relationship between worker and consumer protest is a vital topic that will be addressed in the concluding chapter.

Conclusion
Workers, Consumers, and Independent Monitoring

THIS BOOK has argued that private monitoring has not been successful in ameliorating the sweatshop problem because of flaws in the way monitoring is carried out and the conflicts of interest involved, and also that private monitoring does not address fundamental problems in the structure of the industry such as secrecy, mobility, workers' vulnerability, and pricing. Although monitoring in Los Angeles was a new and innovative approach to the problem of manufacturers' lack of accountability, the program has been fraught with weaknesses, such as erratic monitoring practices, minimal training of monitors, on-site worker interviews, lack of oversight, and failure to follow up on documented violations. Many of these problems have reemerged at the international level.

Most fundamentally, private monitoring in Los Angeles was built on irreconcilable contradictions. These contradictions can be summarized as follows: First, manufacturers are in control of a program meant to discipline them; and second, workers are not participants in a program meant to benefit them. Again, these patterns are mirrored in the majority of international monitoring cases now being conducted.

Codes of conduct were an important step in establishing the concept of corporate responsibility, something that had been negated by the widespread use of the contracting system. Monitoring began to address the hypocrisy of publicly adopting codes, then failing to enforce them. However, codes and monitoring to date have not significantly improved the situation for garment workers around the world. They certainly have not brought about the production of "no-sweat" clothes. However, they do hold promise if the programs are changed to involve workers in meaningful ways and if an independent monitoring component is incorporated into the system. Empowering workers and truly informing consumers could be a powerful combination in fighting sweatshop abuses.

PRIVATE MONITORING AND THE DISEMPOWERMENT OF WORKERS

This study makes clear a number of underlying problems with private monitoring programs. Private monitoring for the most part has not protected workers' right to organize, which is vital to their ability to maintain a monitored work site beyond the brief period of the audit. Moreover, although monitoring may improve conditions, it *cannot* offer assurances of compliance, as companies sometimes claim. In fact, it has been used at times against workers to undermine their competing claims. Thus, monitoring can act as a wedge, rather than a link, between workers and consumers. The GUESS? example highlighted a company's ability to use its monitoring program as a public-relations tool specifically to challenge the legitimacy of the union and more generally as evidence that workers were being treated fairly. Other companies have done the same, both in their public statements to consumers (via the press, mailings, and their websites) and in attempts to defend themselves from lawsuits brought by workers. Such claims of good business practices are rarely reflected in truly good working conditions for workers. The monitoring program could not protect GUESS?'s workers from violations or ultimately from layoffs when the company illegally moved its production abroad.

No single study is comprehensive, but the totality of the literature on international private monitoring makes a convincing case that such self-regulation, like monitoring in Los Angeles, is gravely flawed and involves underlying contradictions. Here, too, monitoring practices are erratic; auditors routinely miss violations; and workers are by and large unaware of programs meant to benefit them. Yet by simply participating in code monitoring, companies have been able to make bold claims about their progressive practices. Reminiscent of GUESS?'s full-page "No Sweat" ads, Nike proclaimed on its website in 1997 that it would "assure best practices in every factory where NIKE products are made, regardless of who owns the factory, or the scale and duration of our presence there" (as quoted in O'Rourke 1997: 12). Such assurances serve to disempower workers by denying the reality of the conditions under which they work.

However, companies are becoming more hesitant to make this kind of sweeping claim. Nike's website is now much more cautious about its claims. The emphasis now is on the effort that is being and will continue to be made rather than on giving assurances. This is a direct result of the scrutiny given its claims and its monitoring systems in literature such as that cited in this book—and, more important, in the activism of advocates and students who have taken Nike to task over the monitoring issue and worked to uncover and bring to the public the abuses that continue to plague the industry.

This book has shown that private monitoring has marginally improved compliance, but violations remain rampant. The latest statistics from the DOL bear out this analysis. In 2000, violations were found at more than half of the most effectively monitored shops in Los Angeles. Likewise, evidence from abroad shows that, despite a decade of codes of conduct and tens of thousands of factory audits, improvements, if they occur, are generally restricted to physical conditions in the plants and rarely affect wage levels and unionization rights, which might guarantee long-term and more significant changes.

Private monitoring does nothing to empower workers largely because it is not substantively concerned with rights to freedom of association and collective bargaining. In Los Angeles, the monitoring program was not geared to inform workers or to scrutinize compliance with laws governing the right to organize. These standards were never part of the agreements and were not added even superficially to monitoring services, as were a battery of other regulations on such issues as health and safety, immigration, workers' compensation, and registration. Internationally, these rights are included in codes, but factories regularly pass inspection while completely disregarding these provisions.

Moreover, it was manufacturers, not workers, that were empowered by the structure of the domestic monitoring program. Although the DOL has moved toward more informal agreements that mirror the voluntary nature of international monitoring accords, manufacturers were given too much control even during the program's height. Monitoring was born of the recognition that manufacturers are responsible for violations by setting low prices and requiring quick turnaround. Yet in a sense, the DOL ignored the ramifications of this fact, setting up a program based on fundamental conflicts of interest in which manufacturers that desired to produce cheap, timely goods also had to enforce labor standards on their contractors. In addition, monitoring was not standardized. Instead, it was offered on a fee-for-service basis by commercial firms. Monitoring firms responded to their clients' (the manufacturers') specifications. In addition, many monitoring firms had their own conflicts of interest in that they worked for the manufacturers or contractors in other capacities.

Private monitoring has—at least, in some instances—put further pressure on workers, partly because it did not support contractors in their pursuit of fair contract prices and stable contracts. Evidence from Los Angeles and reports from around the world show that contractors are made to absorb the costs not only of the improvements required to come into compliance but often of the monitoring itself. Researchers in Thailand found that these expenses were recouped by raising production quotas for workers. It is logical that this will hold true elsewhere. Moreover, because their relationships with manufacturers are on a contract-to-contract basis, factory owners are being asked to invest large amounts of money in improvements with no long-term guarantee of work.

Finally, private monitoring institutionalizes workers' vulnerability through the establishment of an industry and a set of practices built on enforcing manufacturers' accountability for workers without those workers' knowledge or consent. For the most part, workers do not know about monitoring or even about the codes, and the codes are so broad that they are meaningless unless an informational process geared toward workers is instituted. Since interviews take place at the factory, workers who reveal violations are easily identified and thus subject to retaliatory firings. They may also be laid off when the manufacturer finds out that the factory is violating its code. In addition, monitoring is a sporadic and unreliable solution. Private monitoring, as conducted in Los Angeles, entails one or a series of relatively short visits to factories. Such monitoring is not a process that involves workers or others in ongoing vigilance. The confidentiality involved in the process prevents parties other than the monitors, the manufacturers, and the government from even obtaining detailed information about company performance and factory location. This lack of disclosure keeps workers and their advocates from leveraging the system.

The challenges of monitoring abroad are far more complex than those in Los Angeles. Visits are much more infrequent. It is easier to hide violations from monitors, who are often unfamiliar with local dialects, laws, and customs. No government authority is aligned with the program that can demand entrance to a shop. Information can be even more limited, because there is often no oversight body. And workers in some places are subjected to more poverty and repression, making it less likely that they will speak openly to strangers. International monitoring can provide even less certainty of compliance than that conducted in Los Angeles.

The truth is that no monitoring program can guarantee the rights of millions of workers in tens of thousands of factories and hundreds of thousands of workshops and homes spread throughout the world. Given the current structure of the garment industry, assurances are impossible. Yet the FLA, the WRAP program, and the SAI plan all imply such assurances by allowing companies to advertise themselves as participating members and use the FLA or other "service" mark. Praising the announcement of the FLA, U.S. Secretary of Labor Alexis Herman declared: "The Administration is convinced this agreement lays the foundation to eliminate sweatshop labor, here and abroad. It is workable for business and creates a credible system that will let consumers know the garments they buy are not produced by exploited workers."[1] Although the FLA has changed in ways that make it a more credible model of self-regulation, it cannot be cast as an independent guarantor. Moreover, hundreds of factories are currently being certified through the SAI and WRAP programs, which require contractors to directly hire private commercial firms to certify themselves; the brand-name companies then get credit for working with these factories. These two programs offer companies the potential to turn consumers' concern, created by the anti-sweatshop movement, to their advantage with little effort on their own part.

Linking Workers and Consumers

Another related and significant issue should be addressed before concluding: What is the relationship between consumer protest and producer protest when it comes to affecting labor conditions? And how can a better synergy between these forms of protest be developed? This question is clearly part of a broader examination of the effect of globalization on the relationship between First World and Third World activists.

Although many view codes of conduct and private monitoring as a way to address poor labor conditions created by globalization, to a certain degree they actually reinforce power dynamics because they are based on the premise of disempowered workers and governments. They are rooted in a vision of corporations as self-regulating and benign entities. And most significant for the discussion to follow, codes and private monitoring are driven by the notion that First World consumers rather than Third World workers are the loci of resistance.

The burgeoning anti-sweatshop movement has focused much of its energy on an attempt to create alliances between First World consumers and Third World workers. Although this movement has brought the issue of sweatshops into the consuming public's eye, it has had considerably less success in translating this heightened concern into victories for garment workers in their factories. Multiple factors make the realization of concrete gains difficult. The underlying problem is the complete imbalance of power between ever changing legions of garment workers scattered across the globe and the concentrated power of a small number of retailers and manufacturers that dictate prices and schedules to competing factory owners. Problems of communication, coordination, and comprehension among activists in consuming and producing countries hinder efforts to address this formidable imbalance.

Moreover, a focus on conditions rather than on the rights of the workers has put the anti-sweatshop movement in a vulnerable position. Multinationals appear to take the high road by adopting codes of conduct for their contracting facilities and monitoring them for compliance, without changing the basic operating principles of the system. Although conditions may be cleaned up on the day of an audit, or may actually improve, workers by and large are not being allowed to exercise their rights of association, organizing, and bargaining. Therefore, any improvements remain subject to the continued vigilance, and at the grace, of the multinationals and the consumers who pressure them—uncertain assurances, at most. Without the ability to freely exercise their rights to associate and bargain collectively, workers enjoy, at best, small improvements in conditions without a mechanism to guarantee their continuance and without the ability to negotiate for an increase in wages or control over their hours and their lives. At worst, workers continue to toil in miserable conditions and are handicapped in any struggle for change by a misrepresentation of their situation to far-off consumers.

Although the DOL in Los Angeles and some of the international programs discussed have attempted to establish the accountability of profit makers for the conditions of those who produce their goods, they have done so in a way that does not challenge the basic operating principles of global capitalism. Their answer—private monitoring—actually bolsters the position of companies vis-à-vis workers. It creates a social contract without the participation of workers—the social-accountability contract. This configuration stands in sharp contrast to the traditional social contract of the mid-1900s. In this newer version, employers and government are linked to contractors—not workers' organizations—in an agreement. As independent monitoring has developed, it has begun to address this omission by bringing workers back into the picture.

Chapter 7 described the origins and worldwide development of independent monitoring. Because of independent monitoring's preliminary nature, its effectiveness cannot be assessed in a systematic way. Private regulation has reinforced the power imbalance engendered by global capitalism to some degree by turning enforcement over to the private sector rather than demanding that government fulfill its mandate or bolstering the power of workers to negotiate for themselves. However, it is not clear that independent monitoring would not also serve as a buffer, although perhaps a more benign one, between workers and employers. Evidence from the El Salvador case suggests just such an outcome. Moreover, the campaign around this first case, which was originally born of a concern for workers' unionization rights, quickly fell into the trap of focusing on conditions in order to mobilize consumers. However, El Salvador was the first case, and practitioners (including the Salvadorans themselves) have learned a great deal from it—not least, that monitors must define what COVERCO in Guatemala has called a "non-substitutive" role vis-à-vis unions.

Despite the drawbacks and internal contradictions of this first project, the very concept of independent monitoring changed the terms of the debate. As the NLC's Charles Kernaghan describes:

> The companies had in a sense set up an entire framework, with all of the dialogue and all the terminology and the agenda, and they controlled every step of it. Unless we removed their agenda, there was no way worker rights could be protected with the help of international solidarity. So for us, independent monitoring meant that we here in the United States would leap over the top of their entire agenda. We would make this a dialogue between the North American people and the workers in those factories and their representatives and the unions.[2]

In the Kukdong case, independent monitoring did just that: It opened a channel between Third World workers and First World students and activists.

Kukdong turned out to be a landmark case, resulting in the first independent union to sign a collective-bargaining agreement at a garment-exporting plant in Mexico. Within weeks of the successful binational campaign to secure reinstatement, workers formed the Sindicato de los Trabajadores de la Empresa Kukdong International de Mexico on

March 18, 2001. SITEKIM supporters initially faced a virulent anti-union campaign on the part of the company and the official union, CROC, which included intimidation, bribery, strip searches, and physical attacks. The labor board, which was politically tied to the official union, denied legal recognition to the independent union. However, continued organizing by the workers, along with pressure on both the manufacturer and the local government, resulted in an unprecedented victory.

That campaign illustrates the potential of the triangle of resistance discussed in Chapter 2. It demonstrates that pressure on all three points of the triangle of power—manufacturer, government, and contractor—is essential to winning labor victories in the global economy. Consumer pressure on Nike was strong during the reinstatement campaign in terms of both university administrators pressuring Nike headquarters directly and students and activists protesting in front of Nike stores. Although the public demonstrations waned with the return of the workers, universities, the WRC, and the ILRF continued to push Nike to use its influence with the factory to recognize the union and then to return orders to the plant.

Constituencies in both countries also pressured the Mexican government to recognize the union and allow for a fair secret-ballot election. This pressure was exercised to some degree by local groups—labor lawyers, academicians, and the Workers' Support Center—in Mexico. In the United States, the Campaign for Labor Rights organized delegations of labor, Latino, and student leaders to almost forty Mexican consulates and the embassy. The delegations delivered letters that were then sent by diplomatic pouch to Mexico's President Vicente Fox. Perhaps most influential was a visit from Congressman George Miller, a strong supporter of the WRC and its efforts, to Puebla, Mexico, and to the local labor board, which had refused to recognize the union in violation of Mexican laws that governed the process.

Most important, the continuing organizing campaign on the ground quickly moved forward. By September, 399 of the 450 workers employed in the factory at the time signed the application for the independent union. This enormous show of support among the workers, coupled with the pressure exerted by Nike, Reebok, and politicians, convinced both the company and the labor board to recognize the union on September 21, 2001.

The independent monitoring carried out by the WRC had facilitated an exchange of information, an exertion of pressure at key points, and timely support to the workers. It was one crucial component of this campaign. By focusing on the workers' struggle for recognition rather than on their working conditions, the WRC helped the Kukdong workers fundamentally change the nature of labor relations in their plant. The second round of negotiations culminated in a contract on April 1, 2002, that guaranteed significant wage increases, with direct raises of 10 percent, and other increases in benefits and bonuses that could add up to as much as 40 percent. (Workers had been making less than half of the bare mini-mum necessary to feed a family with two children.)

More broadly, independent monitoring's greatest potential is in locat-ing workers at the center of the monitoring system. Where possible, the initiation of an investigation is triggered by workers. Through education programs that increase workers' knowledge of the codes and their abil-ity to report violations, workers become the front-line monitors. More-over, the decision for any investigation to proceed must rest on the desire of affected workers. Thus, workers are not relegated to a passive outsider position in the model; they are the hub. The hope is that independent mon-itoring will also provide workers with resources in their relationships with other constituencies.

Transparency is central to this model. Disclosure of factory locations and reports provides a freer flow of information to consumers, investors, activists, universities, and any other party interested in the situation of the workers. It also provides more information to workers and their advo-cates. Workers can identify the connection between their factory and a particular manufacturer or university through factory lists, and they can challenge the accuracy of a list if they find that their factory is not included when it should be. Advocates can attempt to verify the information col-lected and the claims made in publicly released reports. They can also use such reports as an opening with workers—as an invitation to respond with their own assessment of the situation. Moreover, students are now push-ing for and winning broader disclosure. A few universities have agreed to require their licensees to disclose wage data from contracting factories. The WRC is encouraging, although not requiring, universities to take this step and will help determine how best to present such data in a com-parable format. Companies may thus compete with universities and other consumers on the basis of higher standards rather than just lower costs.[3]

Independent monitoring could provide workers with protection from government repression through denunciation. Moreover, it could strengthen government enforcement by informing workers about their rights under local laws and about local remedies available to them. Inde-pendent monitors could alert local authorities to labor violations, pro-vide a safer environment in which workers can denounce violations with-out fear of losing their jobs, and even report weaknesses in the present system of labor-law compliance.[4]

The ultimate goal of an independent monitoring or verification model is not to create a huge apparatus that can monitor every one of the tens of thousands of apparel factories across the world. Rather, the intent is to help create an environment in which protected workers will be able to function as monitors and enforcers of standards in their own factories.

Workers, after all, are the best monitors. As Marcela Muñoz, who leads the independent union at Kukdong, pointed out: "Someone outside cannot know what it is like to be at a machine ten hours a day, or standing ironing, to be out of your house for fifteen hours. And that person cannot defend our rights."[5] Private monitoring, at best, can offer very sporadic snapshots of conditions in factories; at worst, it can convey only the appearance created by the factory owner on the day of the visit. Workers know the whole picture, day in and day out, visible and hidden, particularly when they have been informed of their rights and trained to detect violations. In this model, outsiders serve principally to verify workers' complaints.

Unionization is an important step in securing both protection for workers and the ability to negotiate decent conditions. By prioritizing freedom-of-association rights as a uniquely important aspect of the codes, the WRC aims to open space for workers to organize. Monitors at both Mandarin and Kukdong focused initially on the return of workers who had been fired for organizing or protesting. This is the point at which consumers' and workers' leverage could converge to shift power if consumers' efforts were refocused from responding to reported conditions to responding to violations of workers' rights to organize and speak out.

The task at hand, then, is to gain access to the workers, inform them of their rights, and implement effective mechanisms of complaint. The more challenging task, in an industry based on mobility, is to offer workers some measure of protection from firings and layoffs if they do defend their rights. Activists must put pressure on the contractors, as well as on the manufacturers, to respect these rights and pressure the manufacturers to stabilize their relationship with the contractor. When manufacturers produce for universities, schools can play a role in promoting such stability.

Structural changes that stabilize factory–manufacturer relationships with fewer but longer-term contracts may give workers leverage by tying manufacturers more closely to specific factories, limiting their ability to cut and run at the sign of organizing or protests against wrongdoing. Longer-term relationships would also give contractors more leverage to negotiate contract prices with manufacturers and thus, possibly, to pay workers better. In turn, workers would be in a better bargaining position with their immediate employers. Such stabilization, combined with efforts to inform workers of their rights, open spaces to organize, and protect workers' rights to do so, may actual contribute to the elimination of sweatshops.

True implementation of codes of conduct would require changing the system of production. No company that contracts to hundreds of changing factories across the globe can possibly *know* whether violations are occurring. The benefit of private monitoring paid for by the manufacturer is that, to some extent, it pressures manufacturers to limit and stabilize their contractor base in an effort to reduce monitoring costs. (This is not true of programs in which the contractors pay.) However, with its exclusion of workers, private monitoring cannot ensure anything. Multi-stakeholder initiatives can also play an important role here by requiring longer-term contracts, delving into the issue of pricing, and obliging companies not just to adopt codes but to make sure workers understand them. Independent monitoring has been most effective when it has acted as a check on manufacturers' commitment to standards—ideally, through a multi-stakeholder initiative or even through a company's own program. Moreover, multi-stakeholder initiatives, such as the FLA, have strengthened their programs in response to the constant pressure of alternative models and of activists who hold their feet to the fire.

However, even an ideal combination of internal and independent monitoring could not dramatically change the situation by itself. Codes of conduct and monitoring must be seen as one tool within the broader context of governmental and intergovernmental actions. As Van Heerden of the FLA says, "We are an ad hoc response to a regulatory vacuum."[6] The present trend must be reversed, and national regulation must be strengthened. Moreover, trade agreements must include strong labor-rights provisions. An international body should be created that can rule on and sanction violations of international labor standards. Such bodies already exist for trade violations.

Although it is not clear how independent monitoring will turn out, it is clear the struggle over private versus independent monitoring concerns a larger conceptualization of the roles of manufacturers, consumers, and workers. Manufacturers are depicted as either partners in social responsibility or the source of exploitation. Workers are viewed alternatively as wards of benevolent manufacturers and active agents of change. Consequently, the implications for the role of consumers and activists shifts between concerned shoppers and participants in worker solidarity. The reality is that the roles may fall somewhere in between, or they may be a combination of both. However, the vision of consumers engaged in an enterprise that supports the *empowerment* of workers is crucial to any effort to return workers to a participatory role in the social contract.

Appendix 1
Confessions of a Sweatshop Monitor
BY JOSHUA SAMUEL BROWN

[NOTE: In 2002, as I was updating and preparing the manuscript of this book for review, I ran across the following article online. I was struck by the consistency between this inspector's 1998 experience in China and my research findings in Los Angeles at the same time. He describes the same lack of oversight, training, standard procedures, and accurate reporting that I found to plague the monitoring industry in L.A. But, more important, I was struck by the futile and helpless position of this young inspector caught up in complex issues beyond his own competence. I think this first-hand account tells all too well, in a few pages, what I have attempted to document on a larger scale.]

HALFWAY over the Pacific it dawns on me that I have no idea what my job is.

It's October 15, 1998 and twelve hours ago, I was in the southern California offices of an independent monitoring company that inspects factories for safety violations and human rights abuses throughout the world. I had been hired over the phone a few days before. My sole qualification for the job? I speak Chinese and have a friend already working for the company. I assumed that there would be some sort of lengthy training process to teach me how to be a human rights inspector. There wasn't.

Arriving in Los Angeles, I'm taken to Denny's by another inspector, then back to the office, where I putter around for a few hours before being driven back to the airport to catch my plane to Taiwan. I tell my manager that I feel a bit unprepared for the task ahead.

"Don't worry, you'll do fine," he tells me, handing me a suitcase full of folders containing the names and addresses of 23 factories in Taiwan and $26 a day for meals.

"You'll meet your partner in Taiwan, he'll show you the ropes," he says, passing me the company handbook. "You can learn about OSHA regulations and the manufacturers' codes of conduct on the airplane."

INSPECTOR HEART ATTACK

My partner's name is John, but everybody calls him Heart Attack. I find him sprawled on the floor of our Taipei hotel room early the next morning. Pieces of reports, violation sheets and photographs of factories are scattered over the floor.

Reprinted by permission of Joshua Samuel Brown. First published in the *Albion Monitor* (http://www.monitor.net/monitor/), September 1, 2001.

John is rooting through the mess, whining that he'd been awakened by a call from Marty at 4 AM, something about a "failure to assess back wages in Saipan." Heart Attack looks extremely tense. "Back wages, John," he babbles in a mocking falsetto. "Assess the back wages, don't forget the back wages." I introduce myself, telling him I'm to be his partner, and he's supposed to train me. He looks up at me, eyes wide with loathing.

"Training you?! Me? They're going to fire me over this Saipan thing, but first they want me to train my own replacement, right? I'm not going to dig my own grave, no thanks!"

Things are tense, and I haven't even dropped my suitcase yet. I try to defuse the situation by offering to buy him a cup of coffee in the hotel lobby, assuring him that I know nothing about Saipan, or of any plans to fire him. Heart Attack seems to relax.

"Sorry about that," he says, getting up to shake my hand. "Nobody trained me to assess back wages, you know."

Not even knowing what he means by "back wages," I nod dumbly. I'm to spend the next two weeks learning how to be an inspector from Heart Attack. Despite his apparent neurosis, he has the instincts of a bloodhound, and proves himself an excellent inspector. On the job just over three months at the time, he's already considered a veteran at the company.

"This company has a turnover rate higher than most burger joints," he warns me over coffee.

BAD REVIEWS MEAN LITTLE
October 18, 1998

I'm learning from Heart Attack how this business works. Inspectors go into factories all over the world looking for signs of worker exploitation, egregious safety violations, child labor and quota violations. We are paid by our clients, major manufacturers whose stores and products are household names. On a good day, our company earns thousands of dollars from a few international inspections. The inspectors themselves are paid minimal hourly wages, with no benefits. Inspectors are expected to work 70-hour weeks, and to be on call 24 hours a day for calls from the L.A. office. The worse a factory is, the more often inspectors are sent, and the more money the company makes.

My first day on the job, Heart Attack and I perform two surprise inspections. The first factory is a re-audit of a factory producing goods for K-mart.

"Man, the last guy they sent really botched this inspection," Heart Attack says. "Look at this report." The report is for an inspection performed a year ago. It's written so generically that the writer could easily have been describing half of the medium-sized cookware factories in Taiwan. The factory had been given a low risk assessment, ending with the often-used line, "The inspector was unable to find any violations that would be considered a risk at this medium-sized factory." I think that maybe we were at the wrong facility, because the one we are in is an unmistakable hellhole—a dark basement factory with poor ventilation and dangerous equipment. There's no first-aid kit, and the fire extinguishers expired around the same time as Chiang Kai-shek.

We interview the workers. They tell me they're paid only half of what they had been promised by contract, and one of the Thai workers confides in me that he wants to run away, but the boss keeps all his documents locked in a safe. I ask them why they didn't tell this to the last inspector, and they stare at me blankly.

"A foreigner visited last year, but he didn't talk to us. Was he from your company?"

I bring these problems up to the factory manager, and he looks at me as if I'm insane.

"What problem?!" the manager says. "Last guy say everything OK! I sign paper, he leave! Why you bother me again!?" Later I call in to our office and ask a manager just how the previous inspector could have given this sweatshop a low risk rating. "That guy didn't work out," I'm told.

A few days later, Heart Attack and I are in central Taiwan, and I'm learning a lot more about the business. There seems to be an absolute lack of consistency in the attitudes of inspectors working for us.

"Everybody has their own focus," John tells me. "Like, there are some who I call eye-wash inspectors. They can go into the worst factory in China and head straight for the first-aid kit. They'll ignore all of the other violations, and write three paragraphs in their report about how there was no eye-wash in the kit. Then they come back home and brag about how they can do five factories a day." I ask him why these eye-wash inspectors don't get fired for incompetence. He smirks and rubs his thumb and forefinger together in the universal symbol for payola. "This company cares about quantity, not quality," John says. We approach the factory, a place producing belt buckles for Calvin Klein. The facility has been under inspection for quite some time, and not by slacking eye-wash inspectors. This place has been thoroughly raked over.

"Look at this last report!" Heart Attack hands me the previous inspection team's violation list. It has some pretty damning violations:

- Dangerous metal-melting chemicals being mixed in vats by workers wearing flip-flop sandals
- Overtime not being paid at legal rate
- Imported workers denied access to their passports
- 90 hour work weeks

There is a tacit agreement that what we write in our reports will be read by the manufacturers, who are supposed to pull out of those factories found to be continually in violation of their codes of conduct. Were this truly the case, we would not even be here: This factory has been on the high-risk list for two years. I ask Heart Attack if he thinks the client will pull out of this factory soon, and he snorts derisively.

"We've been here five times already, and every time the factory gets a high risk," says Heart Attack. "Calvin Klein won't pull out of this factory until we find 9 year-olds chained to arc welders and strung out on speed. The boss knows that we're only paper tigers." Nonetheless, I try to convince the boss to mend his ways. Heart Attack is a crude man, a rare breed of sinophile, able to speak Chinese without an ounce of Chinese manners.

I, on the other hand, have spent much of my adult life in Asia. I understand the use of polite shaming. I appeal to the boss's sense of patriotism and reputation.

"News crews might come here one day," I tell him, switching from Mandarin Chinese to the native Taiwanese dialect. "The poor conditions we've found here might cause a loss of face to both you and the Taiwanese business community. Mainlanders will look at you and tell the world that the Taiwanese have no heart."

The boss nods politely, promises to make the improvements suggested in our report, and invites us to have dinner with him. We decline, explaining that it goes against our own company's code of conduct. We are forced to give this factory yet another high-risk rating. The owner signs our findings sheet without a glance.

Two weeks after our swing through Taiwan began, Heart Attack and I are trying to get all our reports in before returning to America. We have been awake for 30 hours straight. He tells me we've had a successful trip. Of the 23 factories on our list, we found 22 of them, and were only denied access to one. Tallying up our profit and loss sheet, we figure that we've earned the company more than $20,000 profit. I've been working 13-hour days for two weeks, and am looking forward to reaching San Francisco for some R&R.

While I am excited by my new job, I'm beginning to wonder just whose needs I'm serving. Am I helping the industry clean up its dirty laundry, or just to bury it a little further from the noses of the American consumer?

THE DOG MEAT MAN
November 15, 1998

There is a long trench with imposing razor ribbon fences on either side, and one bridge running across it. This is the path that leads from Hong Kong to China. This is where I'll be spending the next three weeks.

It's my second trip as a sweatshop inspector, and my first trip into mainland China. Before leaving the office in L.A., one of the senior inspectors took me aside and told me that "no factory in China should ever get a low-risk rating." It was explained to me that all factories in China were so far against the clients' stated codes of conduct that if one were to be given anything other than a high-medium risk, whoever reviewed the report in the office would assume the on-site inspector hadn't really looked. I naively asked him why we even bothered inspecting factories if we knew that they'd fail; the senior inspector looked at me like I was nuts.

It is also the first trip for my Hong Kong partner, Jack Li. Despite the fact that I've been on the job only one month, I will be training him. Before I leave the office, I'm given a chunk of cash to pay Jack's salary. His pay is half of my own, with no overtime pay. His per diem food allowance is $6 less than mine. How ironic, going overseas to uncover disparity in the workplace while committing it myself on my employer's behalf.

I feel disgusted with myself, and decide to split the difference of our per diems between us.

Jack and I inspect a typical Chinese factory a couple of days later. We find almost every violation in the book. The workers are pulling 90-hour weeks. The place has no fire extinguishers or fire exits, and is so jammed full of material that a small fire could explode into an inferno within a minute. There are no safety guards on the sewing machines, and the first-aid box holds only packages of instant noodles. Most of the workers are from the inland provinces, so I conduct the employee interviews in Mandarin while leaving Jack to grill the owners in Cantonese.

With the bosses out of earshot, I fully expect the workers to pour out their sorrows to me, to beg me to tell the consumers of America to help them out of their misery. I'm surprised at what I hear.

"I'm happy to have this job," is the essence of what several workers tell me. "At home, I'm a drain on my family's resources. But now, I can send them money every month."

I point out that they make only $100 a month; they remind me this is about five times what they can make in their home province. I ask if they feel like they're being exploited, having to work 90 hours a week. They laugh.

"We all work piece rate here. More work, more money."

The worst part of the day for them, it seemed, was seeing me arrive. "I don't want to tell you anything because you'll close my factory and ruin any chances I have at having a better life one day," one tells me.

I ask if they feel like they're being exploited, having to work 90 hours a week. They laugh.

Jack and I tell the owner that she needs to buy fire extinguishers, put actual first-aid supplies in the first-aid kits, install safety equipment on the sewing machines, and reduce worker hours to below 60 per week. We figure if she takes care of the first two tasks, we've helped to make the world a slightly less ugly place.

It's too late to hit another factory, so we sit down for some tea with the owner. We've just finished faulting her for just about every health, safety and payroll violation in the book, but she remains an excellent host.

"Thank you for caring so much about our poor Chinese factory workers," she tells us. "But really, it's all about profit. If I paid my workers more money, I'd have to raise the price to my buyers, the people who are sending you here to inspect my factory. Do you think they would accept that?"

I try to explain to her that a new consciousness is developing among American consumers, and that all of the American garment producers are trying their best to clean up their factories.

"Gua yang tou, mai gou rou," she replies, quoting an old Chinese proverb.

Translated: "Hang a sheep head but serve dog meat."

"Calvin Klein, Wal-Mart, Kathie Lee: They all want the same thing. Chinese labor, the cheaper the better," she smiles, pouring the tea. "They all want to project a smiling face, to appear to be caring and compassionate, because that makes people feel better about buying the products that have their names.

"But we both know that all they care about is money," she continues. "If I did all the things you told me to do, my clothing would become more expensive to the manufacturers. Then they would just use a cheaper factory, one in Vietnam or someplace even less regulated than China."

Finally, it hits me. I understand why my employer doesn't care if we do a good job or not. We aren't here to help change anything; we're only a PR prophylactic. Hiring an industry-friendly "independent" inspection company is the most cost-effective way for the manufacturers to maintain their profits while claiming to care about the people on whose sweat their profits depend.

Jack and I finish our tea, thank the owner for her hospitality, and head back to our hotel, just a couple of sheep heads working for the dog-meat man.

JOSHUA SAMUEL BROWN has written for the *Hong Kong Daily Standard, Taipei Times, China Post, Beijing Scene,* and many other publications.

Appendix 2
Research Methods

To CONDUCT RESEARCH on monitoring, I used a multipronged approach. While I primarily relied on the qualitative methods of in-depth interview, observation (sometimes participatory), and document analysis, I also used quantitative analysis of Department of Labor data and a brief survey to ground my research. Each of these areas is covered in detail.

My case study on Los Angeles (Chapters 3 and 4) is based almost exclusively on primary data collected through the aforementioned methods. As explained at the beginning of Chapter 3, I compared practices observed on actual monitoring visits with information derived from interviews, written monitoring protocols, and DOL survey data. The analysis of international monitoring found in Chapters 5 and 6 is based primarily on interviews with monitoring groups and a large body of secondary literature produced by academics, monitors, workers, and NGOs, as well as the websites of various monitoring organizations. Chapter 7, however, is based on primary data gathered in interviews, document searches, and participant observation. I conducted research in El Salvador during two rounds of fieldwork. The first was a research trip that focused very specifically on the Gap campaign and the case of the Mandarin International factory, where the first ever independent monitoring project had just begun work. The second round consisted of two trips (in 1998 and 1999) and was part of my dissertation research, which focused more broadly on monitoring. I also conducted research trips to New York in 1998 and 1999 and to Washington, D.C., in 1999 and 2002. Participant observation in the development of an independent monitoring model began in late 1998 and continued throughout the process.

INTERVIEWS

My primary method for conducting research was the in-depth interview. I conducted 139 in-depth interviews with people from all of the different constituencies involved in monitoring: monitors, manufacturers, contractors, workers, labor leaders, NGO staff, workers' advocates, and state and federal government officials. This multi-perspective approach gave me a more complete picture of monitoring than I would have otherwise obtained. All interviews, except three telephone interviews, were conducted in person. Interviews lasted between half an hour and two and a half hours. During my pre-dissertation research, conducted in 1996, I audiotaped most of the thirty-eight interviews. During the formal dissertation research, from 1998 to 1999, all ninety-four interviews were audiotaped unless otherwise requested by the interviewee—a rare occurrence. Only two of the seven formal interviews conducted in 2002 and 2003 were audiotaped. Although I used an interview schedule for all interviews, the questions were open-ended.

TABLE 7. Interviews by Category and Country

Category	El Salvador	United States	Total
Academic	5	2	7
Business	3	18	21
Government	8	13	21
Monitors	8	15	23
NGOs	8	15	23
Press	1	0	1
Union staff	5	12	17
Workers	18	8	26
TOTAL	56	83	139

Table 7 provides a summary of the informants I interviewed by category and by country. A full listing of the interviewees (including name, position, and organization with which they are affiliated and the interview date and place) is located in Appendix 3. Most categories are self-explanatory, but I will elaborate on a few. "Business" refers to representatives of apparel companies or sewing contractors and their associations. "Monitors" are from specialized firms, apparel companies, or oversight organizations. The "NGO" category refers to representatives of non-governmental organizations, including religious institutions, women's organizations, legal-aid offices, solidarity organizations, and labor advocates. These totals (and the list of interviews) refer only to in-depth interviews and do not include brief information-gathering phone calls, informal conversations, or interactions during conferences and observations, of which there were many.

OBSERVATIONS

The general secrecy—in the name of confidentiality—surrounding both monitoring and supplier chains impeded access to observations and created some uncomfortable situations. As I explain in Chapter 3, despite my requests I was allowed to observe only two companies conduct a total of six complete audits. At a third firm, Cal-Safety, the executive director agreed to the observation, and I went out on one audit, but we were denied access. I returned to the office to await another audit. However, when the owner, Carol Pender, saw me, she became very upset. She yelled at me that no one went out on visits with Cal-Safety's monitors and that the televisions news program 20/20 had requested permission and she had refused. When I responded that I was an academic researcher, not a journalist, she continued to insist, claiming that she had to protect her clients and her employees. I pointed out that I had signed a confidentiality agreement that the executive director had drawn up promising not to reveal the names or identities of her employees or of the factories and their employees. She was unmoved by this argument and by my subsequent request.

Although the number of observations was limited, I did accompany the most experienced monitors at each firm. Moreover, I had ample opportunity to discuss the various procedures and situations encountered with the monitors and verify what was typical and what was unusual. Many of the observations are also corroborated by other evidence, such as DOL survey data and the testimony of workers, monitors, government officials, and contractors. I also observed at a monitor training session, a DOL forum, and other events in Los Angeles, which gave me additional data for the research.

In El Salvador, I was granted access to the factory in question (the only factory to be independently monitored) on three separate occasions. In 1996, I was given a tour of the factory and allowed to interview workers selected by factory management, all of whom turned out to be members and representatives of the company union.

I was then allowed to return to the factory for a second visit and to interview four workers whom I had randomly selected from among the workforce. However, that visit caused a small uproar. The independent monitor had given me a copy of a report of conditions found in the plant without noting that the report was not a public document. I took the document to the factory to use as a baseline in the interviews. While I was on the shop floor selecting one of the workers, the head of personnel entered the office I had been given for the interviews, apparently looked through my papers, and saw the report. A member of the monitoring group later told me that the factory owner had called an emergency meeting because the report, from his point of view, was confidential. My contact, sensing my embarrassment, tried to assure me that the incident had been quickly dismissed as other more pressing matters overtook the emergency meeting. Even so, the incident taught me that one must always clarify the terms of information given by an informant.

In 1999, I was again given access to the factory but offered the opportunity to speak only to two of the leaders of the company union. I then met with two leaders of the independent union outside the factory during the lunch hour.

In terms of the development of the WRC and the debate on college campuses, I have done a considerable amount of participant observation and applied research. The exact development of this, as well as a discussion of its merits and drawbacks, is covered in the Preface. Here I will only describe the participant observation and the data to which I gained access.

Because of the knowledge I gained during my fieldwork and through my advocacy on the subject, I was selected to become a member of the Advisory Group on Codes of Conduct and Enforcement Issues for the University of California system. I participated in many meetings with administrators, licensing directors, lawyers, faculty, and other students on these issues. As part of the committee, I also attended presentations by all of the monitoring organizations (FLA, WRAP, WRC, and SAI), three of them by their executive directors. These presentations provided the opportunity to ask many specific questions. We also had presentations by and discussion with representatives of several major apparel companies, including Adidas, Jansport, and Nike. Other conferences on codes and monitoring provided opportunities to hear presentations by and speak informally with company representatives, monitors, NGO staff, and workers

Finally, I was involved in the development of the WRC from its inception. This provided me not only with firsthand knowledge of the history of the organization but also with an integral understanding of the controversies and discussions that were entailed in developing the model. I also serve on the WRC's advisory council and governing board, along with students, administrators, and other experts in the field. The discussions among these participants have enriched my understanding of the issues involved, as I believe my own participation has enriched these discussions.

DATABASE

The U.S. DOL conducted a baseline survey of sewing factories in California in 1994. The survey included findings on violations from factory investigations as well as information on employer knowledge and other areas obtained through interviews with the contractors. The department conducted similar surveys in 1996, 1998, and 2000, focusing on the five-county Los Angeles region. In 1996, it expanded the survey to include questions on monitoring activities, and in 1998, to include price negotiations. The DOL analyzed these new data in relationship to violations. Each survey covered between sixty-seven and seventy-six shops. The data are presented in Chapters 3 and 4.

In addition to using the DOL's analysis of its data, I obtained the completed survey forms for 1998 through a Freedom of Information Act request. I used the raw data to construct a database and did supplementary analysis of the information. By cross-checking the manufacturers listed in each contractor survey against the list of ACPA signatories, I was able to determine whether signatories' monitoring activities differed from those of non-signatories. Also, because the DOL collected data on seven monitoring components plus the contractor's ability to negotiate, I was able to do a much more detailed analysis of how monitoring was actually being practiced. These data confirmed the findings from the small sample of observations I was able to conduct.

SURVEY

In October 1998, I conducted a short survey of the six monitoring firms in Los Angeles. The five companies I had been able to interview all responded to the survey, with one company (Labor Law) responding that all information requested was confidential. The purpose of the survey was to get a more accurate account of the breadth and growth of the companies by asking for specific data on where and for whom they had monitored over a six-year period. The head of the monitoring program at PricewaterhouseCoopers also filled out the survey as a follow-up to our interview.

DOCUMENTARY EVIDENCE

As all researchers do, I collected far more documentation than I was ever able to incorporate. Thanks to the Internet and the Lexis/Nexis database, I amassed an enormous amount of information from companies' and NGOs' websites, as well as from newspaper articles. Documentation gathered during fieldwork included sales packets, monitoring protocols, and other information from the top three firms, which agreed to provide this and all the available information from the various international monitoring oversight organizations, such as codes, charters, protocols, membership lists, and staff information. Business organizations such as the California Fashion Association, the Gap, GUESS?, and Mandarin International furnished reports, pamphlets, and other documents. The National Labor Committee furnished me with a documentary history of the entire Gap campaign, as well. NGOs and academics studying maquilas in El Salvador provided a substantial number of publications, educational materials, and unpublished papers. Finally, I collected a number of government documents that were crucial to understanding monitoring as it has developed and is practiced. Foremost among these were the many iterations of the monitoring agreements themselves.

CONCLUSION

This thorough triangulation of the subject matter gave me a very broad understanding of monitoring, from the details of the monitoring process to its political significance for different actors. The strong reliance on in-depth interviews and observation, combined with the statistical analysis in the case of Los Angeles and a review of secondary sources in terms of international monitoring, allowed me to place the detailed information I gathered in a more general context.

Appendix 3
List of Interviews

Name	Position/organization	Place[a]	Date	Sector[b]
Abebe, Sam	General manager, L'Koral	Los Angeles	July 20, 1998	B
Amaya, Irma	Movement of Women Mélida Anaya Montes	San Salvador	July 23, 1996	N
Anner, Mark	Board member, GMIES	San Salvador	July 12, 1996	M
Anner, Mark	Board member, GMIES	San Salvador	Aug 5, 1996	M
Anner, Mark	Board member, GMIES	San Salvador	July 21, 1999	M
Anonymous	Owner, small monitoring firm	Los Angeles*	Sept 25, 1998	M
Athreya, Bama	Deputy director, ILRF	Washington, D.C.	Oct 10, 2002	N
Atilano, Jesse	President/CEO, Labor Law	Los Angeles	June 25, 1998	M
Bernstrom, Bill	Executive Director, Cal-Safety	Los Angeles	June 29, 1998	M
Bissel, Trim	Coordinator, Campaign for Labor Rights	Washington, D.C.	July 6, 1999	N
Blackwell, Ron	Director of corporate affairs, AFL-CIO	Washington, D.C.	July 7, 1999	U
Blanchard, David	Minister involved with GMIES	San Salvador	Aug 8, 1996	N
Blanco, Felix	President, Central of Salvadoran Workers	San Salvador	July 23, 1999	U
Brackley, Dean	Professor, University of Central America	San Salvador	July 15, 1996	A
Briggs, Barbara	Assistant director, NLC	New York	Apr 6, 1999	N
Campbell, Vera	President, Knitworks (division of Design Zone)	Los Angeles	July 28, 1998	B
Castillo, Cecilia	Assistant to the owner, Mandarin International	San Salvador	July 24, 1996	B
Castro, Pablo de Jesus	Professor of sociology, National University of El Salvador	San Salvador	July 11, 1996	A
Chavez, Sergio	Central American coordinator, NLC	San Salvador	July 26, 1999	N
Chicas, Eugenio	Assemblyman, Salvadoran National Assembly	San Salvador	July 25, 1996	G

Name	Position/organization	Place[a]	Date	Sector[b]
Coughlin, Ginny	Coordinator of Stop Sweatshops, UNITE	New York	April 8, 1999	U
Cowell, Susan	Vice-president, UNITE	New York	May 11, 1998	U
de Hahn, Esther	CCC of the Netherlands	Berkeley	July 17, 1998	N
De Magaña, Imelda	Vice-minister of Economy for Commerce and Industry, Ministry of the Economy	San Salvador	July 22, 1996	G
Esmond, Stephen	Owner and director, Garment Compliance Consultants	Los Angeles	July 23, 1998	M
Fuentes, Jiovanni	Organizer, Federation of Independent Associations and Unions of El Salvador	San Salvador	Aug 9, 1999	U
García, Gilberto	Economist, Center for the Study of Work	San Salvador	July 8, 1996	A
García, Gilberto	Economist, Center for the Study of Work	San Salvador	July 22, 1999	A
Gearhart, Judy	Outreach coordinator, SA8000 (SAI)	Berkeley	July 18, 1998	M
Geth, Connie	Coordinator of retailer contact program, DOL	Orange County	Sep 24, 1998	G
Gil, Paul	Senior project manager, MANEX	Berkeley	May 27, 1998	B
Hagelshaw, Andy	Bay area coordinator, Committee in Solidarity with the People of El Salvador	San Francisco	June 28, 1996	N
Hall, Gerald	District director, DOL	Los Angeles	June 12, 1998	G
Harvey, Pharis	Executive director, ILRF	Washington, D.C.	July 9, 1999	N
Henriquez, Marisol	Inspector, Ministry of Labor	San Salvador	July 28, 1999	G
Hernandez, Rosa Virginia	Organizer, COMUTRAS (women's section of the Democratic Workers' Central)	San Salvador	July 5, 1996	U
Horn, Hillary	National associate director of corporate and financial affairs, UNITE	Washington, D.C.	July 9, 1999	U
Howard, Alan	Assistant to the president, UNITE	New York	May 12, 1998	U
Howard, Alan	Assistant to the president, UNITE	New York*	Apr 2, 1999	U
Iraheta, Gerardo	Professor of sociology, National University of El Salvador	San Salvador	July 11, 1996	A

Name	Position/organization	Place[a]	Date	Sector[b]
Jailer, Todd	Member, Coordinating Committee for the Dignification of Employment in the Maquilas	Berkeley	June 27, 1996	N
Jairo, Jaime	Inspector, Ministry of Labor	San Salvador	July 28, 1999	G
Jones, Liz	Senior researcher, UNITE	New York	May 8, 1998	U
Juarez, Concepción	Coordinator of youth program, Movement of Women Mélida Anaya Montes	San Salvador	July 26, 1999	N
Jue, Gary	Director, American–Chinese Garment Contractors Association	Los Angeles	July 23, 1998	B
Kabori, Michael	Program director for business and human rights, Business for Social Responsibility	San Francisco	Feb 8, 1999	B
Kane, Lonnie	CEO, Karen Kane	Los Angeles	July 8, 1998	B
Karp, Roberta	Vice-president and general counsel, Liz Claiborne and Company; chair, AIP	New York	Apr 6, 1999	B
Kaufman, Eileen	Executive director, SAI	New York	Apr 7, 1999	M
Kernaghan, Charles	Executive director, NLC	New York*	June 13, 1996	N
Kernaghan, Charles	Executive director, NLC	New York	Apr 6, 1999	N
Konheim, Bud	CEO, Nicole Miller	New York	Apr 5, 1999	B
Leazar, Jennifer	Local coordinator, Committee in Solidarity with the People of El Salvador	San Salvador	Mar 26, 1998	N
Lee, Jay	Director, Korean American Garment Industry Contractors Association	Los Angeles	July 24, 1998	B
Levinson, Mark	Chief economist, UNITE	New York	May 11, 1998	U
Levy, Stan	General counsel, GUESS?	Los Angeles	July 8, 1998	B
López, Marlene	Lawyer, Movement of Women Mélida Anaya Montes	San Salvador	July 29, 1999	N
Mancillas, Pedro	Corporate director, Mandarin International	San Salvador	July 28, 1999	B
Manubens, Marcella	Director of human rights program, Phillips–Van Heusen	New York	Apr 8, 1999	B
Melawani, Irma	Director of contractor compliance, GUESS?	Los Angeles	Aug 7, 1998	M

Name	Position/organization	Place[a]	Date	Sector[b]
Metchek, Elsa	Executive director, California Fashion Association	Los Angeles	June 26, 1998	B
Miller, Lenore	President, Retail, Wholesale and Department Store Union	New York	May 11, 1998	U
Miller, Spencer	Owner, My Joy (in-house contractor for Little Laura)	Los Angeles	July 21, 1998	B
Molina, Norma	Monitor, GMIES	San Salvador	July 20, 1999	M
Monitor 1	Cal-Safety	Los Angeles	July 1, 1998	M
Monitor 2	Cal-Safety	Los Angeles	July 1, 1998	M
Monitor 3	Labor Law	Los Angeles	July 27, 1998	M
Morales, Kathy	Vice-president of manufacturing, Laundry	Los Angeles	July 14, 1998	B
Morril, Maureen Murtha	Senior adviser to the administrator, DOL	Washington, D.C.	July 6, 1999	G
Murtagh, E. J.	International labor officer, Bureau of International Labor Affairs, DOL	Washington, D.C.	Oct 11, 2002	G
Nangle, John	Solicitor general, DOL	Los Angeles	Aug 5, 1998	G
Navarrete, Dulceamor	Labor lawyer, Human Rights Institute of the University of Central America	San Salvador	July 27, 1999	N
Niepold, Mil	Director of programs, Verité	Oakland	May 18, 1999	M
Nova, Scott	Executive director, WRC	Washington, D.C.	Oct 10, 2002	N
Nutter, Steve	Western regional director, UNITE	Los Angeles	July 1, 1996	U
Nutter, Steve	Western regional director, UNITE	Los Angeles	July 6, 1998	U
Nutter, Steve	Western regional director, UNITE	Los Angeles	Feb 18, 1999	U
Otero, Rolene	District director, DOL	Los Angeles	Aug 6, 1998	G
Posner, Michael	Executive Director, National Lawyers' Committee for Human Rights	New York	Apr 8, 1999	N
Quan, Katie	Labor specialist, UC Berkeley Center for Labor Education and Research	Berkeley	Apr 31, 1998	A
Quinteros, Carolina	Monitor, GMIES	San Salvador	July 22, 1996	M

Name	Position/organization	Place[a]	Date	Sector[b]
Quinteros, Carolina	Monitor, GMIES; board member, GMIES	San Salvador	Mar 26, 1998	M
Quinteros, Carolina	Monitor, GMIES; board member, GMIES	San Salvador	July 30, 1999	M
Quinteros, Carolina	Monitor, GMIES; board member, GMIES	San Salvador	Aug 9, 1999	M
Ramirez, Aleida	Primero de conflictos, Federation of Unions of Salvadoran Workers	San Salvador	July 30, 1999	U
Rankin, Randy	Director of social accounting, PricewaterhouseCoopers	Pasadena	Sep 24, 1998	M
Razo, Joe	Senior deputy labor commissioner, DLSE	Los Angeles	July 31, 1998	G
Reinis, Richard	Apparel industry lawyer; founder, Compliance Alliance	Los Angeles	Aug 13, 1996	B
Reinis, Richard	Apparel industry lawyer; founder, Compliance Alliance	Los Angeles	July 3, 1998	B
Rodriguez, Joe	Executive director, Garment Contractors Association of Southern California	Los Angeles	July 13, 1998	B
Rosenblum, Jonathan	Independent Monitoring Project coordinator, ILRF	Madison, Wisconsin*	Mar 17, 2003	N
Saguero, Roberto	Assistant to Vice-minister of Economy for Commerce and Industry, Ministry of Economy	San Salvador	July 22, 1996	G
Sandoval, Marina	Foundation Boell (publisher of monographs on Central America)	San Salvador	July 28, 1999	N
Shaiken, Harley	Professor, UC Berkeley	Berkeley	Dec 8, 1998	A
Shea, James	International economist, Bureau of International Labor Affairs, DOL	Washington, D.C.	Oct 11, 2002	G
Shilling, David	Executive director, Interfaith Center for Investor Responsibility	New York	Apr 7, 1999	N
Solano, Cesar	Editor, economics section, *La Prensa Grafica* (El Salvador's largest daily)	San Salvador	July 11, 1996	P
Su, Julie	Staff attorney, Asian Pacific Legal Center	Los Angeles	July 29, 1998	N
Suzanne Seiden	General counsel, DOL	Washington, D.C.	July 9, 1999	G

Name	Position/organization	Place[a]	Date	Sector[b]
Tchaklian, Ed	Former state labor inspector	Los Angeles	July 31, 1998	G
Tchaklian, Ed	Former state labor inspector	Los Angeles	Aug 6, 1998	G
Toledo, Lisa	Audit manager, Heller Financial, Inc. (lender to apparel companies)	Los Angeles	Aug 6, 1998	B
Valdiva, Damian	Vice-president and director of monitoring, Labor Law	Los Angeles	June 25, 1998	M
Van Heerden, Auret	Executive director, FLA (at time of interview; currently president and CEO)	Washington, D.C.	Oct 11, 2002	N
Vela Cea, Ronoél	Chief inspector, Ministry of Labor	San Salvador	July 28, 1999	G
Wang, David	Owner, Mandarin International	San Salvador	July, 19, 1996	B
Worker 1	Garment worker	Los Angeles	July 22, 1998	W
Worker 2	Garment worker	Los Angeles	July 22, 1998	W
Worker 3	Garment worker	Los Angeles	July 22, 1998	W
Worker 4	Garment worker	Los Angeles	July 22, 1998	W
Worker 5	Garment worker	Los Angeles	July 29, 1998	W
Worker 6	Garment worker	Los Angeles	July 29, 1998	W
Worker 7	Garment worker	Los Angeles	July 29, 1998	W
Worker 8	Garment worker	Los Angeles	July 29, 1998	W
Worker A	Garment worker	San Salvador	July 8, 1996	W
Worker B	Garment worker	San Salvador	July 8, 1996	W
Worker C	SETMI leader	San Salvador	July 12, 1996	W
Worker D	SETMI leader	San Salvador	July 12, 1996	W
Worker E	Garment worker and supervisor	San Salvador	July 15, 1996	W
Worker F	ATEMISA member	San Salvador	July, 19, 1996	W
Worker G	ATEMISA member	San Salvador	July, 19, 1996	W
Worker H	ATEMISA member	San Salvador	July, 19, 1996	W
Worker I	ATEMISA member	San Salvador	July, 19, 1996	W
Worker J	ATEMISA member	San Salvador	July, 19, 1996	W
Worker K	Randomly selected worker at Mandarin	San Salvador	July 24, 1996	W
Worker L	Randomly selected worker at Mandarin	San Salvador	July 24, 1996	W
Worker M	Randomly selected worker at Mandarin	San Salvador	July 24, 1996	W
Worker N	Randomly selected worker at Mandarin	San Salvador	July 24, 1996	W

Name	Position/organization	Place[a]	Date	Sector[b]
Worker O	General secretary, ATEMISA	San Salvador	Aug 10, 1999	W
Worker P	Secretary of conflict, ATEMISA	San Salvador	Aug 10, 1999	W
Worker Q	SETMI leader	San Salvador	Aug 10, 1999	W
Worker R	Secretary-general, SETMI	San Salvador	Aug 10, 1999	W
Yap, Martin	Internal monitor, BCBG	Los Angeles	Aug 4, 1998	M
Youngblood, Randy	CEO, Apparel Resources Inc.	Orange County	July 6, 1998	M
Yu, Michelle	Legislative assistant to California State Senator Tom Hayden	Los Angeles	Feb 18, 1999	G
Zamora, Aracely	Ombudsman for women's rights, Office of Ombudsman for Human Rights of El Salvador (PDDH4)	San Salvador	July 23, 1996	G
Zepeda, Juan de Dios	Staff member, Democratic Workers' Central	San Salvador	July 6, 1996	U
Zollner, Anne	Labor rights officer, Bureau of International Labor Affairs, DOL	Washington, D.C.	Oct 11, 2002	G
Zuniga, Carlos	Inspector, Ministry of Labor	San Salvador	July 24, 1996	G

[a]Place names followed by an asterisk indicate that the interview was conducted by telephone.

[b]Sectors: A, academic; B, business (manufacturer or contractor); G, government official; M, monitor (specialized firms, apparel companies, or oversight organizations); N, NGO (nongovernmental organization: religious, women's, human rights, or labor advocacy); P, press; U, union staff; W, worker.

Appendix 4
Acronyms and Abbreviations

ACPA	Augmented Compliance Program Agreement
ACTWU	Amalgamated Clothing and Textile Workers Union
AFL-CIO	American Federation of Labor–Congress of Industrial Organizations
AFSC	American Friends Service Committee
AIFLD	American Institute for Free Labor Development
AIP	Apparel Industry Partnership
AIWA	Asian Immigrant Women's Advocate
ATEMISA	Asociación de Trabajadores de Empresa de Mandarin International, SA (Employees Association of Mandarin International)
BSR	Business for Social Responsibility
CCC	Clean Clothes Campaign
CCSC	Cal-Safety Compliance Corporation
CENTRA	Center for the Study of Work (El Salvador)
CEP	Council on Economic Priorities
CEPAA	Council on Economic Priorities Accreditation Agency
CLC	Collegiate Licensing Company
COVERCO	Comisión de Verificación de Codígos de Conducta (Commission for the Verification of Codes of Conduct)
CROC	Confederación Revolucionario de Obreros y Campesinos
DLSE	Department of Labor Standards Enforcement (State of California)
DNV	Det Norske Veritas (Norway)
DOL	Department of Labor (U.S.)
ECP	Employer Compliance Program
EMI	Equipo de Monitoreo (de Honduras)
ETI	Ethical Trading Initiative
FLA	Fair Labor Association
FLSA	Fair Labor Standards Act
FPCA	Full "Hot Goods" Compliance Program Agreement
GATT	General Agreement on Tariffs and Trade
GCA	Garment Contractors' Association of Southern California
GMIES	Grupo de Monitoreo Independiente de El Salvador
GSC	Global Social Compliance
GSP	Generalized System of Preferences
Hong Kong CIC	Hong Kong Christian Industrial Committee

ICCR	Interfaith Center on Corporate Responsibility
ICFTU	International Confederation of Free Trade Unions
ILGWU	International Ladies' Garment Workers' Union
ILO	International Labour Organization
ILRF	International Labor Rights Fund
IMC	Independent Monitoring Component
INS	Immigration and Naturalization Service
IRCA	Immigration Reform and Control Act
IRRC	Investor Responsibility Research Center
ITGLWF	International Textile, Garment, and Leather Workers Federation
ITS	Intertek Testing Services
IUI	Independent University Initiative
LARIC	Labor Rights in China
LCHR	Lawyers' Committee for Human Rights
MANEX	Manufacturing Excellence Corporation
M-CAP	Manufacturer Compliance Assistance Program
MFA	Multi-Fiber Arrangement
MSN	Maquila Solidarity Network
NAFTA	North American Free Trade Agreement
NCCGCA	Northern California Chinese Garment Contractors Association
NGO	Nongovernmental organization
NLC	National Labor Committee
NLRA	National Labor Relations Act
NLRB	National Labor Relations Board
OECD	Organization for Economic Cooperation and Development
OSHA	Occupational Safety and Health Act (or Administration)
PASE	Profesionales por la Auditoria Empresarial (Nicaragua)
PRI	Partido Revolucionario Institucional (Mexico)
RWDSU	Retail, Wholesale, and Department Store Union
SA8000	Social Accountability 8000
SAI	Social Accountability International
SETMI	Sindicato de Empresa de Trabajadores de Mandarin International (Union of Mandarin International Workers)
SGS	Société Générale de Surveillance
SITEKIM	Sindicato de los Trabajadores de la Empresa Kukdong International de Mexico
UCAS	University Coalition Against Sweatshops
UNITE	Union of Needletrades, Industrial, and Textile Employees
USAS	University Students Against Sweatshops
WRAP	Worldwide Responsible Apparel Production (program)
WRC	Worker Rights Consortium
WTO	World Trade Organization
WWW	Women Working Worldwide

Notes

NOTE: Full information for all interviews (including interviewee's name and position and the place and date of each interview) can be found in Appendix 3.

INTRODUCTION

Epigraph: Leslie Kaufman and David Gonzalez, "Labor Progress Clashes with Global Reality," *New York Times,* April 24, 2001.

1. U.S. DOL, press release, August 5, 1992.

2. Enriqueta Soto, testimony before U.S. House Committee on Education and the Workforce, *The Failure and Promises of the California Garment Industry,* 105th Cong., 2d sess., May 18, 1998.

3. Steven Greenhouse, "Sweatshop Raids Cast Doubt on Ability of Garment Manufacturers to Police Factories," *New York Times,* July 18, 1997.

4. In the southern United States, there is a growing percentage of African American workers (Blumenberg and Ong 1994).

5. As early as the 1920s, Los Angeles was the fourth-largest garment-manufacturing area in the country. By the 1950s, there was a growing movement to California (Bonacich et al. 1994). Although garment employment has declined in the rest of the country since the late 1970s, it rose in Los Angeles (Bonacich and Appelbaum 2000). This growth continued until the late 1990s.

6. Retailers increasingly cut out the manufacturer by producing their own private-label clothing. Although retailers are the most powerful enterprises in the industry, for structural and legal reasons that will be discussed later they have generally not been integrally involved in monitoring. Therefore, this book focuses on manufacturers as the locus of power in the monitoring relationships. It should be noted, however, that retailers are increasingly the targets of litigation, publicity, and other corporate-campaign strategies.

7. These terms are used interchangeably, although the word "jobber" arose to refer to those manufacturers that did not have an inside shop and therefore only farmed out the jobs to contractors (Selekman et al. 1925). I choose to use the word "manufacturer" because the brand-name companies are generally referred to this way within the industry and by government officials, unions, and others working in this realm. However, I acknowledge the move to call these companies "marketeers" or "merchandisers" in an effort to name what they actually do and clarify what they do not do (Appelbaum et al. 1994; Gereffi 1994).

8. For example, there have been cases in El Salvador in which workers have come to work in the morning to find the shop closed and the contractor moved to Guatemala or Honduras.

9. "Hot goods" does not apply to shipping goods within the state, and goods can still be sold once shipped.

10. Connie Geth, interview; Gerald Hall, interview. See also U.S. DOL 1995.

11. Lisa Toledo, interview. See also Joanna Ramey, "Labor Urges Lenders to Join Anti-Sweatshop Crusade," *Women's World Daily,* July 20, 1998; Times Wire Report, "Levi Closes Its Last Two Sewing Plants in the US," *Los Angeles Times,* January 9, 2004.

12. The NLC grew out of internal opposition to the AFL-CIO's support of U.S. military aid to El Salvador and Guatemala in the early 1980s because of the human-rights violations against unionists there.

13. A more detailed enumeration of the distinctions and similarities of these types will be the focus of later chapters.

CHAPTER ONE

1. The figures are from U.S. Bureau of Labor Statistics, *Employment and Earnings,* Washington, D.C., 1954. For 2002, statistics are available from the Bureau of Labor Statistics website: http://www.bls.gov.

2. During the writing of this book, manufacturers began to change this practice somewhat to avoid the consequences of new legislation in California. To avoid new liabilities associated with being "manufacturers," these entities began requiring contractors to purchase the cloth themselves, sometimes even financing them to do so.

3. Contracting work in response to growing strength of labor is not limited to this historical example. It can be seen in other industries, as well, such as strawberry farming in the 1960s (see Wells 1996).

4. In 1994, the ILGWU and ACTWU merged to form UNITE. The ILGWU was one of two main unions in the apparel industry. The other was the ACTWU, which specialized in organizing the textile industry and the men's clothing sector of the garment industry. Figures for the merged union after 1994 are not comparable with those for the single union. Therefore, the figure shows membership only up to the merger.

5. It is interesting to note that at the beginning of the twentieth century, the Women's Trade Union League was using the term "living wage" in the campaign for a minimum wage for women (Dye 1980: 147).

6. For a detailed discussion of the ban on homework, see U.S. Senate, *Amending the Fair Labor Standards Act to Include Industrial Homework: Senate Hearings 98-633,* 98th Cong., 2d sess., February 9, 1984.

7. In 1998, the New York State legislature passed a bill (SO7628) that created "hot goods" on the state level and thus a roundabout, but not direct, form of joint liability.

8. The practice of collecting liquidated damages was used in an attack on the union during recent congressional hearings chaired by Representative Pete Hoekstra (R-Mich.). Accusations have been made that the union cares more about collecting these large sums than retaining its members. See Robert Fitch, "Look Behind the Label: How UNITE Learned to Live with Sweatshops," *Village Voice,* January 20, 1998. The union, however, sees such fines as the only deterrent it currently has to keep companies from moving production abroad.

9. A detailed history and coverage of legal challenges to the Garment Industry Proviso is given in U.S. House of Representatives Committee on Education and the Workforce, *Hearing on the American Worker at a Crossroads Project: The Rationale for the Effect of the Garment Industry Proviso under Section 8(e)*

of the National Labor Relations Act, 105th Cong., 2d sess., August 6, 1998. This 1998 subcommittee was pushing to eliminate the proviso, which would have further weakened the declining position of garment workers in the United States.

10. Leslie Earnest, "Levi Strauss to Close Six Plants," *Los Angeles Times,* April 9, 2002.

11. Times Wire Report, "Levi Closes Its Last Two Sewing Plants in the US," *Los Angeles Times,* January 9, 2004; Leslie Kaufman, "Levi Strauss to Close Six U.S. Plants and Lay Off 3,300," *New York Times,* April 9, 2002; Jenny Strausburg, "Workers' Rights Protestors Call for Levi CEO to Resign," *San Francisco Chronicle,* April 12, 2002.

12. Restrictions on China may continue until the end of 2008 because of a special bilateral agreement (CRS 2002).

13. The theory that capital accumulation happens through extraction of value from periphery to core (Wallerstein 1989) has been challenged by theories of global commodity chains recognizing that capital is accumulated at various nodes on the chain, not in a single place (Appelbaum et al. 1994; Gereffi 1994). My point here is to focus on the effect of changing relations on workers, which is not the emphasis of either of these theories.

14. Annie Phizacklea (1983) theorizes that, as migrants gained more rights and became more militant, capitalists regained dominance by moving much of the production to the Third World.

15. Stephen Gregory, "Some Shrinkage in the L.A. Garment Industry; Employment: Cheaper Imports Are Partly to Blame in Loss of 3,700 Jobs in the County's Apparel Sector. But Nationwide, It Was Worse," *Los Angeles Times,* May 12, 1999; "L.A. County Apparel Industry Loses 5,000 Jobs," *Los Angeles Times,* May 25, 2000.

16. Los Angeles Economic Development Corporation, "LAEDC Releases 2002–2003 Industry Outlook for L.A. County Economy," press release, February 21, 2002.

17. The effects of IRCA will be discussed in more detail in Chapter 2.

18. Mary McKnight, garment enforcement coordinator, DOL, Los Angeles, telephone conversation, April 3, 2003.

Chapter Two

1. This question is addressed in Chapter 1.

2. The figures were taken from the DOL's *Garment Enforcement Reports* for 2000. The data were previously available on the DOL website but were removed in 2003 (in author's possession).

3. Comparison of DOL website in 1998 and 2003; also, conversations with DOL staff in Washington, D.C., and California.

4. Nancy Cleeland and Marla Dickerson, "Davis Cuts Labor Law Funding," *Los Angeles Times,* July 27, 2001. This is confirmed by advocates.

5. WTO courts have already handed down decisions that weaken several U.S. environmental laws; they also overturned a ban on beef with certain carcinogenic hormones and a European policy that helps Caribbean banana farmers.

6. Principle no. 3; see http://www.unglobalcompact.org for details.

7. The complaint was filed at the National Administration Offices in Mexico and Canada under the labor side accord of NAFTA. Shortly after the Mexican

National Administration Office accepted the case for review, the INS and DOL issued a new memorandum of understanding limiting their collaboration: see Bureau of National Affairs, *Daily Labor Report,* no. 227, November 25, 1998.

8. In one high-profile case in 1999, eight workers who were union activists and members of the union negotiating team were called into the manager's office at a Holiday Inn Express in Minneapolis, where the workers had recently won a union election. Each worker was detained by the INS, and deportation proceedings were initiated. The INS received considerable criticism for this incident and after considerable media and community pressure allowed the workers to stay in the United States, where they were eventually granted back pay. Most workers have not been so lucky. In fact, the U.S. Supreme Court has since ruled against such compensation.

9. Outstanding examples of this include Justice for Janitors Campaigns with the Service Employees' International Union; workers at American Racing Equipment, who began a wildcat strike and ended up represented by the International Association of Machinists and Aerospace Workers; and hundreds of drywallers who organized on their own but received legal and other support from the labor movement in Southern California (Fisk 2000 et al.; Milkman and Wong 2000; Zabin 2000).

10. In June 1998, the ACPA became the FCPA. However, 95 percent of companies are still under ACPA agreements.

11. Alan Howard, interview, April 2, 1999. Details of this event will be given in Chapter 6.

12. Mark Anner, interview, July 12, 1996. Anner is a long-time labor activist in El Salvador and one of the founding members of GMIES (the Salvadoran Independent Monitoring Group).

13. Although this process is not the focus of this book, examples include Sweatshop Watch, a coalition of union and nonprofit and legal-aid organizations that played an instrumental role in the passage of anti-sweatshop legislation in California (AB 633) in 1999, which provides the state government with new enforcement tools, and the Coordinating Committee for the Dignification of Employment in the Maquilas, a large coalition of unions, women's groups, religious organizations, and others in El Salvador that won revisions to the Law of the Free Trade Zones in the federal assembly.

14. Pharis Harvey, interview. The ILRF was the most labor-oriented NGO to stick with the AIP process (although they withdrew from the FLA board some time later).

15. Although most of the workers affected by the AIP process are not members or even potential members of UNITE, because they reside outside the jurisdiction of this U.S.-based union, UNITE was in a sense representing all garment workers. Some would argue, however, that UNITE prioritized the interests of U.S. workers over the interests of those working elsewhere.

16. For example, Richard Reinis, a garment-industry lawyer and founder of the Compliance Alliance, the largest monitoring consortium, said, "What this is is a privatization of a government function": Richard Reinis, interview, July 3, 1998.

17. Mary McKnight, garment enforcement coordinator in Los Angeles, used this phrase in a training session for manufacturers in Los Angeles on August 5, 1998. "Partnership" appears in the DOL's materials on monitoring.

18. *Stop Sweatshops Act of 1997,* HR 23/SR 626, 105th Cong., 1st sess.

19. Reinis, interview, July 3, 1998. Reinis was approached by Republican legislators about such a proposal. No bill made it through Congress.

20. This practice may be in peril. On May 2, 2002, the California Supreme Court decided that Nike could be sued for false advertising if it untruthfully represented the labor conditions in its factories. The suit (*Kasky v. Nike*), which was not about monitoring but about Nike's claims concerning conditions in Asian factories, had previously been dismissed on the grounds that Nike was exercising its free-speech rights under the First Amendment. The U.S. Supreme Court heard Nike's appeal in April 2003; the company asked the court to determine that such claims are protected as political speech rather than open to false-advertising challenge as commercial speech. However, the court dismissed the appeal on June 26 without deciding the merits of the case, thereby allowing the case to go to trial. However, Nike settled the suit in September 2003, so the issue was not resolved by the court. The settlement included a $1.5 million donation to the Fair Labor Association.

21. Gap's Code of Vendor Conduct, as posted on the International Labour Office website: http://www.itcilo.it/english/actrav/telearn/global/ilo/code/gap.htm (accessed March 4, 2004).

22. Bill Bernstrom, interview.

23. Monitor no. 2 (anonymous), interview.

24. Eileen Kaufman, interview. Social Accountability 8000 is a program of the Council on Economic Priorities.

25. Anonymous DOL official, interview.

26. Kaufman, interview.

27. There are also critiques of each of these campaigns, including the lack of integral involvement of workers and the accusation that by making minimal reforms, the companies managed to gain favorable publicity while conditions remained dismal.

CHAPTER THREE

1. See Appendix 2 for a full description of research methods, including observations.

2. Mary McKnight, garment enforcement coordinator, DOL, Los Angeles, telephone conversation, April 3, 2003.

3. Gerald Hall, deputy regional administrator, western region, wage and hour division, DOL, telephone conversation, March 25, 2003; McKnight, telephone conversation.

4. Bruce Sullivan, district director, DOL, New York, released to me a spreadsheet entitled "NY Manufacturers with Monitoring Agreements Statistics," in September 2002. These figures do not indicate how many of the companies dropped out of the agreement after signing.

5. Louis Vanegas, district director, DOL, New York, conversation, April 6, 2002.

6. In 1999, a firm in McLean, Virginia, signed the agreement, according to the list I received dated 2001. According to the DOL's website, a group of apparel manufacturers in Dallas also did a short-term stint on a monitoring agreement, signing in 1997. However, they were not included in the 1998 or 2000 list I

obtained from the DOL. In 2001, I was told by the DOL's district director in Los Angeles that the industry in Dallas had "dried up" and that he did not believe that there were agreements in other parts of the country: Don Wiley, district director, DOL, Los Angeles, telephone conversation, May 11, 2001.

7. Although the Los Angeles DOL claimed to have no list of those monitoring, the district director in New York told me in 1998 that 149 firms claimed to be monitoring, with only 23 monitoring under agreements at the time.

8. This statistic was released in the DOL's 1998 survey packet.

9. Rolene Otero, interview.

10. However, one internal monitor pointed out that if he failed to detect violations, he would lose his job, whereas an outside monitoring firm might simply lose one client: Martin Yap, interview.

11. Four interviews took place in person; one was conducted over the phone. The director of the one company (the only one the DOL had not known about) was extremely cautious, agreeing only to an anonymous interview, canceling that interview, and then consenting to speak on the phone (it turned out, at quite some length). The person who ran the sixth firm never responded to my messages.

12. In 1999, Cal-Safety merged with Specialized Technology Resources Inc., which offered product-testing services, and became a "full-service" monitoring and testing company: *California Apparel News,* September 3, 1999.

13. Some charged $500 for Mexico.

14. In 2000, the price of an international audit by an accounting firmed ranged from $3,500 to $5,000 per visit.

15. In 1998, Cal-Safety had staff members in New York, and Apparel Resources had staff in Texas.

16. Randy Rankin, interview; and telephone interview with a representative of Stonefield Josephson, September 25, 1998.

17. Otero, interview.

18. Sam Abebe, Vera Campbell, and Spencer Miller, interviews.

19. Contractors, manufacturers, and anonymous monitoring employees all told me about double billing. Spencer Miller of Little Laura described fighting with Cal-Safety over this issue. The heads of all three contractor associations in Los Angeles concurred on how the current system works: Gary Jue, Jay Lee, Joe Rodriguez, interviews.

20. Rodriguez, interview; letter outlining proposal, Joe Rodriguez to Gerald Hall, district director, DOL, November 14, 1996 (in author's possession).

21. Interviews with three principal contractors' associations, as well as with individual contractors.

22. Randy Youngblood, interview. Youngblood was referring specifically to the WRAP model.

23. Paul Gil, interview; IMC document; proposal, "Made by the Bay Compliance Monitoring," provided by Gil (in author's possession). See also Gil, testimony before U.S. House Committee on Education and the Workforce, *The Failure and Promises of the California Garment Industry,* 105th Cong., 2d sess., May 18, 1998.

24. Ester de Hahn, interview; CCC (n.d., 1999); Ascoly and Zeldenrust (n.d.).

25. Arrived at by cross-referencing a list of ACPA signatories with manufacturers from each case.

26. Gerald Hall, telephone conversation, May 8, 2003.

27. Anonymous interview.

28. Randy Youngblood, telephone conversation, July 14, 1998.

29. Bernstrom, interview.

30. Cal-Safety factory-investigation checklist.

31. Ed Tchakalian, interview.

32. Both Tchakalian and Yap, a long-time monitor, argued this in interviews.

33. Reinis, among others, argued that the reason employees do not reveal certain violations is that they actually benefit from a system of hidden payments that allows them to dodge taxes and collect welfare.

34. Anonymous interview.

35. Irma Melawani, interview.

36. Bernstrom told me this on July 7, 1998, after I went on an audit with his staff members and we were refused entrance.

37. Monitor 2, interview.

38. Reinis, interview, August 13, 1996.

39. Table 5 and Figures 9–11 are based on survey data provided to me by the DOL in the form of two tables: "Los Angeles Garment Manufacturing 1996 and 1998 Compliance Survey Findings" (dated May 1998) and "U.S. Department of Labor Compliance Surveys in Garment Manufacturing" (dated August 2000).

40. Don Wiley, telephone conversations, February 2001, May 14, 2001. I checked with both Wiley and Gerald Hall on May 8, 2003, to see whether there were any new, more definite numbers but was told that there were not.

41. If the verbally reported data are correct, this could be as high as 44 percent.

42. In fact, Hall argued that this number is fairly meaningless, because the threshold is so low it should not really be considered monitoring and that the effectively monitored category is what is meaningful.

43. It should also be noted that the effectively monitored column represents only 28 percent of the seventy factories investigated, or twenty shops. This is only a little more than a third of fifty-four sampled factories being monitored.

44. The official data show 44 percent of the most thoroughly monitored shops in compliance and 27 percent of all monitored shops. The verbally reported data basically reverse this. In either case, the highest figure is 44 percent.

45. This figure is arrived at by taking the average back wages owed in monitored shops in one quarter (ninety days) from the DOL data and multiplying that by the four quarters and then by the number of shops that are estimated to be monitored (70 percent of the total 5,000 registered shops). This method of calculation has been used by Hall (Bonacich and Appelbaum 2000).

46. This was largely due to the formation of the Compliance Alliance, a group of Los Angeles manufacturers who "proactively" signed their own negotiated version of the ACPA, although all were under scrutiny or pressure from the DOL for previous violations.

47. There was most likely an actual decrease in compliance between 1996 and 1998 that is not represented in the statistics. While the observable decrease in compliance in minimum wage (57% to 52%) may be attributed to a 21 percent rise in the federal minimum wage during this period, compliance in all areas probably decreased more than is represented by comparing the 1996 and 1998 figures in Table 5. The 1998 survey included only registered shops, the sample being taken from a state list of registered shops. In 1996, the survey sample was taken from tax data from the Employment Development Department, in which "underground"

or unlicensed shops were included. Therefore, the pool for the 1998 survey *should* have lower violation rates, because it is widely acknowledged that there are far more violations in the underground shops that were excluded. Since the pool was not kept constant, the fact that the 1998 figures do not show lower rates of violations would thus actually indicate a rise in violations. Moreover, the 2000 figures may actually also show erroneously high rates of compliance because the DOL took the unusual step of announcing the survey ahead of time, giving contractors a warning to clean up their shops.

48. U.S. Department of Labor, news release, "Only One-Third of Southern California Garment Shops in Compliance with Federal Labor Laws," USDL-112, August 25, 2000. Available at: http://www.dol.gov/esa/media/press/whd/sfwh112.htm.

49. In May 1999, the DOL in New York City won a judgment in such a case ("Garment Enforcement Timeline, June 1995–June 1999," entry for May 25, 1999, http://www.dol.gov/dol/esa/public/forum/timeline.htm, accessed April 26, 2000 [no longer available]). In January 2001, the Los Angeles DOL had won a similar "disgorgement" case against XOXO, and in May 2001 they were expecting a decision against another manufacturer (Don Wiley, telephone conversation, May 11, 2001). It is not likely that this tack will continue under the Bush administration.

CHAPTER FOUR

1. Gerald Hall and Joe Razo, interviews.

2. A former employee who had been there for several years told me this, and it was confirmed by another former employee. See "Confessions of a Sweatshop Monitor" (Appendix 1) for a description of such turnover and its effects.

3. Gerald Hall, speaking at Los Angeles training forum for monitors and manufacturers, August 24, 1998.

4. Razo, interview.

5. Ibid.

6. Randy Youngblood, telephone conversation, March 8, 1999.

7. Hall, interview.

8. Reinis, interview, July 3, 1998.

9. See Chapter 2 for statistics on this.

10. Bill Bernstrom, interview.

11. Sam Abebe, interview.

12. Julie Su, interview. Su was the attorney representing the workers in the El Monte case.

13. Greenhouse, "Sweatshop Raids."

14. Patrick McDonnell, "Industry Woes Help Bury Respected Garment Maker," *Los Angeles Times,* December 1, 1998.

15. Otero, interview. Otero was the DOL district director who originated the monitoring program.

16. List of ACPA signers dated October 2000; Don Wiley, conversation, May 11, 2001.

17. Gerald Hall, telephone conversation, March 25, 2003; Mary McKnight, telephone conversation, April 3, 2003.

18. Greenhouse, "Sweatshop Raids."

19. Otero, interview.

20. Hall, interview.

21. Reinis, interview, July 3, 1998. Reinis put together a group of manufacturers called the Compliance Alliance that signed a joint agreement with the DOL to monitor their own contractors.

22. Many people have used this image to describe monitoring, including California's Labor Commissioner José Millan.

23. Reinis, interview, July 3, 1998.

24. Razo, interview, July 31, 1998.

25. This was told to me by several sources.

26. Reinis, interview, August 13, 1996.

27. Joe Rodriguez, interview.

28. Bernstrom, interview.

29. Otero, interview; Razo, interview.

30. Worker no. 3, interview.

31. I heard this repeatedly in my interviews.

32. Razo, interview.

33. Julie Su, e-mail communication, April 30, 1999. Graciela Ceja also testified at a State Assembly hearing on pending garment legislation.

34. "Los Angeles Garment Workers Win Justice after Exposing Sweatshop Conditions Workers' Case Shows Failure of 'Private Monitoring,'" *Sweatshop Watch* (newsletter), vol. 6, no. 4 (December 2000). Guerra is most likely referring to quality-control staff who enter the factory on a regular, often daily, basis.

35. Jesse Atilano, interview; Damian Valdiva, interview.

36. Abebe, interview.

37. Letter, Jesse Atilano, in sales packet for Labor Law, "Dear Employer" (in author's possession; italics in the original).

38. Prices were not raised, according to the DOL, which wrote letters to the manufacturers about the issue. Information on pricing is also according to contractors' associations and even manufacturers, who explained that the retailers had not raised their prices.

39. ACPA, December 29, 1994.

40. FCPA, June 7, 1998 (the sixth version of the ACPA).

41. Half of the contractors in Los Angeles are Asian and 30 percent are Latinos. Most members of these groups are immigrants (Bonacich and Appelbaum 2000).

42. Otero, interview.

43. Ibid.

44. *Herman v. Fashion Headquarters,* 97 Civ 8806 (SHS) U.S. Dist. Ct. (1998).

45. DOL, press release no. USDL-218, December 7, 1998.

46. Anonymous long-time monitor, interview.

47. Otero, interview.

48. Anonymous, interview.

49. Harley Shaiken, interview.

50. According to the opinion given by John Conley, law professor and specialist in intellectual property law, in the matter of the University of North Carolina's requiring disclosure from its licensees.

51. Auret van Heerden, interview.

52. In a presentation to the University of California's Advisory Group on Codes and Enforcement, a representative of Nike said that the company had a 5–25 percent share of production in most of the garment factories with which it

contracted. The representative could not explain why, beyond broadly citing "business reasons."

53. John Nangle, interview.

54. Sweatshop Watch, "California Adopts Toughest Sweatshop Law of Its Kind in the Country," September 29, 1999. Available at: http://swatch.igc.org/swatch/industry/cal/.

55. Claudia Figueroa, "AB 633 Sends Many Scurrying to Comply," *Apparel News,* November 15, 2002.

56. Leslie Earnest, "Wet Seal is Set to Settle Wage Claim," *Los Angeles Times,* January 21, 2004.

57. Claudia Figueroa, "AB 633 Regulations at Heart of Wet Seal Labor Dispute," *Apparel News,* January 17, 2003; "Labor Panel Holds Retailer Liable," *Daily Journal,* January 15, 2003.

58. In this case, the lawyers also argued that the workers should be considered third-party beneficiaries of the DOL agreement and should be allowed to seek damages based on breach of contract. This was not resolved, because the case was settled out of court. See *Figueroa v. Guess?, Inc.,* State of California, Superior Court, filing BC 155 165.

59. Julie Su, e-mail communication, May 3, 2003.

60. Elsa Metchek and Gerald Hall, interviews.

61. The DOL's materials on the "No Sweat" campaign refer to this as a partnership.

62. According to Mary McKnight, garment enforcement coordinator in Los Angeles, at a DOL training session held on August 5, 1998.

63. Reinis, interview, August 13, 1996.

64. Vera Campbell, interview.

CHAPTER FIVE

1. Gerald Hall, telephone conversation, March 25, 2003. Gerald Hall is now the regional director of the DOL's wage and hour division.

2. Cavanagh specifically cites the involvement of ITT in the coup that ousted Chilean President Salvador Allende in 1973.

3. By 1987, however, Sullivan, a minister in Philadelphia, had abandoned the program, calling instead for full divestment.

4. All statistics in this section are taken from ILO 2000, except where noted otherwise.

5. U.S. International Trade Commission. Available at: http://dataweb.usitc.gov.

6. Descriptions of all of these conditions can be found in Bonacich et al. 1994; BSR 2000; Chapkis and Enloe 1993; CESR 1999; Fuentes and Ehrenreich 1983; Klein 1999; Kwan 2000; Ross 1997; Varley 1998; Verité 2000, and on the websites of various NGO organizations, including WWW, Sweatshop Watch, the NLC, the MSN, LARIC, and COVERCO.

7. Dozens of articles have been published over the past seven years on this case—recently, "Ciudad Juarez Finds More Females Dead," AP/CNN, February 19, 2003. There is also a recent documentary on the cases, called *Señorita Extraviada,* dir. Lourdes Portillo (ITVS, 2001).

8. David Fickling, "Misery of Rag-Trade Slaves in America's Pacific Outpost," *The Guardian,* March 1, 2003.

9. These complaints were alleged and documented in a lawsuit filed against eighteen retailers and their contractors in Saipan, Commonwealth of the Northern Mariana Islands, on January 13, 1999. Information here is from *Doe I v. The Gap,* the original complaint filed in the Central District of California's Western Division.

10. Mary Adamski, "Feds Uncover American Somoa Sweatshop," *Honolulu Star-Bulletin,* March 24, 2001.

11. Robert Collier, "Clothiers Fold on Sweatshop Lawsuit," *San Francisco Chronicle,* September 27, 2002.

12. Fickling, "Misery."

13. John Pomfret, "Chinese Workers Showing Disenchantment: Official Statistics Show Number of Labor Disputes Has Soared as Workers Complain of Late or No Pay, Layoffs and Corruption," *Washington Post* Foreign Service, April 23, 2000, A23. See also, for example, Robert Marquand, "China Faces Growing Labor Unrest," *Christian Science Monitor,* March 25, 2002; Erik Eckholm, "Leaner Factories, Fewer Workers Bring More Labor Unrest to China," *New York Times,* March 19, 2002; Philip Pan, " 'High Tide' of Labor Unrest in China; Striking Workers Risk Arrest to Protest Pay Cuts," *Washington Post,* January 21, 2002.

14. The workers at the PVH plant originally won recognition through an international solidarity campaign and a one-time monitoring effort by Human Rights Watch. For a detailed description of this case, see Armbruster-Sandoval 2000.

15. In 2000, Mexico's ruling party, the PRI, was replaced by a more rightwing party, the Partido Acción Nacional. The main union, the Confederación de Trabajadores Mexicanos, is allied with the PRI, which ruled for seventy years and still holds power in many local areas. Both parties strongly support foreign investment, export processing, and free trade.

16. The Salvadoran labor code states that the workers should give the employer a document containing this information, but in practice the workers file the document with the ministry, which forwards it to the employer: *Codigo de Trabajo,* ed. Ricardo Mendoza Orantes (San Salvador: Editorial Juridica Salvadoreña, 1999).

17. Madquisal produces Russell products for Duke, Purdue, and the University of Michigan, among others.

18. Robert Collier, "Labor Rights and Wrongs: Some U.S. Firms Work to Cut Abuses in Chinese Factories," *San Francisco Chronicle,* May 17, 2000.

19. Ibid.

20. Dexter Roberts, "A Life of Fines and Beatings," *Business Week,* October 2, 2000.

21. From a WRAP program packet (in author's possession).

22. According to a Salvadoran reporter, the costs are more like $7000 (Rosales 2002).

23. Rankin, interview.

24. Pedro Mancillas, interview.

25. The codes are available at the organizations' websites: http://www.fair labor.org, http://www.cepaa.org, http://www.wrapapparel.org, and http://www .workersrights.org.

26. "WRAP Principles (December 16, 1999)," reprinted in *Production Facility Self-Assessment Program* (WRAP, 2000), 7–8.

27. "Bush Picks Cuba Hardliner to Shape Latin American Policy," *Boston Globe,* March 24, 2001.

28. Kaufman, interview.

29. U.S. companies include Dole Food, Chiquita Brands, Eileen Fisher, and Toys "Я" Us. Amana, Avon, and Cutter and Buck have also been involved.

30. "SA8000 Standard Elements." Available at: http://www.cepaa.org/SA8000/SA8000.htm.

31. Bill Bernstrom, letter to the editor, *Bobbin* (February 1999): 6.

32. WRAP's website shows thirty-nine countries, but several of the pages are missing, so the names of the monitors cannot be determined.

33. According to information posted on the FLA's website as of January 2003, although one has reportedly withdrawn.

34. Carolina Quinteros, interview, July 30, 1999.

35. According to PricewaterhouseCoopers' response to my survey, returned in November 1998.

36. SAI has also accredited other firms specializing in systems management and ISO certification based in Italy and Germany.

37. T-Group Solutions is a subsidiary of Triburg, a firm that acts as a buying agent for two FLA member companies, but it is not allowed to monitor for its client brands (MSN 2002a).

38. Intertek Testing Services is accredited by all three organizations; Merchandise Testing Laboratories by the FLA; and Underwriters Laboratories by SAI.

39. For a complete list, see http://www.fairlabor.org/html/monitors/accredited-monitors.html; http://www.cepaa.org/certification_to_sa8000.htm; and http://www.wrapapparel.org/infosite2/index.htm. All list the accredited monitors and have direct links to the websites of those accredited groups.

40. See "Nike Statement Regarding Indonesia Report," press release, Nike, March 7, 2002. Available, along with the entire Oxfam report and response, at: http://www.caa.org.au/campaigns/nike/reports/machines/summary.html.

41. GMIES has received funding from unions in Canada and Spain, as well as from NGOs in the Netherlands, Germany, and Canada and from BSR in the United States.

42. Quinteros, conversation, April 5, 2002.

43. Bama Athreya, interview.

CHAPTER SIX

1. In 1999, six university members of the Collegiate Licensing Company and five U.S.-based licensees launched a pilot project to experiment with implementation of the CLC code of conduct. The six universities are Boston College, Duke University, Georgetown University, the University of North Carolina at Chapel Hill, the University of Wisconsin at Madison, and the University of Southern California. The five companies are College Concepts, Gear for Sports, M. J. Soffe, Jansport, and Zephyr Graf-X.

2. The IUI was conducted by BSR, the IRRC, and Professor Dara O'Rourke of MIT. Five universities participated in the study; PricewaterhouseCoopers was hired to do the factory audits. Project participants also collected general information from other in-country sources, including labor unions, government officials, and NGOs. In addition, BSR conducted a survey of ongoing government,

company, and NGO compliance efforts. Harvard University originally organized the study and paid half the costs; consequently, the research is often referred to as the "Harvard Study." The other participating universities were the University of Michigan, Notre Dame University, Ohio State University, and the University of California.

3. This belief has resulted in provision of services, including those addressed at family well-being, that often exceeds Levi Strauss's code or "Terms of Engagement."

4. Melawani, interview.

5. At the time of his first report, O'Rourke was a research associate with the Transnational Resource Action Center and consultant to the United Nations Industrial Development Organization.

6. O'Rourke told me this in a conversation following the release of his report.

7. Formerly known as international trade secretariats, global union federations are international trade union organizations based on industrial sectors such as the ITGLWF (International Textile, Garments and Leathers Workers Federation).

CHAPTER SEVEN

1. Tracy Wilkinson, "New Questions Arise for Salvadorans in Los Angeles," *Los Angeles Times*, January 12, 1992.

2. In 1988, as part of President Reagan's "Trade, Not Aid" initiative, the U.S. government gave El Salvador $32 million in startup costs to build export-processing facilities. Under Reagan, the US-AID had also underwritten the budget of the Salvadoran Foundation for Economic and Social Development, whose mission it was to promote U.S. investment in labor-intensive assembly production in El Salvador, with a focus on apparel (Kernaghan 1997).

3. Gilberto García, interview, July 22, 1999. CENTRA has conducted several studies of the industry.

4. According to a survey by CENTRA in San Salvador, more than 64 percent of workers have completed primary education. The women earn just below the average urban wage for female workers with the same education level, while men earn about 10 percent over the median urban wage. Men and women usually work in different sections of the maquilas, with men performing the more highly remunerated work of mechanics, shipment handlers, and sometimes quality-control staff (Quinteros 1998).

5. Ronél Vela Cea, interview.

6. This was down from thirty-two inspectors four years earlier.

7. Jaime Jairo and Carlos Zuniga, interviews. In 1996, the Ministry of Labor's entire budget barely surpassed the salary of the CEO of the Gap. Both were reported at just over $3 million (Anner 1998).

8. Among others, Dulceamor Navarrete, labor lawyer with the Institute of Human Rights at the University of Central America, mentioned that the Ministry of Labor is passive in its approach and that there is corruption within its ranks. Jiovanni Fuentes, an organizer with FEASIES (Federation of Independent Associations and Unions of El Salvador), criticized the ministry for its failure to investigate serious complaints and for advising workers to take small amounts of remediation rather than fight in court for all the money owed them. The government's complicity with labor rights abuses is also documented in a 110-page report released by Human Rights Watch in December 2003 (see HRW 2003).

9. *Codigo de Trabajo,* San Salvador, Republic of El Salvador, 1999, 81.

10. This point was also made by Navarrete and Fuentes.

11. In 1996, several sources reported that the ministry provided workers with letters stating that they had never belonged to a union, which employers often demanded. The fact that the ministry was willing to issue such letters involved it directly in the common and illegal practice of blacklisting unionists, who could not obtain such letters. In 2000, the Ministry of Labor released a US AID-funded report documenting abuses in the maquila industry that included blacklisting. The report was immediately retracted due to pressure from employers' associations. See also HRW 2003.

12. García, interview, July 8, 1996.

13. Annual sales have since risen to almost $14 billion.

14. Mandarin later changed its name to Charter, but it is referred to as Mandarin here to avoid confusion.

15. The NLC, previously the National Labor Committee Education Fund in Support of Worker and Human Rights in El Salvador, had originated within the U.S. labor movement in the early 1980s, with the goal of changing AFL-CIO support for U.S. intervention in the region. The NLC also engaged in accompaniment and campaigns to protest the detention and torture of unionists and to expose their executions. After the civil war ended, the NLC concentrated on the growing commercial relationship between U.S. companies and El Salvador. That is, the NLC was working to bring solidarity directly to union-organizing struggles.

16. At times, the Gap had up to 80 percent of the production in the plant. The second biggest client was Eddie Bauer.

17. Charles Kernaghan, interview, April 6, 1999.

18. Anner reports that U.S. newspapers have consistently joined the issue of sweatshops to child labor. At the peak of this trend in 1996, 314 articles appeared in major U.S. papers discussing sweatshops and child labor, whereas only 33 articles included both "living wage" and sweatshops and only 8 included "right to organize" and sweatshops.

19. SETMI was constituted in February 1995. On April 7, the executive committee was fired, and firings of small groups of workers at a time continued over the next few months: Virginia Hernandez, interview.

20. The ILGWU had held a boycott of the Gap the previous year over violations of wage and hour laws and harassment and intimidation of unionizing workers at a contracting factory in San Francisco: Arthur Friedman, "ILGWU Launches Gap Boycott with Rally at San Francisco Unit," *Women's Wear Daily,* October 13, 1994.

21. Cited in letter from Salvadoran activists dated October 13, 1995 (reprinted in Anner 2000).

22. These accounts are taken from reports of investigations conducted by the Legal Aid Office of the Archdiocese of San Salvador between February and June 1995.

23. This law was approved in January 1996 and included provisions stating that if national laws were violated, the company in question would lose certain benefits, including its exemption from various taxes.

24. For example, during the NLC's campaign concerning Disney's production in Haiti, the largest contractor there closed ten plants and moved most of the production to China: Trim Bissel, "A Step Forward," in *Mattel, Levi, Reebok*

Endorse Code, CCC, May 1999. Available at: http://www.cleanclothes.org/codes/5-99woksh1.htm.

25. When I asked ATEMISA leaders in 1999 whether their pay was sufficient, they replied that it was not but that they were not interested in trying to get a collective-bargaining agreement, even though they claimed that they had enrolled 92 percent of the workers. "By trying to get something," they said, "you don't get anything and you lose what you have": Worker O and Worker P, interviews. These statements stood in sharp contrast to the sentiments of other union leaders and even those of non-union workers. A worker from a different free-trade zone said about organizing, "Even though you get nothing, you don't allow them to mistreat you": Worker E, interview.

26. Worker C (SETMI leader), interview.

27. Worker D (SETMI leader), interview.

28. Interviews in 1996 with U.S. participants in these discussion: Minister David Blanchard; Dean Brackley of the University of Central America; and Mark Anner, a long-time activist in the country who was working for Norwegian unions at the time doing labor solidarity.

29. Agreement dated March 22, 1996 (reprinted in Anner 1998).

30. Quinteros, interviews, July 22, 1996, and July 30, 1999. To give a more complete view of GMIES's monitoring methodology: In a report by GMIES put out in May 2002, monitoring of three factories over a one-year period included three announced one-week inspections at each factory, and two to three unannounced visits per month. In this period, GMIES also conducted three personnel surveys, 960 in-depth interviews with female workers, twenty-five payroll checks, eight health and safety inspections, four water-quality checks, and four earthquake-safety inspections (GMIES 2002).

31. Leslie Kaufman and David Gonzalez, "Labor Progress Clashes with Global Reality," *New York Times,* April 24, 2001.

32. This failure to capitalize on the union's existence is in large part due to the fact that the union movement in El Salvador was fractured and weak. Another contributing factor was that the international solidarity campaign died out after the implementation of monitoring and Mandarin was largely forgotten.

33. Jiovanni Fuentes, interview.

34. Mancillas, interview.

35. Worker O, interview.

36. Worker R, interview.

37. Some connected the fact that the Gap now pays GMIES directly to the monitoring organization's inability to verify that the closing of the Tainan factory was related to the union campaign there. GMIES publicly questioned the companies' claim that they had no orders but said that without the union's willingness to share information it could make no definitive finding on the matter (GMIES 2002).

38. The groups were the Committee for the Defense of Human Rights, the Jesuits, the Women's Collective of Honduras, and Caritas Diocesana.

39. Quinteros, interviews. The Campaign for Labor Rights published a series of "position papers" from labor leaders on independent monitoring in 1998. Andy Banks of the teamsters' union lays out a fierce debate occurring in the union movement over the merits of monitoring and whether it can bolster unionization

efforts or simply acts as a type of substitute. He solves the dilemma by suggesting that unionization rights must be the priority in any code and monitoring effort, so that workers can eventually monitor their own conditions (Banks 1998). See also Ballinger 1998; Coats 1998; and Connor 1998.

40. At an August 2001 meeting in El Salvador organized by GMIES to explain the differences between the Northern monitoring programs (FLA, SAI, WRAP, and WRC), one unionists said dismissively, "It's just a bunch of alphabet soup."

41. Rosenblum, interview.

42. It should be pointed out that, according to COVERCO's latest report on two Gap factories, COVERCO received 521 complaints in eight months.

43. In El Salvador, the Gap (through Raggio's Jesuit connections) originally hired Eugene Palumbo, a progressive North American who had been a long-time resident in the country. Workers had positive things to say about Palumbo's role in resolving problems, although he has now left.

44. Worker R, interview.

45. Mancillas, interview.

46. Anonymous Cal-Safety monitor, interview, 1998.

47. According to GMIES, the Gap is planning to expand its use of independent monitoring to Taiwan, and it has already started using EMI in Honduras, PASE in Nicaragua, and COVERCO in Guatemala.

48. SETMI (which became STECHAR when the company moved and changed its name to Charter) is the only union in the maquila sector in El Salvador that is currently growing, according to Quinteros, although it has not been able to get a majority of the workers and win a collective-bargaining agreement. ATEMISA disappeared when the company moved in 2000.

49. Kernaghan, interview, April 6, 1999.

50. See chap. 5, no. 41.

51. According to Pharis Harvey, director of the ILFRF, who also described how the DOL's representatives gave pep talks and even twisted arms to keep the effort going.

52. Roberta Karp and Bud Konheim, interviews.

53. "Stop Sweatshops" bill, 1997 House Resolution 23 and Senate Resolution 626.

54. My Nexis–Lexis search showed that in 1996 alone, 694 articles appeared in major papers mentioning sweatshops in reference to apparel or garment. According to Mil Niepold of Verité, who uses the example of Nike in training for companies, 592 articles about Nike were published over a five-year period, and 92 percent of them were negative: Mil Niepold, interview.

55. L.L.Bean, Nike, Phillips–Van Heusen, Liz Claiborne, Nicole Miller, Patagonia, Hanover Direct, and Reebok. Kathie Lee Gifford was individually involved. Other original members included Karen Kane and Warnaco, which both dropped out before the FLA was formed, largely in protest of the idea that outside NGOs would be involved in monitoring. L.L.Bean dropped out of the FLA in 2000, saying that monitoring costs would be too high. There has been some other turnover in companies, with some members of the AIP not joining the FLA or dropping out—Hanover Direct and Nicole Miller—and new companies joining the FLA, including Adidas, Gear for Sport, Joy Athletics, Polo Ralph Lauren, Eddie Bauer, Zephyr Graphics, and Nordstrom for its private-label clothes. As of February 2003, there were thirteen participating companies, although Levi Strauss had

announced plans to withdraw from the association, citing the slowness of its monitoring program.

56. Michael Posner, interview.

57. "Workplace Code of Conduct," Fair Labor Association. Available at: http://www.fairlabor.org/html/CodeofConduct/index.html.

58. Karp, interview.

59. Floyd Norris, "Report Says PricewaterhouseCoopers Partners Made Improper Investments," *New York Times,* January 7, 2000.

60. Howard, interview.

61. David Shilling, interview.

62. FLA Charter, sec. VII(C).

63. UNITE, "Statement on the Apparel Industry Partnership," November 5, 1998; Steven Greenhouse, "Groups Reach Agreement for Curtailing Sweatshops," *New York Times,* November 5, 1998 ; Howard 1999.

64. Howard, interview, May 12, 1998; Steve Weingarten, UNITE, telephone conversation, March 20, 2003.

65. "Joint Statement on the Apparel Industry partnership by Lenore Miller (RWDSU), Jay Mazur (UNITE), and John J. Sweeney," November 4, 1998. Available at: http://www.sweatshopwatch.org/swatch/headlines/1998/aip_nov98.html #unions (accessed February 8, 2004).

66. In some ways, the split reflected long-standing differences. As Trim Bissel, director of the Campaign for Labor Rights, described the conflict in an interview: "There are crucial debates within the movement between those who believe that capitalism is an inherently reasonable system but the present state with sweatshops has gone too far versus those who think it is inherently flawed and the present state is just an extreme form." For Bissel, the split over the FLA represented a larger debate over the possibility of reforming capitalism. There was a division between those who saw the FLA as a means of finally pushing companies to take corporate responsibility seriously and those who saw it as legitimizing an inherently corrupt system.

67. Comment made at a meeting to discuss monitoring at the University of California, Berkeley, December 3, 1998.

68. This comment was printed in a letter that appeared in a series of responses to the "Sweatwash Award" given to the FLA by Corporate Watch. The "Sweatwash" article included information about connections and funding—for example, that executives from Reebok, the Gap, and Liz Claiborne all served on an advisory board to the Lawyers' Committee; that the National Consumers' League is heavily funded by corporations; that BSR is a membership organization for businesses; and that the Robert F. Kennedy Center works with Reebok on its human-rights award.

69. U.S. House of Representatives, *Floor Statement, Congressman George Miller, Amendment to HR 6: Expressing the Sense of Congress That Universities and Colleges Should Adopt Education Merchandise Codes of Conduct,* 105th Cong., 2d sess., May 6, 1998. http://resourcescommittee.house.gov/105cong/democrat/record/sweatshop.html (accessed February 25, 2003 [no longer available]; in author's possession).

70. California State Senate Concurrent Resolution no. 93, May 12, 1998.

71. Steven Greenhouse, "Activism Surges at Campuses Nationwide, and Labor Is at Issue," *New York Times,* March 29, 1999.

72. Justine Nolan of the LCHR told me that "the DOL is playing a large role in the university recruitment phase of the process": Justine Nolan, telephone conversation, May 3, 1999. Also, Maureen Murtha Morrill of the DOL explained that, although the DOL was not involved in recruiting the companies, it did participate in the recruitment of universities by sending out materials, answering questions, and updating the lists, among other things. In fact, FLA membership and "No Sweat University" were part of the broader DOL program: Maureen Murtha Morrill, interview. After leaving the DOL, Morrill went to work directly for the FLA as a liaison for the universities.

73. Such agreements often involve contributions to the universities, as well as payments directly to coaches. See Klein 1999 for details on some of the conditions of such sponsorship.

74. Steven Greenhouse, "Seventeen Top Colleges Enter Alliance on Sweatshops," *New York Times,* March 16, 1999.

75. Sam Brown reported to the UC Advisory Group on March 14, 2001, that in response to universities' new requirements of their licensees, 640 university licensees had joined the FLA in the preceding few weeks. By February 2003, almost 1,100 licensees had joined the FLA. About 60 percent (663) were in Category D, which consists of small companies with local production that are not required to monitor but are subject to the FLA complaints procedure. Another 410 companies were in Category C—small to medium-size companies whose production facilities would be pooled and monitored as a group. Sixteen companies were in Category B, which comprises large companies that agree to follow FLA's monitoring procedures for their college-licensed goods but not for their other production. Four companies—Adidas, Zephyr Graphics, Gear for Sport, and Joy Athletics—joined as participating companies. It should also be noted that Champion sold its collegiate-license business rather than participate in monitoring.

76. USAS, "Worker Rights Consortium for the Enforcement of University Licensing Codes of Conduct" (also known as the WRC White Paper), October 1999.

77. Conversations with Jeremy Blasi, USAS leader, Berkeley, April and May 2000, who was in direct contact with the decision makers in the UC system throughout this period. By February 2003, the WRC had 113 affiliates. The FLA had 176 university members.

78. By early 2003, USAS had chapters on more than 180 campuses, including in Canada. After their schools passed codes and joined the WRC, many students began to work on issues of living wages for workers on their own campuses, local labor struggles, and antiwar organizing.

79. The University of Pennsylvania later joined both organizations, as did many other schools.

80. The University of Oregon was eventually forced to withdraw from the WRC because the state governing body of public institutions deemed its membership to be in violation of state laws by unlawfully adding conditions to contracts. This decision relieved the university of being stuck between student protestors and Nike, and Knight once again began attending sporting events and giving donations.

81. Philip Knight, "Knight's Statement," published press release, *The Oregonian,* April 25, 2000.

82. Ibid.

83. This sentiment was expressed by UC administrators as well as by other administrators and some faculty around the country.

84. A United Nations summary of multi-stakeholder initiatives also noted the effectiveness of the "name and shame" strategy (Utting 2002).

85. I was present at this meeting as a graduate student representative to the advisory group.

86. The observer was present for a total of eight days.

87. When the FLA later decided to make reports public as a matter of policy, Verité withdrew from the organization as a monitor.

88. Such attention included nationwide protests on college campuses and in front of Niketown stores, as well as press coverage in the *New York Times,* the *Christian Science Monitor,* and London's *Financial Times,* among other publications.

89. The report was released simultaneously with a response from Nike, which had obviously viewed the report prior to release.

90. Scott Nova, interview.

91. The ILRF decided to withdraw, although the retiring director, Pharis Harvey, wanted to remain on the FLA's board. At the last minute, the FLA's director, Sam Brown, clarified that the ILRF had never been on the board but that representatives had served as individuals. Subsequently, the ILRF's name was removed from below Harvey's name on the FLA board list, although other NGO representatives still appeared with their associations.

92. Terry Collingsworth, e-mail communication, March 5, 2003.

93. Letter from Bishop Jesse De Witt, board chair, ILRF, to Sam Brown, executive director, FLA, October 4, 2001.

94. Another concern was raised within the ILRF's board over its association with the FLA. The ILRF's staff had found that their colleagues in producing countries did not trust the FLA and that the ILRF's close association with the organization was problematic.

95. Van Heerden, interview.

96. Approximately twenty-two universities contributed $200,000 in 1999 for a one-year project. In 2001, thirty universities contributed another $250,000. The ILRF has also received federal and foundation grants for this purpose.

97. The FLA's first public report states the belief that informed and aware workers are key to safeguarding codes. Also, Van Heerden, interview.

98. Van Heerden, interview.

99. Scott Nova, e-mail cover letter, March 19, 2003, accompanying the release of the WRC's preliminary report on the Primo Factory in El Salvador. Another example of the WRC's pushing the FLA to meet its standards and the WRC's benefiting occurred in the New Era case in New York. When the union finally achieved a collective-bargaining agreement, the WRC alerted the FLA (to which New Era was applying to become a member) that New Era had inserted a gag clause within the no-strike clause of the contract, under which workers would not be able to speak to not only the media (which is standard) but also to FLA and WRC representatives. Through the FLA's intervention, the company withdrew this addition. Nova, interview.

100. The home page of the FLA's website begins with this description of the organization. The term is repeatedly used in the association's first public report.

101. Derived from a comparison of the lists of affiliates posted on each organization's website. Students do continue to protest for university membership in the WRC. For example, in April 2003, ten students at Akron University in Ohio went on a hunger strike, demanding that their university join the WRC.

102. Nova, interview.

103. As reported by Homero Fuentes of COVERCO at a monitoring summit in Berkeley, California, on April 5, 2002.

CONCLUSION

1. Steven Greenhouse, "Groups Reach Agreement."

2. Kernaghan, interview, April 6, 1999.

3. This is a step toward the ratcheting standards proposed in Sabel et al. 1999.

4. In both the Mandarin and the Kukdong cases, complaints were made to government authorities about their failure to enforce the workers' rights. In El Salvador, pressure is being put on the government over blacklisting.

5. Presentation at the University of Southern California, December 6, 2001.

6. Van Heerden, interview.

References

AFSC (American Friends Service Committee). 2000. "Addressing Corporate Conduct: A Roundtable Exploring Initiatives at the Workplace, National and Multilateral Levels." Hong Kong, May.

Almaguer, Tomás. 1994. *Racial Fault Lines: The Historical Origins of White Supremacy in California.* Berkeley: University of California Press.

Amin, Amirul Haque. 2000. "La Realidad de codigos de conducta en Bangladesh." Pp. 190–202 in *Codigos de conducta y monitoreo en la industria de confeccion. Experiencias internacionales y regionales,* ed. Ronald Koepke, Norma Molina, and Carolina Quinteros. San Salvador: Heinrich Böll Foundation.

Anderson, Sarah, and John Cavanagh. 2001. *Executive Excess 2001: Eighth Annual CEO Comparative Survey.* Boston: Institute for Policy Studies and United for a Fair Economy.

Anner, Mark. 1998. "La Maquila y el monitoreo independiente en El Salvador." Report. GMIES, San Salvador.

———. 2000. "The Dynamics and Unanticipated Outcomes of the Anti-Sweatshop Movement in the U.S. and Central America." Paper presented at the 22nd International Congress, Latin American Studies Association, Miami, March 16–18, 2000.

Appelbaum, Richard. 1999. *Los Angeles Jewish Commission on Sweatshops Report.* Los Angeles: Los Angeles Jewish Commission on Sweatshops.

Appelbaum, Richard, David Smith, and Brad Christerson. 1994. "Commodity Chains and Industrial Restructuring in the Pacific Rim: Garment Trade and Manufacturing." Pp. 187–204 in *Commodity Chains and Global Capitalism,* ed. Gary Gereffi and Miguel Korzeniewicz. Westport, Conn.: Greenwood Press.

Armbruster-Sandoval, Ralph. 2000. "Globalization and Cross-Border Labor Organizing in the Americas: The Phillips–Van Heusen Campaign, the Battle in Seattle and Beyond" Paper presented at the Latin American Studies Association Conference, Miami.

Arnold, Pauline, and Percival White. 1961. *Clothes and Cloth: America's Apparel Business.* New York: Holiday House.

Ascoly, Nina, and Ineke Zeldenrust. N.d. "The Code Debate in Context: A Decade of Campaigning for Clean Clothes." Clean Clothes Campaign. Available at: http://www.cleanclothes.org/codes.htm.

———. 2001. "Discussing Key Elements of Monitoring and Verification." Center for Research on Multinational Corporations, September. Available at: http://www.somo.nl/monitoring/related/disc-key-elements.htm.

Ascoly, Nina, Joris Oldenziel, and Ineke Zeldenrust. 2001. "Overview of Recent Developments on Monitoring and Verification in the Garment and Sportswear Industry in Europe." Center for Research on Multinational Corporations, May.

Bacon, David. 2000. "The AFL-CIO and Immigrant Workers." *WorkingUSA* 3, no. 5.

Bair, Jennifer, and Gary Gereffi. 2002. "NAFTA and the Apparel Commodity Chain." Pp. 23–53 in *Free Trade and Uneven Development: The North American Apparel Industry after NAFTA*, ed. Gary Gereffi, David Spener, and Jennifer Bair. Philadelphia: Temple University Press.

Ballinger, Jeff. 1998. "Monitoring." *Campaign for Labor Rights Newsletter* 12. March–April.

Banks, Andy. 1998. "Monitoring: A Trade Union Perspective." *Campaign for Labor Rights Newsletter*. August–September.

Bardhan, Pranab. 2001. "Some Up. Some Down." *Boston Review*, February–March.

Barnet, Richard, and John Cavanagh. 1994. *Global Dreams: Imperial Corporations and the New World Order*. New York: Simon and Schuster.

Barnet, Richard, and Ronald Muller. 1974. *Global Reach: The Power of the Multinational Corporations*. New York: Simon and Schuster.

Baron, Ava, and Susan E. Klepp. 1984. " 'If I Didn't Have My Sewing Machine . . .': Women and Sewing Machine Technology." Pp. 20–59 in *A Needle, a Bobbin, a Strike: Women Needleworkers in America*, ed. Joan M. Jensen and Sue Davidson. Philadelphia: Temple University Press.

Barry, Tom, and Deb Preusch. 1990. *AIFLD in Central America*. Albuquerque: Resource Center.

Basu, Kaushik. 2001. "The View from the Tropics." *Boston Review*, February–March.

Bickham-Mendez, Jennifer, and Ronald Koepke. 1998. *Mujeres y maquila*. San Salvador: Heinrich Böll Ediciones.

Blasi, Gary. 2001. "Implementation of AB 633: A Preliminary Assessment," report, University of California, Los Angeles, Law School. Available at: http://www.law.ucla.edu?ab633preliminaryreportdraft72601.htm.

Bluestone, Barry, and Bennett Harrison. 1982. *The Deindustrialization of America*. New York: Basic Books.

Blumenberg, Evelyn, and Paul Ong. 1994. "Labor Squeeze and Ethnic/Racial Recomposition in the U.S. Apparel Industry," in *Global Production: The Apparel Industry in the Pacific Rim*, ed. Edna Bonacich et al. Philadelphia: Temple University Press.

Bonacich, Edna. 1973. "A Theory of Middlemen Minorities." *American Sociological Review* 38 (October): 583–94.

———. 1994. "Asians in the Los Angeles Garment Industry." In *The New Asian Immigration in Los Angeles and Global Restructuring*, ed. Paul Ong et al. Philadelphia: Temple University Press

Bonacich, Edna, and Richard Appelbaum. 2000. *Behind the Label: Inequality in the Los Angeles Apparel Industry*. Berkeley: University of California Press.

Bonacich, Edna, et al., eds. 1994. *Global Production: The Apparel Industry in the Pacific Rim*. Philadelphia: Temple University Press.

Brandeis, Louis. 1977 (1915). "Purpose of the Protocol," in *Out of the Sweatshop*, ed. by Leon Stein. New York: Quadrangle/The New York Times Book Company.

Broad, Robin. 2001. "A Better Mousetrap." *Boston Review*, February–March.

———. 2002. *Global Backlash: Citizens Initiatives for a Just World Economy*. Lanham, Md.: Rowman and Littlefield.

Brody, David. 1993. *In Labor's Cause*. New York: Oxford University Press.

BSR (Business for Social Responsibility), Investor Responsibility Research Center, and Dara O'Rourke. 2000. *Independent University Initiative: Final Report.* San Francisco: Business for Social Responsibility.

Burgess, Pete, and Maggie Burns. 1999. *Pilot Interim Review.* London: Ethical Trading Initiative.

Burgess, Pete, and Geoff Lane. 1999. *"Learning from Doing" Review. A Report on Company Progress in Implementing Ethical Sourcing Policies and Practices.* London: Ethical Trading Initiative.

Carnoy, Martin, Derek Shearer, and Russell Rumberger. 1981. *A New Social Contract: The Economy and Government after Reagan.* New York: Harper and Row.

Castells, Manuel, and Martin Carnoy. 1996. *Sustainable Flexibility: Prospective Study on Work, Family, and Society in the Information Age.* Berkeley: Center for Western European Studies.

Castells, Manuel, and Alejandro Portes. 1989. "World Underneath: The Origins, Dynamics and Effects of the Informal Economy." Pp. 11–40 in *Informal Economy: Studies in Advanced and Less Developed Countries,* ed. Alejandro Portes et al. Baltimore: Johns Hopkins University Press.

Cavanagh, John. 1997. "The Global Resistance to Sweatshops." Pp. 39–50 in *No Sweat: Fashion, Free Trade and the Rights of Garment Workers,* ed. Andrew Ross. New York: Verso.

Center for Economic and Social Rights. 1999. *"Treated Like Slaves": Donna Karan, Inc., Violates Women Workers' Human Rights.* New York: CESR.

Chapkis, Wendy, and Cynthia Enloe. 1993. *Of Common Cloth: Women in the Global Textile Industry.* Amsterdam: Transnational Institute.

Chishti, Muzaffar. 2000. "Employer Sanctions against Immigrant Workers." *WorkingUSA* 3, no. 6.

Clean Clothes Campaign. N.d. *Keeping the Work Floor Clean.* Available at: http://www.cleanclothes.org/codes/workfloor.htm.

———. 1999. *Overview of Recent Developments on Monitoring and Verification of Codes on Conduct in the Clothing and Sportswear Industry.* October. Available at: http://www.cleanclothes.org/codes.htm.

Coats, Stephen. 1998. "Reflections on Independent Monitoring." *Campaign for Labor Rights Newsletter.* April–May.

Cobble, Dorothy Sue. 1993. *Women and Unions: Forging a Partnership.* Ithaca, N.Y.: ILR Press.

Commons, John. 1977 (1901). "The Sweating System." Pp. 44–45 in *Out of the Sweatshop,* ed. Leon Stein. New York: Quadrangle/New York Times Book Company.

Compa, Lance. 2001. "Wary Allies." *American Prospect* 12, no. 12 (July 2–16).

Compa, Lance, and Tashia Hinchcliffe. 1995. "Private Labor Rights Enforcement through Corporate Codes of Conduct." *Columbia Journal of Transnational Law* 33, no. 3: 663–89.

Connor, Tim. 1998. "Independent Monitoring." *Campaign for Labor Rights Newsletter,* April–May.

COVERCO (Commission for the Verification of Codes of Conduct). 1999. "First Public Report, Independent Monitoring Pilot Project with Liz Claiborne, Inc." Report, Guatemala City.

————. 2000. "Second Public Report: Independent Monitoring Pilot Project with Liz Claiborne, Inc." Report, Guatemala City.

————. 2001. "A COVERCO Special Report: LCI's Standards of Engagement and the Unionization of Two Supplier Factories in Guatemala." Report, Guatemala City.

CRS (Congressional Research Service). 2002. *Textile and Apparel Trade Issues.* Washington, D.C.: CRS-Library of Congress.

CSDS (Center for Societal Development Studies, Atma Jaya Catholic University). 2001. *Workers' Voices: An Interim Report of Workers' Needs and Aspirations in Nine Nike Contract Factories in Indonesia.* Baltimore: Global Alliance.

Delgado, Hector. 1993. *New Immigrants, Old Unions.* Philadelphia: Temple University Press.

Dent, Kelly. 2002. "The Contradictions in Codes: The Sri Lankan Experience." Pp. 135–45 in *Corporate Responsibility and Labor Rights: Codes of Conduct in the Global Economy,* ed. Rhys Jenkins, Ruth Pearson, and Gill Seyfang. London: Earthscan.

Diao, Xinshen, and Agapi Somwaru. 2001. *Impact of the MFA Phase-Out on the World Economy: An Intertemporal, Globalgeneral Equilibrium Analysis.* Discussion Paper no. 79. Washington, D.C.: International Food Policy Research Institute. Available at: http://www.cgiar.org/ifpri/divs/tmd/dp.htm.

Dicken, Peter. 1992. *Global Shift: The Internationalization of Economic Activity.* New York: Guilford Press.

Dreier, Peter, and Richard Appelbaum. 1999. "The Campus Anti-Sweatshop Movement," *American Prospect* 10, no. 46 (September–October).

Dublin, Thomas. 1979. *Women at Work.* New York: Columbia University Press.

Dyche, John. 1977 (1914). "The Board of Grievances." Pp. 123–24 in *Out of the Sweatshop,* ed. Leon Stein. New York: Quadrangle/New York Times Book Company.

Dye, Nancy Schrom. 1980. *As Equals and as Sisters: Feminism, the Labor Movement and the Women's Trade Union League of New York.* Columbia: University of Missouri Press.

Edelman, Laura, Christopher Uggen, and Howard Erlanger. 1999. "The Endogenity of Legal Regulation: Grievance Procedures as Rational Myth." *American Journal of Sociology* 105, no. 2: 406–54.

Edwards, Richard. 1979. *Contested Terrain: The Transformation of the Workplace in the Twentieth Century.* New York: Basic Books.

Eisenstein, Zillah, ed. 1979. *Capitalist Patriarchy and the Case for Socialist Feminism.* New York: Monthly Review Press.

Enloe, Cynthia. 1993. "We Are What We Wear—The Dilemma of the Feminist Consumer." Pp. 115–19 in *Of Common Cloth: Women in the Global Textile Industry,* ed. Wendy Chapkis and Cynthia Enloe. Amsterdam: Transnational Institute.

Esbenshade, Jill. 1999. "Monitoring in the Garment Industry: Lessons from Los Angeles." Working paper, Chicano/Latino Policy Project, University of California at Berkeley.

Etienne, Jannick. 2000. "Monitoreando a Mickey Mouse en Haiti." Pp. 170–77 in *Codigos de conducta y monitoreo en la industria de confeccion. Experiencias internacionales y regionales,* ed. Ronald Koepke, Norma Molina, and Carolina Quinteros. San Salvador: Heinrich Böll Foundation.

Fantasia, Rick. 1988. *Cultures of Solidarity.* Berkeley: University of California Press.

Featherstone, Liza, and United Students against Sweatshops. 2002. *Students against Sweatshops.* London: Verso.

Fernandez-Kelly, María Patricia. 1983. *For We Are Sold, I and My People: Women and Industry in Mexico's Frontier.* Albany: State University of New York Press.

Fernandez-Kelly, María, and Ana Garcia. 1989. "Informalizaion at the Core: Hispanic Women, Homework and the Advanced Capitalist State." Pp. 247–64 in *Informal Economy: Studies in Advanced and Less Developed Countries,* ed. Alejandro Portes et al. Baltimore: Johns Hopkins University Press.

Finn Scott, Miriam. 1977 (1910). "What the Women Strikers Won." P. 84 in *Out of the Sweatshop,* ed. Leon Stein. New York: Quadrangle/New York Times Book Company.

Fisk, Catherine, Daniel Mitchell, and Christopher Erickson. 2000. "Union Representation of Immigrant Janitors in Southern California: Economic and Legal Challenges." Pp. 199–224 in *Organizing Immigrants: The Challenge for Unions in Contemporary California,* ed. Ruth Milkman. Ithaca, N.Y.: ILR Press.

FLA (Fair Labor Association). 2003. "Fair Labor Association First Public Report: Towards Improving Workers' Lives." Washington, D.C.

Frundt, Henry. 1999. "Cross-Border Organizing in the Apparel Industry: Lessons from Central America and the Caribbean." *Labor Studies Journal* 24, no. 1: 89–106

Fuentes, Annette, and Barbara Ehrenreich. 1983. *Women in the Global Factory.* Boston: South End Press.

Fung, Archon, Dara O'Rourke, and Charles Sabel. 2001. "Realizing Labor Standards." *Boston Review,* February–March.

Gereffi, Gary. 1994. "The Organization of Buyer-Driven Commodity Chains," in *Commodity Chains and Global Capitalism,* ed. Gary Gereffi and Miguel Korzeniewicz. Westport, Conn.: Greenwood Press.

Gereffi, Gary, David Spener, and Jennifer Bair. 2002. *Free Trade and Uneven Development: The North American Apparel Industry after NAFTA.* Philadelphia: Temple University Press.

Gill, Jennifer. 2001. "'We're Back to Serfs and Royalty.'" *Business Week,* April 9.

GMIES (Grupo de Monitoreo Independiente de El Salvador). 1997a. "Primer informe publico del Grupo de Monitoreo Independiente de El Salvador." Report, San Salvador, April.

———. 1997b. "Segundo informe publico del Grupo de Monitoreo Independiente de El Salvador." Report, San Salvador, December.

———. 2002. "Verification of Compliance with Salvadoran Labor Law and the Gap Inc. Code of Conduct in Four Companies in El Salvador." Report corresponding to the third set of visits held between March and April 2002. San Salvador, May.

Gordon, David, Richard Edwards, and Michael Reich. 1982. *Segmented Work, Divided Workers.* Cambridge: Cambridge University Press.

Graubart, Jonathan. 2002. "Giving Teeth to NAFTA's Labor Side Agreement." Pp. 203–22 in *Linking Trade, Environment and Social Cohesion: NAFTA Experiences, Global Challenges,* ed. John Kirton and Virginia MacLaren. Aldershot: Ashgate.

Green, Duncan. 1988. "ETI Southern Participation Conference." Available at: http://www.cleanclothes.org/codes/edu98-09.htm#action.

Hale, Angela. 2000. *Phasing Out of the Multi Fibre Arrangement: What Does It Mean for Garment Workers?* [briefing paper]. Manchester: Women Working Worldwide.

Harrison, Bennet, and Barry Bluestone. 1988. *The Great U-Turn: Corporate Restructuring and the Polarizing of America.* New York: Basic Books.

Hartman, Heidi. 1979. "Capitalism, Patriarchy and Job Segregation by Sex." Pp. 206–47 in *Capitalist Patriarchy and the Case for Socialist Feminism,* ed. Zillah Eisenstein. New York: Monthly Review Press.

Harvey, Pharis J., Terry Collingsworth, and Bama Athreya. 1998. *Developing Effective Mechanisms for Implementing Labor Rights in the Global Economy.* Discussion paper, International Labor Rights Fund, Washington, D.C.

Haworth, Nigel, and Stephen Hughes. 2000. *Death of a Social Clause,* Manchester Papers in Politics Series. Manchester: University of Manchester.

Hossfeld, Karen. 1990. "Their Logic against Them: Contradictions in Sex, Race and Class in Silicon Valley." Pp. 149–78 in *Women Workers and Global Restructuring,* ed. Kathryn Ward. Ithaca, N.Y.: ILR Press.

Howard, Alan. 1997. "Labor, History, and Sweatshops in the New Global Economy." Pp. 151–82 in *No Sweat: Fashion, Free Trade and the Rights of Garment Workers,* ed. Andrew Ross. New York: Verso.

———. 1999. "Why Unions Can't Support the Apparel Industry Sweatshop Code." *WorkingUSA* 3, no. 2 (July–August): 34–52

HRW (Human Rights Watch). 2000. "Unfair Advantage: Workers' Freedom of Association in the United States under International Human Rights Standards." Available at: http://www.hrw.org/reports/2000/uslabor.

———. 2003. *Deliberate Indifference: El Salvador's Failure to Protect Workers' Rights.* Available at: http://hrw.org/reports/2003/elsalvador1203/.

ICCR (Interfaith Center on Corporate Responsibility). 1998. "Footwear Manufacturing Fact-Finding Report: Nike and Reebok Plants in Indonesia, Vietnam, China." New York.

IHS (Insan Hitawasana Sejahtera). 1999. "Peduli Hak: Caring for Rights. An Intensive Research, Evaluation and Remediation initiative in Two Indonesian Factories Manufacturing Reebok Footwear." Report. Jakarta.

ILO (International Labour Organization). 2000. *Labour Practices in the Footwear, Leather, Textiles and Clothing Industries.* Geneva: International Labour Organization.

International Confederation of Free Trade Unions (ICFTU). 2002. *Annual Survey of Violations of Trade Union Rights.* Available at: http://www.icftu.org.

Jeffcott, Bob, and Lynda Yanz. 2000. *Codes of Conduct, Government Regulation and Worker Organizing.* Toronto: Maquila Solidarity Network.

Jenkins, Rhys. 2002. "Political Economy of Codes of Conduct." Pp. 13–30 in *Corporate Responsibility and Labor Rights: Codes of Conduct in the Global Economy,* ed. Rhys Jenkins, Ruth Pearson, and Gill Seyfang. London: Earthscan.

Jensen, Joan M., and Sue Davidson, eds. 1984. *A Needle, a Bobbin, a Strike: Women Needleworkers in America.* Philadelphia: Temple University Press.

Johnston, Paul. 1994. *Success while Others Fail: Social Movement Unionism and the Public Workplace.* Ithaca, N.Y.: ILR Press.

Karl, Marilee and Choi Wen Cheung. 1993. "Resistance, Strikes and Strategies." Pp. 91–98 in *Of Common Cloth: Women in the Global Textile Industry,* ed. Wendy Chapkis and Cynthia Enloe. Amsterdam: Transnational Institute.

Kernaghan, Charles. 1997. "Paying to Lose Our Jobs." Pp. 79–94 in *No Sweat: Fashion, Free Trade and the Rights of Garment Workers*, ed. Andrew Ross. New York: Verso.

Kessler, Judi. 2002. "The Impact of North American Economic Integration on the Los Angeles Apparel Industry." Pp. 74–99 in *Free Trade and Uneven Development: The North American Apparel Industry after NAFTA*, ed. Gary Gereffi, David Spener, and Jennifer Bair. Philadelphia: Temple University Press.

Kessler-Harris, Alice. 1982. *Out to Work: A History of Wage-Earning Women in the United States*. Oxford: Oxford University Press.

Klein, Naomi. 1999. *No Logo: Taking Aim at the Brand Name Bullies*. New York: Picador.

Koepke, Ronald. 2000. "Las Experiencias del Equipo Monitoreo Independiente de Honduras." Pp. 100–119 in *Codigos de conducta y monitoreo en la industria de confeccion. Experiencias internacionales y regionales*, ed. Ronald Koepke, Norma Molina, and Carolina Quinteros. San Salvador: Heinrich Böll Foundation.

Kwan, Alice. 2000. *Report from China: Producing for Adidas and Nike*. Hong Kong: Hong Kong Christian Industrial Committee.

LARIC (Labour Rights in China). 1999a. "Hong Kong NGO Seminar on Codes of Conduct 15 July 1999." Seminar Report, Asia Monitor Resource Center, Hong Kong.

———. 1999b. *No Illusions: Against the Global Cosmetic SA 8000*. Hong Kong: Labour Rights in China.

Laslett, John. 1993. "Gender, Class or Ethno-Cultural Struggle—The Problematic Relationship between Rose Pesotta and the Los Angeles ILGWU." *California History* 72, no. 1: 20–39.

Laslett, John, and Mary Tyler. 1989. *The ILGWU in Los Angeles, 1907–1988*. Inglewood, Calif.: Ten Star Press.

Lee, Seung Hoon, and Ho Keun Song. 1994. "The Korean Garment Industry: From Authoritarian Patriachism to Industrial Paternalism." Pp. 147–61 in *Global Production: The Apparel Industry in the Pacific Rim*, ed. Edna Bonacich et al. Philadelphia: Temple University Press.

Leibhold, Peter and Harry Rubenstein. 1999. *Between a Rock and a Hard Place: A History of American Sweatshops, 1820–Present*. Los Angeles: UCLA Asian Ameican Studies Center and Simon Weisenthal Center Museum of Tolerance.

Levinson, Mark. 2001. "Wishful Thinking." *Boston Review*, February–March.

Light, Ivan, and Edna Bonacich. 1988. *Immigrant Entrepreneurs: Koreans in Los Angeles, 1965–1982*. Berkeley: University of California Press.

Louie, M. C. 1992. "Immigrant Women in Bay Area Garment Sweatshops." *Amerasia Journal* 18, no. 1: 1–27.

Martens, Margaret, and Swasti Mitter. 1994. *Women in Trade Unions: Organizing the Unorganized*. Geneva: International Labour Office.

Martinez, Julia, and Carolina Quinteros. 1997. *Situacion de la mujeres en las organizaciones laborales salvadoreñas: Una aproximación*. San Salvador: Proyecto Escuela de Formación Sindical en Centroamerica.

Marx, Karl. 1978 (1849). "Wage Labour and Capital." In *The Marx-Engels Reader*, ed. Robert Tucker. New York: W. W. Norton.

Mazur, Jay. 1998. "Testimony before the Subcommittee and Investigations of the Committee on Education and the Workforce." *Hearing on the American Worker at a Crossroads Project: The Rationale for the Effect of the Garment Industry*

Proviso under Section 8(e) of the National Labor Relations Act, 105th Cong., 2d sess., August 6, 1998. U.S. House of Representatives Committee on Education and the Workforce

Meier, Matt and Feliciano Ribera. 1993. *Mexican Americans, American Mexicans.* Hill and Wang.

Milkman, Ruth. 1985. "Women Workers, Feminism and the Labor Movement since the 1960s." Pp. 300–322 in *Women, Work and Protest,* ed. Ruth Milkman. Boston: Routledge.

———, ed. 2000. *Organizing Immigrants: The Challenge for Unions in Contemporary California.* Ithaca, N.Y.: ILR Press.

Milkman, Ruth, and Kent Wong. 2000. "Organizing the Wicked City: The 1992 California Drywallers Strike." Pp. 169–98 in *Organizing Immigrants: The Challenge for Unions in Contemporary California,* ed. Ruth Milkman. Ithaca, N.Y.: ILR Press.

Mitter, Swasti. 1994. "A Comparative Survey." Pp. 3–16 in *Women in Trade Unions: Organizing the Unorganized,* ed. Margaret Martens and Swasti Mitter. Geneva: International Labour Office.

Moberg, David. 2001. "Unions and the State." *Boston Review,* February–March.

Molina, Norma, and Carolina Quinteros. 2000. "El Monitoreo independiente en El Salvador." Pp. 82–99 in *Codigos de conducta y monitoreo en la industria de confeccion. Experiencias internacionales y regionales,* ed. Ronald Koepke, Norma Molina, and Carolina Quinteros. San Salvador: Heinrich Böll Foundation.

MSN (Maquila Solidarity Network). 2001. "Codes Memo: Number 8." Toronto, August. Available at: http://www.maquilasolidarity.org.

———. 2002a. "Codes Memo: Number 12." Toronto, November. Available at: http://www.maquilasolidarity.org.

———. 2002b. "Codes Monitoring and Worker Organizing, Challenges and Opportunities," Seminar report (from Puebla, Mexico), Toronto. Available at: http://www.maquilasolidarity.org.

———. 2003. "Codes Memo: Number 13." Toronto, January. Available at: http://www.maquilasolidarity.org.

NICWJ (National Interfaith Committee for Worker Justice). 1998. "Cross Border Blues: A Call for Justice for Maquiladora Workers in Tehuacán." Chicago.

NLC (National Labor Committee). 1999. "Fired for Crying to the Gringos: The Women in El Salvador Who Sew Liz Claiborne Garments Speak Out Asking for Justice." Report, New York.

———. 2000. *Made in China: The Role of US Companies in Denying Human and Worker Rights.* Report, New York.

Omi, Michael, and Howard Winant. 1986. *Racial Formation in the United States: From the 1960s to the 1980s.* New York: Routledge.

Ong, Paul, Edna Bonacich, and Lucie Cheng, eds. 1994. *The New Asian Immigration in Los Angeles and Global Restructuring.* Philadelphia: Temple University Press.

O'Rourke, Dara. 1997. *Smoke from a Hired Gun: A Critique of Nike's Labor and Environmental Auditing.* San Francisco: Transnational Resource and Action Center.

———. 2000. "Monitoring the Monitors: A Critique of PricewaterhouseCoopers' Labor Monitoring." White paper, September 28. Available at: http://web.mit.edu/dorourke/www/PDF/pwc.pdf.

———. 2003. "Outsourcing Regulation: Analyzing Nongovernmental Systems of Labor Standards and Monitoring." *Policy Studies Journal* 31, no. 1: 1–30.

Oxfam GB, FLACSO, PIFIC-PUCMM, and CIPAF. 1998. "Evaluation of Levi Strauss and Company's Terms of Engagement Process." Santo Domingo.

Pearson, Ruth, and Gill Seyfang. 2002. "'I'll Tell You What I Want . . .': Women Workers and Codes of Conduct." Pp. 43–60 in *Corporate Responsibility and Labor Rights: Codes of Conduct in the Global Economy,* ed. Rhys Jenkins, Ruth Pearson, and Gill Seyfang. London: Earthscan.

Petersen, Kurt. 1994. "The Maquila Revolution in Guatemala." Pp. 268–86 in *Global Production: The Apparel Industry in the Pacific Rim,* ed. Edna Bonacich et al. Philadelphia: Temple University Press.

Phizacklea, Annie. 1983. *One Way Ticket: Migration and Female Labour.* London: Routledge.

Piñeda, Magali. 2000. "El Caso de Levi Strauss and Company en la Republicá Dominicana." Pp. 120–39 in *Codigos de conducta y monitoreo en la industria de confeccion. Experiencias internacionales y regionales,* ed. Ronald Koepke, Norma Molina, and Carolina Quinteros. San Salvador: Heinrich Böll Foundation.

Piore, Michael. 1997. "The Economics of the Sweatshop." Pp. 135–42 in *No Sweat: Fashion, Free Trade and the Rights of Garment Workers,* ed. Andrew Ross. New York: Verso.

Portes, Alejandro, Manuel Castells, and Laura Benton. 1989. *Informal Economy: Studies in Advanced and Less Developed Countries.* Baltimore: Johns Hopkins University Press.

Portes, Alejandro, and Robert Manning. 1986. "The Immigrant Enclave: Theory and Empirical Examples." Pp. 47–69 in *Competitive Ethnic Relations,* ed. Susan Olzak. Orlando: Academic Press.

Prieto, Marina, and Jem Bendell. 2002. "If You Want to Help Us, Then Start Listening to Us!" Occasional Paper, New Academy of Business, Bath, U.K., December.

Quinteros, Carolina. 2001. "Union Sundown?" P. 63 in "The NGO-Industrial Complex," by Gary Gereffi, Ronie Garcia-Johnson, and Erika Sasser. *Foreign Policy,* no. 125 (July–August): 56–65.

Quinteros, Carolina, Gilberto García, Roberto Góchez, and Norma Molina. 1998. *Dinamica de la actividad maquiladora y derechos laborales en el Salvador.* San Salvador: Centro de Estudios del Trabajo.

Reich, Robert. 1991. *The Work of Nations.* New York: Vintage Books.

Reimers, David. 1985. *Still the Golden Door: The Third World Comes to America.* New York: Columbia University Press.

Roberts, Lesley. 2002. "Beyond Codes: Lessons from the Pentland Experience." Pp. 79–89 in *Corporate Responsibility and Labor Rights: Codes of Conduct in the Global Economy,* ed. Rhys Jenkins, Ruth Pearson, and Gill Seyfang. London: Earthscan.

Rosales, Metzi. 2002. "Un cambio forzado." *Enfoque,* October 27.

Ross, Andrew, ed. 1997. *No Sweat: Fashion, Free Trade and the Rights of Garment Workers.* New York: Verso.

Ross, Robert. 2002. "The New Sweatshops in the United States: How New, How Real, How Many, and Why?" Pp. 100–122 in *Free Trade and Uneven Development: The North American Apparel Industry after NAFTA,* ed. Gary Gereffi, David Spener, and Jennifer Bair. Philadelphia: Temple University Press.

Rothstein, Richard. 1989. *Keeping Jobs in Fashion: Alternatives to the Euthanasia of the U.S. Apparel Industry.* Washington D.C.: Economic Policy Institute.

Sabel, Charles, Dara O'Rourke, and Archon Fung. 1999. *Open Labor Standards: Towards a System of Rolling Rule Regulation of Labor Practices.* Discussion paper presented at the Annual Meetings of the World Bank Seminar on Labor Standards, Washington, D.C., September 28, 1999.

Safa, Helen. 1994. "Export Manufacturing, State Policy and Women Workers in the Dominican Republic." Pp. 247–67 in *Global Production: The Apparel Industry in the Pacific Rim,* ed. Edna Bonacich et al. Philadelphia: Temple University Press.

Sajhau, Jean-Paul. 1997. *Business Ethics in the Textile, Clothing and Footwear (TCF) Industries: Codes of Conduct* (working paper). Geneva: International Labour Organization.

Sassen, Saskia. 1994. *Cities in a World Economy.* Thousand Oaks, Calif.: Pine Forge Press.

———. 1998. *Globalization and Its Discontents.* New York: The New Press.

Sassen-Koob, Saskia. 1989. "New York City's Informal Economy." Pp. 60–77 in *Informal Economy: Studies in Advanced and Less Developed Countries,* ed. Alejandro Portes et al. Baltimore: Johns Hopkins University Press.

Schoenberger, Karl. 2000. *Levi's Children,: Coming to Terms with Human Rights in the Global Marketplace.* New York: Atlantic Monthly Press.

Schofield, Ann. 1984. "The Uprising of the 20,000: The Making of a Labor Legend." Pp. 167–82 in *A Needle, a Bobbin, a Strike: Women Needleworkers in America,* ed. Joan M. Jensen and Sue Davidson. Philadelphia: Temple University Press.

Scipes, Kim. 2000. "It's Time to Come Clean." *Labor Studies Journal* 25, no. 2.

Seidman, Joel. 1942. *The Needle Trades.* New York: Farrar and Rhinehart.

Selekman, B. M., Henriette Walter, and W. J. Couper. 1925. *The Clothing and Textile Industries in New York and Its Environs.* New York: Committee on Regional Plans of New York and Its Environs.

Shaiken, Harley. 1993. "Going South: Mexican Wages and U.S. Jobs after NAFTA." *American Prospect* 4, no. 15, 58–64.

———. 1994. "Advanced Manufacturing and Mexico." *Latin American Research Review* 29, no. 2: 39–71.

Shaw, Linda, and Angela Hale. 2002. "The Emperor's New Clothes: What Codes Mean for Workers in the Garment Industry." Pp. 101–12 in *Corporate Responsibility and Labor Rights: Codes of Conduct in the Global Economy,* ed. Rhys Jenkins, Ruth Pearson, and Gill Seyfang. London: Earthscan.

Shaw, Randy. 1999. *Reclaiming America: Nike, Clean Air and the New National Activism.* Berkeley: University of California Press.

Siahaan, Emelia Yanti Mala Dewi. 2000. "Códigos de conducta y organización de trabajadores en las plantas de la industria de la confección en Indonesia." Pp. 178–89 in *Codigos de conducta y monitoreo en la industria de confeccion. Experiencias internacionales y regionales,* ed. Ronald Koepke, Norma Molina, and Carolina Quinteros. San Salvador: Heinrich Böll Foundation.

Sklair, Leslie. 1994. *Sociology of the Global System,* 2nd ed. Baltimore: Johns Hopkins University Press.

Sokoloff, Natalie. 1988. "Contributions of Marxism and Feminism to the Sociology of Women and Work." Pp. 116–29 in *Women Working: Theories and*

Facts in Perspective, ed. Ann Stromberg and Shirley Harkess. Mountain View, Calif.: Mayfield Press.

Standing, Guy. 2001. "Human Development." *Boston Review*, February–March.

Stein, Leon, ed. 1977. *Out of the Sweatshop*. New York: Quadrangle/New York Times Book Company.

Stepick, Alex. 1989. "Miami's Two Informal Economies." Pp. 111–34 in *Informal Economy: Studies in Advanced and Less Developed Countries*, ed. Alejandro Portes et al. Baltimore: Johns Hopkins University Press.

Su, Julie. 1997. "El Monte Thai Garment Workers: Slave Sweatshops." Pp. 143–50 in *No Sweat: Fashion, Free Trade and the Rights of Garment Workers*, ed. Andrew Ross. New York: Verso.

Sweeney, Kevin. 2000. "Voting with Their Pocketbooks: The Strengths and Limits of Consumer-Driven Codes of Conduct." Pp. 253–65 in *Global Codes of Conduct: An Idea Whose Time Has Come*, ed. Oliver Williams. Notre Dame, Ind.: University of Notre Dame Press.

Thomas, Robert. 1985. *Citizenship, Gender and Work: Social Organization of Industrial Agriculture*. Berkeley: University of California Press.

Tiano, Susan. 1990. "Maquiladora Women: A New Category of Workers?" Pp. 193–224 in *Women Workers and Global Restructuring*, ed. Kathryn Ward. Ithaca, N.Y.: ILR Press.

Tsogas, George. 2001. *Labor Regulation in a Global Economy*. Armonk, N.Y.: M. E. Sharpe.

U.S. DOL (Department of Labor). 1995. *Apparel Industry Source Booklet*. Washington, D.C.

———. 1996. *The Apparel Industry and Codes of Conduct: A Solution to the International Child Labor Problem?* Bureau of International Labor Affairs, Washington, D.C.

———. 1997. *By the Sweat and Toil of Children*. Washington, D.C..

———. 2000. *Wages, Benefits, Poverty Line, and Meeting Workers' Needs in the Apparel and Footwear Industries in Selected Countries*. Washington, D.C.: U.S. DOL, Bureau of International Labor Affairs.

U.S. GAO (General Accounting Office). 1988. *Sweatshops in the U.S.: Opinions on Their Extent and Possible Enforcement Options*. Washington, D.C.

U.S. ITC (International Trade Commission). 1998. *Annual Statistical Report on U.S. Imports of Textiles and Apparel: 1997. Investigation No. 332-343.* Washington, D.C.

———. 2002. "U.S. Trade by Geographic Regions: Annual U.S. Merchandise Imports, Selected Partners in Western Hemisphere" [data report]. Available at: http://dataweb.usitc.gov. (accessed June 24, 2002).

Utting, Peter. 2002. "Regulating Business via Multi-Stakeholder Initiatives: A Preliminary Assessment." In *Development Dossier: Voluntary Approaches to Corporate Responsibility*. Geneva: United Nations Non-Governmental Liaison Service, May. Available at: http://www.un-ngls.org/documents/publications.en/develop.dossier/dd.07%20(csr)/Section%20II.pdf (accessed March 8, 2004).

Varley, Pamela. 1998. *The Sweatshop Quandary: Corporate Responsibility on the Global Frontier*. Washington, D.C.: Investor Responsibility Research Center.

Verité. 2000. "Pilot Project for Licensing Labor Code Implementation: Final Report." Amherst, Mass.

Waldinger, Roger. 1985. "Another Look at the International Ladies' Garment Workers' Union: Women, Industry Structure and Collective Action." Pp. 86–109 in *Women, Work and Protest*, ed. Ruth Milkman. Boston: Routledge.

———. 1986. *Through the Eye of the Needle: Immigrants and Enterprise in New York's Garment Trades*. New York: New York University Press.

Wallerstein, Immanuel. 1991. "The Ideological Tensions of Capitalism: Universalism versus Racism and Sexism." Pp. 29–36 in *Race, Nation and Class*, by Immanuel Wallerstein and Etienne Balibar. London: Verso.

Ward, Kathryn. 1990. *Women Workers and Global Restructuring*. Ithaca, N.Y.: Cornell ILR Press.

Wells, Miriam. 1996. *Strawberry Fields: Politics, Class and Work in California*. Ithaca, N.Y.: Cornell University Press.

Wells-Dang, Andrew. 2002. "Linking Trade to Labor Standards: Prospects for Cambodia and Vietnam." *Foreign Policy in Focus Policy Report*. June. Available at: http://www.fpif.org/papers.

WWW (Women Working Worldwide). 1998. "Women Workers and Codes of Conduct: Asia Workshop Report." Manchester, U.K.

———. 1999. "Women Workers and Codes of Conduct: Central America Workshop Report." Manchester, U.K.

———. 2001. "Reports from Final Codes Project Workshop." Manchester, U.K., November.

Yanz, Linda, and Bob Jeffcott. 2001. "Bringing Codes Down to Earth." *International Union Rights* 8, no. 3. Available at: http://www.maquilasolidarity.org/resources/codes/downtoearth.htm.

Yanz, Lynda, Bob Jeffcott, Deena Ladd, Joan Atlin, Maquila Solidarity Network. 1999. *Policy Options to Improve Standards for Garment Workers in Canada and Internationally*. Ottawa: Status of Women Canada's Policy Research Fund.

Yimprasert, Junya, and Christopher Candland. 2000. *Can Corporate Codes of Conduct Promote Labor Standards? Evidence from the Thai Footwear and Apparel Industries*. Bangkok: Thai Labor Campaign.

Zabin, Carol. 2000. "Organizing Latino Workers in Los Angeles' Manufacturing Sector: The Case of American Racing Equipment." Pp. 150–68 in *Organizing Immigrants: The Challenge for Unions in Contemporary California*, ed. Ruth Milkman. Ithaca, N.Y.: ILR Press.

Zolberg, Artistide. 1990. "Reforming the Back Door: The Immigration Reform and Control Act of 1986 in Historical Perspective." Pp. 315–39 in *Immigration Reconsidered*, ed. Virginia Yans-McLaughlin. New York: Oxford University Press.

Index

interviews for this work: number and type conducted, 10, 215*t*, 219–27*t*; research methods, 214–15

investment, transnational: attractiveness to developing nations, 27; in El Salvador, 26

investor(s): power of, 33; in triangle of resistance, 53–56, 54*f*

Investor Responsibility Research Center (IRRC), 111, 147

Iran, union suppression in, 128

ISO. *See* International Standards Organization

Jamaica, monitoring programs in, 132

Japan, labor costs in, 124

Jay's Fashions, 1

JC Penney, 126

Jeans Plus, 2, 94

Jessica McClintock, 58

jobber contracts. *See* manufacturer contracts

John Paul Richard, 101

Joint Board of Sanitary Control, 17

joint liability: efforts to legislate, 56; establishment of principle, 19–20, 101, 112–15; monitoring and, 56; private monitoring and, 112–15; webs of production and, 35*t*

Jordan, U.S. trade agreements with, 42

Justice for Janitors Campaigns, 232n9

Karp, Roberta, 179

Kaufman, Eileen, 57

Kearney, Neil, 132, 135

Kellwood, 133

Kenan Institute Asia, 141–42

Kenan Institute of Private Enterprise, 141–42

Kennedy, Edward, 56

Kennedy School of Government, Innovations in American Government award, 3

Kenya, union suppression in, 128

Kernaghan, Charles, 170, 177, 203

KIMI, Inc., 175

K-Mart, 210

Knight, Philip, 188

Koret of California, 30

KPMG, 138–39

Kukdong International factory, 188–91, 197, 203–6

labeling of sweatshop products, 16

labor, forced, 126–27

labor costs: efforts to minimize, 124–30; by nation, 124

Labor Council on Latin American Advancement, 134

labor law(s): enforcement of (*see* enforcement of labor laws); globalization and, 42; New Deal reform of, 18–19; post–World War II expansion of, 20

Labor Law, Inc., 64–65, 103

labor law violations: increase after globalization, 4; in Los Angeles, 82–86, 83*t*, 85*f*, 87*f*; manufacturers' ignoring of, 1–2, 94, 96; in Salvadoran maquilas, 168. *See also* private monitoring: effectiveness of

labor relations, private monitoring and, 9

Labor Rights in China (LARIC), 158, 162–63

labor rights organizations, independent monitoring by. *See* independent monitoring

labor rights protections, in international trade agreements, 42–43

Latin America: GUESS? decision to outsourcing to, 3; immigration from, 28; impact of free trade on, 27; labor costs in, 124; U.S. trade policy and, 26

Latinos, unions and, 49

Law of the Free Trade Zones (El Salvador), 171

Lawyers' Committee for Human Rights (LCHR), 178, 185

Lesotho, union suppression in, 128

Levi Strauss Co.: closure of domestic factories, 23–24, 30; code of conduct, 120, 122, 160; monitoring program, 127, 142, 150–51; production chain of, 111

liquidated damages, 20, 230n8

literature on codes of conduct and monitoring: conclusions of, 146–47, 163–64; critiques and proposals, 161–63; cross-company/country studies, 147–50; implementation research, 150–56; reports from NGOs and multi-stakeholder projects, 156–58; reports from NGOs and workers, 158; types of, 145–46

Liz Claiborne: AIP and, 179; code of conduct, 162; FLA and, 244n55; monitoring program, 140, 141; moving of production overseas, 30; production chain of, 35–36, 111; unionization and, 175; use of monitors reports, 57

L.L. Bean, 244n55

Los Angeles: compliance firms in, 63, 64–66, 65*t*; DOL program in, 58; effectiveness of private monitoring in, 82–86, 83*t*, 85*f*, 87*f*, 94–95, 95*t*, 235–36n47; enforcement of labor laws in, 39–40, 82–86, 83*t*, 85*f*, 87*f*, 235–36n47; as focus of DOL enforcement, 6–7; garment industry in, 28–29; garment workers in, 4, 29–30, 30, 30*f*; GUESS? sweatshops in, 1–3; immigrant enclaves and, 51; INS enforcement in, 48; level of compliance in, 199; as model for international monitoring, 119; monitoring practices and standards, 69–80; monitoring programs in, 7, 8, 52–53, 198; payment for monitoring in, 66–67; union membership in, 30, 30*f*; unionization in, 48–49; unregistered shops in, 126; workers' salaries in, 21–22

Macalester University, 187

MacBride Principles, 121

Macy's Department Stores, 117

Made by the Bay program, 69

Made in China (NLC), 130

Malaysia, union suppression in, 128

Mancillas, Pedro, 174, 176

Mandarin International factory, 140, 169–74, 176, 206

Mandela, Nelson, 122